Two Hundred Years at the Falls of the Ohio:

A History of Louisville and Jefferson County

Copyright © 1987
The Filson Club
1310 South Third Street
Louisville, Kentucky 40208

Library of Congress Catalogue
Number: 87-82003
ISBN: 0-9601072-3-1

First Edition, September 1979
Second Edition, October 1987

Through the courtesy of the publish-
ers, excerpts from the following books
have been used: Elliott Paul, My Old
Kentucky Home, Random House, copyright 1949; Gilbert Chase, America's
Music: From the Pilgrims to the Present,
McGraw-Hill Book Company, copyright
1955; Abraham Flexner: An Autobiography, Simon & Schuster, copyright
1960; Dorothy Park Clark, "Louisville's
Invisible Benefactor": The Life Story
of James Graham Brown, James Graham
Brown Foundation, copyright 1978.

Dedication
To all the men and women of all races
who during the past two centuries have
helped build a community at the Falls of
the Ohio.

Two Hundred Years
at the Falls of the Ohio:
A History of Louisville
and Jefferson County

George H. Yater

*This publication was made
possible through a grant by the
Liberty National Bank and Trust
Company of Louisville, Kentucky.
Published by The Filson Club.*

1987

Preface

It has been only eight years since the first edition of *Two Hundred Years at the Falls of the Ohio* was published, but the developments in that short space of time have been significant. The trends in evidence in 1979 have become more sharply focused and help to delineate the shape that future developments are likely to take in the next decade or so, at least. Rarely does an author have the privilege of extending the time frame of any historical work, but this second edition gives that opportunity.

The shift from a predominantly blue-collar to a predominantly white-collar economy is more evident than ever. In the years following the Civil War Louisville became a manufacturing city — a process that began about 1870. In one of those neat divisions of the time frame that history occasionally offers, the new turn in economic direction began about 1970 — although it took some time to recognize the underlying trend. The shift is to the information/knowledge/service sector.

The change in economic base is fundamental and will likely bring equally fundamental changes in the community's persona. When manufacturing was dominant, Louisville became basically midwestern in temperament, although it assiduously cultivated a romantic image of southern gentility. It managed to convince the nation that this was so. It has been found difficult to erase that image, which also (as an unintended consequence) conjured up an image of drowsy languor under the magnolias. The erasing process is, however, under way. In fact, Louisville's recent responses to its challenges have earned it a level of national attention that it has not known for many years.

As the urbanized area has spread beyond the nominal city boundaries, it has become impossible to speak of Louisville as only the area encompassed within those boundaries. The interrelationship spreads beyond the Jefferson County boundaries, as well. The Metropolitan Statistical Area as defined by the United States Census Bureau now includes seven counties, three of them in Indiana.

Understanding how this community faced past problems and responded to them — sometimes well and sometimes poorly — provides a framework for understanding the present and approaching the future. Even so, treating contemporary events is always difficult for the historian, since time has not yet brought its gift of perspective. The past is never a blueprint for the present or the future. Nevertheless, it provides general lessons, including the vital ones of responding early and creatively to problems and sensing when changing situations require a change in leadership style.

This edition of *Two Hundred Years at the Falls of the Ohio* was made possible by the unprompted initiative of Liberty National Bank and Trust Company when it learned that the first edition had gone out of print. That bank also made the first edition possible through a grant to the Heritage Corporation of Louisville and Jefferson County. This edition is published by The Filson Club, which for more than a century has been active in preserving materials relating to the history of Louisville and Kentucky and has developed an eminent and growing collection, open for research to all.

My debt to those who commented on the manuscript for the original edition is as great as ever, and to them must be added those who performed the same role for the new Chapter Seventeen. Foremost was Jack Trawick, whose work with Louisville Central Area, Inc., and currently as head of the Louisville Community Design Center, gives him a special insight into developments of the past several years. Staff members of The Filson Club also lent their expertise: James R. Bentley, director; Rick Bell, assistant to the director; and Mary Jean Kinsman, curator of photographs and prints.

George H. Yater, *October 1987*

Contents

The rocky rapids were a bar to navigation/Filson Club

The Falls of the Ohio before the 1927 dam/Caufield & Shook

Prologue

In the early spring of 1778, nearly two years after the United Colonies had boldly proclaimed themselves the independent United States of America, George Washington's ragged, hungry Continental Army welcomed the end of a hard winter at Valley Forge. As his troops warily trailed the British army moving out of Philadelphia, loosing sporadic volleys into the long columns of Redcoats, the Virginia planter-turned-general contemplated his coming summer campaign.

A thousand miles away another Virginian, a newly appointed lieutenant colonel of the State Militia, commanded a small convoy of vessels drifting quietly down the twists and turns of the Ohio River. George Rogers Clark, too, contemplated his coming summer campaign that would take the Revolutionary War to the far reaches of the Illinois country and to the shores of the Mississippi River. It was territory that Virginia claimed, territory where the British least expected an incursion of American rebels.

Clark led a small force of Virginia militia—about 150 men—and a group of perhaps eighty settlers: family groups and a few adventurous young single men. The militiamen were (so they thought) on their way to defend Kentucky; the civilians on their way to settle in Kentucky. Unknown adventures and dangers lay ahead as they drifted down the torturous miles of what the French before them had called *La Belle Rivière*.

Never was that Gallic name more appropriate than in spring, and in this May of 1778 Clark's convoy moved down a rippling river alive with fish, and through the tiny, evanescent sounds of spring. There was the rustling of new leaves stirred by river breezes, the clear call of songbirds, the gobbling of wild turkey flocks, the droning of bees busy taking nectar from the spring wildflowers. The shores were lined with majestic cottonwood trees, just now casting their cottony seeds onto the waters; sycamores so huge that their hollow interiors could be used as shelter; willows and red cedars, and all festooned with wild grape, honeysuckle, and Virginia creeper.

At one place another and more compelling sound joined the quiet chorus, a sound heard no other place along the Ohio on its nearly 1,000-mile sweep from western Pennsylvania to its meeting with the Mississippi. It was the sound that marked the only impediment to navigation in the entire length of the stream, or in the nearly 1,000 additional miles of the Mississippi flowing lazily to New Orleans and the Gulf of Mexico. By 1778 it was already known as the Falls of the Ohio, though it actually was a lengthy, rock-strewn rapids and not a waterfall at all.

Rapids or falls, it had a special sound. Early accounts say a distant murmur could be heard long before the source was seen. As one drew closer, the volume of sound increased, though it varied with the seasons. In the summer, when the water was low, there was only a rippling and splashing. As the volume of water increased with spring and fall rains, the rippling became a roar. Sometimes the water was so high that the falls disappeared entirely and the river flowed placidly and quietly southward.

The Falls was a sight to see as well as hear. Naturalist John James Audubon recalled that "The beauty of the situation on the banks of *La Belle Rivière*, just at the commencement of the famed rapids, commonly called the Falls of the Ohio, had attracted my notice.... The prospect from the town is such that it would please even the eye of a Swiss.... The rumbling sound of the Falls as they tumble over the rock-paved bed of the rapids is at all times soothing to the ear."

Before the month of May was out, things would change at the Falls and the new sounds of man would be heard. George Rogers Clark was carrying secret military orders that only he and a handful of others, including Patrick Henry and Thomas Jefferson, knew. To carry out those orders he needed a base on the Ohio River. His flotilla drifting down the placid Ohio carried more than met the eye. It also carried the seeds of a city at the Falls.

Chapter One

Genesis: Clark and Corn Island, 1778-79

"I observed the little island of about seven acres oposite to whare the Town of Lewisville now stands[,] seldom or never was intirely covered by the water, I resolved to take possession and fortify[,] which I did…." In that laconic prose George Rogers Clark described the founding of Louisville in the spring of 1778. It also is testimony to Clark's erratic spelling and punctuation, and to the original (mis)pronunciation of Louisville's name. The "little island," which has long since vanished, was a short distance off the Kentucky shore near the foot of present-day Twelfth Street. It soon gained the name Corn Island (presumably for a crop of corn raised there in the summer of 1778) and has become a touchstone of Louisville's history. Yet it was not Clark's objective to found a town at the Falls of the Ohio or anywhere else. That a city would rise here at the break in navigation was inevitable; that it began in 1778 is one of those seeming 'accidents' of history, one of the unexpected consequences that often follow when men set out to accomplish other purposes.

Clark's purpose was grandiose, nothing less than striking down British and Indian power in the country northwest of the Ohio River, a vast stretch of territory called the Illinois country. Clark's plan was to drive the British from their posts at Kaskaskia and Cahokia far away on the Mississippi River, Vincennes on the Wabash River, and finally from the most redoubtable stronghold of all, the fort at Detroit. This bold, even breathtaking plan, conceived by the 26-year-old Virginian, ranks as perhaps the most daring of all American expeditions during the Revolutionary War. Kaskaskia and Cahokia were nearly 1,000 difficult miles from Virginia, even 300 miles beyond the few tiny, new and scattered settlements in Kentucky that were already beginning to feel the bloody sting of Indian raids from north of the Ohio River.

It was these raids against the new settlements in Kentucky that inspired Clark to his bold plan. He knew the raids at first hand, having spent time cooped up in Fort Harrod (today's Harrodsburg) in 1777 when it had been attacked by Shawnees. Undoubtedly that was when Clark first conceived the idea of an offensive into the enemy's own territory. It was not long after the 1777 raids that Clark, already achieving stature as a leader among the handful of Kentucky settlers, set off for the Virginia capital at Williamsburg to lay his thoughts before Governor Patrick Henry. It is a measure of the man that he was able to convince Henry that only by striking in force, taking the offensive in the enemy's own territory, could Kentucky be made safe. With an American show of strength and a British defeat, Clark argued, the Indians would be persuaded that it was prudent to remain north of the Ohio on the 'Indian side' of the river. Clark's real orders were secret; publicly he was only recruiting Virginia militia to protect the Kentucky settlements from attack.

Once the campaign was approved, Clark immediately set plans to put it into motion. By the end of January 1778, he had recruiters all across Virginia, but in the end he had to rely mainly on the northwestern area of the state (today a part of Pennsylvania) to supply the bulk of his force. By early May, Clark, who had been given the Virginia rank of lieutenant colonel as commander of what was to become known as the Illinois Regiment, had collected only about 150 men.

In the Fort Pitt area, claimed by both Virginia and Pennsylvania, there was even more difficulty for Clark's recruiter, Captain William Harrod (older brother of James Harrod, the founder of Kentucky's pioneer settlement at Fort Harrod). Pennsylvania partisans were reluctant to enlist in the Virginia forces, and there was strong feeling that taking troops to Kentucky would weaken the defense of the thinly populated upper Ohio Valley. Nevertheless, some adventurous frontiersmen did enlist, most coming from the country between the Monongahela and the Ohio; others came from upland Virginia along the Blue Ridge and from the Shenandoah Valley.

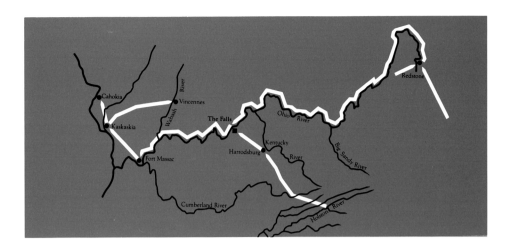

The three companies assembled at Redstone, the little settlement south of Fort Pitt at the point where Redstone Creek flows into the Monongahela. (Today it is Brownsville, Pa.) Clark had hoped for a larger force, but the far southwestern Holston Valley settlements promised more men who would join him in Kentucky. He would still be short of the 500 men he wanted, but undaunted he "set Sail for the Falls" on May 12.

Clark's small flotilla of perhaps ten vessels included an unwanted contingent of some ten to twenty civilian families. Kentucky had become a magic word east of the Appalachians, a land wide open for settlement, reputedly fertile beyond imagining, a land of milk and honey where land-hungry settlers might achieve independence and plenty. "What a Buzzel is amongst people about Kentuck? to hear people speak of it one Would think it was a new found Paradise...." one Virginian exclaimed as early as 1775. But by 1778 it was evident that the Indians would not easily give up their hunting grounds to this first great American land rush. What safer way for settlers to get to the promised land than under the protection of armed soldiers? There is also evidence that some of the settlers were related to the newly enlisted militiamen. Clark had little choice except to let the entreating civilians come. He could not reveal that his secret orders called for the capture of "Kaskasky" in the Illinois country, and families coming with their few worldly goods provided a perfect cover for his real intentions.

The trip was made without incident. In fact, Clark called it a "very pleasant Voyage to the falls of Ohio." Such quiet trips were not to last for long now that a British order to encourage Indian attacks had reached Fort Detroit. But though the voyage itself may have been pleasant, there were disappointments along the way. Clark stopped at the mouth of the Kentucky River to meet the reinforcements recruited in the Holston Valley. The news was bad. "...you may easily guess at my mortification," he wrote to George Mason, "on being informed that [they] had not arrived; that all...had been stopt by the insessant labours of the populace, except part of a Compy that had arrived [in Kentucky, but not at the meeting place] under the command of one Captain Dillard." The Holston settlers were as opposed to sending away prime defense forces as were the Pittsburgh settlers.

Now, he added, he was "as Desperate as before I was Determined." But he knew that Governor Henry was being criticized for sending troops to protect Kentucky and that the Governor had put himself into this position because of his faith in Clark. "That, and some other secret impulses, occationed me, in spite of all Council, to risque the Expedition to convince them of their error...." Clark had intended to erect a fort where the Kentucky flows into the Ohio, but with fewer troops than he expected, he realized he could not afford to keep two posts. "...Of course[,] the Falls was the more Elligible spot," he wrote to Mason, "as it would answer all those desireable purposes and in a great measure Protect the Navigation of the

Above: Clark took this route from Redstone, Pennsylvania, to the Illinois country by way of the Falls of the Ohio. Arrows indicate the two sources of his recruits. Those from what is now western Pennsylvania and West Virginia congregated at Redstone and those from the Holston Valley joined the group at the Falls.

Left: George Rogers Clark, in this memorial by Felix de Weldon, points to the Falls of the Ohio. The bronze statue, a gift from the Arthur E. Hopkins bequest, is on the Belvedere of Louisville's Riverfront Plaza.

River as every Vessel would be obliged to stop sometime at that place[.] they would always be exposed to the Indians[.]"

So the little flotilla set out again downriver, the troops still not knowing they were bound far beyond Kentucky. That is why he chose the island: "…to stop the desertion I knew would ensue on the Troops knowing their Destination[,] I had encamped on a small Island in the middle of the Falls…." The date was May 27, 1778. We know it only through a deposition made many years later by James Patten. The civilians, whom Clark had reluctantly taken along, were now of real service. "…they ware of little expence, and with the Invalids would keep possession of this Little post untill we should be able to Occupy the Main shore…." Louisville, as yet unnamed, had been founded.

Busy days followed: felling the huge sycamores and cottonwoods, cutting the thick cane to clear a spot for planting, and putting in a crop of corn and vegetables. A blockhouse and cabins had to be erected. Then there was the most difficult task of all: turning the independent frontiersmen into a semblance of a military unit. But Clark was not only disciplining his troops; he was waiting for whatever reinforcements might finally arrive from the Holston Valley, plus some from the stations in the interior of Kentucky. Finally, toward the end of June, they came, conducted by John Todd, Jr., from Fort Harrod. The whole enterprise excited Todd. "Never did so many occurences croud one another as does now in this country," he wrote back to Virginia, and added that "…we have spared [Clark] about 60 men to make a stroke at Cascasky [and] a garrison of about 30 men…."

Now Clark revealed the secret orders to his officers. "After my Making known my Instructions almost every Gentn. [the officers] warmly Espoused the Enterprise…and supposed they saw the salvation of Kentucky almost within their reach but surely repined that we ware not strong enough to put it beyond all doubt. the Soldiery in Genl. Debated on the subject but determined to follow their Officers." Soldiers debating a proposed campaign is not a picture of the most disciplined of troops, but these were not the most disciplined of times.

Now that he was proposing to go on to the far-away Illinois country, Clark correctly presumed some would want to desert, and some did, despite being on an island, despite guards at the boats. They were the recruits from the Holston, whose departure had caused such an uproar there. Captain Dillard had returned home, leaving the men under the command of a Lieutenant Hutchings. Learning of their destination, part of the company asked permission to return home. It was refused.

Then, as Clark ruefully admitted, he "got out Generald by their Lieutenant, whom I had previously conceived a very tolerable opinion of." The reluctant soldiers of Hutchings' company had discovered that in one place it was possible to wade from Corn Island to the mainland, and at dawn one morning most of them did just that. Fortunately, the detachments from Fort Harrod had brought some horses, and Clark sent pursuers on horse and on foot, with orders to put to death any deserters who attempted further escape.

"They overhauled them in about 20 miles," Clark recalled. "the deserters, discovering them at a distance[,] scattered in the w[o]ods[;] only 7 or 8 were taken[.] the Rest made their way to the different posts[.] Many that was not woodsmen almost perished[.]" This incident delayed Clark's departure for the Illinois, but finally, on June 24, all was in readiness. With the handful of reinforcements from Kentucky and the Holston Valley, he had about 175 men.

"We left our little island," Clark wrote, "and Run about a mile up the River in order to gain the main Channel, and shot the Fall at the very moment of the suns being in a great Eclipse[,] which caused Various

Above and opposite: Murals at the Clark National Memorial, Vincennes, Indiana, portray Clark's adventures. "Kentucky—Entering the Great Valley," above, presumably shows Clark on the white horse. In "The Wabash—Through Wilderness and Flood," opposite, Clark leads his troops in the Illinois campaign. Filson Club

conjectures among the superstitious." Astronomical records confirm the eclipse. The boats must have passed over the Falls about nine a.m.

The troops had gone and the settlers on Corn Island, plus the thirty militiamen, some incapacitated, some apparently deemed a bit over-age for hard campaigning, were on their own. Their fate, as well as that of the Illinois Regiment, now hung on Clark's generalship. Relatively secure on their island (the nearest Indian settlements were in Ohio and today's Indiana; usually only occasional hunting parties appeared at the Falls), the small band of pioneers settled down to tending their corn and vegetable plots, hunting expeditions to the mainland, and looking around the country with an eye to future homesteads. A site with a good spring or along a watercourse was especially desirable, and the future Jefferson County abounded in such locations. The population on Corn Island may have increased by at least one during this time, too. Isaac Kimbley, visiting Louisville in May 1852, told *Louisville Journal* editor George D. Prentice that he had been born on Corn Island in 1779, the son of Andrew and Sallie (Bromley) Kimbley, and was, therefore, the first white child born in Jefferson County.

The daily round of pioneer domesticity on the island was quickly enlivened with startling—and cheering—news from across the Atlantic. France had signed a treaty of alliance with the struggling United States; a powerful military weight had been added to the American side. It might seem this would be of little practical value to the tiny settlements, or stations, in the Kentucky wilderness; French grenadiers were not likely to appear on the frontier. Yet it would be a psychological boost to the Kentucky settlers and news of major importance to the Illinois Regiment, as John Campbell, a Pittsburgh merchant and trader, realized. Clark's military targets, the towns of Kaskaskia, Cahokia, and Vincennes, were actually old French settlements. They were part of the vast Mississippi Valley territory that, along with Canada, the French had lost to England only fifteen years earlier in the French and Indian War.

Though the English had placed colonial officials at the former French towns, the closest British regulars were at Fort Detroit; the British relied locally on militia recruited from the residents. The news of the French alliance with the Americans could be expected to have a powerful influence on the French *habitants*. The urgency of the information still radiates from Campbell's dispatch: "Mr. Wells [the messenger] is just waiting[.] he can inform you of some of the particulars of these glad Tidings…." The treaty had been signed on February 16 in Paris and the news arrived at remote Corn Island in about four and one-half months—practically instantaneous transmission in 1778. There was only one problem. Clark and his troops had left several days earlier.

Because the news was useless unless it got to Clark, one of the civilians, William Linn, an experienced frontiersman, took the precious document and set out in a canoe to catch up with the Illinois-bound troops. Linn stayed with the expedition, eventually becoming a major in the Illinois Regiment. A valuable addition to Clark's small force, Linn was a former lieutenant in the Virginia Militia, a member of a group that made the long river trip to New Orleans two years earlier to secure four tons of Spanish gunpowder badly needed by troops on the frontier and delivered it safely to Wheeling. Now he delivered a trump card to Clark, one that the young commander would use well with the French *habitants*. For Clark's purposes, the American and French diplomats couldn't have timed the alliance better.

With total surprise in its favor, Clark's little army took Kaskaskia without firing a shot. Oddly, the American force came in sight of the town on July 4, exactly two years after the American declaration of independence. Moving in quickly under cover of darkness, Clark's troops had total control of the town by the early hours of July 5. The next day, Cahokia, too, fell in a bloodless conquest. It must have been about mid- or late July when the Corn

Recollections of Corn Island
Patrick Scott, only four years old when his family joined the group of settlers who accompanied Clark to Kentucky, recounted many years later what his father told him of those early days. Scott was living in Bourbon County at the time.

"My f[ather] came down in 1778 with Clark's Co[mpany]. I stopped at the falls of Ohio....They planted corn on Corn Island. Have heard my f[ather] say as he used to set of night in his cornfield, that he thought he could hear the corn go tick-tick—it grew so fast....13 families came down....Clark settled these 13 families on Corn Island....One was the Patten's, who died [1815] in Louisville some years ago. Another was the Lynn's."

Scott added that his family moved to Harrodsburgh in the late summer of 1778, traveling for safety with some of Clark's discharged troops.
Draper Manuscripts, 11CC5-7

Island settlers learned of Clark's successes. The good news was delivered by famed frontiersman Simon Kenton, returning as an "express," a messenger who made his way alone through the wilderness, dodging Indians and living off game.

The startling news of the American exploits did not reach Lieutenant Governor Henry Hamilton, the top British official at Fort Detroit, until August 6. To Clark's troops, the thought of Hamilton's discomfiture may have been worth all the hardships and risks involved in their perilous enterprise. All the deep-seated fear of Indian attacks that was shared by the frontiersmen from western Pennsylvania to Kentucky had been focused on Hamilton. Settlers called him the "Hair Buyer," firmly convinced that he paid the Indians a bounty for each American scalp presented at Detroit for redemption.

Meanwhile, Clark turned his attention to Vincennes, 240 miles back to the east on the Wabash River. French *habitants* from Kaskaskia, led by Father Pierre Gibault, offered to go to Vincennes to intercede in the Americans' behalf. By the end of July the American colors were flying over the sturdy log fort at Vincennes and the Americans had gained their first artillery pieces. With the easy taking of Vincennes, Clark's bold plan had been crowned with astonishing success in less than two months since he had left the Falls of the Ohio. Not a man had been lost, not a shot had been fired. Even the Indian tribes were impressed. At Cahokia in July and early August of 1778, Clark made treaties with "ten or twelve different nations." Affairs were moving along smoothly.

Now it was time to think of the settlers back on Corn Island. In addition, the eight-month terms of enlistment of many of the militiamen were coming to a close. Those who did not want to remain in service were sent back to the Falls under the command of William Linn to be discharged. Linn also brought Clark's orders to remove the post to the mainland, the second step in the founding of a town.

On this return trip the troops marched overland, following the age-old Buffalo Trace, a clear track made through the wilderness to the Falls of the Ohio by these huge animals on their migrations from the prairies to the salt licks of Indiana and Kentucky. Work on the new fort on the shore probably began immediately on receipt of Clark's orders from Kaskaskia. The new stockade, built nearly opposite Corn Island near today's intersection of Twelfth and Rowan streets, was occupied by the fall of 1778.

While the new stockade was under construction, there was a different kind of activity some 350 miles away at Fort Detroit. Hamilton now had news of the total debacle in the Illinois country, including the defection of most of the *habitants*, the confusion among the Indian tribes, and the loss of Vincennes. Obviously the British lion could not sit idly by while its tail was twisted this way by a handful of rebel militia. Hamilton had to make a move. He chose to strike at Vincennes, coming down from Detroit with British regulars, French militia from Detroit, sixty Indians, and a brass six-pounder to batter down the fort's walls. Vincennes was an easier target than Hamilton knew. The local French militia melted away, leaving the fort manned by only one American officer and perhaps three privates. On December 17, 1778, this small force surrendered in the face of rather overwhelming odds.

It was not long after the surrender that prying, curious eyes scrutinized the new fort at the Falls. The settlers and militiamen never knew how narrowly the little outpost escaped tragedy. But the story is recorded in the quill-penned words in Hamilton's daily Journal. He told how the little fort was observed by British Captain Matthew Elliott and a scouting party of Miami and Shawnee Indians sent out to discover what was happening at the Falls. Clark, in pure bluff, had hinted to the Indian tribes that he had a large garrison there to call on at any time. Hamilton wanted to collect information

Drawing of Corn Island by Carol A. Rush, 1979

The settlers on Corn Island

A complete listing of the individuals who remained on Corn Island after Clark's departure on June 24, 1778, will probably never be made. The first list appeared in Dr. Henry McMurtie's 1819 work, "Sketches of Louisville and Its Environs," as "the account we have from the earliest settlers." It contained only five names, which have been included in all subsequent lists.

A comprehensive list was compiled in 1880 by Reuben T. Durrett at the time of Louisville's centennial. He counted ten married couples, most with children; one widower and his children; four unmarried males; and one black slave, for a total of forty-nine individuals. But even this list is incomplete.

Accounts of participants only compound the confusion. Clark himself wrote in 1779 that "about 20 families" accompanied the expedition. Colonel Joseph Bowman of the Illinois Regiment, writing in 1778, said "eight or ten" families were left on Corn Island. John Todd, Jr., writing the same year, said "twelve families is settled at the Falls" and indicated there were at least thirty men in the garrison.

Some of those traditionally listed as settlers later received land in the Clark Grant (present Clark County, Indiana,

and parts of adjacent counties) for their service as members of the Corn Island garrison. However, since most of these individuals brought their families with them, it may be that they were enlisted as garrison troops only after the expedition arrived at the Falls. Yet, Edward Worthington, who served as a captain in the Illinois campaign, is said (by Durrett) to have brought his family.

Coupling Durrett's list with later research yields the following names. Those who received land for military service are shown in roman.
James Patten, his wife Mary, and their children, Martha, Peggy, and Mary. Richard Chenoweth, his wife Margaret, and their children, Mildred, Jane, James, and Thomas. John McManus, Sr., his wife Mary, and their children, John, Jr., George, and James. John Tuel (or Tewell), his wife Mary, and their children, Ann, Winnie, and Jessie. William Faith, his wife Elizabeth, and their son John. Jacob Reager, his wife Elizabeth, and their children, Sarah, Mariah, and Henry. William Scott, his wife (name unknown), and their four-year-old son, Patrick. William Linn (a widower) and some, at least, of his six children. Edward Worthington, his wife Mary, and his son, Charles. James Graham and his wife Mary. (Their son,

Christopher Columbus Graham, born in 1784 near Danville, achieved fame for, among other things, living to the age of 100.) John Donne, Sr., his wife Martha, their son, John, Jr., and their slave Cato Watts. Andrew Kimbley and his wife Sallie, parents of Isaac Kimbley, who claimed to have been born on Corn Island. Joseph Hunter (a widower) and his children, Joseph, David, James, and Ann. Neal Doherty, Samuel Perkins, John Sinclair, and Robert Travis.

There were thus perhaps sixty individuals on Corn Island. This was a close-knit group, many members having ties of marriage and long friendship. James Graham and Jacob Reager, for example, were married to sisters of Edward Worthington. John Donne, Sr's wife was a daughter of Joseph Hunter. James Patten's wife, the former Mary Doherty, was probably a sister of Neal Doherty, and of Frederick Doherty, who went on the Illinois campaign.

Other newcomers in the fall of 1778 and spring of 1779 also had ties to the original group. Marsham Brashears was a brother of Captain Richard Brashears of the Illinois Regiment. John Corbly, who made the survey of Louisville in the spring of 1779, was a long-time friend of William Linn and later married his niece, Nancy Ann Linn.

and perhaps some prisoners. But the Indians, who thought they had been seen, "could not be prevailed upon to proceed," Elliott reported. These Indian scouts must have been hovering about the Falls shortly after Christmas, departing about January 9.

Hamilton, meanwhile, felt secure in the fort at Vincennes. He obviously was informed by his Indian scouts that there was no threat from American troops at the Falls. Moreover, Clark and what Hamilton called his "bandetti" were in Kaskaskia, seemingly locked in by the frigid Illinois winter. They would be easy prey, Hamilton thought, when warmer weather came and after the flooded Wabash River, a virtual shallow lake several miles wide, receded. This plan proved to be a major tactical error.

When Clark learned (about the end of January) of the British recapture of Vincennes, he realized his only hope lay in surprising Hamilton. And, despite winter and flood, Clark's small force crossed Illinois and the Wabash, catching the British totally unaware, in what two eminent contemporary American historians have called "…the most splendid chapter in the history of the early West, and one of the more illustrious chapters in the history of the Revolution." This time it was Hamilton's turn to surrender. Now the Americans had the brass six-pounder that had been laboriously transported from Detroit, the British regulars, and the greatest prize of all, Henry Hamilton, the "Hair Buyer" himself. He and other British officers and officials from Detroit and the regulars would soon be on their way through Kentucky and across the mountains to imprisonment at Williamsburg. From Hamilton's first-hand account we learn that the governor and twenty-six prisoners were taken up the Ohio in the very boat constructed especially in Detroit to bring the six-pounder down the Wabash to Vincennes.

British troops had finally been met head on in the West and easily defeated, and British prestige among the Indians had been badly damaged. It must have seemed certain that Indian attacks on Kentucky would cease. The joy was to prove premature, but for now it was not clouded by knowledge of the hard days that lay ahead. Spring was coming, time to think of the future, of new homesteads in this new land of Kentucky.

All Kentucky was one county in 1779, a unit set up in December 1776 to provide a better defense through a locally based militia and also to provide some measure of local administrative and judicial functions. The County Court, the governing and judicial body, was modeled on the courts which administered the older counties on the eastern side of the mountains. Theoretically, the Kentucky court was the same as any other in Virginia, but it had to deal with problems unknown in the older parts. One problem was the huge territory it administered; another was the Indian presence.

The Kentucky County Court, having considered the Indian situation, issued from Fort Harrod on April 7, 1779, an earnest plea to its increasing number of constituents, "The Court of Kentucky doth recommend to the inhabitants that they keep themselves as united and compact as possible, one other year, settling themselves in Towns and Forts…and that the intended Citizens choose three or more of the most judicious of their body as Trustees, who shall be invested with authority to lay off such town with regularity… [and] that they return to this Court to be recorded a fair plan of their Town…." A town was seen as a defensible place of refuge, harking back to an important role of the urban community in Medieval Europe.

At the Falls there was immediate response to the Court's request; so immediate, in fact, that it might seem the settlers already were about the business. The "fair plan" they made still exists, dated April 24, 1779. It is signed by John Corbly, surveyor. Most interesting of all, it is labeled "Plan of the Town of Louisville on the Ohio." The town was laid out and it had a name more than a year before it received a charter. The settlers at the Falls were now residents of Louisville, Kentucky County, Virginia. Though it was

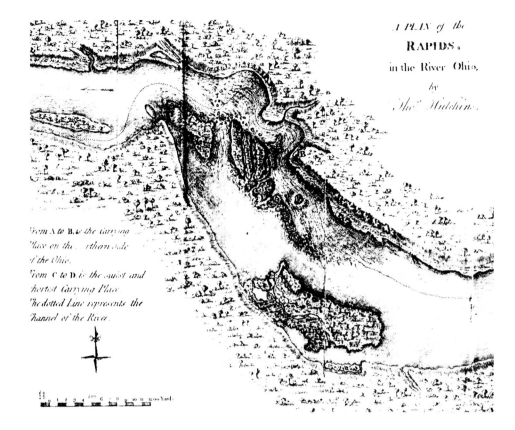

only a small log stockade and a paper town on the American frontier, it bore the illustrious name of the French monarch, Louis XVI. The King's assent to the French alliance with the American revolutionists was acknowledged by the finest gesture these town builders could make.

The order to choose town trustees had been complied with even more quickly than the making of the plan. Seven trustees were chosen at an April 17 meeting held by the "intended citizens of the Town of Louisville at the Falls of the Ohio." It had been only eleven months since the little band of adventurers, unsure of their destination, had landed on Corn Island. Surprisingly, only two of those traditionally listed as the first settlers were among the seven elected trustees: James Patten and Richard Chenoweth. Also chosen was William Harrod, who had been exercising both military and civilian jurisdiction at the Falls. The other four names appear in the Louisville record for the first time: Marsham Brashears, Edward Bulger, Henry French, and Simon Moore. Obviously the little outpost was already beginning to attract newcomers. Some, including Bulger, were from the group of Clark's soldiers who had left the Illinois Regiment in the summer of 1778 when their initial enlistments were up. Others came from the country around the headwaters of the Ohio.

Now in the greening of the spring of 1779 and a winding 607 river miles from Fort Pitt, these elected trustees drew up a remarkable document, one that reflected not only the revolutionary temper of the times, but their own background. They were not Tidewater Virginians, not large landowners. They were mostly of Scotch-Irish or German backgrounds, some first- or second-generation Americans, fiercely independent, from upland Virginia and the Shenandoah Valley. They were rooted as much in New Jersey or Pennsylvania or mountain Maryland as in the Old Dominion. Those from Virginia generally had not been there long. They were an embryo middle class and as apt to distrust the Continental Congress as the British crown.

Marsham Brashears was named secretary to the new trustees. His brief recording of the minutes of their first meeting April 24 still conveys the freshness of new beginnings and an equal chance for all. The plan for land ownership provided: "That each adventurer draw for only one lot by equal

Top: A remnant of Corn Island remained until the Falls dam and hydroelectric generating station were built in the late 1920s. This photograph was made by R.C. Ballard Thruston in 1922.
Filson Club

Bottom: No accurate drawing exists of the fort on shore, but it surely resembled Fort Boonesborough as pictured in this sketch based on research into original records. The standard form of a Kentucky station was a rectangle with the rear walls of the cabins forming part of the stockade and the roofs slanted toward the inside of the fort, providing a vantage for riflemen.
Filson Club

chance. That every such person be obliged to clear off the undergrowth and begin to cultivate part thereof by the 10th of June, and build thereon a good covered house, 16 feet by 20, by the 25th of December. That no person sell his lot unless to some person without one, but that it be given up to the Trustees to dispose of to some new adventurer on pain of forefeiture thereof."

These pioneers saw the new town of Louisville as a community of freeholders, each with his small property, a community whose inhabitants had won a measure of control over their lives by emigrating to the far western frontier. The drawing of numbers for lots was held April 24, perhaps by the trustees themselves as part of the business of their first meeting. Precisely how rapidly the land was cleared and cabins erected we do not know, but we do have one tantalizing eye witness glimpse of the town in the fall of 1779. "....there is a great number of Cabbins here and a considerable number of inhabitants..." Most of these early cabins were built in the vicinity of the Twelfth Street fort, an area that eventually acquired the name White Home.

The handful of early settlers liked entertainment, too. When Clark returned to Louisville in August 1779, his plans for a strike at Detroit stymied by lack of troops, he proposed a "feast" to celebrate the victories in the Illinois country. Settlers from Fort Harrod and nearby Logan's Fort were invited to attend; fifteen men and three women made the trip, despite signs of Indians on the way. Among the visitors were James Harrod and his wife, Ann. Rum and sugar had been brought by keelboat from Kaskaskia and a new room with puncheon floor had been added to Bachelor's Hall in the rude fort. One guest from Fort Harrod was Daniel Trabue, who recalled that "when these Fort Ladys came to be dressed up they did not look the same. Everything looked new; we enjoyed ourselves very much." A dance was also held with the Harrods leading "the first Gig." If there was a dance, there had to be music, but Trabue doesn't say who provided it. Probably most of the settlers owned fiddles, the universal instrument of the Scotch-Irish, as William Linn did. Or perhaps the guests danced to the tunes of Cato Watts, a black slave owned by settler John Donne. Tradition makes him a fiddler.

In any event, the little town with the democratic hopes was coming along, but not without flaws. Slavery was one. Cato Watts was a man held in life-long bondage, Louisville's first black resident, but denied the status of citizen. Very soon other black slaves would be brought to the new settlement. Some would be French-speaking blacks owned by Vincennes merchants who came to Louisville to open trade between the new American town and the old French one. The labor of the blacks was as basic to building a community as that of the whites who first flooded down the river and of the later waves of immigrants from Europe.

Then there was another and more immediate problem of which the hopeful adventurers were hardly aware. Somebody else owned the land where they were founding a town.

Chapter Two

A Question of Titles, Clouded and Otherwise

The speed with which John Corbly surveyed and produced a map of the proposed town of Louisville—apparently seven days at most—may mean some of his work was done for him. He may have used survey marks that were already made—axe chops on trees, piled-up stones, perhaps even some stakes. Though the new settlement was now the cutting edge of the American westward movement, its site had been picked for a town (unnamed) five years earlier, a survey made, lots marked out and offered for sale by proprietors John Connolly and John Campbell, both of Pittsburgh.

Their advertisement in the Williamsburg *Virginia Gazette* of April 7, 1774, extolled the site as "formed by Nature as a temporary Magazine, or Repository...for Produce [and] Merchandises." Behind the Eighteenth Century prose is the clear recognition that the land at the Falls was a natural spot for warehousing and distribution. But with Indian unrest stirred by the increasing flow of Anglo-American settlers into the Ohio Valley (1774 was the year of the first abortive attempt to settle Harrodsburg) plus the outbreak of the Revolution, there had been no takers.

If John Corbly, who produced the 1779 plat of Louisville, indeed used Connolly's survey, it was one of the ironies of Revolutionary history. The two Pennsylvanians represented in microcosm the two opposing forces in the American struggle for independence: Connolly, of Scotch-Irish ancestry, land speculator with powerful connections, seeker of wealth and power, Anglican (when he bothered with religion), arch-Tory and ardent opponent of independence; Corbly, from England, a former indentured servant, proponent of the small freeholder, Baptist preacher, a soldier in Captain William Harrod's company, arch-Revolutionary. At its very inception, Louisville became a meeting ground for diverse currents in American society.

Connolly was to end his days in Canada, embittered and frustrated, one of the perhaps 60,000 Tories who were forced to flee the American colonies; Corbly would return to the Monongahela country by 1780 and the log Baptist churches where his magnetic preaching and warlike sermons had gained him frontier renown. He continued to espouse the cause of the small farmer and freeholder, becoming a leader of the Whiskey Rebellion in 1794, the protest against the federal excise tax on whiskey. (Goshen Church, at Garard's Fort, Pennsylvania, his chief pastoral charge, is now the John Corbly Memorial Baptist Church.) Connolly's and Campbell's prior title to the land at the Falls was the first crisis, aside from the chronic fear of Indian attack, that the fledging settlement of Louisville faced. The question of who owned the land posed a continuing threat to the titles of early settlers and interfered with the sale of lots, one factor that may account for the town's relatively slow growth in its earlier days.

John Connolly was a man of more than passing importance on the American pre-Revolutionary frontier. He was ambitious and, as a favored nephew of George Croghan, also had connections and used them. Croghan, a native of Ireland, was the key British agent in dealing with the Indians. His early experience as the foremost trader with the tribes prepared him for his role of foremost negotiator. He was the man most responsible for gaining the allegiance to the British of the Indians in the Ohio Valley territory that England wrested from France in 1763.

Small wonder, then, that when Governor Dunmore arrived in Virginia in 1772 and was quickly caught up in the western land fever, he cultivated Croghan as an ally. As part of this alliance, Dunmore named John Connolly as his representative in charge of both military and civil affairs on the Upper Ohio. Croghan later came to regret his recommendation of his nephew, who immediately began acting the role of petty despot. But Dunmore, Croghan, and Connolly all sought big profits in the seemingly endless expanse of land west of the Alleghenies.

Thus, when the Virginian Thomas Bullitt led a surveying party into

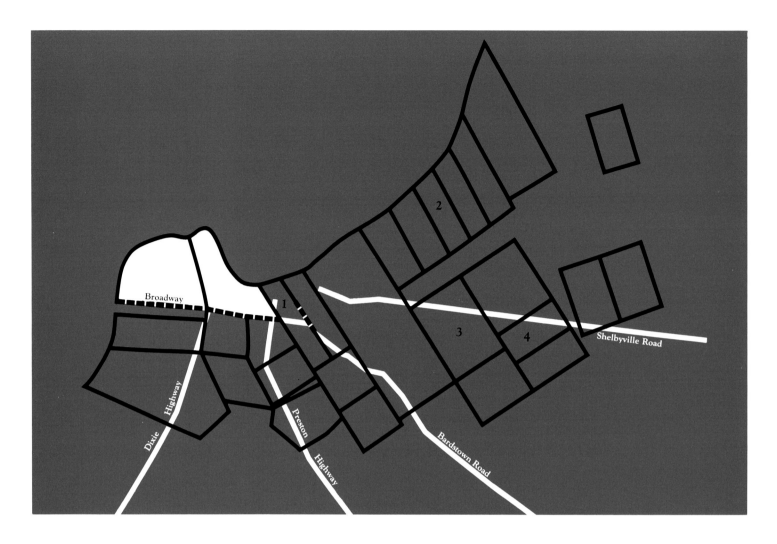

Broadway

Dixie Highway

Preston Highway

Bardstown Road

Shelbyville Road

1

2

3

4

The official 1774 Fincastle County survey of land claims at the Falls of the Ohio reaffirmed John Connolly's 1773 claim (white area), which became Louisville's central business district and West End. The survey lines through the wilderness set the general orientation of later property boundaries and even of many streets and roads.

Some of the other tracts shown are:
1. William Preston's 1,000 acres was directly east of the original Louisville boundary. The northern portion became Preston's Enlargement of 1827, the first territory annexed by Louisville.
2. William Peachey's 1,000 acres became the site of the Taylor family home, Springfield, and of President Zachary Taylor's grave. Hancock Taylor, an uncle of the future president and a member of the 1774 surveying party, was killed in an Indian raid before the surveyors returned to Virginia.
3. John Floyd's 2,000 acres included what is now the heart of St. Matthews.
4. John Ware's 1,000 acres passed through various hands. By 1787, when it was purchased by Alexander Scott Bullitt, it was already known as the 'Oxmore Tract.' Part of the site is now occupied by Oxmoor shopping center.
Map based on research by Neal O. Hammon.

Kentucky in 1773, he almost certainly had Dunmore's blessing. Bullitt was acting as agent for Virginia officers who had been awarded land grants for service in the French and Indian War. One group of Bullitt's party laid out claims at the Falls of the Ohio. Most of the thirty tracts of 1,000 to 2,000 acres each were granted by Dunmore to associates of George Croghan. The choicest one of all, directly on the Falls, went to Connolly, whose service with British regulars as a surgeon's mate gained him a military claim to land. Connolly's land patent, dated December 16, 1773, gave him 2,000 acres that were to become the heart of Louisville. At the same time another 2,000 acres west of Connolly's land went to Pennsylvanian Charles DeWarrensdorff. That tract is now Louisville's West End north of Broadway. Because of questions about the legality of this survey, it was repeated in 1774 by deputy surveyors of Fincastle County.

Connolly had perhaps picked out the spot he wanted during his wide travels in the western country. In a lengthy conversation with George Washington at Pittsburgh in 1770, Connolly described the Ohio Valley, claimed to have been 400 miles up the Cumberland River, and talked of a fourteenth colony in Kentucky. Washington, who was looking for profits in western land, recorded the conversation in detail in his diary, calling Connolly "a very sensible Intelligent man."

Though the founders of the town of Louisville in 1779 knew of Connolly's claim, there was one important transaction of which they were not aware. After Connolly had secured his 2,000 acres at the Falls, he wanted more. He had obviously picked this as an important spot. Immediately west was the 2,000-acre tract that had been awarded to DeWarrensdorff. To acquire that tract, too, Connolly turned for financial aid to John Campbell, the man who would later dispatch news of the French alliance to Corn Island. Campbell

The 1773 town survey

Isaac Hite, later a resident of Jefferson County, was a member of Thomas Bullitt's 1773 surveying party at the Falls. His daily Journal shows that a town was laid out at the Falls five years before Clark and his company arrived at Corn Island.

"Aug. 5th & 6th at the Town at the Falls."

"Friday 27th [August] went & marked out lots in the Town & went up to the 1st Island."
Journal of Isaac Hite, 1773.

The 1774 survey

Thomas Hanson, a member of John Floyd's party which resurveyed the tracts at the Falls in 1774, kept a daily Journal, just as Hite did the previous year. His entry for May 30, 1774, indicates that John Campbell was very much a silent partner in Connolly's land venture. Douglass was another surveyor.

"Mr. Douglass made a survey at the falls for Dr. Connelly, of 4,000 acres. Here is a large body of flat land, which is indifferent next to the River, but a Piece back it is very good land."
Thomas Hanson's Journal, 1774.

was another important man at Pittsburgh and, like many there, a Scotch-Irish immigrant who had found profit in the fur trade with the Indians. Campbell agreed to a joint purchase of the DeWarrensdorff acreage, a transaction completed early in 1774. In return for advancing Connolly's share of the purchase price, Campbell received a half interest in Connolly's original 2,000 acres and a mortgage note. The advertisement of town lots followed soon after.

The settlers first learned of this significant twist in the land title in the summer of 1779 from Campbell himself. He came to Louisville, probably because of news reaching Pittsburgh of the town beginning to rise on the land in which he had an interest. Without doubt, he informed the trustees of his transaction with Connolly, whose Tory activities had put him in an American prison. Whatever the discussions, Campbell left Louisville in late September, joining a convoy of keel boats bound upriver with Spanish gunpowder for Fort Pitt. On October 4 the flotilla was ambushed near the present site of Cincinnati by several hundred Indians, led by Simon Girty and Matthew Elliott (the same Elliott who had led the unsuccessful scouting party to the Falls in January). The ambush was a major disaster for the Americans. Practically the entire party of seventy men was killed and John Campbell was taken prisoner.

Connolly's and Campbell's claims to the land where Louisville was gaining the look of a small, but permanent, settlement, did not extend to the land south and east. That land belonged to others as a result of the 1774 survey. It was inviting land, especially to the east on Beargrass Creek. In 1779 the first moves were made to settle there—by squatters and by one man who already owned his land—John Floyd. Though Floyd had not come to the Falls with Clark, he was no stranger to the area. He had been here in 1774 as head of the surveying party sent out by William Preston to legalize Dunmore's 1773 surveys. Like hundreds of others, Floyd had fallen under Kentucky's spell. He wanted to have part of this Kentucky empire for himself, and on the 1774 surveying trip he got it.

Floyd purchased the rights of two Virginia officers to their 1,000-acre tracts, evidently before he left Virginia with the surveying party, then laid them out adjacent to each other so that he had 2,000 acres encompassing present-day St. Matthews and southward to a little beyond the present Watterson Expressway. Five years later, with a town rising at the Falls and settlers beginning to stream in, Floyd decided it was time to occupy his land. On November 8, 1779, he arrived at the Falls with his new wife and infant son. As was frequently the case among the settlers, he was accompanied by numerous other kin: three of his brothers and his two brothers-in-law, Eleazer LeMaster and James A'Sturgus and their families, plus a black slave named Bob. With high hopes, Floyd immediately set to work to erect a cabin nearly in the center of his 2,000 acres.

The thoughts of the black man are lost forever, but he was never to see the coming of spring to Kentucky. "…the first tree Bob cut down on the place lodged and slipped back on the stump and tore off his right foot, or at least all the skin and flesh from his ankle down," Floyd wrote to William Preston, his former employer and the man who had been his wife's guardian. The Floyds cared for Bob as best they could, but there was actually no remedy. He died about the first of February, probably from gangrene, and lies in an unmarked grave somewhere in the St. Matthews area, probably the first black man to die in what is now Jefferson County.

The following spring Floyd erected a stockade that was known as Floyd's Station, though he himself called it Woodville. (Its hilltop location is near the Jamestown Apartments, west of Breckinridge Lane.) He had arrived on his property none too soon. Before he got there, eleven cabins had been built by squatters, testimony to the emigration that had begun in 1779 and would soon reach floodtide proportions. John Floyd was the first person

Above: John Floyd, who headed the Fincastle County surveyors on their 1774 mission at the Falls, became a permanent resident of the area in 1779 on land he had chosen during the surveying expedition. After his death in a 1783 Indian ambush, his widow married Alexander Breckinridge. The road leading to Floyd's former home site became Breckinridge Lane. A tributary of Salt River was named Floyd's Fork by the 1774 surveyors to honor their chief.
The Filson Club

to occupy land in what is now Jefferson County who had a clear title to his property.

This Jefferson County pioneer was of a somewhat different background than most of the townspeople at the Falls. His family had been in Virginia for generations; indeed his swarthy complexion was attributed to his descent on his mother's side from the grandaughter of Pocahontas. He was born in Amherst County on the eastern side of the Blue Ridge, though within sight of that blue-shrouded mountain range. Floyd came from a planter family. His father, though not a Tidewater planter, had not been forced to the rugged mountain country. Floyd was evidently able to pay the price that the two Virginia officers demanded for their land claims, or to secure the claims on credit.

Floyd's hopes for a future in Kentucky were recalled years later by his close friend and fellow-Virginian Nathan Reid, "Frequently have Floyd and myself sat down on a log or at the foot of a tree and giving a free rein to our heated imaginations, constructed many a glorious castle in the air. He would, on such occasions, contrast the many discomforts that then beset us with the pleasures we should one day enjoy in the possession of boundless wealth."

Significantly, the Floyd party came to the Falls through Cumberland Gap, riding horseback, driving cattle with them. Geography made the overland route more convenient than the river for Virginia and Carolina newcomers arriving from east of the Alleghenies. Floyd represented a group that was to dominate the county in its early years—the rising, well-landed gentry, as opposed to the generally less-affluent settlers of Louisville.

The little town, which had learned from a flood in the spring that the Ohio River could be a foe as well as a friend, soon had another example of nature's unpredictability in the Ohio Valley. Few of the cattle brought in by new settlers during the summer survived the frigid weather that caused the river to freeze over, coated the surrounding forest in shimmering ice, and brought frequent blinding snow storms in what became known in local tradition as "the hard winter." On Beargrass Creek the Floyds (and the squatters, soon to be turned into tenant farmers) suffered through the cold. In February 1780, Floyd wrote William Preston that when "I attempted to write in Dec'r the Ink froze in the pen and it is no better yet, as the snow has never melted off the south side of the cabin since the first of last month." This "hard winter" demonstrated the close relationship between the Ohio River and Louisville's economics. Corn was in short supply, and by January, when the frozen Ohio made it impossible to bring in corn from the upper Ohio, the price had climbed to $165 a bushel in depreciated Continental currency. By May, after the river was open, the price dropped to $30.

The extremely cold weather had only one advantage to Louisville and Kentucky: it kept Indian raids to a minimum as the red men, too, huddled against the cold in the villages north of the Ohio River. But spring plus British encouragement would bring them out in force. The winter was hard. The summer of 1780 would be harder.

Chapter Three
Settling In

Though 1780 dawned frigid and snowy at the Falls, spring finally made its way to the Ohio Valley, bringing with it the vanguard of a veritable army of newcomers. The new settlers began arriving as soon as the ice disappeared from the river, some as early as March. Virginia's new land law, adopted in 1779, and George Rogers Clark's success in the Illinois country had combined to open the floodgates of settlement. On May 5, Floyd wrote that "near three-hundred large boats have arrived at the Falls this spring with families…. We have six stations on B. Grass with not less than 600 men. You would be surprised to see 10 or 15 waggons at a time going to & from the Falls every day with families & corn."

In the Jefferson County-to-be, the most desirable lands lay east of Louisville on the Middle Fork of Beargrass Creek, called "the garden of the state." William Linn, the man who delivered the news of the French alliance to Clark, had moved out to Beargrass by May 1779, establishing Linn's Station at what is now the Hurstbourne Country Club. It was one of the six stockaded stations that were established by the spring of 1780.

Three of the new stations were on land leased from Floyd. Hogland's was on the creek, just 2,000 feet west of Floyd's stockade, perhaps on the very spot now occupied by the club house of the Big Spring Country Club. The Low Dutch (or New Holland) Station, near where Brown's Lane now crosses Beargrass Creek, was home to a group of Pennsylvania Germans. Spring Station was north of the creek on high land where a spring still issues forth, forming a small stream flowing into Beargrass. The stockade may have been built by Samuel Beal, for whom the stream was named Beal's Branch. He built an imposing home on the site in 1795 when the Indian menace and the need for "forting" was past.

The sixth stockade was the A'Sturgus Station, built by Peter A'Sturgus a little south of the present Oxmoor shopping center. The land passed through several hands and was already called Oxmoor when Alexander Scott Bullitt became master of the estate in 1787. Linn's, beyond the A'Sturgus Station, was the easternmost point of local settlement until Squire Boone built a stockade at Painted Stone in what is now Shelby County.

Though the Middle Fork of Beargrass Creek was "the garden," other parts of the future Jefferson County abounded in excellent land, including the area along the South Fork of Beargrass, where the well-to-do Speed family from Virginia was later to settle on acreage they named Farmington. In the spring of 1780, a stockade was erected by James Sullivan on or near the present site of the Heritage House nursing home at 3411 Bardstown Road.

Back at the Falls, the "Burrough of Lewisville," still operating under the year-old directive of the Kentucky County Court, was so concerned about the "many villanys" that it took judicial matters into its own hands, elected six magistrates in June 1780, and designated the home of Captain William Oldham as a Court House. From one of the magistrates' first acts, setting rules for selling whiskey, we learn that three residents were already engaged in distilling: Evan Williams, Marsham Brashears, and Jacob Myers. There was also concern about the title to the land. A recent Virginia law permitted the State to escheat (seize) and sell property of Tories. With John Connolly a known Tory and John Campbell vanished into the wilderness, there was real danger that the land would be taken and sold right from under those who had drawn for lots and paid the price to the Town trustees. In fact, a jury met in Lexington, considered the evidence against Connolly, and found on July 1, 1780, that he was a British subject and that his land could be seized.

This threat to the settlers' titles may have been the spark that caused them to appeal rather forlornly to the Virginia legislature for a town charter and for confirmation of ownership so that they would not be "turned out of the houses we have built." Of thirty-nine signers of the petition, only two were among the Corn Island settlers: James Patten and John Tewell. The

A Breckinridge letter

Virginian Alexander Breckinridge, who came to the Falls area soon after his release from a British prison ship in 1781, established residence along Beargrass near Floyd's Station. Here are extracts from a letter Breckinridge wrote in August 1783 to his half-brother, John Breckinridge, in Virginia.

"Since I wrote you last…we have the disagreeable news of Mr. [Walker] Daniels being killed and a Mr. Knightly, (Merchant at the Falls); Mr. [William] Johnston, Clerk of this County slightly wounded and made his escape and three prisoners taken with several horses. This happened on the road between the Falls and the Salt Works and within about a mile of where our friend Col. Floyd was wounded.

"By a late account from a prisoner among some of the Wabash tribes informs there are as many [as] 200 Indians out with an intention to do murder and it generally supposed they are to come to this quarter…that now we have every reason to suppose that party has paid us a visit but it is supposed chiefly with an intention to steal horses."

Filson Club History Quarterly, July 1965

Assembly responded favorably with a State charter that invested title in the trustees so that Louisville became its own proprietor.

But the charter changed political affairs in the settlement. Now the trustees were appointed by the legislature, not elected by the inhabitants, and the early hope that each "adventurer" would own only one lot was lost forever. Also, the legislators, looking to help fill the Virginia treasury, empowered their new trustees to sell lots "for the best price that can be had." Under the charter the land was safe from seizure, but the bulk of the purchase price went to the State. There was now no restriction on the amount of land that could be owned by one individual. By early 1786 a total of 300 lots had been sold, with numerous persons owning several.

William Johnston had acquired thirty-five by 1786. Johnston, a native of Virginia, educated at William and Mary College, arrived here in 1782, and about 1785 acquired acreage on the high lands east of town, which he called Cave Hill Farm. (Today it is Cave Hill Cemetery.) With the new charter and newcomers arriving almost daily, it might have seemed that all was well at the Falls of the Ohio. But if the settlers thought Clark's Illinois campaign had intimidated the Indians, 1780 was to show how wrong they were.

Hit-and-run raids must have started early. Timothy Corn, a member of a large family who arrived by flatboat in March from Redstone, recalled that upon landing near Beargrass Creek (then emptying into the Ohio between Third and Fourth streets) the family was "informed by some of the men belonging to the Fort that if we did not immediately hurry to the Fort and take shelter that we would all be killed by the Indians."

By May, John Floyd wrote from his station to William Preston that "Hardly one week pass[es] without some one being scalped between this and the Falls and I [have] almost got too cowardly to travel about the woods without company." In mid-May, Captain Abraham Chapline, escaping from Indian captivity in Ohio, brought news of worse to come. He grimly reported that the British were mounting a major invasion of Kentucky from Detroit. The force of some 600 Indians and British regulars, under the command of Captain Henry Bird, a Virginia Tory, was to bring artillery with it. The principal objective was the fort at Louisville along with the stockades on Beargrass Creek.

The new settlers were scarcely prepared for such a reception. While George Rogers Clark was busy at the mouth of the Ohio establishing the short-lived Fort Jefferson, Colonel George Slaughter, who had recently arrived from Virginia with 150 militiamen as a replacement garrison for the Louisville fort, sent a frantic plea for 1,500 more troops, a quota the state probably could not have supplied even in the best of times.

Captain Bird and his large force appeared on schedule, the boats coming down the Great Miami River and reaching the Ohio near present Cincinnati in June. From here the British and Indians could float down to the Falls in thirty hours with practically no opposition. Louisville, still worrying about land titles, seemed to be on the verge of destruction before it received its cherished charter. The little log fort would be no match for artillery. These were tense days at the Falls, but then the unpredictability of the Indian warriors saved the day for Louisville. Tory Alexander McKee, John Campbell's former business associate, who accompanied the British force, explained to the commander at Detroit what happened. "…it was proposed and strongly urged by us, to proceed down the river against the Enemies Forts at the Falls of the Ohio…which would have been a fatal stroke to the Enemies settlement in that country, the Indians could not be prevailed to come into it…."

The Indians from the Ohio country had good tactical reasons for their reluctance. They feared that while they left their own villages undefended, Kentuckians from the settlements on the Licking would swoop down on them. So the British force, even larger than Chapline had guessed, number-

Above: In an attempt to discourage Indian incursions into Kentucky, George Rogers Clark built an armed galley to patrol the stream. The life of this vessel, probably the first ever constructed at Louisville, was short. The recent painting, commissioned by the U.S. Marine Corps, is based on contemporary descriptions. The history of the galley is told in the documents quoted below.

"We are going to Build armed Boats to station at the Mouth of Miami to dispute the navigation of the Ohio either up or down...find out and encourage Boatbuilders and good workmen to repair to this place immediately, they shall have good wages in hard Money. Ship Carpenters...shall have almost what wages [they] will ask."
Clark to Joseph Lindsay, March 5, 1782.

"We have...a Galley on the Stocks that will be furnished in about twenty days, that I think will do business: She is seventy three feet keel...to have forty six oars [,] one hundred ten men...gunnels...play on hinges and raise her side so high that she can lay within pistol shot of the shore without the lease danger."
Clark to Virginia Governor Benjamin Harrison, May 2, 1782.

"I enlisted in Captain [Jacob] Pyatt's company of Marines...and was in service on board said boat guarding the Ohio River till about the 1st of September [1782] when our boat sunk at the mouth of a creek called Bear Grass at the Falls of the Ohio."
Deposition of Cornelius Darnell in 1832 in his application for a military pension.
U.S. Marine Corps

ing perhaps 1,200, marched up the Licking Valley, winning ridiculously easy victories with the artillery at Ruddle's and Martin's stations near present-day Paris. It was the worst defeat Kentucky suffered during the Revolution. The British officers, probably disappointed because they could not persuade their Indian allies to march on Louisville, withdrew the invading army after these two attacks, taking prisoners to Detroit. Louisville was saved through sheer luck.

That Kentucky could survive and grow despite such massive losses is an indication of the tremendous desire for land and independence that animated a colonial society throwing off old shackles. Settlers continued to pour in, especially to the lush Bluegrass area of central Kentucky. Clark's decision to locate his outpost at the Falls, a better location for the management of his Illinois expedition than an outpost at the Kentucky River, also laid the groundwork for the Louisville area and central Kentucky to develop separately. The Falls was not geographically situated to serve as a protective shield for the Bluegrass and thus developed no ties to this chief focus of early settlement. Instead, the Falls region looked only to its own defense, since its exposed position made it more subject to frequent Indian forays. Lexington grew more rapidly in population and wealth in the early days. The long rivalry of the two towns was thus set from the beginning.

The rapid growth of 1780 strained the ability of the Kentucky County Court to deal with the increasing multiplicity of administrative and legal problems, and before the year was out petitions went off to the Virginia legislature asking that Kentucky County be divided into smaller units. The petition "of the inhabitants at and near the Falls of the Ohio" claimed "at least 800 settlers and daily increasing" and pointed out that they were "near 100 miles from the Court House" at Harrodsburg, a trip of four or five days on foot. Fifty-eight persons signed the petition, including Daniel Boone.

The Assembly responded favorably, voting (apparently in November) to approve the division of Kentucky into three counties: Fayette, with Lexington as the county seat; Lincoln, with Harrodsburg as the seat; and Jefferson (named for Thomas Jefferson, who had succeeded Patrick Henry as governor), with Louisville as the seat. Kentucky County had been huge; Jefferson was still large, extending generally from the Kentucky River on the east to Green River on the west. (Since then, twenty-eight other counties or parts of counties have been carved from this original territory.) Though Louisville was the county seat, court sessions were also held at various stations for the convenience of the residents. John Floyd was named County lieutenant on the recommendation of George Rogers Clark.

Though the greater tide of settlers poured into the Bluegrass, Louisville also continued to grow. In November 1780 Clark, proposing that some boats be built for military use, suggested that they be made at the Falls "as here is saw mills plenty." The little settlement was beginning to develop rudimentary industrial operations, including the production of salt. Jefferson County, in fact, became the most important center for the production of salt for the whole western country until early in the Nineteenth Century. Without the presence of salt, a food preservative, the settlement of the Falls area would have been much slower.

The salt-making conducted at Bullitt's Lick (in present Bullitt County west of Shepherdsville) and at Mann's Lick (now Fairdale) eventually employed hundreds of workers in around-the-clock operations. By 1787 Lexington merchants were advertising in *The Kentucky Gazette* "A Constant supply of the best of salt, from Mann's Lick." French botanist Andre Michaux watched the salt-making process at "Manslick" in 1795 and described how the salt water was raised from wells by horse-operated pumps and boiled in long lines of iron kettles over wood fires tended by black slaves. Portions of the road to this early industrial site still bear the historic name of Manslick Road.

Above: The easily constructed flatboat brought thousands of Kentucky settlers downriver. This example, from a French publication of 1796, is probably a "Kentucky boat," designed for a trip no farther than the Falls of the Ohio. Naturalist-artist John James Audubon, who was also a prolific writer, described the craft in action.

"But have [travelers] told you, kind reader, that…a boat thirty or forty feet in length, by ten or twelve in breadth, was considered a stupendous fabric; that this boat contained men, women and children, huddled together, with horses, cattle, hogs and poultry…while the remaining portion was crammed with vegetables and packages of seeds? The roof or deck of the boat was not unlike a farmyard, being covered with hay, ploughs, carts, wagons, and various agricultural implements [and] spinning wheels. Even the sides of the floating-mass were loaded with the wheels of the different vehicles, which themselves lay on the roof."
St. Louis Mercantile Library

Above right: The interior of a flatboat provided not only space for cargo or family possessions, but also provided living and sleeping quarters. Some were even equipped with a crudely constructed fireplace for cooking and for warmth.
Tulane University

In addition to this beginning of industry, the Falls area began to attract its first substantial 'foreign' community—the French. Though but a dot on the map of frontier America, Louisville's position on the river and at the Falls promised a bright commercial future. Probably the first of these French-born immigrants to Kentucky was Barthelémi Tardiveau, who arrived by 1781, perhaps earlier, supplying flour to Clark's regiment and receiving in pay the one thing Virginia had in abundance—Kentucky land. He used the land to trade for marketable products, especially tobacco, which very early became an important Kentucky product.

Soon Tardiveau was in Louisville, bringing his European mercantile experience to the frontier community, where he established a firm trading in furs, flour, and land. The trade patterns of Tardiveau and other early merchants tell much about Louisville's long-distance trade connections—to Philadelphia and New Orleans—dictated by its river location. Philadelphia merchants reached the Ohio Valley overland to Pittsburgh (route of the famed Conestoga wagons).

Trade the other way was another matter. Taking boats upstream to Pittsburgh by manpower was a slow and costly business. The only economically feasible way to get Kentucky's goods to market was down the river by flatboat to Spanish New Orleans. And the Spanish paid in gold and silver coin, a boon to money-starved Kentucky, where the wild depreciation of both Continental and Virginia currency brought the ancient art of barter back into fashion. Tardiveau and another early French trader, Jean Honoré, were the first to exploit the New Orleans trade, beginning in 1782.

But while Louisville and Jefferson County slowly began to take on the look and characteristics of a community that had come to stay, the British at Fort Detroit still had other ideas. Bird had not been able to get the Indians to

Above: During the Nineteenth Century Locust Grove was 'modernized' in the architectural fashion of the time. Purchased jointly by the Commonwealth of Kentucky and Jefferson County, it was opened as a historic home in 1964.
Filson Club

Opposite: The early attempt to recreate Virginia's plantation economy and society in Jefferson County has left two handsome survivors, both now museum homes open to the public. Locust Grove (top), on Blankenbaker Lane, was built about 1790 by Major William Croghan, whose wife, Lucy, was a sister of George Rogers Clark. Following the amputation of a leg in 1809, Clark lived here until his death in 1818. Farmington (bottom), on Bardstown Road, was erected in 1810 by John Speed and his wife, the former Lucy Fry, using architectural features favored by Thomas Jefferson. Their children included James Speed, who served briefly as attorney general in Abraham Lincoln's cabinet, and Joshua Speed, a Springfield, Ill., friend of Lincoln. Joshua became an original developer of Louisville's Highlands neighborhood.
Photography by John Beckman

attack Louisville in 1780, but 1781 offered another chance. It was also the year that Clark again attempted his long-cherished plan to capture Detroit, receiving a brigadier general's commission from Virginia and recruiting reluctant troops from war-weary Virginia and western Pennsylvania.

In the middle of August both the British and Clark's troops were on the move and collided unexpectedly on that dangerous stretch of the Ohio River below Cincinnati, where the Great Miami, route of Indian parties, comes into the Ohio. The British and their Indian allies let Clark's main force of nearly 400 men pass, then lay in wait for a smaller following group of Pennsylvania volunteers headed by Colonel Archibald Lochry. Caught by surprise, the Americans were quickly defeated and all survivors taken prisoner. Ironically, this defeat probably spared Louisville because it convinced the Indians (correctly) that Clark was now too crippled to make a move.

The British force was smaller than the huge 1780 force, but it was still formidable—more than 400 Indians plus 100 British rangers. Alexander McKee again commanded the Indians. Still anxious to draw Clark's troops "into an action near the neighborhood of the Falls," McKee prodded the somewhat reluctant warriors southward. In early September the settlers at Squire Boone's station in present Shelby County, alarmed by the increasing 'Indian signs,' decided to go back to the Beargrass for greater safety. As the refugees approached Long Run Creek on September 15, they and their lagging militia escort stumbled right into an Indian ambush that became known as the Long Run Massacre. Seven settlers were killed, including some women, but the Indians were driven off. The rest of the party managed to get to Linn's before nightfall with the news.

This was the climax of a bad season for the settlers. Linn himself had been killed in an Indian ambush in early spring while on the way to Louisville to attend a session of the new Jefferson County Court. Floyd, as County lieutenant, dispatched a report to Governor Thomas Jefferson in April that declared, "We are all obliged to live in Forts in this Country, and notwithstanding all the Caution that we use, forty-seven of the Inhabitants have been killed & taken by the Savages. Besides a number wounded since Jany. last—Amongst the last is Major William Lyn." After the Long Run attack, Floyd gathered militia and volunteers to bury the dead and pursue what he called the "execrable Hell hounds." He found his quarry near present-day Eastwood. Famed Indian fighter Bland Ballard, who was along, later recalled that Floyd "was decoyed onto a ridge in pursuit of some indians that showed themselves and the indians just fired on them from both sides...." It was another American defeat. Of Floyd's twenty-six men, seventeen were killed, one of them his brother-in-law, Eleazar LeMaster. A monument marks the site of what the pioneers called Floyd's Defeat.

McKee reported to the commander at Fort Detroit that after the attacks at Long Run and on Floyd's force "The Lake Indians...thinking they had scalps and prisoners sufficient, did not even halt on the ground." So Louisville squeaked through again because of the Indians' independent ways.

Though McKee does not mention it, another reason the Indians did not want to press on might have been the new Fort Nelson at Louisville, the first section of which had been completed six months earlier by Richard Chenoweth under a £15,000 contract with the military authorities. The construction of this new fort between Main Street and the river, with the main gate near Seventh Street, was a response to news of the planned British invasion of 1781. The fort was begun in January 1781 and completed in March.

Fort Nelson represented a vast improvement over the hastily thrown together stockade at Twelfth Street. Undoubtedly the strongest fortification in the West aside from Fort Pitt, it was probably constructed to withstand artillery, though its capabilities were never tested. Fort Nelson, because it was moved upriver from the site of the first fort, hastened the development of the area by the harbor as the heart of the city.

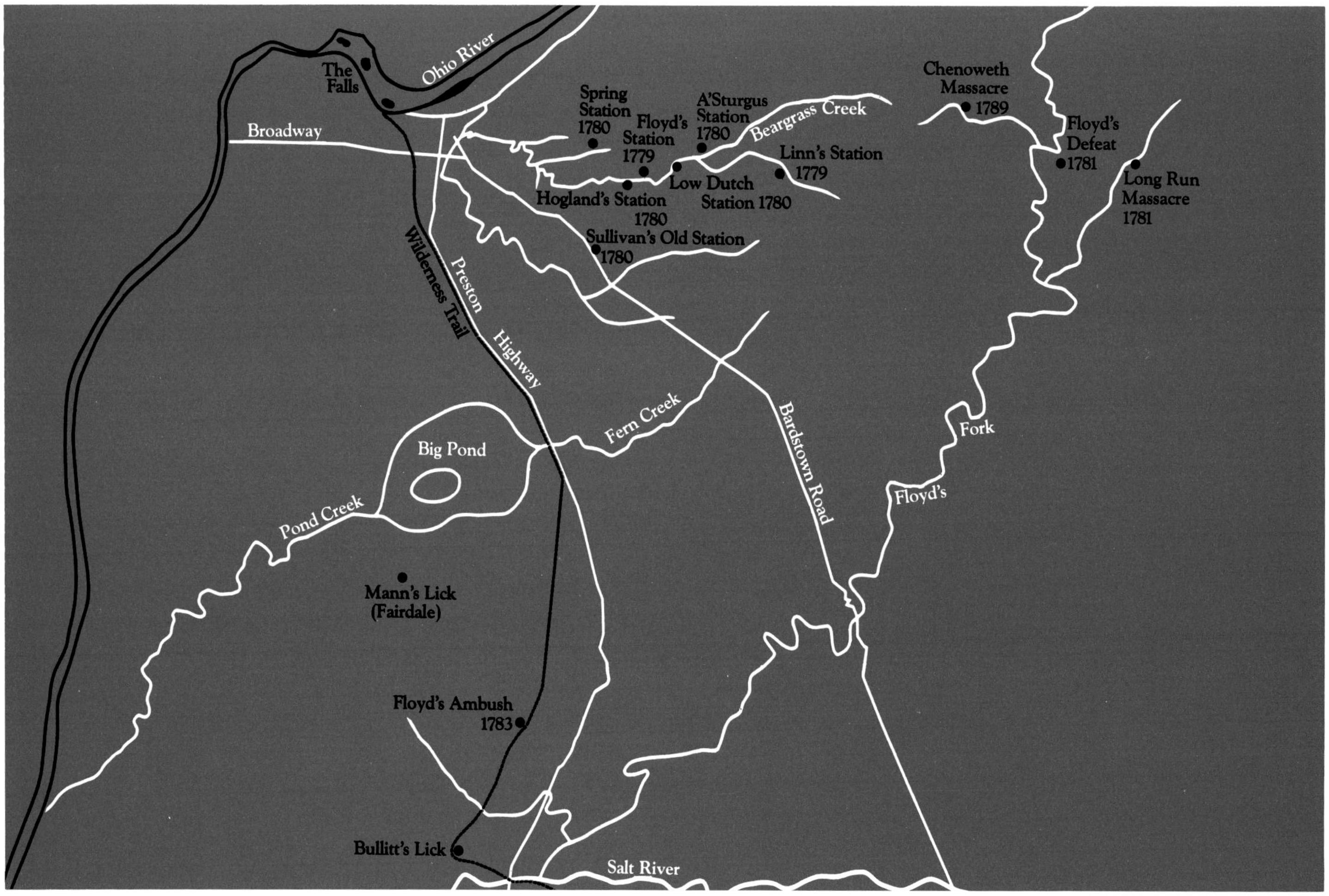
Ohio River
The Falls
Broadway
Spring Station 1780
Floyd's Station 1779
A'Sturgus Station 1780
Beargrass Creek
Linn's Station 1779
Low Dutch Station 1780
Hogland's Station 1780
Sullivan's Old Station 1780
Chenoweth Massacre 1789
Floyd's Defeat 1781
Long Run Massacre 1781
Wilderness Trail
Preston Highway
Bardstown Road
Fern Creek
Fork
Floyd's
Big Pond
Pond Creek
Mann's Lick (Fairdale)
Floyd's Ambush 1783
Bullitt's Lick
Salt River

Above: The six stations along Beargrass Creek east of Louisville were all settled by 1780. Together with Louisville they formed the population center of early Jefferson County. This map also shows the location of other important places and events in the area's pioneer history. The Wilderness Trail, which entered Kentucky at Cumberland Gap, ended at the Falls. Broadway, Preston Highway, and Bardstown Road are shown as reference points only.

In any event, the Long Run Massacre and Floyd's Defeat proved to be the last time the Indians approached Louisville in force, though they continued to "infest the roads" for the rest of the decade, capturing or killing lone travelers or small parties, stealing horses, and killing cattle. John Floyd himself became a victim in the spring of 1783, killed just twelve days before the birth of a son, named John for his father and destined to become a governor of Virginia. Floyd, who some think might have become Kentucky's first governor, was buried not far from the new brick dwelling he had under construction at his station.

Most of the settlers killed, ambushed one by one, are faceless and nameless today, their very graves lost and forgotten; men of small means, their hopes were not as sweeping as those of a John Floyd, but pulsed as intensely. One is remembered only because his grandson became the sixteenth president of the United States. Abraham Lincoln, a native of Pennsylvania, who had migrated to the Shenandoah Valley by the late 1770s, staked out his claim on Long Run Creek in 1780, several years before he moved onto his land with his family. A convinced Baptist, Lincoln gave part of his land as the site of the Long Run Church. Then, on a day in May 1786, as he and his three young sons were returning from planting, an Indian bullet suddenly brought his hopes to an end. Tom Lincoln, only ten, watched his father die. It was a story he passed on to his children, including young Abraham, as the family moved about Kentucky, to Indiana, and then to Illinois.

Despite these and hundreds of similar incidents, Louisville itself was never attacked. That may have been because of Fort Nelson; more likely it was because of the final American victory in the Revolution and the end of British attempts to organize the Indians into large fighting forces. The British surrender at Yorktown came on October 17, 1781—one month after the Long

Run Massacre and Floyd's Defeat. With the coming of peace, the world wore a different and happier aspect for the outposts at the Falls. Change was in the wind for the little town and the stations founded in the midst of a long and often discouraging war for independence. As early as 1782 a school had been started by William Johnston with perhaps as many as twenty-five students. In 1783 the first retail store was opened by Daniel Brodhead in a large log building on the north side of Main between Fifth and Sixth.

Brodhead would accept in payment the certificates of deposit issued by John Sanders, who had established a "keep" in 1780, taking in furs and skins and issuing certificates for them—promises to pay as soon as the furs could be sold, usually in Pittsburgh. Since the certificates were transferable, they helped fill the need for a circulating medium of exchange. In 1785 a log Court House was built in Louisville (it burned in 1787 and was replaced in 1790 with a stone building) and the Court no longer continued its circuit around the stations. By 1786 a Mr. Nickle was conducting a dancing school.

But an old problem popped up again before 1783 was out. The end of the Revolution brought John Campbell back on the scene, asserting his interest in the Connolly lands. Campbell had not been heard from since the fall of 1779, when he had been captured by the Indians. Now it turned out that Campbell had been a British prisoner so openly defiant of royal authority that he had been refused parole or exchange. He had been held nearly four years and was not released until after the preliminary articles of peace had been signed by the Americans and English in November 1782.

Once released, Campbell turned his attention immediately to his land holdings, which were threatened with sale under the verdict of the 1780 jury of escheat. He had valid title not only to the half of Connolly's land excluded from the grant to Louisville but also to the 2,000 acres that is today's West End, which he had purchased from Connolly, though the deed had not been recorded. Campbell hastened to Richmond in the spring of 1783 and cajoled the Virginia Assembly into suspending the sale of lots in Louisville until a division line could be run to mark off his 1,000 acres.

Campbell's reappearance may account for the fact that a new town plat was made in 1783, adding Jefferson, Market, and Green streets, though none of these thoroughfares were formally named until later. The new plat was of a grid pattern that could be extended indefinitely over the flat plain. The green outlots to the south were perhaps the reason for the name Green Street. Later, a "slip" of ground 180 feet wide and just south of Green from First to Twelfth was set aside to be "common lots," presumably for pasturage of householders' livestock. The division line between Campbell's acreage and the Town's was run July 20, 1784, after a certain amount of squabbling between Campbell and the trustees, and was admitted to record by the Jefferson County Court on August 2, 1785.

The new line became the western boundary of the Town for many years, running from the river at Twelfth Street southwest to the southern boundary of Connolly's land, which became Louisville's southern boundary and today's Broadway. This street still undulates slightly from true east and west—a legacy of the 1774 surveyors, who apparently had a little trouble keeping the line straight through the wilderness. The eastern Town boundary angled southeast from the river at about First Street to the future Broadway, following the original survey of Connolly's land. The resulting shape was a bit unusual for it made Louisville a trapezoid in the wilderness. But at last the Town knew where it began and where it ended.

Campbell was able to prove his purchase of the West End tract, and the Jefferson County Court of Quarter Sessions awarded him title in 1790. He also pursued plans for a town on his 1,000 acres of the Connolly grant. He picked the "Lower Falls" (later to become Shippingport) as an eligible site and began advertising lots for sale as early as January 1784. He had already, in 1783, built a tobacco inspection warehouse there, but it was not profitable and in 1791 Campbell was back in Richmond seeking compensation for his losses. His petition was turned down on the advice of the State auditor, who noted that "if the Inspection doth not support itself it is therefore discon-tinued." Campbell's attempt to found a town was also discontinued about the same time, doubtless because it, too, failed to support itself.

Had circumstances been different, Louisville today might well honor John Campbell as its founder. He had seen the potential of the site in 1774 and backed up his belief with his money. His message on the French alliance dispatched from Fort Pitt to Clark had been a prime factor in the success of the Illinois campaign and, thus, the move from Corn Island to the mainland. The charter of Louisville had appropriated the most valuable half of the Connolly tract while Campbell was a British prisoner and unable to assert his claim. He had to settle for the less valuable portion. He finally left Louisville in the early 1790s for the Bluegrass. Not until after his death in 1799 did his land find a market.

The failure of Campbell's town venture is not surprising considering Louisville's slow growth in these years. Though the little town advanced, gaining more merchants and craftsmen, the Court House, and even a few brick dwellings among the cabins and frame houses, it did not move ahead during the 1780s and 1790s the way its geographical position promised. The reasons for Louisville's slow development, contrasted, say, to Lexington's more rapid growth, were numerous: Indian raids and threats of British attack frightened off settlers during the earlier years; legislative action suspended sale of lots for a time; and finally, the vagaries of Spanish policy on naviga-tion of the Mississippi seriously hampered the development of river trade. Louisville's position on the river dictated that it become a commercial city and until the river could achieve its full potential, Louisville grew slowly.

There were also more localized problems the town had to deal with. A petition by the residents to the Virginia Assembly in 1789 declared that they were "very much aggrieved by the appointment of new Trustees...who reside some distance from the town and....the Town & its interest would be much better regulated by men who live in it." Another problem emerged that caused many potential newcomers to avoid Louisville. As the town grew, there was a noticeable increase in sickness in the summer: fevers and chills called the 'ague'. Modern medicine ascribes this malaria-like illness to the mosquitoes breeding unchecked in the numerous ponds as frogs and other natural predators disappeared. Not until other epidemics, including small-pox, became so severe that they earned Louisville the name of "Grave-yard of the West," were steps taken to drain and fill the ponds.

Despite these obstacles to development, it seemed to most observers that Louisville had a bright future. In 1784 Hector St. John Creve Coeur, a

native of France, best known for his *Letters of an American Farmer,* arrived
at Louisville, a tourist on a flatboat load of newcomers. "What was my
surprise," he wrote, "when, in place of the huts, the tents, and primitive
cabins, constructed by mere chance and surrounded by palisades, of which
I had heard so much during the last five years, I saw numerous houses of two
stories, elegant and well painted, and (as far as the stumps of trees would
permit) that all the streets were spacious and well laid out."

In 1796 Moses Austin was not impressed. He described Louisville as
a town of about thirty houses, none "elegant," but may have been excluding
cabins from that count. He was unhappy with the accommodations, too,
finding no tavern that deserved "a better name than that of Grog Shop." How
subjective these impressions are is shown by an English visitor who came
through the next year and commented that there were "about 200 houses,
chiefly frame-built" and "pleasantly situated." By 1797 a few brick houses
were already rearing their red walls among the log and frame structures. The
first was erected by Frederick Augustus Kaye in 1789 (the same year as the
Chenoweth massacre) on the south side of Market between Fifth and Sixth
streets. Others soon followed and the town began to take on something of a
substantial air as the Nineteenth Century approached. But it was still a small,
compact community, and by 1800 had a population of only 359. Lexington
was far and away the metropolis of Kentucky with a population of 1,759.
Louisville, as a matter of fact, was only the fifth largest town in Kentucky, also
being eclipsed by Frankfort, Washington, and Paris.

The population of Jefferson County as a whole in 1800 also shows the
early ascendancy of central Kentucky. Jefferson's total of 8,754 fell far below
Fayette's 14,028. Jefferson County was thinly populated considering its area,
which included today's Shelby, Henry, Oldham, and Trimble, plus parts of
Franklin, Bullitt, Spencer, Carroll, and Anderson counties. But other little
towns were springing up in the Falls area, where most of Jefferson's population was still concentrated. In 1797 the County Court approved the petition
of Philip Buckner to lay out Middletown on part of his 500 acres, and of
Abraham Bruner to found Jeffersontown (called Brunerstown in its early
days) on his 122 acres.

All this activity showed the shape of the future in the Falls area. The
final defeat of the Indians in Ohio at the Battle of Fallen Timbers in 1794 had
forever removed the threat from that quarter. The Beargrass stations and the
other fortified points had disappeared by 1800 and remained only as memories of a fearful past. Even Fort Nelson was gone, its usefulness ended when
the United States Army built a strong fortification in 1786 on the north side
of the river. Now Louisville could turn its full attention to its greatest asset:
the winding, muddy, capricious, mighty Ohio River.

Chapter Four

The River That Made Louisville a Town

The Ohio River makes a great lazy double curve at Louisville, embracing the city, setting the northern and western limits, confusing strangers who find that both north-south and east-west streets have one end at the river's edge. The river shaped Louisville's early growth pattern, forming a community strung out along the river from Portland on the west to Butchertown and the Point on the east, crescent shaped to follow the river's curve. The great flat plain to the south and the high lands (a term early telescoped to Highlands) to the southeast remained mostly farm holdings until after the Civil War.

Founded when it was, where it was, Louisville could have developed no other way. It hugged its river lifeline, the river that brought troops for its fort, newcomers to buy its lots and found its trade and industry, and goods to stock its stores. The flatboats came by the hundreds, bringing settlers, their furniture, their wagons, their livestock, their poultry. No wonder the boats of settlers were called 'arks'. And whether the newcomers stayed in Louisville or trekked into Jefferson County or farther inland, their very boats helped build the town. Assembled along the Monongahela or around Pittsburgh, the ungainly, flat-bottomed, keelless vessels were sold for a few dollars after they had served their transportation purpose, providing inexpensive sawn timbers and boards for Louisville's early framed wooden structures.

The keelboat had one advantage over the flatboat; because it had a traditional hull, it moved through the water easily and could be rowed or manhandled upstream against the current, though it was a slow, laborious and expensive task when the keel was loaded with cargo. Sometimes, though, the keel could be moved by sail. The square-ended flatboat, designed to float with the current, could not be taken back upriver. It was built for a one-way trip.

But the flat, which required only a folk knowledge of carpentry for its construction, soon became the workhorse of the river; in fact, it remains so today in the form of the barge. Because of its simple construction, the flat could be built anywhere along the Ohio to take a locally assembled cargo. Many were probably built at Louisville, but early entrepreneurs here had an advantage; they could purchase flatboats that had ended their journey at the Falls and send them on to New Orleans, although there was a certain amount of risk in this. Flatboats built around Pittsburgh to carry settlers or cargo only as far as Kentucky—called Kentucky boats—were smaller than those built for cargo going to New Orleans and were usually rather flimsy.

With the end of the Revolution and a peace treaty in 1783 that promised free navigation of the Mississippi, Louisville seemed primed for growth. Located at the Falls, it stood to profit from portaging the produce of the rich lands of the Ohio Valley. But the Spanish put a sudden end to this first blooming. Before 1784 was over, a royal proclamation banned American navigation of the Mississippi through the territory where the Spanish claimed both sides of the river (Vicksburg and below). The Spanish looked with alarm on the relentless westward push of American settlement. Free navigation of the Mississippi, they feared, would only accelerate this mass movement that was not likely to halt at the border of Spanish territory.

When the Mississippi was closed, the shock waves were felt throughout Kentucky and were not to subside for nearly a decade, merging with the discontent of landless settlers, who found the bureaucratic red tape and loopholes in the land law worked mainly to the advantage of land speculators. Together, the two issues, the first political upheavals to wrack this western part of Virginia, would make Kentucky a separate state by 1792. The ineffectual efforts of Congress to deal with the issue of free navigation pushed Kentuckians' patience to near the breaking point. When rumors reached Kentucky of Secretary of Foreign Affairs John Jay's suggestion before a closed Congressional session in 1786 that the United States propose to Spain to suspend the right of Mississippi navigation for up to twenty-five years, there was

a political explosion. Some Kentuckians saw the proposal "as the workings of Eastern jealousy to smother us." Plans were openly discussed for raising a Kentucky military force, led by George Rogers Clark, to open the river by force. Despite the furor, some merchants remained hopeful.

Louisvillian Thomas Green, however, who felt that action was required immediately, became an outspoken leader in the effort to cut the Gordian knot. In a letter, allegedly to an unidentified New Englander but probably written only for propaganda in Kentucky and the Tennessee settlements, he declared that "Our situation is as bad as it can be; therefore every exertion to retrieve our circumstances must be eligible, manly and just." Military action, he proclaimed, was the only way to open the river, and if that is "not countenanced or succored by the United States (if we need it), our allegiance will be thrown off....Great Britain stands ready with open arms to receive and support us."

Strong words, but Green had lots of support, including pioneer Louisville settlers Marsham Brashears and James Patten, who were among those who paid to send an express with a similar letter to Georgia, which then extended to the Mississippi River. Clark, still seeking the full measure of military glory that eluded him through the failure of his two attempts to muster an army to take Detroit, also supported Green. Clark had been at rather loose ends ever since Virginia had dismantled its military establishment in the summer of 1783. The move not only left Clark without employment, but with a huge personal debt he had incurred during his campaigns. Virginia, also saddled with debt, found numerous excuses for not reimbursing its hero of the Illinois. Now it seemed Clark might substitute New Orleans for the lost opportunities at Detroit. But others, too, saw an opportunity in the explosive situation, especially the flamboyant James Wilkinson. The former Continental Army general had come to Lexington in late 1783 as representative of a firm of Philadelphia merchants. When the Mississippi was closed, the devious Wilkinson concocted a scheme that would enhance his purse, make him a hero in Kentucky, and lay the groundwork for what became known in Kentucky history as the Spanish Conspiracy. Military action against Louisiana did not fit into Wilkinson's neat plans. If Clark's

Clark in decline

"Saw Genl Clark, who is still more of a sot than ever, not company scarcely for a beast; his character, which once was so great, is now entirely gone with the people in this country; failed in his campaign last fall against the Wabash Indians…."
Erkuries Beatty Diary, April 19, 1787

General Clark has a visitor

"I had the pleasure of seeing this celebrated warrior at his lonely cottage seated on Clark's Point [in Clarksville]. This point is situated at the upper end of the Falls, particularly the lower rapid, commanding a full and delightful view of the falls, particularly the zig-zag channel which is only navigated at high water. The general has not taken much pains to improve this commanding and beautiful spot, but it is capable of being made one of the handsomest seats in the world. General Clark has now become frail and rather helpless but there are the remains of great dignity and manliness in his countenance, person and deportment, and I was struck with perhaps a fancied likeness to the great and immortal Washington."
Journal of Josiah Espy, 1805

A "frolick" on Corn Island

"We…saw the genteeler sort of people in numbers coming in from the country, each with a young girl behind them or woman on the same horse (the way of riding in this country), to a great Barbecue on the Island opposite Louisville, and to conclude with a Dance in town in the evening…Suppose there will be near 100 men and women at this frolick; saw some of the young ladies in town dressed in all their finery for the honor of the treat; some of them middling handsome, rich enough dressed but tawdry."
Erkuries Beatty Diary, April 19, 1787

reputation could be undermined, the pressure for armed intervention would also be undermined and a possible rival removed. Wilkinson, a master of innuendo and underhanded dealing, managed his campaign perfectly. He aimed unerringly at all Clark's weak spots, picturing him as a *former* but no longer competent military genius, one growing too fond of the bottle. Privately Wilkinson boasted that "the sun of General Clark's military glory has set, never more to rise."

While he was helping destroy Clark's reputation, Wilkinson launched his Spanish plan. In June 1787, despite the ban on navigation, he dispatched a convoy of flatboats from Louisville loaded with tobacco, salted hams, and butter gathered from a number of planters. When Wilkinson returned in early 1788, he announced to a delighted Kentucky that he had not only sold the cargo, but had arranged with Governor Estaban Miro for trade to be resumed. There was only one proviso: all trade had to be conducted through Wilkinson as agent. But he did not tell his Kentucky admirers all; he had taken a secret oath of loyalty to Spain and had agreed, for pay, to work for the separation of Kentucky from the Federal union with the ultimate aim of adding it to the Spanish dominions with himself as governor. Thus, when Wilkinson was named a Louisville Town trustee the following year by the Virginia legislature, he was a secret Spanish citizen.

His trade agreement with Miro was a juicy plum for a man who had arrived in Kentucky only four years earlier. It made Wilkinson perhaps the most powerful man in Kentucky, but there were few complaints. The way to New Orleans was again open and the threats of military action vanished. (Some Federalists, notably Humphrey Marshall, suspected treason behind the trade agreement but were unable to prove it.) Once again the Louisville harbor resounded to the boatmen's call, and the tempo increased even more after 1789 when Miro unexpectedly removed all barriers to Mississippi navigation and lowered import duties, provided the goods shipped were from the "western country" and not from east of the Alleghenies. (Congress thought this might mean a quickening flow of goods upriver, too, and that same year authorized a collector of customs for the "district of Louisville.")

The other political issue agitating Kentucky and especially Jefferson County was the discontent of the small army of settlers lured across the Alleghenies by cheap land, only to find that most of the good acreage had already been claimed by Virginia speculators who expected to sell at a handsome profit. The disappointed land seekers, who formed a loose quasi-political group called the partisans, were mostly non-Virginians. They had no political, social, or family ties to the Old Dominion as did, for instance, the Bullitts, Floyds, and Johnstons. The partisans had little in common except their dismay with the workings of the Virginia land law, a discontent they began to share as early as 1779. They were men of small means and large hopes, the kind John Floyd found established on his land on Beargrass Creek by the fall of 1779. By the middle 1780s they probably represented over half the population. Most were from Pennsylvania or North Carolina, but a number also came directly from Europe. Their political aim at first was to separate Kentucky from Virginia through action by Congress that would wipe out the Virginia land grants.

The movement was especially strong in Jefferson County because the river gateway brought an unusually large number of non-Virginia settlers who had braved Indian dangers and suffered hardship and misfortune on their voyages. One victim of a sunken boat recalled that "Although we saw a great many of our things a swimming off, their appeared to be not a murmur or regret, but only thankfull it was no worse than it was." After such trials, these settlers were in no mood to accept the special position of sometimes impecunious but well-landed young Virginians who hoped to make a fortune from land sales.

28

Early day farming
David Meriwether, whose family came to Jefferson County from Virginia in 1805 when he was a very young child, remembered the trip from Redstone to the Falls by flatboat and his first farm chores. The Meriwethers lived near the site occupied today by the Cane Run Generating Station of the Louisville Gas & Electric Company.

"In 1805 my father...purchased a farm on the banks of the Ohio River about eight miles below Louisville... There was but one house between our place and the city of Louisville and but one between us and the mouth of Salt River...When I was but a few years older, it was made my business to protect the growing crops from the depredations of wild animals. In the early spring of the year I was awakened before daybreak to take the dogs and chase the deer out of the wheat patches; when the grain of wheat had formed, I had to remain in the field all day to keep the wild turkeys from eating it. Then when the corn began to yield roasting ears, I had to go around the farm repeatedly every day to keep the squirrels out; at night before going to bed, I had to take the dogs and go around the field to scare the raccoons out to keep them from damaging the corn."
My Life in the Mountains and on the Plains

In a group so diverse and recently formed as the partisans, there were no obvious leaders. They exchanged laments during the days when Indian threats kept them "forted" in stations, feeding on each other's discontent and seeking someone who could speak for them all. In August 1780 George Rogers Clark wrote his father from Louisville that "The partizans in these Cuntries are again Soliciting me to head them as the Governor General as all those from foreign states are for a new Government[,] but my duty obliging me to Suppress all such proceedings I consequently shall loose the Interest of that party."

But the vacuum of leadership was eventually filled. John Campbell became the Jefferson County spokesman of the partisans almost immediately after his arrival in 1784. It was an alliance of convenience. He probably did not agree with the partisans' demand that uncultivated land be taxed (to lower its price and force its sale) since he himself hoped to own large uncultivated tracts. Neither was he in sympathy with the demand of some that slaves be freed without compensating their owners. But Campbell, through his Philadelphia commercial connections, represented would-be land speculators in the Keystone State who were being kept out by the Virginia speculators. Separation from Virginia suited the needs of Campbell's clients. Later the partisans, largely because of Campbell's influence, opposed separation when it appeared the Virginians would control the new government and keep all land claims intact.

The partisans had enough political strength to elect sympathetic delegates to the series of conventions held in Danville beginning in 1784 to discuss the question of statehood. John Campbell went from Jefferson County to two of the conventions as their representative, and the same group elected him a member of the convention that drew up Kentucky's first Constitution in 1792. Other Jefferson delegates included such large landholders as Richard Taylor (father of President Zachary Taylor) and Alexander Scott Bullitt. The partisan spirit had ebbed by 1792, though, as the landless began acquiring acreage that came on the market or drifted elsewhere—some to Spanish Louisiana. Others stayed in Kentucky, grubbing a living as best they could by doing the rough work of making salt at Bullitt's and Mann's Licks, tenant farming, hiring out for odd jobs. They were the people of whom a 1796 visitor to Kentucky commented, "...exhausted and worn down with stress and disappointment [they were] at last Obliged to become hewers of wood and Drawers of water."

John James Audubon

John James Audubon, (opposite), the famed naturalist-artist whose monumental Birds of America has become a classic, spent the years 1807-1810 in Louisville as a (not too successful) storekeeper. It was to Louisville that he brought his bride, the former Lucy Bakewell of Pennsylvania, in May 1808. The couple made their home in John Gwathmey's Indian Queen Tavern, where their first son, Victor Gifford Audubon, was born the following year. In Louisville Audubon spent more time tramping the woods and shore and sketching than in tending the store, and he cherished his memories of those years.

"Louisville in Kentucky has always been a favorite place of mine. The beauty of its situation on the banks of "La Belle Rivière," just at the commencement of the famed rapids…had attracted my notice, and when I removed to it…I found it more agreeable than ever….The rumbling sound of the waters as they tumble over the rock-paved bed of the rapids is at all times soothing to the ear….But, above all, the generous hospitality of the inhabitants and the urbanity of their manners, had induced me to fix upon it as a place of residence….

"I wish here to name those persons who so unexpectedly came forward to make our stay among them so agreeable ….The Croghans, the Clarks (our great traveler included), the Berthouds, the Galts, the Maupins, the Tarascons, the Beals, and the Booths, form but a small portion of the long list….We lived for two years at Louisville, where we enjoyed many of the best pleasures this life can afford; and whenever we have since chanced to pass that way, we have found the kindness of our former friends unimpaired."

Audubon, Ornithological Biography, 1831

But soon another opportunity opened for the landless, an opportunity for a man to find a place for himself on the river that tumbled through the rocky rapids at Louisville's front door. When the dispute with Spain over the northern extent of Spanish territory east of the Mississippi was finally settled (at the present northern border of Florida) by the Pinckney Treaty of 1795, the navigation question was officially settled as well. No longer would trade be at the whim of the New Orleans governor. Spain agreed not only to free navigation, beginning in 1798, but also to the "right of deposit," which eliminated Spanish import duties on goods shipped abroad. New Orleans became a free-trade zone and the positive impact rolled up the river and bathed all Kentucky. Now the state's produce could be sold to the world and not just to Spain. The river trade, picking up ever since Miro's relaxation of restrictions in 1789, began to boom. Louisville, right at the point of portage, began at last to reap the benefit of its geography.

In 1795 Louisville got a tobacco warehouse to replace John Campbell's earlier unsuccessful venture. This time it was on the town's own waterfront at the mouth of Beargrass Creek near Third Street. The legislative act that authorized the warehouse also permitted the town to levy a property tax earmarked for clearing out "the harbor in the mouth of Beargrass" and gave Louisvillians the right to elect their own trustees. Increasing river traffic caused the Kentucky legislature to create the post of Falls pilot in 1797 because of the "many boats lost in attempting to pass the rapids of the Ohio for want of a Pilot." The Jefferson County Court named Corn Islander John Patten to the post. And in 1799 Congress, anticipating an increase in foreign imports upriver from New Orleans, enlarged the territory of the Louisville customs office to include "all trade" on the Mississippi as well as the Ohio. There was even talk of a canal to bypass the Falls. But the most unusual result of the elimination of port duties into Spanish Louisiana was the brief boom in building ocean-going sailing vessels on the Ohio. Since goods did not now have to go through customs, there seemed no need to unload river craft at New Orleans and reload for foreign shipment. Even before the import duties were lifted, a few ocean-going vessels had been built on the river.

One of the first of these sailing ships was a Louisville product, the schooner *Caroline*, built in 1794, probably below the Falls. Richard Clough Anderson, Sr., owner of Soldier's Retreat, a plantation on Beargrass Creek that is today's Hurstbourne area, built the unlucky *Caroline*—she made only one trip to Europe before she was wrecked in the Bahamas. But with the new treaty, builders on the Monongahela and around Pittsburgh began building ocean vessels in earnest, blithely ignoring the obstacle of the Falls to such deep-draft ships. The first of these small but seaworthy craft, the *Monongahela Farmer*, arrived at Louisville June 16, 1800, then had to wait until the following January for winter rains to raise the river enough to enable the craft, of 100 tons burden, to brave the Falls. Other ships soon followed, and Louisville's harbor took on the look of a real seaport as these vessels unloaded cargo (to ride higher in the water) and waited for a good chance to shoot the foaming rapids.

This improbable venture of building ocean-going vessels on the Ohio so excited the imagination of a firm of French merchants in Philadelphia, John Tarascon and his brother Louis, that they moved operations to Pittsburgh in 1802 and quickly established one of the most important shipyards there. They soon took into partnership one of their clerks, James Berthoud. Combining shipbuilding with merchandising, the Tarascons sent their own goods in their own vessels, as well as building ships on contract. The career of one Tarascon-built ship, the *Louisiana*, reveals some of the problems encountered by an ocean vessel from the Ohio. She ran ashore near the present site of Paducah and was stuck for two weeks until the river rose, was becalmed in the Mississippi below New Orleans, then ran into a

storm that made her river crew so sick she was forced to put in at Norfolk. Despite all, however, the *Louisiana* finally got to Liverpool (perhaps with a different crew).

All of these deep-draft ocean vessels had delays and narrow squeaks at the Falls of the Ohio. In 1805 a Tarascon ship was totally wrecked in those treacherous waters, which led its builders to conclude "…that we have been convinced by a dear-bought experience [that] it is below the rapids that vessels fit for the sea must be constructed and laden." With French verve, the Tarascons and Berthoud decided to move all operations below the Falls. They had apparently been considering the move earlier, for in 1803 they had purchased a large tract of what had been John Campbell's land. Now, in a grand entrepreneurial move, they established a town and planned a shipyard, borrowing thousands of dollars in Philadelphia for the project. Thus Shippingport was born in 1806, a child of the ultimately unsuccessful marriage of river and ocean navigation.

By the time the Tarascons made their move, New Orleans had been an American port for two years—in fact, all the vast territory of Louisiana was American, including St. Louis. The Louisiana Purchase of 1803, which took the entire nation by surprise, had headed off another potential explosion in Kentucky. The problem was once again the navigation of the Mississippi. Despite the Pinckney Treaty, which had seemed to solve the problem, navigation was suddenly cut off again by the Spanish in late 1802 in a prelude to the transfer of the Louisiana territory to France. The Federal government, under President Thomas Jefferson, acted rapidly. The American objective was to purchase New Orleans and the country surrounding it to solve the question of free navigation once and for all. The French countered by offering the entire Louisiana territory. The transfer to the United States took place in March 1804. To Louisville the immediate meaning was the end of interference with navigation. Now all the western waters that flowed from the Falls to the Gulf were American and river commerce began a phenomenal expansion.

The ocean-going vessel experiment was over by about 1808, creating an even greater need for muscle on the rude flats to keep them off sandbars and snags and to bring the keels back upriver with Louisiana sugar, cotton, molasses, and imported luxuries. It was rough, hard work, but interspersed with hours of lazing down the Ohio and Mississippi. Besides, there was

always wide-open New Orleans at the end of the trip. It was far better than the "fair Hell on earth" of the hot, smoky salt licks. Many a former 'Salt River roarer' joined those legendary boatmen whose exploits live on in the stories of Mike Fink, the Paul Bunyan of the western waters.

But it took a whole crew of Mike Finks three to four months to get a keelboat from New Orleans to Louisville, with at least another month to Pittsburgh. The time and labor involved made the freight charges inordinate. During keelboat days upstream freight traffic on the Mississippi, most of it destined for Louisville, averaged only 6,500 tons a year, while traffic down averaged 60,000 tons a year. By 1806 eight keelboats handled all the upstream business to the Falls. Louisville's customs collector was not overworked in the late Eighteenth and early Nineteenth centuries.

It was that 60,000 tons downstream, practically all of which went by flatboat, that began building Louisville's prosperity. Some of the cargo came directly from the Louisville area, farm produce wagoned in over the network of roads starting to radiate from the Falls to the hinterlands. Most of it came to Louisville in flatboats that had begun their journeys on the Monongahela, or at Pittsburgh, or in the fertile Ohio country where settlers were streaming in following the removal of the Indian tribes westward. Other flats brought Kentucky's contribution by way of the Licking or the Kentucky rivers.

By 1807, only three years after New Orleans became an American port, some 2,000 boats arrived there from upriver. This trade turned Louisville into what S.P. Hildreth, an 1805 visitor, termed "a brisk little town." The reason, he noted, was that "the obstruction to navigation by the Falls made it necessary for the barges to land a part if not all their freight before attempting" the Falls. No loaded flat or keel dared go over the Falls except at the highest stages of the river. Sometimes empty keels were even pulled by manpower upstream over the Falls if the current was not too swift, but it was a toilsome task.

All of this activity kept the Louisville harbor busy and the rough road between Louisville and Shippingport full of wagons portaging cargo, an activity that provided employment for a small army of teamsters. There was often a need for temporary storage of goods, and warehousing began to enhance Louisville's economic base. Warehousing led naturally to wholesaling. The increasing tonnage of valuable cargo also created a need for marine insurance, secured at first from private individuals, usually merchants. Probably the first Louisville insurance contract on a cargo was written by pioneer merchant Daniel Brodhead in 1784 on a shipment from Pittsburgh to the Falls by James Wilkinson. The premium was £42 on a cargo valued at £700, a steep rate of 6% of the value.

The river trade was indeed making Louisville "a brisk little town." Small but lively, the community welcomed the Nineteenth Century with the launching of its first newspaper, a weekly sheet called the *Farmer's Library or Ohio Intelligencer* that appeared in January 1801. Anti-Federalist to the core (it printed some of Tom Paine's work), the paper was published by New Englander Samuel Vail, who brought the press and type from Fair Haven, Vermont. In 1807 Louisville's name appeared for the first time on a newspaper masthead when Joseph Charless began publishing the weekly *Louisville Gazette*. These two publishing ventures were short lived, but in 1810 both *The Western Courier* and *The Louisville Correspondent* appeared, and from then on the town was never without its own newspaper to provide a focus for community feeling and to organize perceptions about the town, thus helping to organize the town itself.

Physically the community was rapidly shedding its log-house and frame-building look. In 1808 the English visitor Fortescue Cuming described it as having "one principal and very handsome street [Main] ...and the houses generally superior to any I have seen in the Western country, with

Right: William Clark, younger brother of George Rogers Clark, was the co-leader with Meriwether Lewis of the 1803-1806 Lewis and Clark Expedition to the Pacific Coast. Though St. Louis is usually credited as the starting point for the journey of exploration, Clark recruited many of the expedition's members around Louisville and the two leaders joined forces here. Clark's black "servent," York, accompanied the expedition on its three-year trip.
Filson Club

Far right: Kentucky Gazette, Lexington, 1803

LOUISVILLE, October 15.
Captain Lewis arrived at this port on Friday laſt. We are informed, that he has brought barges &c. on a new conſtruction, that can be taken in pieces, for the purpoſe of paſſing carrying-places; and that he and captain Clark will ſtart in a few days on their expedition to the Weſtward.

NOTICE.
THE Standing Committee of the

Clark's leg is amputated

In the winter of 1809 when George Rogers Clark was nearing sixty and living alone in his log home near Clarksville, he fell in front of the fireplace, severely burning one leg. When infection set in, Clark was brought to Louisville to have the leg amputated by Dr. Richard Ferguson. This account of the amputation was recorded in 1883 by 99-year-old Christopher Columbus Graham as told to him by Dr. Richard Ferguson, Jr., son of the surgeon.

"Col. Geo. Rogers Clark while in an intoxicated condition fell in the fire (it is said but he [Dr. Ferguson's son] does not say positively he was intoxicated). his relatives and friends as a matter of course not wishing to have this said against the old pioneer held that he had a paralytic stroke.

"His leg was taken off on South side Main St. between third and fourth Sts. by the old Dr. Ferguson (and not at Locust Grove as reported) when Col. Geo. Rogers Clarke Floyd...had the drum and fife brought just outside the room in which the amputation was to take place[.] when Dr. Ferguson began to cut off the limb[,] at a signal the drum and fife started and played while the operation was going on[,] Col. Clark keeping time with his fingers (to the music on the table)....

"As all reports are hearsay, and contradictory...and from all I can learn and what I know of the man, I report that he fell in a fit of epilepsy in the fire. I was absent from here for eighty years[,] otherwise I would have been present & known all about it."
Draper Manuscripts, 35J39

the exception of Lexington. Most are handsome brick, and some are three stories...." Though Cuming does not mention it, one of those three-story brick buildings was Louisville's first theatre, erected about 1808 on the north side of Jefferson Street, then near the edge of town, today part of the site of the Commonwealth Convention Center. One actor remembered it as "dark, dingy and dirty," but a new management in 1818 changed that. The theatre, like the newspaper, became a fixture of Nineteenth Century Louisville life.

A further indication of growth was the construction of churches to replace services held in Steele's Meeting House or in private homes. The Methodists reportedly built the first in 1809 on the north side of Market between Seventh and Eighth, perhaps the one in which Bishop Francis Asbury preached in 1812. He described it as "our neat brick house thirty four by thirty eight feet." The second church building was Catholic, the chapel of St. Louis, built in 1811 on Eleventh near the river. A Catholic church this early in Louisville's history is testimony to the growing French community, strengthened when the Tarascons and Berthoud moved their operations from Pittsburgh to Shippingport. The Tarascons gave the land for the church, a gift sizeable enough to allow for a cemetery as well. Louisville had also grown large enough to require a market house, erected about 1805 in the middle of the street immediately south of Main (thereafter known as Market) between Fourth and Fifth. And by 1811 there were residences on Walnut.

The briskness of these years is revealed most dramatically, however, in the U.S. Census for 1810. The population had increased a rather amazing 400%, up from the 359 of 1800 to 1,357 in Louisville and ninety-eight in the new town of Shippingport, plus the uncounted but lively transient population of boatmen, traders, and just plain tourists. Now Louisville had the makings of a real city: river trade, a business establishment, a market house, newspapers, churches, even a theatre. It needed only a catalyst to bring about the transformation from brisk town to Kentucky's metropolis. That catalyst arrived one midnight near the end of 1811, waking most of the town with its unearthly sound.

Chapter Five

The Steamboat That Made Louisville a City

Some Louisvillians thought the great comet riding the night sky that autumn of 1811 had fallen into the Ohio right at the Falls. What else could account for such a roaring and hissing from the river? Others, no doubt, guessed correctly what it was that caused the sounds that cut through the still midnight air on October 28, rousing many in the small town. Soon a crowd of the curious appeared at the Beargrass landing. There, revealed by a brilliant moon—"it was light as day almost"—was the most unusual vessel ever seen at Louisville. There were sails, familiar from some keelboats and the ocean-going vessels that had tarried at Louisville. But this vessel, though it had a hull similar to the brigs and schooners, also sprouted a tall pipe jutting into the air with a lazy curl of smoke emerging from it; attached to each side of the hull was something akin to the wheel of a water mill. This vessel, the *New Orleans*, was a steamboat. The missing element needed to transform Louisville into a city had arrived.

Probably none of the throng at the waterfront realized the full significance of what they witnessed. The general opinion was that such a curiosity as a steamboat would never be seen in Louisville again. A steamboat could obviously do well coming downstream—it had come from Pittsburgh in the record time of eight days—but could it go upstream against the strong currents of the Ohio and Mississippi? Since the *New Orleans* had to wait for a rise in the river to go over the Falls, Louisville used the opportunity to give a public dinner for Nicholas Roosevelt, who had superintended the boat's construction and brought it safely this far. Despite the complimentary toasts offered, the general tenor, as recalled by Roosevelt and his wife, was "She can't go back up."

But the town quickly learned that she could. Roosevelt, returning Louisville's hospitality, invited his hosts to dine aboard the *New Orleans.* While the guests were enjoying this novel repast there were sudden "unwonted rumblings accompanied by a very perceptible motion in the vessel." The alarmed guests forgot dinner as they rushed onto the deck, convinced the *New Orleans* had lost anchorage and was drifting to destruction on the Falls. Instead, she was paddling upstream, making such progress against the Ohio's current that Louisville was soon out of sight. If Louisvillians were not convinced by this *tour de force*, they should have been by the series of excursions to Six Mile Island and back (the same excursion route of today's *Belle of Louisville)*, followed by the most solid proof of all—a trip upriver to Cincinnati. Shortly after the *New Orleans'* return to Louisville, the river rose just enough for the mechanical marvel to cross the Falls in mid-December. She arrived in her namesake city early in January and began regular service between there and Natchez.

The long-sought mechanical propulsion for boats on the western waters was now a reality, for the *New Orleans* represented a technological revolution on the river that soon brought about a commercial revolution on shore. The quickened pace was felt almost immediately after the first steamer upriver from New Orleans—the *Enterprize*—arrived at Shippingport on May 30, 1815. The arrival of the *Enterprize* also heralded that competition would rule the western rivers rather than the monopoly that Robert Fulton and his wealthy financial backer, Robert Livingston, had hoped for when they sent the *New Orleans* on her 1811 voyage. Fulton (who had proved that steamboats were practical with his famous *Clermont* of 1807 on the Hudson River) and Livingston had been granted exclusive privileges for steam navigation in the state of New York. They sought the same monopoly from the states and territories in the Ohio and Mississippi valleys. Only Louisiana, still a territory in 1811, agreed, but that was enough to create a situation similar to James Wilkinson's monopoly of trade with Spanish New Orleans in 1788. That westerners would leave such a tempting prospect as steam navigation to an eastern monopoly was hardly to be expected.

The battle began almost immediately, with Henry M. Shreve, soon to

A New Yorker's view
"I can not say that the manners of the people are the most moral or the most agreeable in the world. The Kentuckians are not industrious. They are too fond of whisky and negroes. In this town, however, are a considerable number of Yankees and Pennsylvanians, who serve to sweeten society."
Letter from Louisville, March 14, 1817

become a distinguished citizen of Louisville, as the most visible representative of the anti-monopoly forces. Shreve, who had grown up in Brownsville (old Redstone) on the Monongahela, began his river career on keelboats, quickly becoming a boat owner with a reputation for navigation skill and shrewd business sense. When Daniel French of Pittsburgh, who patented a steam engine far different from the English design used on the Fulton boats, built a steamboat in 1814 to challenge the monopoly, he chose Shreve as her captain. This vessel was the *Enterprize*, her name obviously chosen to reflect her monopoly-breaking mission. Though she was small (only forty-five tons' capacity compared to the 400 tons of the *New Orleans*), she was the entering wedge that destroyed Fulton and Livingston's exclusive grant and made Shreve the hero of the new steamboat age in the West. Anticipating legal action by the monopoly group when he arrived in New Orleans in late 1814, Shreve was ready with bail money when the *Enterprize* was seized. Though her departure was delayed by military service (Shreve arrived at New Orleans shortly before the unsuccessful British attempt to capture the city, the final battle of the War of 1812), she finally sailed north on May 6, 1815, and was the first steamboat ever to arrive at the Falls from New Orleans.

When she cast anchor at Shippingport on May 30, 1815, the *Enterprize* proved that steamboats could, indeed, come back up river. Her time of twenty-five days, compared to three to four months by keelboat, added luster to her laurels. Then, when Shreve took her *up* the Falls, and on to Pittsburgh, Louisville and Kentucky realized that the steamboat age had actually arrived. Despite the monopoly, a group of Louisville businessmen in 1816 built the town's first steamboat, the *Governor Shelby*, expressly for service between Louisville and New Orleans.

Meanwhile, Shreve built a boat of his own at Wheeling in 1816, incorporating his own ideas of what a western rivers steamer should be. He

had watched the *New Orleans* being built in 1811 and realized, from his keelboat knowledge of the rivers, that the deep hull, shaped like those of Fulton's Hudson River boats, was wrong for the Ohio and Mississippi. Th[e] hull, holding the machinery, was too deep in the water with too great a chance of grounding on sandbars or being damaged by tree trunks that formed dangerous and difficult-to-see 'snags' and 'sawyers' in the river. Shreve built the *Washington* with a shallower hull by putting the machinery on the main deck, which provided room for two engines. Since the shallow hull did not permit cargo to be carried below deck (in the 'hold'), Shreve compensated by raising the cabin so that the *Washington* was a double-decker, with cargo on the main deck and passengers above. Shreve's design soon became the model for all western river boats, the progenitor of all the graceful, tall-stacked steamers—work-a-day packets and floating palaces alike—that delighted the eye as they transformed the economy.

The monopoly question was still unsettled when, on March 3, 1817, Shreve set out from Shippingport for New Orleans on the trip that would finally settle the issue, the trip that early rivermen considered "the commencement of steam navigation in the Mississippi Valley." This time the monopoly offered him a partnership if he would permit the court case to be decided against him. Arrested and released on bail after he spurned the offer, Shreve started out for Louisville with a full load of passengers and 155 tons of freight. He departed two or three weeks behind the Fulton boat *Aetna* on her fourth trip to Louisville. After the bitter rivals made port at the Falls in April, only a week apart, a public dinner was held for Shreve, more to honor his flouting of the monopoly than for his mechanical exploits. At the last minute it was decided that Captain Robeson DeHart of the *Aetna* should also be invited, though it was made clear that the honor was for DeHart alone and not the Fulton-Livingston interests. During the festivities, Shreve astounded his skeptical audience with the prediction that the trip from New Orleans to Louisville would eventually be made in ten or twelve days. (Within a few years the normal time was fourteen days; by 1850, it was seven days.) While Shreve was in Louisville, a Federal district court had decided on April 17 that it had no jurisdiction over the monopoly issue. Though the case would drag on into the higher Federal courts, where the monopoly would lose, the April 17 decision was as good as a victory. The way was open for all steamboats to sail to New Orleans. The era of Mike Fink and his fellow keelboatmen drew to a close and the era of Mark Twain dawned.

The former outpost of Louisville, once concerned about Indian raids and British invasions from Detroit, was now full of merchants concerned about the price of coffee and sugar and spirits and cooperage; about commissions and forwarding fees, banks, discount rates, and adding dollar to dollar. It was, young Richard Clough Anderson, Jr., commented in 1817, a place "where improvement & prosperity...rapidly changes the face of things." His contemporary, Henry McMurtrie, described Louisville a bit more acidly as a town marked by "frugality, attention to business and an inordinate attachment to money," a place where "as soon as a boy can read, write and cast up a bill, he is withdrawn from school and placed at a desk...." But McMurtrie also admitted that it was a town without beggars in the streets and that there was "always plenty" of employment.

These were years of growth for the communities around the Falls, despite the economic disruption that followed British 'dumping' of manufactured goods in the United States after the end of the War of 1812. Though this caused some monetary crisis in Louisville, it was not too serious a problem in the mercantile town where manufacturing was a small part of the economic base. But to a few manufacturers it caused near disaster. Thomas W. Bakewell, who formed a partnership in 1817 with Scottish millwright David Prentice in a foundry and steam-engine business, recalled those days "when

Above: The huge water-powered Tarascon Mill in Shippingport, completed in 1819 by John Tarascon, introduced automated production to the Louisville area using the design of Oliver Evans, one of the most important early American inventors. Tarascon's financial affairs became so hopeless, however, that he committed suicide in 1825, leaving the mill to his four children. He designated his brother Louis to operate it on their behalf, but creditors relentlessly pursued the heirs and the mill was lost. In 1842 John Hulme and Francis McHarry converted it to the manufacture of cement, with the limestone rock of the Falls of the Ohio as the raw material. Their operation was the predecessor of the Louisville Cement Company, which operated the mill until it was destroyed by fire in 1892.
Louisville Public Advertiser,
November 3, 1819

on Saturday morning I knew not where to look for money for the week's wages for the Hands…most of my dreams even now [1873] revert with painful vividness to that period." Other manufacturing enterprises had appeared in Louisville, though most did not produce goods likely to be affected by imports. There was a soap and candle factory, said to be "the largest establishment of its kind in the western country;" the Hope Distillery, financed by New England capital and described as the largest in the United States; a sugar refinery; tobacco processors; and saw mills and a flour mill powered by steam engines. At Shippingport the Tarascons began construction in 1815 of an imposing water-powered flour mill along the river, completing it four years later. Shippingport also boasted a ropewalk 1,200 feet long and called "one of the finest…in the United States."

By 1820 Louisville's population had tripled over 1810 to 4,012, plus an uncounted but numerous, and often rowdy, transient river population. Shippingport had jumped from a tiny village to a respectable town with a population estimated at 600 "including strangers," and two new towns had appeared below the Falls: New Albany (1813) on the Indiana side and Portland (1814) on the Kentucky side. In an era when population growth had become the standard indicator of any community's prestige and prosperity, the Falls was on the way to ascendancy over the land-locked Bluegrass. Jefferson County's 1820 population of 16,756 was coming close to Fayette's 17,791. Though Louisville still trailed Lexington's 5,279, the trend was clear. By 1830 it would be Kentucky's largest city. An 1826 visitor to Louisville commented that: "The warehouses, the stores, the smell of the landing even, the ship-yards, all indicated the mercantile character, the great and growing importance of the place." Now Louisville's eye was fastened on other river towns as its trade rivals, especially burgeoning Cincinnati, equally stimulated by the steamboat and already more than twice Louisville's size.

The steamboat created the firm base of Louisville's mercantile economy, expanding the opportunities for the wholesalers and commission merchants through whose hands passed the prodigious agricultural produce and rising volume of manufactures from the upper Ohio Valley. This flow of goods, plus later additions from the upper Mississippi, would make New Orleans the premier port of the nation in the value of its exports after 1834, running ahead of New York City for nearly a decade. The Falls was a valve in the river lifeline, a valve controlled by mercantile Louisville. Goods transshipped around the Falls were stored in its warehouses, insurance on cargo and vessels was written in its insurance offices, its new banks helped finance the rising tide of commerce. Travelers stopped in its hostelries, refreshed themselves in its 'coffe houses', ran up losses in its gambling houses, and bought pleasure in its bordellos.

Louisville soon grew large enough to attract visits of circuses and to support a race track. As early as 1815 races were held "below town in the Bottoms," probably the beginnings of the track called the Louisville Turf at the foot of Sixteenth Street near the Hope Distillery. Out in the county the Beargrass Track on Peter Funk's property near present Hurstbourne Lane (once Funk's Lane) was in operation by the middle 1820s. The early popularity of racing is indicated by an 1829 letter from John Cleves Short to his brother, the well-known Kentucky physician, Dr. Charles Wilkins Short. A passenger in a stagecoach trip from Frankfort to Louisville, John Short complained that at Middletown he was "annoyed by an accession of dirty mechanics who crowded in…all anxious to get on to the Louisville races." Change infused the former frontier. "With the arrival of the steamboat," one river historian has written, "the West as such began to lose much of its native freshness [and] naivete."

For Louisville, the arrival of the steamboat also brought to the fore the issue of a canal to bypass the dangerous Falls. Though the idea of a canal was not new, the enormous increase in river traffic generated by the steamboat made it of mounting importance to the whole Ohio Valley above Louisville. Upriver cities, particularly Cincinnati, were convinced that Louisville was deliberately obstructing construction of a canal in order to protect its key position as the transfer point for cargoes. The canal issue not only affected Louisville's good name, but also became a three-way tug of war among Louisville, Jeffersonville, and Cincinnati. The opening of the Louisville & Portland Canal in 1830 marked the final chapter in a long story of frustration among the three protagonists.

The first serious attempt at construction dated back to 1805 and involved the notorious Aaron Burr, then in the final year of his vice presidency, his political future clouded by the duel that year that resulted in the death of his political antagonist, Alexander Hamilton. The canal, to be built on the Indiana side, had numerous local backers, including George Rogers Clark (recently moved to a log house on his Clarksville property) and William Croghan, Clark's brother-in-law and master of Locust Grove in eastern Jefferson County. The charter provided what Burr and his associate, James Wilkinson, now Governor of the Louisiana Territory, wanted: the opportunity to assemble a large group of men to carry out the secret scheme that has become known in history as the Burr Conspiracy. The plan apparently was to use Louisiana as the springboard for an expedition to take over Spanish territory in the Southwest, perhaps even Mexico.

Burr's activities aroused such suspicions that the scheme fell apart and the former vice president was arrested in early 1807 on the lower Mississippi by Wilkinson's own orders and charged with treason. This bizarre end to a bizarre undertaking (with Wilkinson once again casting himself as hero of the piece) also spelled the end of the Indiana canal project. Meanwhile, the Kentucky legislature had approved in late 1804 a charter for the Ohio Canal Company to build a canal on the Kentucky side. This company's preliminary engineering survey provided the basis for the later construction of the Portland Canal, but at the time the project languished for lack of funds.

An attempt to revive the canal idea was made by William Lytle of Cincinnati shortly after the steamboat made its appearance on the western rivers. Purchasing most of the land that would become the route of the canal, plus the land below the Falls, he laid out the community of Portland in 1814. He expected to profit mightily from this speculative venture, since the canal would bypass Shippingport and end that town's monopoly of the lower end of the carrying trade around the Falls. Despite another—and favorable—survey, Lytle and his associates failed to accomplish their purpose: the sale to eastern "monied men" of the canal land and stock. A discouraged Lytle wrote in 1817, "If I could command my debts now due me, I would open that canal my self," since "merchants of Cincinnati and else where assure me they would prefer paying from 4[00] to 600 dollars per Barge or Steam Boat rather than unload below the Falls and drag their boats over the rapids...."

Despite Lytle's lack of success, his activity spurred Hoosiers to revive their project in 1818, adding a new approach—a lottery—to help raise construction funds. Most support, however, was expected to come from Cincinnati investors. Alarmed at this threat, Lytle led the move to form a new Kentucky corporation, the Kentucky Ohio Canal Company. The *Liberty Hall and Cincinnati Gazette*, charging the enterprise was "a mere feint," added that "The future growth of Louisville depends upon the obstruction.... Remove it and Louisville dwindles into insignificance...." But even with infusions of money from Cincinnati investors and the lottery, work on the Indiana canal sputtered along almost imperceptibly. The private resources of the Ohio Valley simply were not equal to an engineering project of this magnitude. The panic of 1819 finally brought a quiet end to the Indiana effort. A Cincinnati paper sadly concluded that "the idea of making a canal at Jeffersonville...must be abandoned."

The startling success of the partially completed Erie Canal in New York probably caused renewed Louisville interest in the Falls canal. Moreover, the Louisville location received an impetus when the report of a joint commission representing Pennsylvania, Virginia (which then bordered on the Ohio River), Ohio, and Kentucky endorsed the Kentucky side, estimating construction costs at one-third of those on the Indiana side. Canal fever in Louisville was whipped up by a Town meeting in 1824, a lobbyist was named to seek federal aid, and the Louisville & Portland Canal Company was chartered by the Kentucky legislature in early 1825 with Nicholas Berthoud of Shippingport and James Guthrie among the directors. Canal backers quickly invited DeWitt Clinton, who, as governor of New York, had initiated the Erie Canal project, to visit the Falls and give his opinion of the Portland Canal. It was a master stroke. The father of canals in America said that the Kentucky location "had been pointed out by the finger of nature." Stock sold well, with most of the capital coming from Philadelphia, anxious to protect its long-time trade relations with the Ohio Valley.

Finally opened in December 1830, though some work remained to be done, the Portland Canal cost nearly $743,000 to build, compared to the original contractor's bid of $370,000. Despite the high cost, this project was successfully completed because of one factor none of the others had: federal aid. Congress, finally swayed by statistics of losses to shipping at the Falls, authorized the United States in May 1826 to purchase 1,000 shares of stock, and in 1829 an additional stock purchase was approved for a total investment of $233,500. This final appropriation was made during the last year of the presidency of John Quincy Adams; just in time, as it turned out. Early in the following year Andrew Jackson, implacable foe of federal aid for internal improvements, moved into the White House. The federal investment was profitable, however, with dividends on the government's holdings totaling $257,778 during the first decade of the canal's operation—more than the cost of the stock. Private stockholders fared equally well.

The steamboat not only dictated the building of the canal, but also ordained that the town would become dominant over the county. Already, in the early years of the Nineteenth Century, the sons of the landowning gentry, who had hoped to make Jefferson County a reasonable replica of the plantation-slave society of Tidewater Virginia, felt the lure of commerce and the town. Richard Clough Anderson, Jr., reflected these opposing forces in his diary. After a boyhood on his father's plantation, Soldier's Retreat, he received legal training at William and Mary College in Williamsburg and began the practice of law in Louisville. But his diary shows his heart was elsewhere. On April 15, 1815, he wrote: "My imagination has for 12 mos. formed the kind of life most pleasing to me—a small farm, excellent orchards, vineyards, meadow &c., butter, cheese, &c. in abundance—everything all ways prepared for a friend." But little more than a month later, on May 24, he had other thoughts: "I am impressed that I could make money by entering into Merchandizing....Although I dislike placing my property at hazard...a year or two hence...I will convert part of my property into mercantile capital...." On November 1, 1817, he bought five acres in the new town of Portland "at the extravagant price of $2,000." Two days later, when he bought a lot in Louisville, Anderson wrote that: "I think I shall make money but it is not so great a speculation as many have lately made."

When the bottom dropped out of the speculative market in the panic of 1819, Anderson, like many others, was caught in the financial squeeze. He lost $40,000. This dramatic rise and fall in property values was only one of the severe problems that rapid growth brought to Louisville during a period that opened not only with the first steamboat, but also with a series of earthquakes, centered on New Madrid, Illinois, that shook much of the Ohio and Mississippi valleys. Louisville felt the first tremor of the "New Madrid shakes"

A critical 1815 view
You know I informed you when I landed here,
This town was not handsome and living darned dear,
The streets were all ponds, and I'm told the Trustees
Had sooner wade thro' them, quite up to the knees,
Than incur the expense to have them drained off.
Complain to their honors, they sneer, laugh or scoff,
And say, we've no money; and you very well know,
Without this intercessor the mare will not go.
Casseday, History of Louisville till the Year 1852

Steam Boat For Sale.

ONE fourth of the Steam Boat George Madison, is offered for sale; she is now lying at the mouth of Cumberland, and is on her way to Shippingport by the first rise of water; she is a substantial well built vessel in good repair, and has the reputation of being as good a running boat as any on the river. Terms of sale will be made easy to the purchaser. For further particulars apply to
BARCLAY & WILSON.

at 2:15 a.m. on December 16, 1811. On Cane Run in southwestern Jefferson County, the Meriwether family thought some of the wooden blocks keeping their modest cabin above ground level had given way. At Soldier's Retreat large cracks appeared in the stone walls of the Anderson home. In Louisville a few brick walls were cracked and the tops of some swaying chimneys fell. This first shock, lasting from three to four minutes, created waves in the river of such size that the steamer *New Orleans*, which had just come over the Falls the day before on its downriver trip, was rocked as it lay at anchor at Shippingport. The shocks continued at irregular intervals into the spring of 1812, a kind of symbolic forerunner of the social and economic shocks that were to accompany the transition from town to city.

At the governmental level these new problems were handled by the Board of Trustees, a group of seven men elected annually by the white male

LITERARY AND MUSICAL MAGAZINE,
A. P. HEINRICH, OF KENTUCKY,
Proposes to publish, by Subscription, the Musical
Effusions of his Leisure Hours, under the Title
of the

DAWNING OF MUSIC
IN KENTUCKY,
OR,
The Pleasures of Harmony
IN THE
SOLITUDES OF NATURE.

The work will comprise a variety of original Songs
and Airs, Waltzes, Cotillons. Minuetts, Polonaises,
Marches. Variations, Sonatas, Duetts, with some
pieces of a National Character, adapted to the
Voice. Piano-forte, Violin, Flute. &c.—A. P. H.
being greatly patronized by his friends, especially
in Kentucky, would be particularly gratified to find
the same liberality in other parts of the Union. The
publication will contain about 200 pages of music
paper, executed in a superior style, and delivered
to subscribers, at thirteen dollars, in two numbers,
(being one half cheaper than the usual price.)
A List of Subscribers will be attached to the volume, with an appropriate Address, expressing the
grateful acknowledgments of the Composer.
Persons holding subscription papers are requested to forward them to A. P. Heinrich, Philadelphia,
as soon as possible, as the work will be completed
in about two months.
Philadelphia, Jan. 1820.
☞Subscriptions received at this office.

Above: This advertisement ran in the Louisville Public Advertiser *during the early months of 1820, seeking subscriptions for the first published works of the man who introduced serious music to Louisville in 1819 through concerts at Samuel Drake's Louisville Theatre. German immigrant and amateur musician Anton Philip Heinrich composed many of the pieces in* The Dawning of Music in Kentucky *in 1819 while a house guest of Judge John Speed at Farmington. The title piece received its first performance in Louisville January 26, 1820. Before his Louisville sojourn, Heinrich had conducted the first performance of a Beethoven symphony (Number One) in America at Lexington in 1817. His later musical career in Boston, New York, and Europe won him the title "Beethoven in America."*

inhabitants of Louisville over twenty-one years of age who had paid the poll tax. (As late as 1829 there were only 800 qualified voters.) Given the developing mercantile base of the Louisville economy, it is not surprising that merchants dominated the board and that election contests were based more on personality and social standing than on widely differing views on issues. Since the trustees were unpaid, that itself tended to limit office to the more affluent—the merchants. This rising urban group began to take on characteristics of its planter contemporaries, described by one Kentucky visitor as feeling "that they have an hereditary claim to command, place and observance." The issues, as the merchants saw them, were chiefly those concerned with fostering trade, so that the bulk of the limited Town funds was more likely to be spent on projects to that end: clearing the harbor rather than keeping the streets clean; building a market house rather than draining the ponds, generally acknowledged to be a source of the annual summer bouts of sickness. Henry McMurtrie admonished Louisvillians as early as 1819 that: "As long as the trustees or other officers are chosen from among mercantile men...so long will the town have to take care of itself." The remedy, he suggested, was to provide full-time, paid officers, "or, in other words...an act of incorporation" as a city. Within a decade his advice would be heeded, but until then, the trustees continued to govern a town growing faster than its ability to cope with its growth. It always took a genuine emergency to produce action, and even then it could be slow. The provision of health facilities is a case history.

In mid-June 1817 an epidemic of smallpox struck the community, hitting hardest at the poor, whose crowded living conditions helped it spread rapidly. In a town without hospital facilities, most victims were carted off to hastily improvised facilities in John Gwathmey's cotton textile mill at the edge of town, while the well-to-do received attention at home. Ironically, plans had been set afoot early in the year for the Louisville Marine Hospital, not so much for the citizens as to solve another problem plaguing Louisville: the care of "those engaged in navigating the Ohio and Mississippi...who... become sick and languish at Louisville." In spite of the problem revealed so dramatically by the smallpox epidemic, work on the hospital, built with State funds, was slow. When an even more severe epidemic (perhaps yellow fever) struck the town in 1822, the hospital was still unfinished. One eminent medical practitioner declared that Louisville was "scourged almost to desolation," and Richard Clough Anderson, Jr., who lost a son and nine other relatives, called it "the most afflicting season that ever came to this country." One of the victims was Dennis Fitzhugh, head of the hospital project. The death toll reached at least 140 in Louisville and Shippingport.

This summer of tragedy finally awakened the trustees "from their lethargy," a mid-Nineteenth Century Louisville historian asserted, and the final assault was begun on the ponds, while the hospital, though uncompleted, was ready for some patients in 1823. Draining and filling the ponds required trimming or postponing other expenditures, and additional funding came from a $60,000 lottery authorized by the State in 1823. The Louisville Theatre held benefit performances for the "Pond Fund," a Town engineer was appointed to head the draining effort, and for the next six years this enterprise was the chief Town business.

The Louisville Marine Hospital, located in a somewhat isolated area on Chestnut near Preston, was completed about 1825 and the following year was transferred to the control of the Town. The selection of the site had great consequences for Louisville of today, since it was largely responsible for the development of the Medical Center in that area.

Though the unpaid trustees were often castigated for their management of Town affairs, part of the problem resided in the relationship of Kentucky towns in general to the State government. Municipal authority came from the Kentucky legislature, which stringently limited taxing power.

Above: George Rogers Clark died at Locust Grove February 13, 1818, after being confined to a special roller-equipped chair for nearly a decade. Buried first in the Croghan family grave yard at Locust Grove, Clark's remains were reinterred in Cave Hill Cemetery in 1869.
Photography by John Beckman

German farmers
The Low Dutch Station of 1780 was the nucleus of the early concentration of German-speaking farmers in the Taylorsville Road area of eastern Jefferson County. Charles Anderson, who grew up at Soldier's Retreat on Beargrass Creek, remembered them from his childhood years during the 1820s.

"On the southern side of Soldier's Retreat lived a solid settlement of Dutch [Germans] from Pennsylvania and Maryland, containing probably a majority of the voters in the county...And while owning scarcely any slaves and performing, therefore, all of their farm and household works by their own diligent hands, they had not only the best cultivated and the most profitable farms in the county, but they were (still better) as a class of citizens, quite distinguished for their superior diligence, economy, sobriety and their good order and conservatism, in all customs and duties...their plain education (of reading, writing and arithmetic — mostly in low Dutch) were quite as general and as good of those of the other citizens."
The Story of Soldier's Retreat: A Memoir

Louisville, as a result, was almost a yearly supplicant to Frankfort seeking greater tax authority. By 1812 the Town was allowed to collect only $2,000 annually in taxes, far short of the sum needed to keep pace with the needs for expanded municipal services. By persistent pressure on the legislature, the trustees eventually were permitted to levy forty cents on each $100 worth of personal property, plus a $1.50 poll tax on all free adult males. Even so, the panic of 1819 cut revenues so sharply that some civic projects were postponed. Yet by the mid-1820s, with the monetary crisis over and the tax base increasing, revenues climbed upward. By 1828, when the population was approaching 10,000, Louisville operated on an annual budget of $40,000 and undertook a much-needed program of grading and paving streets. In 1822 an unhappy citizen observed that "there is not a worse mud-hole within 20 miles of Louisville than our much admired MAIN STREET." Things had not improved by 1828 when an English visitor, who was favorably impressed with most things about Louisville, commented that it had "the worst paved streets I ever saw."

Fire protection was another early civic concern, and in 1820 the primitive system of relying on citizens armed with leather buckets (which all householders were required to have) to provide water for extinguishing fires was augmented by three hand-pumper engines "of tolerable performance." The town was divided into three districts, each with its engine and volunteer firemen. Even so, fire constituted a constant threat and in 1827 the town's first large conflagration destroyed most of the south side of Main between Third and Fourth, causing $200,000 in losses. Only a providential rain saved Louisville from what could have been a major disaster.

Louisville's pioneer chronicler, Henry McMurtrie, noted among the town's deficiencies in 1819 that "a watchman is a character perfectly unknown," a condition made worse by the lack of street lighting. This lack of police was remedied the next year, though not in response to McMurtrie's scolding. Rather, it was partially a response by the white majority to its gnawing worry about tight control of a substantial percentage of the town's residents — its blacks. The federal census of 1820 showed that 1,124 Louisvillians were black (1,031 slave and ninety-three free), or 28% of the total population. The fact that a portion of the Town's revenues, pinched by the panic of 1819, would be devoted to establishing even a tiny police force indicates how damaging slavery was psychologically to whites, as well as blacks. The blacks, of course, had no voice in the decision to establish a watch, even though the free blacks had to pay taxes: the poll tax at the minimum and property tax if they had been able to accumulate some small goods of their own.

Slavery was indeed a "peculiar institution," and more so in an urban environment that loosened the relatively tight control that could be exercised on plantation or farm. Living conditions, for example, were different. Rather than being grouped together in "quarters," blacks in town tended to be scattered, living where their owners lived — usually in outbuildings at the rear. With no common quarters, socializing took place in the streets, at the homes of free blacks, or in grog shops — a development that alarmed many whites. There was fear of crime and fear that free blacks would implant notions of escape in the minds of slaves. This fear was reinforced by the many runaways from the interior who used Louisville as the springboard to freedom, which was tantalizingly close — just a river's width away.

Town life relaxed tight control over slaves in other ways, too. The typical slaveowner in Louisville was likely to be a merchant, more lenient than his planter counterpart if for no other reason than the time he devoted to his business. Furthermore, he had little real need for slaves except as house servants, coachmen, and the like. A complicating factor was State law, which, as time went on, made it more difficult to set slaves free. Two other

alternatives were open to the urban slaveowner: sell his excess slaves "down the river" to meet the unending demand in the cotton states, or hire them out to others who needed large amounts of labor.

Louisville slave traders were ready to buy this "merchandise" to sell south or to auction slaves on the streets. In 1821 a sale of a woman and child aroused public indignation, but only because they were "as white as any of our citizens." In 1826 German Prince Karl Bernhardt, a Louisville visitor, witnessed another street sale: "A pregnant mulatto woman was offered...at public auction with her two children...the auctioneer...indulged himself in brutal jests upon her thriving condition and sold her for four hundred dollars." Hiring out was the more common practice, however. Blacks were rented as roustabouts on the wharf, as laborers on street grading and repair, for construction projects of all kinds (including the Portland Canal), and as domestics in hotels and restaurants.

This black labor pool was a factor, too, in the relatively early appearance of manufacturing in a town devoted principally to commerce. Blacks were used in many industrial operations: one ropewalk employed as many as "forty or fifty negro boys." The practice of hiring out loosened the owner's control and even led to many slaves hiring themselves out, seeking jobs in what came perilously close, to the worry of many whites, to a free labor market. "Those who hire their own time, not only act without restraint themselves, but their example induces others to believe that they can take the same liberties...that they can work or play as they please," one agitated white Louisvillian complained. Though the hired-out slave brought his pay home to his owner (he was usually allowed to keep part of it), he was "developing the habits of a wage earner."

The urban environment produced a black population qualitatively different in its outlook and behavior than most rural blacks. Frederick Douglass, one of the foremost black leaders of the Nineteenth Century, and a former slave, pointed out in his *Narrative* that the independence provided by the city, plus the kindness of his master, only increased his self-awareness and longing for real freedom, factors that prompted him to flee. It may have been the developing lack of subservience, plus competition with whites in the lowest economic brackets for jobs, that produced growing white prejudice against blacks. Lafayette, during his 1825 tour of the United States (Louisville was one of his stops), expressed astonishment at the increase in racial prejudice among whites since the days of the Revolution, recalling how black and white soldiers served together then, even preparing and eating their meals together.

Little is known of blacks and their relationships with whites in the early days of Louisville and Jefferson County. Cato Watts has become, in effect, the token black of Louisville history, assigned a suitably subservient role as the smiling fiddler who makes music to keep the white folks happy. But there were blacks at the Beargrass stations, at the salt works, and in pioneer Louisville. As early as 1786, when the town was still on the frontier, it was reported that "some negroes ran away from this place," even though there was scarcely a place of refuge. Most of the slaves came from Virginia, brought by the large landowners, although some of the less affluent "adventurers" from the Monongahela Valley also owned a few slaves, sometimes only one. Many of these whites, especially those who owned no slaves, had favored immediate emancipation and a legal end to slavery in Kentucky even before statehood was achieved. Backed by many clergymen, particularly Presbyterian and Baptist, they had made their strongest stand against slavery when the first Kentucky Constitution was adopted. Though they mustered sixteen votes to prohibit human bondage, the pro-slavery faction carried the issue with twenty-five votes. As slavery became firmly entrenched, especially in the cattle and hemp culture of the Bluegrass and the tobacco culture of western Kentucky, the white voices against the institution represented a

Visiting a slave dealer

Margaret Hunter Hall, who accompanied her husband, Basil Hall, on a two-year tour of the United States, wrote a series of letters to her friends back home in England. From Louisville Mrs. Hall described a trip out the Bardstown Road to the home of John W. Hundley, who owned a 1,200-acre farm near Beulah Church Road. (He built Beulah Church on his property.) The letter is dated May 11, 1828.

"The house we went to was distant about five miles over a most shocking road but thro' a rich and well cultivated country. The proprietor, Mr. Hundley, is a rich, sickly bachelor, aged about fifty, I should think, who has built himself a capacious and commodious house which he occupies in solitude, or the next thing to it, having no other companion than a very dull brother....He has made every dollar he possesses by buying and selling slaves. He is, or was, in the most literal sense of the term a slave dealer, one who scruples not to separate mothers and children, husbands from their wives; such is the account given of him by a person who has known him since he began his career by working for a dollar a day and by that means having acquired money sufficient to purchase one slave he went off to the South where having sold him for a sum large enough to enable him to buy two on his return to the West [Louisville], he again went off to the same ready market.... He is mighty religious in his talk, too...."
The Aristocratic Journey, 1931

Flogging a slave

Increase Allen Lapham worked as an engineer's clerk and assistant on construction of the Louisville & Portland Canal beginning in 1827 when he was only sixteen. On February 21, 1828, he made the following entry in his daily journal.

"I went to Louisville this morning.... While I was going I beheld a scene, which, though very common here, I have never before seen. It was a negro slave belonging to the company [canal contractors], followed by his overseer on horseback who was lashing him every other step with a large cow-hide....He had left the work without permission which was the crime for which he was so cruelly beaten."
The Journals of Increase Allen Lapham for 1827-1830

Right: Louisville Public Advertiser, *November 13, 1824*

50 DOLLARS REWARD.

Ran away from the subscriber, about the 17th inst. a negro man slave, by the name of

REUBEN,

Twenty-five or thirty years of age, five feet ten and a half or eleven inches high, square and strongly built; very black; his eyes rather inclined to be red or yellow, occasioned from dissipation and night strolling. He has rather a shy, down look, and shews guilt very quick; has had a piece bit out of one of his ears, by fighting; and had on when he went away, a tow linen shirt and pantaloons and an old white fur hat, broad brim—he has other clothes, no doubt, but I do not know what kind they are He is an artful fellow, calculated to do a great deal of mischief, by roguishness, which he is much addicted to. He has a wife at Mr. Fitzhugh Thornton's, in this county; and, no doubt, will make the principal part of his stay in that neighborhood, being uncommonly fond of his family

I will give fifty dollars, Commonwealth paper, for Reuben, if taken out of the state; ten dollars, Commonwealth paper, if taken in the county, and twenty dollars, Commonwealth paper, if taken out of the county, and delivered to me, or secured in any jail, so that I get him again

FRANCIS TALIAFERRO.

Oldham county, Ky. August 28.   615ow

100 DOLLARS REWARD.

Ran away from the farm of A K Alexander, in the county of Franklin, and state of Kentucky, a mulatto man slave, named

GEORGE,

The property of A K. Marshall George was hired to said Alexander, and some quarrel having taken place with the overseer, he absconded, about the 19th of November, 1823. He is a light mulatto, formerly belonged to the estate of Violett, who, by his will, devised him free; but, said Violett being in debt, George was sold under execution, and purchased by J. J. Marshall, of the town of Frankfort. George is about 5 feet 9 or 10 inches high; has a slight, genteel person; a brisk, intelligent countenance—but he can be identified beyond dispute, by a scar, which has deprived him of all hair on a large part of his head. He wears his hair long, and attempts to conceal the scar, by combing it smooth over it. He has probably a copy of Violett's will with him, and passes as free; but he is a slave, as above stated. He has been seen in the steam boat Maise, and probably continues in it. The above reward will be paid, upon delivery of said George, in Frankfort, to the subscriber, or by confining him in jail, at Maysville or Louisville, so that he comes to the possession of the subscriber.

J. J. MARSHALL.

august 28   615ow

20 DOLLARS REWARD.

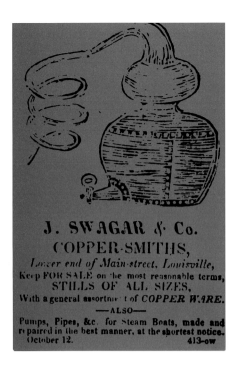

Above: Louisville Public Advertiser, *December 21, 1822*

A fire on Main Street
In 1827 all citizens were still expected to join in to fight fires, but sometimes the work was left to those who were not accorded full citizenship.

"Great credit is due the colored people who displayed great zeal and persevering industry—the Trustees take a pride in acknowledging on behalf of the Citizens the Manly conduct of the above persons and wish they had cause to extend their acknowledgement to all—But they are compelled to say there were many persons present from whose station in Society they would have expected the noblest exertions, and who looked calmly on the ravages of that most destructive element, without making one solitary effort to arrest it; who when appealed to turned indifferently away: Some of those were men of property."
Minutes of the Louisville Town Trustees, *March 9, 1827*

smaller and smaller minority. They were never silenced, however, especially in Louisville.

But of the throng of anonymous black humanity in Louisville and Jefferson County through these early years, some few slaves emerge now and then into clearer light, displaying their own personalities. One was York, who accompanied the Lewis and Clark Expedition on its remarkable three-year journey to the Pacific Coast and back. He first appears, typically for blacks, in a will. On October 1, 1799, the will of John Clark (father of George Rogers Clark) was probated in Jefferson County Court. One provision of the document reads: "I also give unto my son [William] one negro man named York, also old York and his wife Rose...." William, a younger brother of George Rogers Clark, was to become one-half the team of Lewis and Clark at the joint invitation of President Thomas Jefferson and Meriwether Lewis. Clark, who recruited many of the expedition members from the Louisville area, also took York along as his "servant." When the keelboat flotilla departed from the Falls on October 26, 1803, York was the only black member. He was to prove both a valuable addition and an object of wonder to the far western Indians.

A year after the departure, when the party had reached North Dakota, Clark noted in his Journal: "...the three great chiefs [of the Arikaras] and many others came to see us to day...much astonished at my black Servent, who did not lose the opportunity of [displaying] his powers Strength &c. &c...." The next day Clark recorded that the Indians were "much astonished at my black Servent, they never Saw a black man before...he carried on the joke and made himself more turribal than we wished him to doe." York's dancing also intrigued the Indians, who were surprised "that So large a man should be [so] active...."

The Nez Percé, not knowing what to make of York, called him the "black white man" and tried to see if the color would rub off his skin. After such adventures and taste of near-freedom, York's return to domestic drudgery in Louisville must have seemed an even more constricted existence than before the Pacific expedition. Perhaps that was why Clark freed York, giving him a wagon and six horses, with which he is said to have carried freight between Nashville and Richmond.

In the 1820s and 1830s Louisville and Jefferson County blacks were still largely anonymous, but a new generation was being born which was to have a different experience than any previous generation of blacks in America. It would see the transition from slavery to freedom following the Civil War. It was this generation that would become visible and provide much of the leadership for Louisville's black community as it began a journey on a new road, often as rocky as slavery itself. The sketchy formal education these youngsters received for their coming role was recalled by one of those leaders, Horace Morris, in 1873. "Then a motley throng was gathered in a dingy, low-ceiling room in the neighborhood of that classic region, 'Chinch Row', and had the celebrated 'three R's' driven into them, bottom-end up with a leather strap with a buckle on it. I can never forget those days...old Mr. [Peter] Booth was a grand old teacher for the times. When we got as far in Webster's elementary spelling book as b-a, ba, k-e-r, ker, baker, we were ready to graduate! Peter Booth, though a famous scholar, couldn't spell Constantinople, or Philadelphia, either. They had too many syllables for him."

Though it was but a smattering of education, the fact that anything resembling formalized education was available for blacks in a slave state is a tribute to the urban environment versus the more constrained rural setting. It was an indicator that Louisville, legally still a Town, was becoming a city with its attitudes and institutions. As early as 1818, Henry Schoolcraft recalled, "The town had all the elements of city life."

The next step was to become a City in fact.

Chapter Six
The Smile of Wealth

Above: In addition to the Louisville Hotel and the Galt House, there were numerous more modest establishments offering accommodations to the traveling public. The Wall Street House, which issued this lithograph in 1840, advertised itself as "a few rods from the Steam Boat landing." Wall was the old name of Fourth Street between Main and the river.
Filson Club

In 1832, when excavations were under way for the foundations and cellars of Love's Row (a row of commercial buildings on the north side of Main between Sixth and Seventh), workmen unearthed a line of old buried wooden pilings. They were soon identified as part of the remains of Fort Nelson, and Louisville for a moment was reminded of its beginnings little more than a half century earlier. By now, a third of the way into the Nineteenth Century, the community had taken on a solid air. Traveler Caleb Atwater in 1829 observed that Main Street displayed a "smile of wealth," while private homes were "splendid, substantial, and richly furnished. I saw more large mirrors in their best rooms than I ever saw anywhere else…all the furniture is splendid and costly." Obviously Atwater did not visit the "Chinch Rows," the essential underpinnings of this impressive display, but nevertheless provided a valuable report of an active town where "the ringing of the bells and the roaring of the guns belonging to the numerous steamboats in the harbor, the cracking of the coachman's whip, and the sound of the stage-driver's horn salute the ear."

Impressed as Atwater was with Louisville, he saw it only on the eve of a period of dazzling prosperity. Having achieved solidity, the community now aspired to an elegance that was earlier found only in the homes of Jefferson County's pioneer landed gentry. Soon large new hotels, banks, churches, and even more splendid mansions would bring a touch of grandeur to the cityscape. Flushed with its commercial success, Louisville dared dream of becoming the State capital. Its most ambitious building project yet, an expansive City Hall and Court House, begun in the mid-1830s in the new Greek Revival form, was to be the lure—a structure that could serve as the Capitol building. The move was a tactical error, doomed to fail. Louisville, new to the business of exercising dominant economic power in Kentucky, had not yet realized that its new position failed to impress a rural state or a Bluegrass area in eclipse; had not yet realized that its new economic muscle created jealousy and suspicion, rather than respect. Despite this, one happy result was the structure that still serves as the Jefferson County Courthouse, *grand dame* of all the later government buildings that surround it.

It was a heady time at the Falls of the Ohio, and some of the grandiose projects, overly ambitious for their time, had to be delayed: a bridge across the Ohio (there was a later proposal for a tunnel under the river), a water works, and the completion of the imposing Court House. But they were projects born of success and self-confidence, as well as'examples of the complex public decisions that Louisville had to make because of its growth and success. In the middle 1820s, with a population approaching 7,000—a sizeable town for the day—it was being forced to develop a new political process for weaving public decisions from the tangled skein of private interests, attitudes, traditions, and opinions. Some of the older vexing problems were on the way to solution: the ponds were being drained, streets were being paved and graded, the hospital was serving citizens and river mariners alike. There was even a Board of Health to recommend and supervise sanitation measures. An attempt to light the streets by requiring property owners to erect posts with oil lamps proved less successful; owners were dilatory and lamps were frequently vandalized.

But other needs and other problems demanded solutions. Some citizens recognized the need to provide schools for those children—the majority —whose parents could not afford the numerous private academies. And, despite the night watch, crime continued to be a problem in a town where the river brought a constant influx of humankind in all its varieties. Even when arrests were made, justice was often slow. The Town's charter did not permit it to exercise a judicial function, and all cases originating within the Town limits had to be tried in County Court. As early as 1823 the *Public Advertiser* aired community dissatisfaction with this system. Editor Shadrack Penn acidly observed that many of the magistrates who composed the court, especially

those who lived in the county, were "not punctual, or do not attend."

As a counterpoint to these issues, the canal agitation helped bring disparate elements together in a new sense of community self-awareness. It also created the first public debate on Louisville's future, pitting those who feared the canal would have an adverse economic impact against those who argued that the community should be prepared to pursue other economic paths, such as manufacturing, if necessary.

In all, the canal question was a potent factor in creating a new sense of community, which, joined with dissatisfaction over the limited powers of Town government, created a move for City status, especially among the professional groups—attorneys and physicians—and other non-mercantile elements. The backers of the move began their campaign in 1824. This first effort failed, in part at least, because some citizens feared the possibility of higher taxes. The *Advertiser*, enthusiastically behind the incorporation effort, conceded taxes would probably go up, but argued that "There are few, indeed, among us, who cannot pay an additional tax of a few dollars." Then, striking at a sore spot, Penn declared that opponents of incorporation should realize that greater municipal revenue would mean an "efficient police."

This first move toward incorporation also brought to the fore a new type of citizen, the kind of man the Nineteenth Century would call a "community leader," the man who actively sought and achieved leadership through ability, in contrast to the usual style of the Eighteenth Century in which civic roles were seen as the duty of the well-born. Outstanding in this emerging leadership group was attorney James Guthrie. Recently arrived from Bardstown, he made his debut on the civic scene in 1824 as a member of the committee to draft an act of incorporation. That same year he was elected a Town trustee, soon became board chairman, and would remain a principal actor in Louisville affairs for the next forty years.

Despite the 1824 failure, incorporation remained a lively issue. Penn's *Advertiser* (which became Louisville's first daily in 1826), continued to push for it, as did an 1826 addition to local journalism, *The Focus*. Violently opposed in politics, the two journals closed ranks on issues affecting Louisville's future. By late 1827 the community was ready to move and another public meeting produced near-unanimous support for incorporation, though Shippingport and Portland declined to become part of the new City. Again, Guthrie was a member of the committee that drafted the legislative bill, which was easily approved in Frankfort on February 13, 1828. Louisville became the first Town in Kentucky to achieve City status.

State government conferred limited judicial power (less than was asked) and greater taxing authority on the former Town, but retained a strong measure of control. The mayor, who served only a one-year term, was not elected directly by the voters; rather, the governor selected him from the two candidates who received the highest total of votes, and the choice was confirmed by the State Senate. The new City was divided into five wards, each with two councilmen, who were elected directly. The first election was held March 4, only nineteen days after the act of incorporation. Chosen mayor in a close contest was John C. Bucklin, merchant and native New Englander. James Guthrie, for nearly four years Chairman of the Board of Trustees, now became a councilman. Bucklin apparently pleased the voters of the new City; he was re-elected annually to serve five consecutive terms.

Though the choice of mayor continued the old tradition of mercantile dominance, the new Council included proprietors of small businesses, a physician, a steamboat captain, and even a carpenter. The new City also gained its "more efficient" police power, with a marshal (elected annually) who could appoint a deputy in each ward. Yet by 1832 there were no deputies and only six watchmen. An official warning to the watch indicates that it was often less than efficient; watchmen were told not to "frequent the theatre, circus or any exhibition during watch hours."

Opposite top: This manuscript map of the Falls of the Ohio is among the papers of William Clark, younger brother of George Rogers Clark, and dates from about 1836. The younger Clark was by then a St. Louis resident.
Missouri Historical Society

Opposite bottom: Louisville Hotel in 1849.
Louisville Free Public Library

Below: The most memorable experience for travelers on Ohio River steamers was the dangerous descent of the Falls at Louisville. The original caption on this drawing read "Going over Falls of Ohio. [Not exaggerated.]"
Harper's New Monthly Magazine, December, 1858

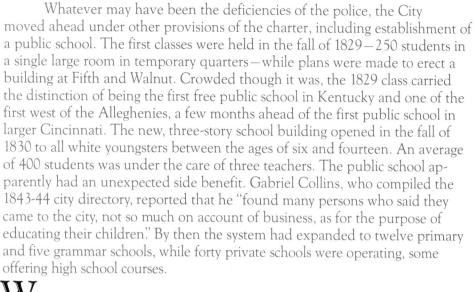

Whatever may have been the deficiencies of the police, the City moved ahead under other provisions of the charter, including establishment of a public school. The first classes were held in the fall of 1829—250 students in a single large room in temporary quarters—while plans were made to erect a building at Fifth and Walnut. Crowded though it was, the 1829 class carried the distinction of being the first free public school in Kentucky and one of the first west of the Alleghenies, a few months ahead of the first public school in larger Cincinnati. The new, three-story school building opened in the fall of 1830 to all white youngsters between the ages of six and fourteen. An average of 400 students was under the care of three teachers. The public school apparently had an unexpected side benefit. Gabriel Collins, who compiled the 1843-44 city directory, reported that he "found many persons who said they came to the city, not so much on account of business, as for the purpose of educating their children." By then the system had expanded to twelve primary and five grammar schools, while forty private schools were operating, some offering high school courses.

With its "stone front of four stuccoed columns, in the Roman Ionic order," that first public school building was intended to be a handsome addition to the urbanizing community. It was the first of numerous public and private buildings erected in the next few years that expressed in brick and stone the community's growing sense of self-esteem. This community consciousness was also revealed by the publication in 1832 of the first city directory, which contained descriptions of new buildings in progress, each with a claim to architectural merit: the Unitarian Church, in Greek Revival style, on the southeast corner of Fifth and Walnut; the nearby St. Louis Catholic Church in Gothic style (on the site of the present Cathedral); the Louisville branch of the Bank of the United States, on Main near Second, boasting a portico in "handsome Tetrastyle Ionic;" and the new Louisville Hotel, on Main between Sixth and Seventh, with a facade "ornamented by a Colonnade of ten Ionic columns." The hotel, the directory assured its readers, "will surpass in elegance and arrangement, any in our Western country."

The hotel and the Catholic church were designed by Hugh Roland, the first architect to open practice in the community. Louisville's aspirations to elegance could now support such a professional.

Proudly described as being larger than the fashionable new Tremont House in Boston, the hotel signified that Louisville had come of age as an urban center. However fine the service at Washington Hall and its contemporaries, they were essentially inns: small and unable to cope with large numbers of guests, serving meals to all guests at one sitting, making no provision for such specialized services as barber and tailor shops. They were cozy, comfortable, and out-of-step with a growing city thronged with out-of-town merchants buying at its wholesale marts, tobacco planters selling their crops, travelers making the transfer between boats mandated by the Falls, adventurers seeking new opportunities, and the merely curious. The elegant Louisville Hotel, with its dining room, bar, baggage room, parlor-bedroom suites, and shops was a symbol of the new era. No longer would travelers record their stay at Throckmorton's or Gwathmey's, but at the Louisville Hotel or the Galt House.

The Galt House, destined to gain the reputation as Louisville's finest Nineteenth Century hostelry, was Aris Throckmorton's reply to the Louisville Hotel. The reputation is based on a later Galt House, built in 1869, but the name dates from about 1835 when the home of Dr. William Galt, on the northeast corner of Second and Main, was acquired and demolished to make way for the new hotel, which was almost directly opposite Throckmorton's old Washington Hall. The memory of the physician's home, with its "hanging gardens" cascading down the terraced river bank at the rear, was perpetuated in the name Galt House. Neither as large nor as impressive as the Louisville

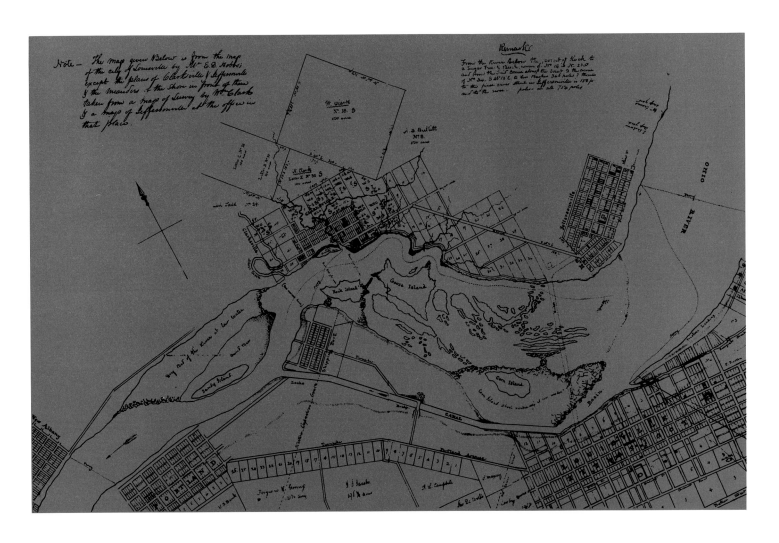

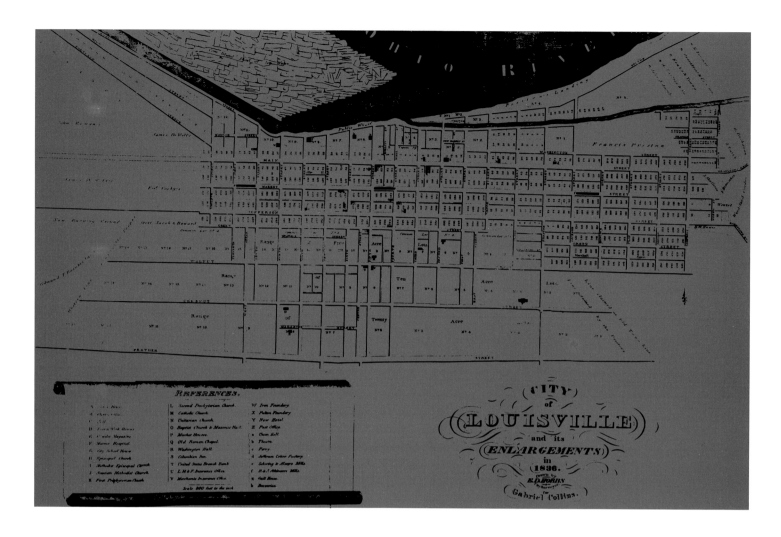

Top: By 1836 Louisville's streets extended eastward beyond the old Town boundary. Prather Street is today's Broadway. The map was made by City Surveyor E.D. Hobbs.
Library of Congress

Bottom: James Dakin's rendering of the proposed Bank of Louisville building on Main Street reveals the kind of architectural elegance Louisville sought in the 1830s. Today the building serves as the lobby of Actors Theatre of Louisville.
New Orleans Public Library, Louisiana Division

Hotel, the Galt House nevertheless gained an early reputation. It housed—and pleased—English novelist Charles Dickens when he visited Louisville in 1842 on his American tour. As trade spread east and west along the wide thoroughfare, the simple dignity of the residences and gardens that lined East Main were beginning to give way to expanding commercial needs.

The Louisville Hotel and the original Galt House have long since vanished from Main Street, but a third example of the rising community pride of the 1830s remains as a tie between past and present. Today the exquisitely proportioned building at 316 West Main houses Actors Theatre of Louisville, but it was built as the Bank of Louisville, chartered February 2, 1833. The structure is not only a rare survivor of Greek Revival design in a Louisville commercial building, but also a stone-and-mortar reminder of the single most controversial action of President Andrew Jackson: the 1832 veto of the renewal of the charter of the Bank of the United States. This bank, a semi-public corporation, served as the nation's central bank. As a depository for all federal funds, it was able to provide the credit required by mercantile and manufacturing interests. Its Louisville branch was the potent financial engine of Louisville's rising affluence and for a few years after 1830 it was the only chartered bank in the city, though there were smaller private banking firms.

Jackson's 1832 veto, followed by his re-election to the presidency that year, doomed the Bank of the United States and opened the way for scores of state-chartered banks to fill the gap. Thus was born the Bank of Louisville in 1833. The next year bank president John S. Snead went to New York seeking an architect to design a building that would reflect the importance of the new financial institution. He chose James Dakin, a promising young designer who had recently set up his own office. Work started in 1835, with a newcomer to the Louisville architectural scene, Gideon Shryock, supervising construction.

Shryock arrived in Louisville in 1835 after completing Morrison Hall

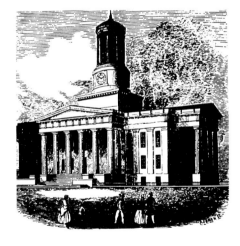

at Transylvania University at Lexington and with the laurels for the design and construction of the Kentucky State House at Frankfort still fresh. Shryock, at the height of his career, was lured to the river city by a commission to build James Guthrie's special project—a building to house City and County offices, the building that Louisville hoped would become the State Capitol. As chairman of the City Council's finance committee, Guthrie played a leading role in acquisition of property and construction of buildings by the municipality. The saga of what would be known for years as "Guthrie's Folly" started innocently enough on April 6, 1835. On that date Guthrie introduced a motion before the Council that the finance committee be empowered to procure a plan and cost estimate for a building of "hewn stone" to be erected at Sixth and Jefferson to house City offices. Guthrie had in mind from the beginning that it should also house the County Court, still occupying the nearby 1811 Court House. By September, Guthrie reported that a design had been completed by Shryock and that the County had agreed to participate in the construction. Work, however, did not begin until 1837, the very year of the worst economic depression yet known in the United States. The panic of 1837 was the natural result, many anti-Jacksonians asserted, of the dizzying increase in bank credit and inflation that followed the Jackson veto of the renewal of the charter of the Bank of the United States.

There was suitable irony in one result of the financial panic; it brought an end to the Court House project in 1839 after it was only partially completed. Guthrie, a Jacksonian and supporter of the bank veto, saw his dream stand unfinished for nearly twenty years, used in its lower floors only. Another problem was the limestone construction material, quarried at Marble Hill on the Indiana shore of the Ohio River below Madison, which proved to deteriorate badly when exposed to weather. While the panic of 1837 rocked the nation's economy and in Louisville "Main Street was like an avenue in some deserted city," the new home of the Bank of Louisville was completed, but that institution felt the financial stringency, too, and delayed paying the bill for the elliptical skylight that graces what is now the lobby of Actors Theatre. Dakin, by this time practicing architecture in New Orleans, was forced to sue for his pay.

The depression, which put the national economy on a roller-coaster until the mid-1840s—sometimes up, but more often sickeningly down—failed to halt another of Guthrie's dreams for his adopted city: an institution of higher education. The most advanced level of instruction available in Louisville was offered by the Jefferson Seminary, a State-endowed institution that had begun operation in 1813, though its State charter was granted in 1798. Managed by the Town trustees and located at Eighth and Cedar on a tract of nearly three acres, the Seminary was more high school than college. Henry McMurtrie commented in 1819 that it was not "so well patronized as it deserves." Less than ten years later, class distinctions began to show themselves in the growing town with complaints that the Seminary educated only a few middle-class boys for the professions. The "Mechanics and Laborers of Louisville" in a communication to the *Public Advertiser* in 1826 declared that the school taught "nothing we want our children to know." Yet, curiously, the Seminary, though it held its last classes in 1829, was to play a part in Guthrie's moves to establish what became the University of Louisville.

The opportunity came through an 1836 dispute among the medical faculty at Transylvania University, most of whom wanted to move that school's medical department to Louisville. Guthrie, who headed a City Council committee to investigate the possibility of establishing a medical school, encouraged the disgruntled Lexington professors to move. The *Public Advertiser* helped the campaign along. "What a valuable addition to our population would four or five hundred respectable students form!—think of the mass of money they would expend here!—and then of the fame and influence we

Above: Engraving of the Medical Department at the University of Louisville, 1846.
Louisville Panorama, *1954*

Below: In its later years it was the Elks Club, but originally the home of George Keats, younger brother of poet John Keats. The 21-year-old George and his 16-year-old bride left England for America in 1818, settling in Louisville. He invested part of an inheritance in a lumber mill, built a flour mill in 1825, and speculated profitably in real estate. He built this home, often called "the Englishman's palace," about 1835 on the south side of Walnut between Third and Fourth. He died only six years later, but not before he provided an original manuscript copy of his brother's "Ode to Apollo" to the Western Literary Messenger, *published in Louisville and edited by Unitarian minister James Freeman Clarke.*
The Filson Club

should acquire." With the promotional groundwork laid, Guthrie arranged for Dr. Charles Caldwell, one of the leaders of the disenchanted Transylvania faculty, to speak at a mass meeting to whip up public enthusiasm. Caldwell performed magnificently, arguing so persuasively for a complete university with medical, law, academic, and mechanical departments that the assembled citizenry unanimously endorsed the sweeping proposal. The meeting was held March 30, 1837. With the public mandate still ringing in its ears, the Council accepted the proposal on April 3.

Guthrie, as chairman of the finance committee, then unveiled his scheme for funding construction of the school, to be known as the Louisville Medical Institute and envisioned as the first unit of the new university. The City Work House and Pest House, built only in 1827 (at Guthrie's urging), was totally inadequate for a city with a population approaching 20,000, he said. In addition, its site of several acres, stretching south and west from Eighth and Chestnut, was prime real estate needed by a community starting to fill in the empty spaces toward Prather Street (Broadway). Reserve one square block on Chestnut between Eighth and Ninth streets as the site for the university, Guthrie urged; sell the rest and use the proceeds to erect the medical school. It was a neatly conceived plan, quickly adopted by the City Council. By November Guthrie had in hand Shryock's plan for the new school, and on February 22, 1838, less than a year after the mass meeting, the cornerstone was laid. The first classes were held in the new building that fall with 204 students and eight faculty members, including the prestigious Dr. Daniel Drake, who had been attracted from Cincinnati. In 1840 an amphitheatre for clinical lectures was completed at the Louisville Marine Hospital, the first such facility west of the Alleghenies. With its capacious new building, a fine library and laboratory equipment, the new medical school ranked among the finest in the United States and attracted an increasing number of students.

This whirlwind campaign that produced results so quickly, despite a depressed economy, reveals a self-confident city moving under extraordinarily active and competent leadership to accomplish lasting results. Impressive as these accomplishments were, other lightning-like moves by Guthrie and his fellow civic leaders were to follow. With the Louisville Medical Institute assured by the fall of 1837, Guthrie immediately introduced a motion in the City Council to establish the Collegiate Institute as an academic counterpart of the Medical Institute. No new construction would be needed, he argued: the old Jefferson Seminary Building could be used. Again, the Council agreed, and the academic institution opened in May 1838 while the medical school was still under construction. The Collegiate Institute, however, fell short of the hopes for it. The Seminary building was inadequate, the number of students was too low (even though the City agreed to pay tuition for thirty selected graduates of the public schools), and the disturbed economy of the early 1840s compounded the problems. In 1844 the ambitious venture closed.

The actions of Guthrie and his fellow Louisville enthusiasts were probably seen in immediate retrospect as pushing the city beyond its resources. When Dickens visited Louisville in 1842 he observed that "...some unfinished buildings and improvements seemed to intimate that the city had been overbuilt in the ardour of 'going a-head', and was suffering under the re-action consequent upon such feverish forcing of its powers." Yet, despite the temporary setbacks with the Court House and the Collegiate Institute, foundations were laid for important projects that are vital parts of today's urban fabric. The Collegiate Institute, for instance, was the forerunner both of the University of Louisville's College of Arts and Sciences and of Male High School, while the Medical Institute became the University's School of Medicine. These transitions, however, were not made easily.

The old dream of a university continued to haunt the community's leadership. Finally, with the return of a stable economy in the mid-1840s, all

Dr Bayless

Obtaining Material

these streams came together with the chartering of the University of Louisville, empowered to take over the Medical Institute, revive the Collegiate Institute as its academic department, and to open a law school. The charter was granted in 1846; in 1848 James Guthrie became president of the University, a post he held until his death in 1868, even while he served as railroad president, in the U.S. Senate, and in the cabinet of President Franklin Pierce as secretary of the treasury.

The establishment of the University dictated the need to erect a home on University Square for the academic department. The new building was begun in 1848, its cost largely financed through sale of the old Seminary property. But financial problems continued, and the only appointment was a professor who taught mathematics on the top floor and complained of a leaky roof. Meanwhile the Law School moved into the building from its former unsatisfactory quarters on the ground floor of the uncompleted Court House. The academic department languished (though medicine flourished and law was modestly successful). After a brief association with Male High School, part of the City school system, the academic department existed only on paper, until it was revived in 1907.

The two public buildings on University Square, built in the modish Greek Revival style, further exemplified the community's sense of self-esteem expressed in architecture. This concern with elegance extended in the private sphere even to the new race track that about 1832 replaced the old Louisville Turf on the riverfront at Sixteenth Street. The new track, Oakland Racecourse, located in a sylvan setting south of the city, boasted a three-story columned clubhouse, Oakland House, in Greek temple form. Oakland House faced Oakland Turnpike (Seventh Street) just south of present Magnolia Avenue, with the track and grandstand farther south. An 1839 visitor found

"the course and fixtures...beautiful, the former singularly shaped, with no long stretches." Oakland was a further stage in the development of horse racing as Louisville's premier sport of the Nineteenth Century, an interest shared by the whole community. Though the Bluegrass region took an early lead in breeding Thoroughbreds, eclipsing the efforts of Jefferson County's landed gentry, racing itself continued to gain in popularity in the city by the Falls. In the middle 1830s the Rev. Samuel Osgood, assistant minister of the Unitarian Church, observed how a meet at Oakland affected Louisville with "a furor...the whole city in commotion," while "the rage of betting infected even the servants and slaves. The little fellow that brushed our clothes at the boarding house...staked his half-dollar with a comrade of like hue and stature...". Though this native New Englander thought the races "semi-barbarous," he went to Oakland where "the august head of Henry Clay... towered up among the sporting magnates on the stand erected for the judges of the course."

Oakland came near to making Louisville a nationally known racing city as early as the 1840s, long before Churchill Downs and the Kentucky Derby, though it faltered financially during that economically depressed period and closed in the mid-1850s. But for a few brief years under the imaginative direction of Yelverton C. Oliver, a Louisiana racing entrepreneur, the track acquired a lustre that caused the national sporting paper, *The Spirit of the Times,* to comment that "Turfmen should guard [Oliver] as a rich pearl, for he is doing everything to make Old Kentuck the race horse region." Oliver's most spectacular effort was the 1839 match race between the Louisiana horse, Wagner, and Grey Eagle, Kentucky's pride. These Thoroughbreds, two of the most famous horses in the United States, raced for the then-unheard-of purse of $14,000. "The number of ladies in attendance was estimated at nearly eight hundred, while nearly two thousand horsemen were assembled in the field,"

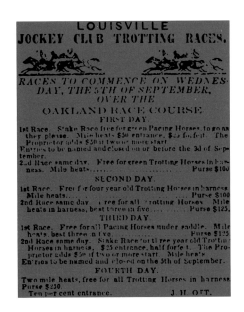

A letter from Lincoln

When Joshua Speed, born at Farmington, tried his hand at business in Springfield, Ill., he made the acquaintance of a rising young lawyer named Abraham Lincoln. A lifelong friendship developed. Lincoln accompanied Speed to Louisville in 1841 and spent six weeks at Farmington. Shortly after, he wrote to Mary Speed, Joshua's half-sister.

"We [Speed and Lincoln] got on board the steamboat Lebanon, in the locks of the Canal....Nothing of interest happened during the passage, except the vexatious delays occasioned by the sand bars be thought interesting. By the way, a fine example was presented on board the boat for contemplating the effect of condition on human happiness. A gentleman had purchased twelve negroes in different parts of Kentucky and was taking them to a farm in the South. They were chained six and six together...strung together precisely like so many fish upon a trot line. In this condition they were being separated forever from the scenes of their childhood...and going into perpetual slavery where the lash of the master is proverbially more ruthless and unrelenting than any other where; and yet... they were the most cheerful...creatures on board. One, whose offence for which he had been sold was an over-fondness for his wife, played the fiddle almost continually...."
Roy P. Basler, Lincoln's Writings

according to a contemporary report. "The stands, the fences, the trees, the tops of carriages, and every eminence overlooking the course were crowded. The Bench, the Bar, the Senate and the Press, the Army and the Navy, and all the et cetera that pleasure and curiosity attracted were here represented...." The Kentuckians were doomed to disappointment, though. Three 'heats' of four miles each were set for the two horses; Wagner won the first two handily, and there was no need for a third. In a rematch a week later, Grey Eagle won the first heat by a length, lost the second by only a neck, and in the third came up lame, never to race again. Although the loser, the gallant horse remained high in the affection of Kentuckians and a succession of boats of the Louisville and Cincinnati Mail Line kept Grey Eagle's name fresh for more than a quarter of a century.

While Louisville reveled in its river-borne prosperity, lighting its streets with gas lamps in 1839 (the first city in the West to do so), creating Cave Hill Cemetery in 1848 as the proper final place of rest for well-to-do citizens, spawning over-ambitious projects for water works, bridges, and tunnels, Lexington fared far differently in the age of the steamboat. Population figures tell the story most dramatically: by 1830 Louisville's population was 10,341 (plus another 1,000 in Shippingport and Portland); Lexington counted only 6,087. A decade later Louisville had nearly doubled in size and was the twelfth largest city in the nation with a population of 21,210 (including Shippingport and Portland); Lexington had barely held its own—6,997. But in 1830 the one-time "Athens of the West" was not ready to let the contest go to Louisville—or Cincinnati—by default. Since it could not embrace the steamboat technology directly, Lexington had to find a means of connecting itself to the river by something better than hard-surfaced turnpikes. In a bold move, the Bluegrass community opted for the new and still-tentative technology of the railroad. It was the right decision at the wrong time.

When the charter of the Lexington & Ohio Railroad was granted in 1830, there were scarcely twenty-five miles of railroad in operation throughout the United States, but Lexington's desperate plight called for unusual measures. The plan was to build the line to Portland, reaching the river below the Falls. Portland's 398 citizens were elated; Louisville was wary. If the railroad proved practical, this mercantile city decided it should stop at Louisville, not Portland. The city at the Falls saw the railroad as a way to tap the Bluegrass; Lexington saw the route to Portland as salvation. The Lexington & Ohio set out bravely, but by early 1834 it halted at Frankfort where the formidable and costly task of bridging the Kentucky River faced it. Then, oddly, Louisville came to the rescue in 1835 with the purchase of $200,000 worth of stock. But there was a condition: that the railroad terminate at Louisville, not Portland. With the condition accepted and Louisville now represented in the management, the railroad commenced grading toward the Falls, planned a bridge, and ordered two steam locomotives from England to replace the plodding horses that pulled the trains of cars. Yet, even with new capital, financial problems continued, particularly when the panic of 1837 dried up the money market. All construction ceased. Louisville would not get its railroad to Frankfort for another fourteen years, but in 1838 it did get a railroad of sorts, complete with one of the tiny English-built locomotives. Moreover, the railroad turned out to be a package arrangement that included, first, the annexation of Portland, and later, support for the Kentucky School for the Blind.

Portland had been growing slowly since William Lytle founded it in 1814, so slowly that in 1830, its 398 residents were still fewer than neighboring Shippingport's 606. But it had a busy wharf and warehouses, and in 1834, perhaps in anticipation of its expected role as a railroad terminus, it obtained a Town charter. The halting of railroad construction in 1837 was an irritant to Louisville, but a crushing blow to Portland. The Lexington & Ohio, now headed by Louisvillian Levi Tyler, wanted to build a separate stretch of rail-

road between Louisville and Portland to capture the profitable transfer business around the Falls. Louisville wanted to annex Portland. From these diverse aims came an agreement: Louisville agreed to let the railroad be built along Main Street to reach its wharf; in return, Portland agreed to become part of the larger city.

The railroad began operation in April 1838, the locomotive *Elkhorn* trundling its train from Sixth Street along Main to Thirteenth, over to Portland Avenue and to the wharf. But the little line's promising career was cut short by an injunction after only five months of operation. Annoyed by the locomotive, a group of Main Street businessmen and residents went to court with their grievances: the locomotive was noisy, it frightened horses, the rails obstructed the street, wagoners refused to make deliveries on Main along the railroad. When the injunction was granted the line stopped service altogether, to the evident joy of the hack drivers who had enviously watched the primitive enterprise carry an average of 550 passengers a day. (Freight services had not yet commenced.) This turn-about so incensed Portland that it went to the legislature and secured its independence again in early 1843, remaining a separate community until it finally agreed once more to annexation in 1852.

Though Portland was denied the wharf-to-wharf railroad it wanted (as a prelude to a railroad to Lexington), the Portland line itself was not a permanent casualty of this urban in-fighting. By 1840 it was running again, using horse cars and keeping its rails off Main Street by stopping at Twelfth. An 1844 German visitor described the line: "The local train is noteworthy in that one of the two cars that go here is drawn by a horse, the other by a small mule. The cars are covered and hold 12 persons each; nevertheless, the stretch is covered at a continual trot."

The little cars did more than provide Louisville's first local transit; they

Above: This portrait of George D. Prentice, made by Louisville photographer Edward Klauber, is probably the last taken of the editor whose local journalistic career spanned nearly 40 years. Louisville Past and Present, 1875

George Prentice arrives
A bright new star appeared in Louisville journalism as the decade of the 1830s opened. George D. Prentice, recently arrived from Connecticut, established the Whig Louisville Journal *as the city's second daily and challenged Shadrack Penn's Democratic* Public Advertiser *for supremacy. It was a contest of editorial wit and Whig versus Democratic principles. The battle raged until 1841 when Penn departed to edit a St. Louis newspaper. Prentice, backed by supporters of Henry Clay, proclaimed his allegiance to the Kentucky presidential hopeful in the* Journal's *first issue, November 24, 1830.*

"We hold it inconsistent with the genius of a Republic that the officers of government should use their official power to reward or punish any citizen for his political preferences….

"For the next Presidency of the United States we shall support HENRY CLAY, steadily, and without a shadow of turning …because we are convinced there is no other man in the nation, who, with a voice like him, could say to the tide of corruption…'here shall thy proud waves be stayed.'"

also helped build the first home of the Kentucky School for the Blind, an educational venture that owed its inception in 1842 to Louisvillian William F. Bullock, attorney, civic leader, and a representative in the General Assembly. But with only $10,000 from the State (plus pledges of assistance from Louisville), the institution required additional funds. The Portland line became the financial key. When the Lexington & Ohio venture finally collapsed totally under financial adversity, becoming State property, the future of the orphan Portland line was anything but bright until a group of Louisvillians came up with a solution. They would operate the trackage, which became the Louisville & Portland Railroad, for the financial benefit of the school. Curiously, one of the architects of this plan was Elisha Applegate, who had instigated the court suit that stopped operation on Main Street. The new company also began operating horse-drawn omnibuses (Louisville's first) on Main Street to connect with trackage at Twelfth Street. The act setting up the railroad specified that the "directors…shall buy land and erect a building" for the school, which they did immediately on the south side of Broadway between First and Second.

The blind school was moved to a rural location on the Shelbyville Pike (now Frankfort Avenue) in 1855 and the Louisville and Portland Railroad became a totally private venture and a link in the city's later extensive streetcar system. Though this urban route never fulfilled Lexington's dream of a connection directly to the river, it provided Louisville its first experience with a railroad, an experience that would blossom in a farsighted plan to tap the South with iron rails only a dozen years after the *Elkhorn* steamed along Main Street.

The Portland railroad was not designed to haul local manufactures to a distant market, since in Louisville, an outside observer noted in 1837, "The spirit of manufactures is not manifested to any extent." A local commentator, Gabriel Collins, discussed the same phenomenon: "It is remarkable, that the population of Louisville depends almost entirely upon her commerce. No other city perhaps in the world…employs as little capital in other Occupations…[yet] the few manufactories that have been established here, have succeeded eminently well…her cotton mill, jeans manufactory, paper mill, carriage and wagon factories, &c…." Strangely, Collins neglected to mention the city's heaviest industries: its foundries and shipyards. The Louisville Foundry, for instance, built nearly forty steam engines in 1836, mostly for use in flour mills, while four other large foundries turned out steamboat engines and boilers, stoves, architectural ironwork of the type that still characterizes New Orleans, and a variety of miscellaneous items. Shipyards are more difficult to quantify, since they were easily moved and phases of the work were often performed in different locations. A hull might be built in Jeffersonville, the engines installed in Louisville, and the cabin work completed in Portland. (These vessels would be claimed by the Louisville press as "Louisville-built," to the continual irritation of the city's Indiana neighbors.) Altogether, thirty-five steamboats were built around the Falls in 1843. But, despite foundries, engine builders, and shipyards, only $864,000 was invested in Louisville manufacturing in 1839, including the simple processing of raw materials involved in making bricks, candles, soap, tanning leather, milling flour, butchering hogs and cattle, sawing lumber, and the like. The groundwork for industry had been laid, however, and manufacturing began to increase in importance through the 1840s, the chief factor, some felt, in the city's continued population growth. The investment in manufacturing grew to over $4 million by the middle 1850s, much of it in small enterprises, a foreshadowing of the diversity that has marked the Louisville industrial scene ever since. During the 1830s and 1840s, too, a number of newcomers laid the foundation for an expanded iron-working industry that would become the major element of the city's economy in the booming post-Civil War years. James

Bridgeford, born in Jefferson County, had moved to Louisville in 1829; James S. Lithgow arrived from Pittsburgh and William H. Grainger from England in 1832; Dennis Long, a native of Londonderry, Ireland, arrived from Pittsburgh in 1838; and Benjamin Avery, a native of New York state, in 1847. Collectively, they became Louisville's "iron men," and important civic leaders. William B. Belknap, a native of Massachusetts, whose name is associated with Louisville hardware wholesaling, was engaged in iron smelting in western Kentucky before he arrived in Louisville in 1840. In 1847 he and Thomas C. Coleman opened a riverfront rolling mill that became an important Louisville industry.

The multiplying foundries (there were fifteen by 1850), plus the increasing use of coal for heating homes and businesses, brought the city's first air-pollution problem in its wake. As early as 1839 a Pennsylvania traveler curtly dismissed Louisville in one sentence: "Louisville is a city of some note and a place of considerable business—but one of the dirtiest and filthiest places I have yet met with—and if its citizens are unhealthy and often swept into a premature grave they are themselves to blame for it." Some three years later, Dickens was a bit more tolerant: "The buildings are smoky and blackened, but an Englishman is well used to that appearance, and indisposed to quarrel with it."

As the workshops increased in number and the sound of industry began gradually to compete with the bustle of the wharf, the number of "mechanics" began to increase and Louisville's social structure took on complex stratifications, while class lines sharpened. In this, the city reflected a nationwide development when the term "laboring class" appeared for the first time in a national context. Yet, in Louisville there was a complicating factor: the presence of slave labor. Occupations requiring manual labor, or even skilled hand work, were low in the urban social scale in all parts of the United States, but

Wheel about, turn about,
Do jes so,
An' ebery time I wheel about,
I jump Jim Crow.

The term "Jim Crow," which came to mean segregation of blacks, had its origin in a performance at Samuel Drake's City Theatre (the former Louisville Theatre) on May 21, 1830. Thomas D. Rice, who appeared in The Kentucky Rifle, or a Prairie Narrative *as "Sambo (the Negro boy)," added a song and dance described in the program as "the comic Negro song of 'Jim Crow.'"*

Accounts vary as to the song's origin, but most agree that near the City Theatre on Jefferson Street was a livery stable kept by a man named Crowe, who owned an arthritic slave named Jim Crowe. Rice, observing the way the black man sang and shuffled his feet in a peculiar dance while tending the horses, imitated it on stage.

The song was published in Pittsburgh in 1830 by William C. Peters, who later published Stephen Collins Foster's first minstrel songs and who also operated a music store in Louisville. "Jim Crow," which paved the way for the blackface minstrel show, was an almost instant success, catapulting Rice to fame and earning him the title of "father of American minstrelsy."
Drawing from collection of West T. Hill, Jr.

in Louisville, where such work was further equated with the "servile" labor of slaves and free blacks, white mechanics felt a double stigma. As a result, whites tended to avoid such occupations if they could, or to avoid Louisville. When Sir Charles Lyell, the eminent English geologist, visited the city in the late 1840s, he found several merchants of the opinion that slavery and a considerable black population had retarded Louisville's growth. "Kentucky," Lyell observed, "suffers from the decided preference shown to the right bank of the Ohio by the best class of settlers from the northeastern states," who wanted to stay away from "the Slave State on the left bank." Lyell probably overstated the case, but he found a growing strain of disenchantment with slavery among some influential whites in Louisville, whom, he observed, "believe and hope that the time of emancipation is near at hand." The black presence was beginning to cause tensions in white society.

Some occupations in Louisville were practically restricted to blacks. Hack drivers, barbers, waiters, cooks, hotel domestics, draymen, roustabouts on the wharf, well-diggers, and laborers in general were overwhelmingly black. In some few instances blacks and whites worked together, performing the same tasks. At the steam-powered Louisville Woolen Factory "Both *whites* and *blacks* are employed…no difference [in productivity] being perceptible." It was an unusual enough situation for the commentator to use italics. Louisville was, after all, a city where one writer could seriously state that "God, in his providence, has appointed the white man to be a guardian over the blacks…," a city in which the elite displayed "the easy gait of people accustomed to being served by slaves." Because of the presence of slavery, the movement for "association," or embryo unionism, among white wage-earners was not as strong as in Cincinnati or Pittsburgh (and was weakened further by the exclusion of free blacks), but moves in this direction were made as early as the 1830s. By 1835 seven different crafts had organized benevolent associations for mutual financial aid: printers, tailors, shoemakers, coach makers, saddlers, cabinetmakers, and tinplate workers. The first true trade union did not arrive until 1839, when the printers organized the Louisville Typographical Association, formed, its founders said, "upon entirely different lines" from the benevolent societies. Louisville journeymen printers were active in organizing the first national printers' union in 1850.

The expansive mood of the 1830s and 1840s had produced a more impressive city and, inevitably, a more complex one with internal tensions bubbling beneath the surface. The construction of the Portland Canal had contributed to the development of this complex, striated social structure by attracting a labor pool to the city. The project also undoubtedly encouraged the transfer of some mercantile capital to other pursuits, including manufacturing, following the disruptive effect of the canal on the transshipment and forwarding business. But the canal did not sound the death knell of Louisville's growth, as some local pessimists had feared. It even spurred the development of an important new industry. The discovery of cement rock during its construction was the beginning of cement manufacture in the area.

Moreover, as river vessels increased in size, the canal was seen "equally with the falls, a barrier to navigation." In addition, high maintenance costs caused tolls to be raised from the initial twenty cents per ton to sixty cents by 1837. (They were later reduced to fifty cents.) For the largest boats that could pass through the canal, the toll could be as much as $1,000 for each round trip. As river traffic increased, the transshipment business probably at least regained its own, despite the canal. When the level of the river permitted, many boats continued to chance the Falls rather than face the delays and pay the tolls to go through the canal. Poet Walt Whitman, bound downriver to New Orleans in 1848, described one such trip: "Our captain, with Western hardihood, determined to go over the 'boiling place'.…The bottom of the boat grated harshly more than once on the stones beneath, and the pilots showed

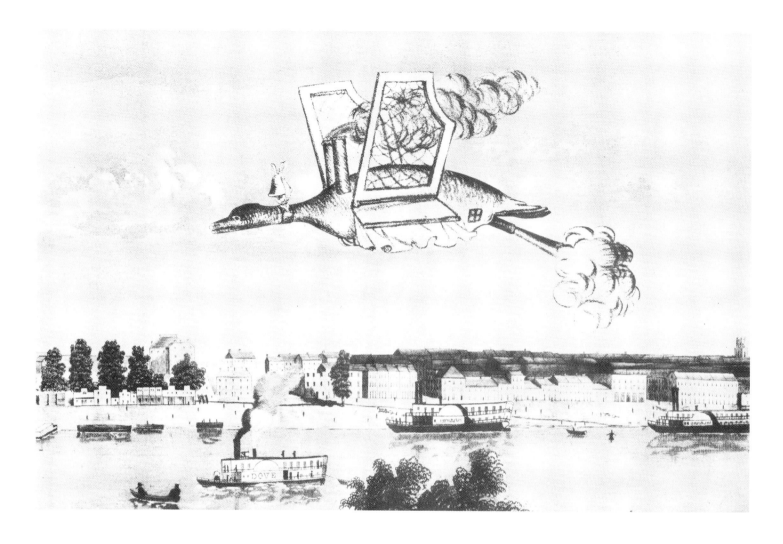

Above: A satire of a contemporary proposal for 'aerial navigation,' the Great Steam Duck was concocted in 1841 by Louisvillian John Ross Browne under the pseudonym of the Louisville Literary Brass Band. The lithograph accompanied a booklet by Browne that was the second publication west of the Alleghenies on the topic of aviation. The first was the booklet it satirized, published in St. Louis in 1840. Browne later became an important California literary figure.
Louisville Free Public Library

plainly that they did not feel altogether as calm as a summer morning."

At the very time the great poet of American democracy was sailing downriver to New Orleans, events in Europe were setting the stage for a great tide of humanity to come streaming across the Atlantic. The unsuccessful democratic revolutions of 1848, plus famine in Ireland, sent tens of thousands of liberal Germans and penniless Irish to the United States, seeking the democracy that Whitman celebrated. They were the Forty-Eighters, coming up the river from New Orleans and westward from the eastern seaboard, following the established travel routes, flooding into the Ohio Valley. They infused the river cities with a new vitality even while their sheer numbers upset the old order of things. As Louisville's share of the hopeful new immigrants stepped off the boats at the wharf or at Portland, it was a replay of the great emigration of the 1780s, but with a new cast and with steamboats instead of flatboats. Then the struggle had been between Indians and American settlers. Now the struggle would be between old Americans and new Americans.

Chapter Seven

Glorious Years, Bloody Years

Louisville, which in 1850 became the tenth largest city in the United States, soon discovered that the higher it rose in urban rank and prestige, the sharper were the external challenges and the internal stresses. This last, and in many ways golden, decade of the antebellum years, was a period of contrasts in the city by the Falls. On the one hand, there was clear recognition of the external challenges involving trade and economic health, and they were met with vigorous action. On the other hand, the internal problems involving touchy social issues became hopelessly entangled in party politics and religious prejudice.

As Louisville entered the 1850s, it seemed well equipped to meet whatever challenges the new decade might offer. The forward strides of the 1830s and 1840s, based largely on the soul-searching engendered by the Portland Canal debate, had been matched by impressive growth: population climbed (in round figures) from 10,000 in 1830 to 43,000 in 1850. Manufacturing began to take root in the 1840s, the city already was an important tobacco market and pork-packing center, and general wholesale trade totaled over $20 million in sales in 1850. Never had the river carried so much traffic. The Louisville-New Orleans route held top rank on the entire western river system in freight and passenger traffic, while the short Louisville-Cincinnati stretch was one of the most crowded and most prestigious. The wharf, inadequate for the number of boats it had to handle, was to be made larger before the end of the decade simply by diverting the mouth of Beargrass Creek, historic landing spot of the pioneers, into the river two miles upstream via the 'Cutoff,' the man-made route it still follows.

The 1850 census returns give a clear look at river activity. On one day that year there were forty-five boats in port, twenty-two exclusively in the Louisville-New Orleans trade. Statistics for the one-year period from August 25, 1848, to August 31, 1849, show that sixty-six different steamboats made 213 trips from Louisville to New Orleans; some only once, others as many as fourteen times.

By the 1850s these steamers had become the 'floating palaces' of river legend, their captains important personages in gold-braided splendor, their pilots the envy of small boys, their comings and goings fully reported in the press. Individual boats were noted for their size, or service, or speed. One of the most famous of this decade was the *Eclipse* (built in New Albany in 1852). In a famous race in 1853 the *Eclipse* and *A.L. Shotwell* (named for a prominent Louisville merchant) set a record from Louisville to New Orleans that still stands: four days, nine hours, and thirty minutes. The race was a dead heat, but the *Eclipse* was the winner in luxury. Her cabin, full of paintings and tapestry, suggested an art gallery. At one end of the cabin was a gilt statuette of Andrew Jackson; at the other, a similar figure of Henry Clay. She boasted forty-eight bridal chambers, scores of staterooms, and sleeping quarters for servants. In 1858 the all-time speed record was set on the Cincinnati-Louisville run by the *Telegraph No. 2* (built in Louisville), which made the downstream trip in only six hours and twenty-six minutes for an average speed of twenty-one miles per hour.

During the 1850s the river was still the city's life line. It is, then, not strange that the river was largely responsible for the two most important issues the community had to face: absorbing thousands of European immigrants and building a major railroad southward.

The rising tide of European immigrants—predominantly German and Irish—who arrived in Louisville and the Ohio Valley in the late 1840s and the 1850s were refugees from economic and political trouble in their homelands and looked to democratic America as the land of new hope. Foreign immigrants were not new to the region; what was new was the sheer number, plus the fact that most were Catholic. Total European immigration into the United States during 1830 had been an easily absorbed 23,322. But the figure increased year-by-year, reaching 84,066 in 1840, spiraling rapidly upward to

Fighting for business

River boat crews took their rivalry seriously. Items similar to this one appeared now and then in the Louisville press.

"A fine pugilistic display came off at the wharf last evening between the officers of two Pittsburg boats. The fight was commenced by the barkeepers of the boats and originated about a passenger who both were trying to get. The fight led to an encounter between the pilots, then between the clerks, and lastly between the captains. We did not learn which party remained in possession of the field."
Louisville Daily Journal, *December 10, 1852*

369,980 in 1850, and 427,833 only four years later. Though the Irish were by
far the largest single group (outnumbering the second-place Germans almost
two to one), the national statistics were reversed in the Ohio Valley. By 1850
there were 7,537 German-born immigrants in Louisville (including some
German-speaking Swiss) compared to 3,105 Irish.

Newcomers of Germanic background had been in the Louisville area
since the beginning of settlement. One of the Corn Island settlers, Andrew
Kimbley, was reputedly a native of The Netherlands. The group of Pennsylvania Germans who founded the Low Dutch Station in 1780 grew and
prospered, turning the Taylorsville Road area into an enclave of mostly
German farmers. In 1812 Methodist Bishop Francis Asbury noted in his
journal: "Came to Brunerstown [Jeffersontown]. We had preaching in
German and English...I saw a native of Saxony who had lately arrived, and
who had joined us." These pioneer Germans were Protestant—unlike the
later, heavily Catholic wave of German immigrants—and established
Jefferson County's first Lutheran church in 1819. (Not until about 1850 was a
Lutheran church established in Louisville.)

The early Germanic settlers came downriver, but after the introduction
of the steamboat, a steadily increasing number of immigrants from all parts of
Europe, but mostly from the strongly Catholic southern German states, came
upstream from New Orleans, whose role as a port of entry is often overlooked.
Steamers carried 25% more passengers upstream than down, and the large
number of German immigrants aboard imbued upriver cities such as St. Louis,
Louisville, and Cincinnati with a distinct Teutonic flavor. After a difficult
ocean voyage, the immigrants took deck passage on river steamers, unpro-
tected from the weather, cooking their own food, and finding sleeping space
amidst the cargo. When the steamer *Winfield Scott* arrived in Louisville in
the spring of 1849 with more than 400 Germans aboard, the *Democrat*
reported that "many...looked as though they were in a dying state," and added
that thirty of the group had died during the river trip.

Immigration produced a sizeable German population in the Louisville
area by the middle 1830s; by 1836 German Catholics were numerous enough
to establish their own congregation, St. Boniface, giving the city its second
Catholic church. By 1838 German Catholics "in and around" Louisville were
estimated to number 2,000. Two years later the total German-born population
within the city rose to 3,616. There were enough Protestants among them by
1842 to establish a German Methodist church and St. John's German Evangelical Church. Louisville's first German newspaper, the short-lived *Louisville
Volksbühne* (Tribune), was founded in 1841, followed in 1844 by the
Beobachter am Ohio (Observer on the Ohio). The *Louisville Anzeiger* (Advertiser), long-lived stalwart of the local German press, began publication
in 1849.

This growing body of German newcomers (and Irish, who in 1840
numbered about 1,000) was being assimilated, though with some difficulty,
into Louisville life, when 1848 put a sharp sting into the already somewhat
strained relations. The social, nationalistic, and uniformly unsuccessful revolutions that broke out all over Europe that year not only pushed American
immigration statistics sharply upward, but injected a new element into the
ranks of German newcomers: the well-educated liberal and radical leaders of
revolution. Unlike the bulk of German immigrants, these Forty-Eighters were
politically oriented social reformers who considered themselves more exiles
than immigrants, and who brought their political ideas with them. Many
came to the Ohio Valley and a significant number to Louisville, which they
promptly chose as national headquarters of a (for the times) radical group,
the Bund Freier Männer (League of Free Men). Anti-clerical, contemptuous
of 'Puritan' American culture, espousing agnosticism and rationalism, and
politically active, the Forty-Eighters offended both native Americans and the

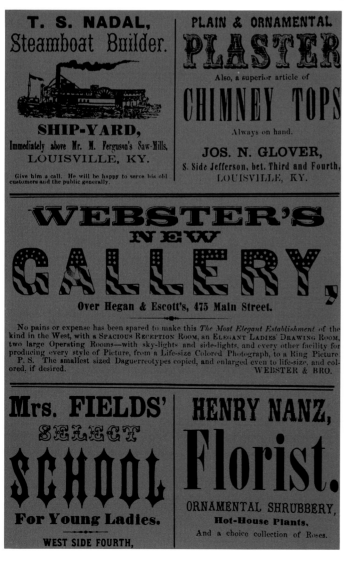

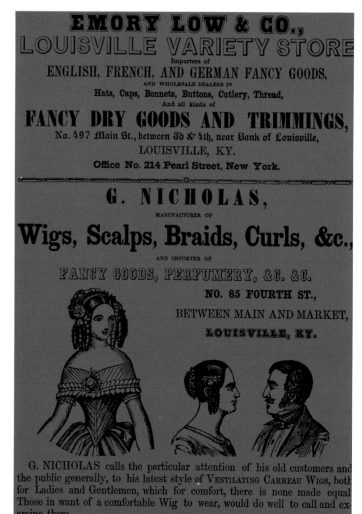

Above: Louisville went wild with excitement when Jenny Lind, the 'Swedish Nightingale,' presented three concerts at the new Mozart Hall in April 1851 as part of her American tour managed by P.T. Barnum. Tickets, auctioned for each concert, sold at up to $175 each. Editor John H. Harney of the Louisville Daily Democrat *was enthralled by Jenny's singing and wrote on April 10:*

"We now feel that we have heard a specimen of the greatest of all musical composers [Handel] sung by the greatest of all vocalists and it is something for the memory to cherish with undying affection. We have heard the triumphant faith of the resurrection of the body expressed in tones of purity that are almost angelic in their sublime sweetness and harmony." Portrait, Filson Club

Opposite top: A moment in time on pre-Civil War Main Street is captured in this old lithograph. The scene is the south side of Main Street east of Third about 1857. A curtain blows through an open window, wagons unload at the curb, and a carriage waits — perhaps while the mistress of an affluent household shops for fabrics at Bent & Duvall. Views of Louisville since 1766, *1971*

Bottom left: Louisville City Directory & Business Mirror, *1858-59*

Bottom right: The Louisville Business Register, *1850*

pious German Catholic, Evangelical, and Lutheran immigrants, as well as the handful of German Jews who were part of the tide.

The outstanding German radical in Louisville was Karl Heinzen, who arrived in 1853 to edit the *Herold des Westens* (Herald of the West), which boldly attacked slavery. But it was the League of Free Men's Louisville Platform of 1854, published in both German and English, that roused native antagonisms, especially among the conservative Whigs. Designed to be the basis of a new reform party, the document called for emancipation of slaves, women's rights, abolition of the death penalty, direct election of the president and senators by the voters, a minimum wage, a one-house Congress, and drastic curtailment of the powers of the presidency. To native Americans the Louisville Platform was a flagrant example of the dangerous doctrines that immigrants imported into America.

With the arrival of the Forty-Eighters, the anti-foreign, anti-Catholic fear and prejudice, which had been steadily rising with the upward curve of immigration, took on fever proportions. In Louisville both the growth of the city and its rising Catholic immigrant population prompted the move of the bishop's seat from Bardstown to Louisville in 1841 and the construction of a new Cathedral, completed in 1852.

The flood of poor Irish, solidly Catholic, coinciding with the rise of German immigration, added fuel to the fire of American nativist prejudice. The inrush followed the Potato Famine in the Emerald Isle, caused by complete failure of the potato crop in both 1845 and 1846. Over two million Irish died of malnutrition. Though the great Irish immigration was confined chiefly to the Atlantic seaboard, some Irish spilled over into the Ohio Valley. Louisville's 1,000 Irish of 1840 had increased three-fold by 1850 and the city's first Irish Catholic church, St. Patrick's, was built in 1853.

As with the Germans, the Irish had been migrating to America for years, but in earlier days little distinction was made in the statistics between Scotch-Irish (almost uniformly Presbyterian, with a sprinkling of Anglicans) and Irish (almost uniformly Catholic). The Potato Famine Irish, however, were a different economic group than earlier Irish settlers; they were mostly tenant farmers arriving almost penniless, flocking to the cities to take any kind of unskilled work that was offered. In this milieu the Irish were at the bottom of the white social structure, saved from the lowest rung of the ladder only by the presence of free blacks and (in the South) slaves, with whom they often competed directly in the labor market.

Louisville historian Samuel Casseday did not feel the Irish worth mention in his 1852 volume, but he praised the Germans, whom he described as "careful, pains-taking and industrious people, of quiet, unobtrusive and inoffensive manners: and...in a majority of instances, men of some education and ability." There was not a hint in Casseday's work of the anti-foreign, anti-Catholic spirit boiling through the nation that would give rise to the Know Nothing party almost as his book was on the press.

The Know Nothing party (it called itself the American party) received its name from secrecy about the party's policies; one aim, however, was quite clear — to keep Catholics and foreigners from holding public office. The new political group's nationwide rise was spectacular, feeding on prejudice and the fear that the constant influx of Catholic immigrants would lead to control of the United States by the Pope and the Catholic hierarchy. Stories of arms, powder, and ammunition cached in Catholic churches found ready acceptance among the credulous. This irrational response was particularly strong among Whigs since the immigrants, once naturalized, flocked in large numbers to the Democratic party. As early as 1844 the German Democratic Association of Louisville issued something of an ultimatum: "We request every German to register his name on the protocol book; and everyone who leaves the party without giving his reasons before a public meeting shall be pub-

Above: Builder and real-estate developer James S. Speed, who became mayor in 1852, was ousted in an illegal April 1855 election called by the dominant Know Nothing party. Four months later the Know Nothings instigated the Bloody Monday riots on the day State officers were elected. In 1856 Speed moved his family to Chicago, where he spent the rest of his life.
Records and Memorials of the Speed Family, 1892

lished in the press as a fellow worthy to be recognized as a *conteumner* of the German Nation." The Irish, too, feeling the Whig party represented property, of which they had none, provided fertile recruiting ground for the Democrats. In Louisville, where Whigs had been dominant for twenty years, this was threatening to shift the balance of political power.

By 1854 the Know Nothings, aided by Whig votes, were strong enough to gain control of County government. American nativistic tendencies were fanned furiously by former Whig Walter N. Haldeman's *Louisville Daily Courier*, which frankly supported the Know Nothings, firing almost daily barbs at Catholics and foreigners. (To Haldeman, naturalized citizens were still "foreigners.") The *Courier's* frequent reports of Democratic organizational meetings insinuated that all were held in German-owned taverns while the liquor flowed freely. Those attending one such meeting were described as "those dear exotics with the perfume of the faderland and the bog mud of the 'ould counthry' lingering about them."

Accompanied by Haldeman's constant encouragement to the political lunatic fringe, Louisville approached the City election of April 7, 1855, a contest complicated by the dispute as to whether the City was to elect a mayor that year. James S. Speed, partner in a real-estate firm, who had served as mayor since April 1852, contended his term did not expire until April 1856, but Know Nothing members of the City Council disagreed. Louisville Chancery Court Judge Henry Pirtle had ruled early in 1855 that Speed's contention was correct. The Know Nothings, a majority and unhappy with the opinion, ordered an election for mayor, an order which Speed promptly vetoed. Undeterred, the Know Nothings announced that John Barbee, a wholesale dry-goods merchant, would run as the American party's candidate. Armed with the opinion of the Chancery Court, Speed did not declare himself a candidate and did not campaign. Unspoken—at least in print—was the fact that Speed, though a Whig, though a member of a pioneer Jefferson County family with Virginia roots, though second cousin to James Speed of Farmington (who would become attorney general in Lincoln's cabinet), though a capable mayor with solid achievements, had committed an unforgivable sin in Know Nothing eyes. He was a convert to Catholicism. Haldeman's *Courier* threw its influence behind Barbee and the Know Nothings, exhorting readers in this typical burst: "The foreign vote in Louisville is a powerful element and when it is directed almost entirely one way [Democratic], and when to it is added the many votes of the many Americans of the Catholic faith, its strength is not to be despised."

Meanwhile, the giant of Louisville journalism, George D. Prentice, watched developments uneasily, endorsing no candidates in the municipal election, ignoring the explosive mayoralty issue, keeping a low profile on nativism. It was un-Prentice-like behavior for the man who had made the *Louisville Daily Journal* a potent factor in Kentucky politics and whose comments were quoted nationwide. The man later blamed for August's Bloody Monday riots was strangely reserved in April. Prentice was, in fact, a man without a party, who realized the Whig organization was defunct, torn in two by the rapidly emerging slavery dispute and left without a unifying force by the death of Henry Clay in 1852. Prentice was to become Louisville's shrillest voice for Know Nothingism, but now he still castigated the violence already being directed at Catholic institutions. Louisville's two other dailies, the *Democrat* and the *Times* (no connection to the present paper of that name), were strongly anti-Know Nothing. Thus, only Haldeman's *Courier* took a nativist stance in the early months of 1855, a policy the Kentucky-born editor had been following for ten years.

Election day brought some violence, and victory for Barbee, who received 3,078 votes, although the American party City Council candidates received generally only a 300-vote edge over their Democratic opponents. Louisville now had two men claiming to be mayor, one flying in the face of an

A sample of Prentice
"...*a large majority of our political opponents in this canvass in the city of Louisville are Germans, Irishmen, and other foreign-born citizens....Their hate knows no bounds. Their revenge exhibits the revenge of a wild beast. Their insolence is unbearable. If they had the requisite courage and strength they would drive forth into the wilderness every native that refuses to let them set their feet upon his neck....No sound in the whole world...would be half so painful to our ears as Dutch and Irish shoutings on the night of the first Monday in August over a victory of the foreign hordes in our midst.*"
Louisville Daily Courier, July 9, 1855

adverse court decision. While the wheels of municipal government spun in confusion, Speed filed a suit in Jefferson Circuit Court challenging Barbee's election. Judge William F. Bullock acted quickly, ruling on May 8 that Speed was mayor until April 1856 and ordering Barbee to step down. Again the Know Nothings ignored the court order while the case was taken to the State Court of Appeals, where Barbee was finally confirmed in office in June.

During all this maneuvering, politics had taken on an even uglier aspect. On May 5, an election was held for magistrates (justices of the peace), who jointly comprised the County Court, the governing body for Jefferson County. On election day Haldeman's *Courier* admonished the voters: "...let us keep the magistracy pure from any taint other than American." This time the escalating violence shocked even Haldeman, who admitted that "foreigners...passing along the street, when in their own houses, when distant from the polls, were attacked and beaten most unmercifully. The houses of some Germans were entered and their property destroyed; others were pursued by infuriated men and boys."

By May, Know Nothingism gained another journalistic voice. Shortly after the municipal election that put Barbee into office, Prentice's *Journal* suddenly became Louisville's and Kentucky's loudest voice in support of the American party, a move of obvious desperation. For a quarter of a century Prentice's newspaper had been the leading Whig organ in Kentucky, indeed, in much of the West and South. Now the Whig party that had carried him to success was in ruins. The *Journal's* circulation was slipping, too. To Prentice, as to many other Whigs—and some Democrats—the American party seemed a way out of the dilemma of the growing bitterness over slavery. Know Nothingism provided a 'straw man' on which both sections could vent their hostilities and appear to create national unity. In early 1855, even before he finally abandoned the lost Whig cause, Prentice wrote that "...it is evident that

The Sabbath defiled
   *"There are others [who do not attend
church], and that class is constantly
increasing with every new infusion of the
foreign element, who make no conceal-
ment of these detestations of the old-
fashioned, hum-drum, puritan method
of opening the first day of the week.
These make each Sunday a Saturnalia,
and with all their might are attempting to
Europeanize our population. Americans
are ever fond of novelties, especially if
brought from across the water, and it is
amusing to see how they perfectly adapt
themselves to enjoying German music
and Lager beer, and Hockheimer and
Bremen cigars, in a pleasant retreat like
that of the Woodland."*
Louisville Daily Courier, *June 12, 1855*

this foreign question is to override all others, even the slavery question, as we
see men of the most opposite views on slavery, forgetting their differences and
acting together." It was a cheap way out for the veteran editor who less than a
year earlier had condemned "the general exclusion of foreign-born citizens
and Roman Catholics from office."

It was also an attempt at the impossible. The issue was whether slavery
would be contained within its existing boundaries or be extended into new
states and territories, such as Kansas and Nebraska; more directly, the issue
was the balance of power between slave and free states, the very issue that
wrecked the Whig party. Behind the frantic political maneuverings of the
1850s and the compromises designed to save the Union loomed the figure of
the black slave. Know Nothingism could not dispel the black presence nor the
sectional rivalry. Haldeman realized this and abandoned the American party
just as Prentice was coming aboard. As committed to the perpetuation of
slavery as Prentice was to the preservation of the Union, Haldeman abandoned Know Nothingism shortly after the national convention of the American party in June 1855 revealed that the Know Nothings, too, were likely to
founder on the slavery issue. Haldeman's departure came just at the right
moment to save his reputation; Prentice's espousal of the party at just the right
moment to blacken his. After the horrors of Bloody Monday on August 6,
Haldeman was the most vociferous of Prentice's rival editors in charging him
with responsibility. (Obviously the Democratic editors of the *Democrat* and
Times did not find it expedient to call attention to the previous record of
their new-found ally.)

Know Nothing street violence increased all through the summer of
1855. Louisville newspapers reported numerous attacks on "foreigners" and
on July 18 an American party rally, provocatively held in the heavily Irish
Eighth Ward (extending from Tenth Street westward), turned into a kind of
dress rehearsal for Bloody Monday. After Irish onlookers hooted the speakers,
a mob attacked Irish residents, damaging property, entering homes and ter-
rorizing the occupants, beating men, and, in at least one instance, wounding
a woman with gunfire. A rumor that arms were stored in the new St. Patrick's
Church led the pastor, the Rev. Thomas Joyce, to open the building for a
search. None was found. Another indicator of the irrationality gripping the
city was the action of the School Board during the summer in refusing to
rehire Catholics as teachers.

THE ELECTION RIOTS.

BLOODY WORK.

MURDER AND ARSON.

TWENTY MEN KILLED.

Top: Louisville Daily Courier,
August 7, 1855

Bottom: No contemporary illustrations of the Bloody Monday election riots of August 6, 1855, are known. This 1897 drawing from the Courier-Journal *is the next best; it was made from a sketch and description furnished by an eyewitness to the destruction of a German bakery in the Preston Street area.*
Courier-Journal, *November 7, 1897*

As August 6 approached, the day on which Kentucky would elect a governor and members of Congress, it was obvious that serious trouble was to be expected in Louisville. The Know Nothing City Council took no action, however, to provide security. Prentice blandly suggested that the Know Nothings should prevent election riots through a "sufficiently strong force for the purpose from their own order." The *Democrat* urged its readers to go to the polls with "unblanched cheek and unfaltering step, relying on no official protection." A confrontation was inevitable. But, even now, the results of that confrontation are shocking.

It is impossible to tell from the subjective, party-oriented newspaper reports exactly how the riots began; only that serious disorder first started in the easternmost First and Second wards (roughly from Floyd Street eastward through Butchertown) where most Germans lived. Long before the polls opened at six a.m. 'executive committees' of the American party took control of the single voting places in each of the city's eight wards, backed by selected police officers, all party members. Their instructions: admit only those who showed a yellow ticket, the sign of American party membership. Naturalized citizens, carrying their citizenship papers, waited impatiently in long lines in the hot August sun while Know Nothings, carrying their yellow tickets, were admitted by back doors. In the lines of waiting voters fights broke out between naturalized citizens and Know Nothing 'bullies'. By noon the Germans and Irish had given up attempts to vote. In the First and Second wards only about 10% of potential voters were able to cast ballots, though the Irish in the westernmost Eighth Ward managed to push the total there to nearly 33%.

Exactly where or precisely how the rioting started is a moot point. The intersection of Shelby and Green (Liberty) streets is the likeliest 'where'; the 'how' could have been the tiniest spark. The tinder caught fire instantly and soon Know Nothing mobs were raging through the city's East End pursuing hapless Germans on the streets. Before long gunfire was directed from the upper windows of houses at the pursuers, who retaliated by setting houses afire on Shelby Street, ransacking German-owned taverns, and beating and shooting any German unlucky enough to be caught. The newly built St. Martin's Catholic Church was saved from destruction only by the intercession of Mayor Barbee and George Prentice. When another group of Know Nothings appeared, bringing a cannon, the united force headed for William Ambruster's brewery in the triangle between Baxter Avenue and Liberty Street, stormed the building despite rifle fire, and set the structure ablaze (though not before consuming copious drafts of the establishment's product). Ten Germans in the building were burned to death while the rioters fired at random into nearby houses, some of which caught fire from the blazing brewery. Some violence even spilled over into Butchertown on the east, where both Germans and Irish were involved in butchering and related trades.

Leaving the smoking East End, the rioters turned their attention westward to the heavily Irish Eighth Ward. The violence here was concentrated on Quinn's Row, a line of wooden tenements on the north side of Main between Eleventh and Twelfth that had been stoned during the July 18 disturbance. This time the row was set ablaze. Some tenants were burned to death, others killed by gunfire as they attempted to escape. One man who, despite thirteen bullet wounds, survived the hail of gunfire was roughly carried off to jail. Owner Francis Quinn's desperate offer of money to the rioters was of no avail. He was killed and his body thrown into one of his blazing buildings.

As night fell, the Louisville skies glowed red, reinforced by additional fires set in the German wards. At the Church of the Immaculate Conception, at Eighth and Cedar, the Rev. Karl Boeswald received an urgent summons to the bedside of a dying parishioner. As he hurried along the street he was fatally wounded by a hail of flying stones. It was after midnight when a huge mob threatened the offices of the *Times*, the *Democrat*, and the *Courier*, all on downtown Third Street. Only the intervention of George Prentice prevented serious damage from the rioters, whom he estimated to number as many as 500.

It is anti-climactic to note that the American party won the election handily, not only in Louisville, but across Kentucky. Charles Morehead became governor and Humphrey Marshall went to the U.S. Senate. The Democrats carried only the Shardein Precinct in Jefferson County, an area filling rapidly with German farmers.

Any Louisvillians fortunate enough to sleep through the night found shocking sights the next morning. The *Times* looked about in outraged disbelief. "While we write, the hot sun of this August day is drinking the vapors of literal pools of human blood that stagnate in our familiar streets." The *Democrat* prophesied that August 6 "will long be remembered as the Bloody Monday." The *Anzeiger* surveyed a city where "Death and desolation is everywhere around us; the heat is debilitating; the inactivity, in business, quiet as death, is depressing." There was never an accurate count of the death toll, but it was at least twenty-two and probably higher. Contemporary estimates were that two-thirds of the dead were foreign-born. Neither was there an accurate assessment of the enormous property damage that, like a gaping wound, still showed two years later.

Only George Prentice seemed unmoved by the spasm that had ravaged the city. The next morning he announced coolly that "We...are sure it will be proved by respectable witnesses that every act of bloodshed was begun by foreigners [on] direct instructions of men with fiendish hearts who...are able to dictate to the Germans and Irish who made these attacks."

Yet to blame Prentice for Bloody Monday, as his rival editors did immediately and many historians have since, is too simple an explanation. Undoubtedly Prentice's invective, more malevolent than any of Haldeman's nativist strictures, inflamed the situation. But examples of violence predated Prentice's opportunistic conversion to Know Nothingism; the whole of the 1850s was a violent decade. To blame Prentice is to ignore the fact that the weight of the Louisville daily English-language press was anti-Know Nothing by three-to-one. In addition, Prentice's outpouring of nativist diatribes was relatively short in time: scarcely more than three months. The root causes of Bloody Monday must be sought elsewhere.

During the following year the *Times* inadvertently gave a clue. "The inhabitants of this state [Kentucky] are a very different people from the inhabitants of New England," the *Times* declared. "In their sympathies and habits they are more like the people of the south...." This was a novel thought for the residents of a city that still called itself western, even though the West had moved to the Pacific Ocean. The Civil War was soon to prove that the city was not northern, but also to demonstrate that neither was it southern. It was both. Bloody Monday was, among other things, an early demonstration of that difficult, divided position.

Unlike most southern cities, Louisville had a substantial foreign population. Unlike northern cities, Louisville had black slavery. And it had trade ties to both North and South. It was pro-slavery and pro-Union (with dissenting voices on both these issues). The Know Nothing movement, which promised to gloss over the North-South dispute, was especially suited to such an environment. Moreover, as a border city, Louisville was buffeted by both the northern and southern divisions within the American party. The southern wing directed its fire chiefly against immigrants in the North and West (because they gave a population advantage that permitted those sections to outvote the South in Congress). Northern nativists stressed anti-Catholicism (because the sheer number of newcomers threatened to swamp traditional Protestant dominance).

Above: Built in far-away Philadelphia, this chunky little freight locomotive was delivered to the Louisville & Nashville Railroad in 1858, in time to see yeoman service during the Civil War hauling Union Army materiel southward. This is the earliest L&N locomotive of which an accurate image exists, though the photograph was made about 1880 in Louisville.
L&N Railroad

Next page: This remarkable color lithograph of Louisville, with meticulous delineation of each building, was published in 1855 by J.T. Palmatary of Cincinnati. It encompasses an area from Shelby Street on the east to Twelfth Street on the west. Corn Island (lower right) was still evident and Beargrass Creek still flowed into the river near the foot of Fourth Street. Several sawmills line the riverfront on the Point and a train from Frankfort arrives on Jefferson Street. Beyond Broadway lies open country, penetrated by the L&N track from Ninth and Broadway.
Liberty National Bank & Trust Company

Louisville nativists saw the "foreign hordes" pouring into their city; they also saw Catholicism increasing rapidly. By 1852 Louisville Catholics, overwhelmingly immigrants, numbered nearly as many as all members of Protestant denominations combined. The presence of German radicals in Louisville was an added irritant. Prentice inflated their numbers: "...a very large proportion of the Germans, who compose a very large proportion of the anti-American party, are infidels, who scoff at the idea of God as the mere figment of an addled brain." Louisville imbibed the Know Nothingism of both North and South and produced an explosive mixture. On August 6, 1855, the mixture went off.

But before the month of August was out, Louisville at last had something to cheer about: tangible evidence of its success in dealing with external problems, despite its internal ones. On August 25 the locomotive *Hart County* steamed southward from Ninth and Broadway, greeted "with loud huzzas" along the way, carrying the first passengers on the Louisville & Nashville Railroad. They did not go far, only eight miles to a rather dismal spot at the northern edge of a low-lying, sparsely populated, swampy area known as Wetwoods. Yet it was an occasion for celebrating. The long-hoped-for railroad to the Tennessee capital was taking concrete form at last.

The passengers on this first train were a mixed throng: "railroad dignitaries, the Mayor of the city, municipal officers, Know Nothing Councilmen, Paddies by the dozen, and a half score of Afric's tawny children, with private citizens in abundance." At Wetwoods they found Irish track gangs busily at work, pushing the twin ribbons of iron forward half a mile a day. There were 178 miles yet to go.

The L&N Railroad, chartered in 1850, was Louisville's solution to the changing transportation patterns that threatened the city's economic underpinnings. The steamboat that had brought a technological revolution to the western rivers, assuring Louisville's rapid growth, now faced a technological revolution on land. Railroads were spiderwebbing across the landscape, stretching farther and farther west from the Atlantic coastal cities. Philadelphia was connected to Cincinnati in 1853. A year later Cincinnati and Louisville achieved rail connection by way of Seymour, Indiana. Almost at once, river tonnage and passengers began to decline. The early railroad warning sign, "Look out for the Cars," had an especially sinister implication for the stately river packets.

Above: Sallie Ward, imperious Louisville fashion setter and daughter of a wealthy commission merchant, created a sensation in 1850 when she divorced her husband of less than two years, prominent Bostonian Timothy Bigelow Lawrence. Enamoured of the tinsel world of fancy dress balls and social adulation, she found intellectual Boston unsuited to her temperament. Connecticut-born Susan Silliman, wife of Dr. Benjamin Silliman, Jr., faculty member of the University of Louisville Medical Department, described Sallie thus in 1849: "[She] is really very pretty, of winning address, but she rouges shockingly! ....Oh, there is so much misjudgment in the education of children here, even those of Christian parents!" Sallie outlived three additional husbands before her own death in 1896.
J.B. Speed Art Museum

Louisville, though, first saw the railroad as a way to tap new territory, not to replace the river. The long-delayed railroad to Frankfort had finally been resuscitated in 1847 with the energetic James Guthrie an enthusiastic backer. Work commenced in the spring of 1849, with financial assistance from Louisville helping push the track eastward along the Shelbyville Turnpike (Frankfort Avenue), through Gilman's Point (St. Matthews), and on to Frankfort and a connection with the pioneer railroad to Lexington. In December 1851 the line was completed, entering Louisville on Jefferson Street as proposed twenty years earlier. The track discreetly ended at Brook Street, though. Louisville still refused to build a railroad to the river at Portland. Guthrie soon took over presidency of the Louisville & Frankfort Railroad, but resigned in 1853 to accept the post of secretary of the treasury in the cabinet of President Franklin Pierce.

Before he took over management of federal financial affairs, however, and even while he was involved in the Frankfort railroad project, Guthrie also busied himself with promoting the Jeffersonville Railroad (incorporated in 1846) north through Indiana. Completed to Columbus in 1852 and Indianapolis in 1853 (with financial aid from both Louisville and Jeffersonville), the line fittingly named one of its early locomotives the *James Guthrie*. New Albany, meanwhile, alarmed at the prospect of the Jeffersonville Railroad, laid plans for its own rail project in 1847 and set to work with such energy that it steamed up its first locomotive in late 1849, ahead of its rival. Though New Albany originated the project, which put rails all the way to Lake Michigan by 1854, Cincinnati viewed it suspiciously as another Louisville-inspired move. After all, Louisville tended to claim it, as it did New Albany-built steamboats, as its own.

Railroad technology was sharpening the intense commercial rivalries among Ohio Valley cities that had grown to maturity dependent on the river. Before long, the railroad, which could go anywhere and at any season, thrust a host of new contenders into the contest. Indianapolis, located on the merest excuse for a river, soon called itself the "Railroad City," and Louisville, looking to railroads to develop new trade territories in the Bluegrass and to the north, found it faced a surprise threat on its seemingly secure southern flank.

Nashville, perched at the head of navigation on the Cumberland River, quickly utilized iron rails to give it better penetration of the southern market, and by 1859 could wheel freight all the way to Atlanta. To further enhance its position, the Tennessee city proposed a railroad northward into Kentucky (encouraged by both Bowling Green and Glasgow) to tap trade that flowed to Louisville. This was a development the city by the Falls could not ignore. Following an enthusiastic public meeting, the City purchased $1 million worth of L&N stock (which proved extremely profitable) and later provided other financial aid. The proposed rail line would not only thwart Nashville's project, but also allow Louisville merchants and manufacturers to tap the Tennessee city's rail route to Atlanta. It would short-circuit the 506 river miles to Nashville with 186 rail miles. By the middle 1850s, when Louisville was enlarging its wharf, railroads built and projected already showed the shape of the future, a future in which the focus of activity would shift from the wharf to the railroad station.

One of the strongest supporters of the Nashville railroad project was Leven L. Shreve, like James Guthrie an important Nineteenth Century Louisville civic leader. One of the entrepreneurs who helped make Louisville a force in the Ohio Valley iron industry, Shreve later expanded his operations to wholesaling and distributing iron and hardware products and was a promoter of the Louisville Gas Company in the 1830s. Ironically, he was a cousin of the intrepid Henry M. Shreve, who had opened steam navigation from New Orleans to Louisville in 1815 with the *Enterprize*. Now, thirty-five years later, Leven L. Shreve became the first president of the L&N Railroad.

Shreve and the Louisville promoters of the L&N were concerned not

This elegant double house, (above right) with its stylish Boston 'bow fronts', was erected about 1840 by brothers Leven L. and Thomas T. Shreve, who grew wealthy in the foundry and wholesale business. Leven (above) was also the first president of the L&N Railroad. The house, the first in Louisville to be lighted with gas, also was home to Jenny Lind during her Louisville concerts in 1851. Louisville Gardens (formerly the Jefferson County Armory) now occupies the site.
Filson Club

only with Nashville's trade threat, but also with the shortcomings of the river that periodically brought a halt to trade throughout the Ohio Valley—low water in the summer and ice in the winter. All the cities and towns along the Ohio from Pittsburgh to Cairo operated on a two-season business cycle tied directly to the river. One cycle was opened by the spring rise, the other by the fall rise. If either was delayed, merchants, manufacturers, and farmers quickly felt the financial stringency. That situation occurred often enough to make Louisville receptive to the railroad as alternative transportation, river city though it was.

When the L&N reached New Haven, Kentucky, in 1857, the *Courier* noted that a carload of Louisville-made furniture had been dispatched to that Nelson County community. The event revealed both the deepening penetration of the iron rails into the Kentucky countryside and the fact that Louisville had come a long way from being merely a handler of products made elsewhere. The export of its own manufactured goods on its own railroad symbolized the increasing importance of industry, which now could draw on the large labor supply created by immigration.

The railroad itself was also a customer for existing heavy industry, purchasing bridge girders and rails from the Louisville Rolling Mill, for example. Louisville-made cotton machinery was being sold to southern customers, while steamboat building, despite the railroads, continued to create a demand for boilers and machinery. In the fifteen-month period from July 1854 through October 1855 a total of forty-one steamers was constructed by the Louisville yards, located upstream from the wharf in the area known as the Point. (The name originated from the point of land created by Beargrass Creek as it flowed into the river near the foot of Third Street and the term remained firmly fixed even after the creek was diverted.) The concentration of steamboat building here was related to the equal concentration of sawmills, handy to large rafts of logs floated downriver. An increasing demand for steam power in factories, in addition to the steamboat market, prompted expansion of the city's iron-working industry. In the middle 1850s Ainslie, Cochran & Company erected a plant at Tenth and Main that produced steam engines, cotton gin machinery, and wheels and castings for railroad cars, and claimed it was "the largest in the West."

Meat packing, principally pork, became big business during the 1850s with Louisville the second largest packing center in the nation (Cincinnati was first), butchering an average of 300,000 hogs each year. The large packing houses exported pork to the South and even Europe, while smaller enterprises (mostly German-operated) supplied fresh meat to local tables. And Louisville led the nation in the manufacture of hemp rope and cotton bagging. The latter item, made of hemp, was used to bale cotton before metal bales were developed. Hemp, not yet widely known as marijuana, was Kentucky's leading

Cockfighting in Louisville

Cockfighting, although illegal, was common in Louisville in the ante-bellum years. Slave Henry Smith, writing in the third person, describes one such event. The locale was probably near Beargrass Creek at the foot of the hill on Baxter Avenue (then Jefferson Street).

"A cock fight took place on Jefferson street at Hamilton pork house at the foot of a street, on a spot of ground where after years was a brick yard. Both whites and blacks repaired to gamble and cock fight. At the time of this transaction there were assembled…hundred[s] of rich white men mingled with scores of negroes engaged in fighting cocks, and many more gambling….They had been warned at different times not to fight or gamble on this ground, often some were shot or stabbed quarreling…when all were in their height of enjoyment there was discovered coming nearly a thousand citizens and officers to arrest the offenders….Those who were not willing to be arrested, were knocked down and handcuffed and the greatest confusion prevailed, fine broadcloth coats, money, revolvers, were all left on the ground…. Smith discovering the danger, at once started for the toll gate…passed on through the gate out on the pike in safety, up the pike road and reaching the top of the hill saw hundreds marching up the street. Smith was the only one who escaped."
Fifty Years of Slavery in the United States

agricultural product from 1840 to 1860 and Louisville was the nation's leading hemp market. The manufacture of jeans cloth, used to make work clothing for slaves, and of woolen fabric expanded during the decade, and the manufacture of ready-made clothing was launched.

There were unexpected manufacturing enterprises too; Peters, Cragg & Company made pianos, employing fifty-two skilled craftsmen. Printing and book publishing also assumed some importance, the largest firm being John P. Morton & Company. Printing and publishing created a demand for paper, an enterprise that lured two brothers from the powder-making du Pont family of Delaware to Louisville in 1854. Alfred Victor and Antoine Bidermann du Pont purchased the paper mill at Tenth and Rowan, owned by Isaac Cromie, enlarging the plant and producing both book paper and newsprint. The du Ponts were best known at this time, however, for the artesian well, an accidental by-product of drilling for water for the mill. Spouting twenty or thirty feet into the air, the water (unsuitable for paper making) was utilized for a fashionable medicinal bath.

This burgeoning wave of manufacturing created for the first time a large labor force in Louisville; at mid-decade blue-collar workers in Louisville numbered perhaps as many as 10,000, including many women. As might be expected, labor-management disputes multiplied. No sooner, for example, had construction work begun on the L&N than the Irish laborers struck for a ten-hour work day. When journeymen curriers struck W.E. Stokes' leather-finishing shop in 1857, they placed an advertisement in the newspapers to air their grievances and ask other working persons not to take their jobs. Yet labor was still largely unorganized and would remain so until after the Civil War. In 1855 there were only two unions: the iron moulders and the printers, both headed by officers with Irish names. Work stoppage was sometimes used as a generalized social protest. After Bloody Monday, fifty stonemasons stopped work on the new Custom House and Post Office at Third and Green streets (today the Commerce Building) "because of violence committed against their countrymen."

The rising curve of industrialism, actively encouraged by the Louisville Chamber of Commerce, was temporarily interrupted by the Panic of 1857 that left 3,000 workers unemployed by the end of the year. Recovery was relatively rapid, however (though the Chamber itself was a casualty). Not a single Louisville bank stopped redeeming its own notes for gold and silver. The L&N Railroad continued to push its rails not only toward Nashville, but Memphis as well, striking toward that river city from its main stem at Bowling Green. The extent of recovery is shown by statistics of 1858 and 1859. In the former year 4,531 "hands" were employed in 214 manufacturing establishments turning out products valued at $7.8 million. A year later employment had climbed to 7,369 (including 1,080 women) in 436 establishments turning

Above: Louisvillians agreed to proposals for a water works in 1856 only after they were assured the corner pumps would remain for public use. The pumps were not eliminated until early in the Twentieth Century when they were declared a health hazard.
The Great South, *1875*

Right: A primeval beech forest along River Road had to be cleared to make way for the Louisville Water Company pumping station, completed in 1860. The structures and engineering details were the work of hydraulic engineer Theodore R. Scowden, who earlier had designed water systems for Cincinnati and Cleveland. The ten zinc statues atop the tower's columned base, installed in 1861 at a cost of only $271.75, were replaced after the 1890 tornado destroyed eight of them.
Lin Caufield

out products valued at $14.1 million. Louisville's new destiny was written clearly in the figures; it was becoming an industrial workshop.

But, as it had once been a trapezoid marked out in the wilderness, Louisville now was becoming a workshop in the midst of one of the more important agricultural counties in Kentucky. Jefferson led all others in market gardening and orchards, having a hungry urban market right at hand. The cash value of the county's farms, $11.1 million, was exceeded only by Bourbon and Fayette in the heart of the rich Bluegrass area. Jefferson also had become an area of relatively small farms, in contrast to its pioneer days when a few speculators and the landed gentry owned much of the county's acreage. By 1860 only one farm exceeded 1,000 acres. The greatest number (576) were in the range of only twenty to ninety-nine acres.

In the city the noticeable shift to an industrial economic base was accompanied by other changes. The Know Nothings, once in office, proved to be more lambs than lions. Though they continued to give lip service to "American" dominance, no changes were made at either the City or State levels legally to keep Catholics from holding office or to lengthen the naturalization period for immigrants. (Not until 1906 did naturalization become a federal function.) In Louisville the American party continued the improvement of public services that was under way when it came to power.

The construction of a water works, which Mayor Speed had proposed the City itself undertake, was finally begun in 1857 by a private corporation. The City aided the project, as it did railroads, through purchase of stock. For a community that had relied on wells (even to supply water to steam boilers) and public pumps on numerous street corners, this was a giant step, though not one taken lightly. Voters had turned down Speed's proposal in 1853 and 1854, but finally agreed to the stock purchase plan in 1856 after they

Above: Albert Fink, like Gideon Shryock before him, had grandiose plans for completion of the Jefferson County Court House, as this sketch shows. He had to settle for a more modest version.
Library of Congress

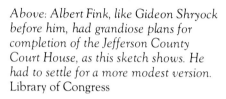

Above right: The Post Office and Custom House, completed in 1858 at Third and Liberty streets, fronted on Third Street. In the days before carrier distribution of mail the Post Office lobby was the daily meeting place of Louisville businessmen waiting for incoming mail to be sorted. Federal courts were on the second floor and offices on the third. The basement was used for storage of whiskey in bond. Today the massive stone structure is an office building.
Edwards' Annual Louisville City Directory, 1868-69

were assured the corner pumps would not be removed; the citizens made it plain they did not want to drink Ohio River water. Promoters of the Louisville Water Company stressed the aid it would provide in fighting fires and in supplying water to industry.

Chief Engineer Theodore Scowden built a pumping station in classic form, more Roman than Greek, and placed the reservoir high atop the nearby river bluff, a site now occupied by the Veteran's Administration Hospital. The first water was pumped in October 1860, fittingly by two steam engines made in Louisville by the Roach & Long Foundry. The quality of workmanship was such that the engines pumped all the city's water until 1893, when they were augmented by larger engines.

When the Water Works began operation, Louisville had also finally completed "Guthrie's Folly," the unfinished Court House that caused the *Courier* to comment in 1855 that: "As a grand old ruined pile, it has an exceedingly fine appearance of a moonlight evening...." Coming to the somewhat reluctant conclusion that it was more economical to complete the building than to tear it down and start over, City and County supplied the funds to finish the work. Even more remarkably, though both City and County governments were dominated by Know Nothings, they turned for an architect to a German-born engineer, a Forty-Eighter, thus tacitly admitting that the new immigrants had something valuable to offer their adopted country after all. Albert Fink came to Louisville in 1857, with a formidable reputation as a bridge designer, to become construction engineer for the L&N Railroad. That same year James Guthrie returned from Washington, his term as secretary of the treasury completed. Almost immediately he was named vice-president of the L&N, with the intent that he become president (which he did in 1860).

Fink and Guthrie, an oddly assorted pair—the brilliant, 30-year-old engineer with the German accent, and the still energetic, 65-year-old financier and Kentucky native—understood each other immediately. Impressed with the ability of the 'Teutonic Giant' (Fink stood six feet, seven inches tall), Guthrie not only maneuvered the completion of the Court House, but had Fink named to head the work. Though the engineer, like Shryock before him, was not able to get his total plan built, the Court House was completed at last in 1859. It had taken twenty-two years, but Guthrie had erased the 'Folly' associated with his name. One other large and impressive public building had been added to the Louisville cityscape by the end of the decade. The Custom House and Post Office at the southwest corner of Third and Liberty was the first federal building erected in Louisville. The solidly built stone structure, designed in what was called the Anglo-Norman style, was completed in 1858.

With its massive stone walls and iron floor girders and columns, the new Custom House was regarded as fire proof, but other buildings in Louisville were not. Costly fires had become such a serious problem that it was obvious

Above: A professional fire department equipped with steam pumpers drawn by horses spelled the end of Louisville's volunteer fire companies and their hand-operated engines as the 1850s drew to a close. This specimen of volunteer days has handholds on the tongue for four men to pull the engine and a fearsome array of handles for pumping water. It is preserved by The Filson Club.

the volunteer firemen pulling their tiny engines to conflagrations, then furiously pumping by hand to get a stream of water, were an anachronism in an age that prided itself on its technological progress. Volunteer fire companies, too, were far from cooperative, each seeking to outshine the other in fighting a blaze. When the newly built public school at Fifth and York was totally destroyed by fire in the spring of 1855, spectators said the loss was due "more to lack of harmony among the several fire companies than want of water." But the immediate problem was to replace the colorful, but woefully inadequate, hand apparatus with the new steam-powered pumpers that were revolutionizing fire fighting.

The newly organized Louisville Board of Fire Underwriters (today the Louisville Board of Independent Insurance Agents) made the use of steam-powered pumpers its first order of business, nudging the City toward purchase of this kind of equipment. The General Council responded favorably, but after two locally-built machines proved failures, local insurance agents turned to a Cincinnati manufacturer in 1858 and presented the steam pumper *Eclipse* to the City. The new engine did all its name implied, eclipsing not only the hand-operated engines, but the eleven volunteer fire companies as well. In 1858 the City General Council disbanded the volunteers, replacing them with paid personnel.

The public school system, too, was greatly improved. The new City charter of 1851 provided that a school be built in each ward and that the schools be placed under the control of an elected School Board of Trustees (two from each ward). In 1852 the new trustees took a bold step, deciding to establish the Female High School as a counterpart to the Male High School. Another kind of institution for Louisville youth founded in the 1850s indicated the unruly temper of the times was not confined to adults. First called the House of Refuge when it was formed by a private group in 1854, it was

A day at the races
Oakland Race Course ran its last about
1855 and was succeeded in 1858 by the
Woodlawn Course, some miles east of
Louisville along the railroad to Lexington. The opening day in May 1860 was
marred by a tornado which caused
several deaths and much damage in the
city, but only heavy rain and wind at
the track.

"Yesterday's sun rose in a cloudless sky
and ushered in a beautiful day – the first
of the spring meeting at the Woodlawn
course....The early trains were crowded
....But at noon it was sultry and oppres-
sive, and later the distant thunder, the
electric flash and the clouds that came
rolling in from the West betokened a
storm. The blast came, terrible as the
simmon that sweeps across the desert,
and following the hurricane, rain fell in
torrents....But the race had to be run,
rain or shine, so Jas. K. Duke, Esq., the
Judge, rang the bell for the horses to be
brought out."
Louisville Daily Courier, May 22, 1860

designed "to prevent our youth from becoming adepts in crime and subjects
for the penitentiary." Not until 1860, however, was progress made in securing
a site and erecting buildings, when the City made available 82.5 acres south of
Louisville, land reserved for Oakland Cemetery. (In the distant future it
would become Belknap Campus of the University of Louisville.)

The great sectional conflict that had been brewing for years between the
industrializing North and the plantation South, symbolized most dramatically
(though hardly exclusively) by the issue of human bondage, was arriving at
the point of no return by the end of the decade. The Know Nothing aber-
ration had only briefly obscured this issue. Humphrey Marshall hardly had
time to take his seat in Congress after the Bloody Monday election than he
announced that he would defer "managing the Dutch and Irish until he had
the niggers safe." Ironically for Louisville and Jefferson County, the rising
discord came at a time when the local black population (slave and free) was
at the lowest percentage it has ever been, except perhaps the very earliest
years of settlement. In 1860 blacks constituted only 11.5% of the population
of Jefferson County as a whole, a mere 10% in Louisville. These low percent-
ages represented a combination of two trends:

   • The huge tide of immigration that pushed Louisville's white population sharply upward to a total of 61,213, an impressive 59% increase over 1850;

   • A 10% decline during the decade in the number of Louisville slaves,
from 5,432 to 4,903.

   Slaves, as opposed to the total of all blacks, were only 7.5% of Louisville's 1860 population. In the county outside the city, slaves numbered 5,402,
or 25% of the total population, down from 32% a decade earlier. Jefferson
County's solid agricultural position thus was based less on slave labor than
ever before. The "peculiar institution," these figures suggest, was dying a

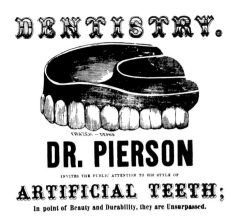

Above: Louisville City Directory
& Business Mirror, 1858-59

natural death in the area around the Falls. One explanation for the decline of urban slavery has been that the institution was incompatible with the urban milieu and unprofitable for slaveowners.

There is some evidence in the Louisville record of an increasing volume of Kentucky slaves sold southward during the 1850s, especially the greater number of "Slaves Wanted" advertisements in Louisville newspapers and the first reports of 'pens' kept by slave traders to collect their human merchandise. One white youngster of the 1850s recalled how he and his friends were intrigued by "Garrison's nigger pen" on Second between Market and Main. The ugly name reflected the ugly business, one of several such businesses where small boys could watch as slaves "were handcuffed in twos and driven to Portland to be shipped to New Orleans by boat to be sold."

And yet Louisville was a city with pronounced divisions of opinion on the practicality and morality of slavery. The 1849 election for delegates to the convention to revise Kentucky's constitution produced two opposing Louisville slates on this very issue. The mercurial Walter N. Haldeman, later a secessionist, in 1849 called emancipation "a cause that has the light of heaven blazing upon it." So strong was emancipation sentiment in Louisville that George Prentice declared that the rest of Kentucky looked upon it as an "abolition hole." In the election itself 46% of Louisville's voters chose the emancipation slate, a losing but remarkable total. The other 54% voted for the pro-slavery ticket, headed by James Guthrie. The new constitution that Guthrie had a large hand in drafting actually tightened the bonds of servitude.

Meanwhile, Louisville's free blacks (fewer than 100 lived outside the city) increased slightly in numbers during the 1850s, totaling 1,917 by 1860. A handful actually acquired substantial property. Washington Spradling, freed from slavery in 1814 when he was a child, was the most successful. He became a barber, a high-prestige occupation for blacks, and by the 1850s owned property assessed at $30,000. At his death after the Civil War he left an estate valued at $100,000. Free blacks, the elite in Louisville's Negro community, were the mainstay of the black churches, which also numbered slaves among their members. Though the churches were the center of black social life, other social events marked Louisville as different from most cities farther south.

In 1857, for instance, free blacks and slaves not only held a New Year's Eve ball, but rented the facilities of the Falls City Hotel for the event. "The immense dining hall was filled…by representatives of the peculiar institution," the *Democrat* reported, adding that they went through "the gentilities of the dance, the promenade, and supper table…with commendable ease and grace." Thus, on the eve of the Civil War, Louisville had developed an export slave trade on the one hand and allowed blacks unusual freedom on the other. It was industrializing, as was the North, but lived on trade with the South.

Now this city, of both North and South (and still acutely conscious of its earlier role as part of the West), approached the most difficult period it has ever faced in its history. Fixed on the border of the South and of the North, it was to be caught in war between them.

Chapter Eight

The Civil War: Louisville's Bad Dream Turns Real

The spring of 1861, dreary and rainy, mirrored Louisville's mood and seemed to reflect the political pain wracking the border city as the "irrepressible conflict" became a fact. Seven southern states had already severed their ties to the Union when the telegraph crackled with more ominous news. The final desperate hopes for peace had been shot down: the newly proclaimed Confederate States of America had begun shelling Fort Sumter in Charleston harbor.

The report had a special poignancy for Louisville. Fort Sumter was commanded by one of the community's own. Major Robert Anderson, son of Jefferson County pioneer Richard Clough Anderson, Sr., had spent his childhood at Soldier's Retreat in the green, rolling land along Beargrass. His family, with its Virginia roots, was part of the landed gentry that had made Kentucky a slave state at the beginning of settlement. When the Confederates demanded that he surrender or be bombarded into submission, Anderson's plight was symbolic of Louisville's. He tried compromise, but in the end he had to decide, and he chose to stay with the Union. On April 14 a battered Fort Sumter ran up the white flag. Major Anderson and his troops evacuated and sailed away to New York.

The attack on Fort Sumter, galvanizing the North to righteous anger and the South to righteous jubilation, was the lancing of a boil, the lifting of a great weight. For both North and South it was the release of emotional tensions that had grown too great to bear. The game of compromise upon compromise and patches upon compromises was over; a momentary exultation of relief swept both North and South. But Louisville, its bad dream of a war between the sections now a reality, stood in unhappy indecision, pulled both ways. Its first reaction was not surprising: the impossible hope that Kentucky might somehow remain neutral amid the flames of conflict. "Kentucky...," the *Democrat* declared, "is at liberty to consider what is best for herself, and let miserable factions fight their own battles."

But geography was against neutrality for Kentucky and especially for Louisville. The city by the Falls was also now the city at the river break in the critical north-south rail route that was to prove a key element in the Union victory in the western theatre of war. Louisville became the staging area for troops moving south and, along with Jeffersonville, the supply base for the incredible volume of materiel needed by armies in the field. The city also became a temporary holding point for thousands of Confederate prisoners, a vast medical center, and a tempting military target.

Louisville first tried compromise and found it did not work. In the presidential election of the previous fall, the only one in American history with four major candidates, the city's voters rejected Abraham Lincoln, Kentucky-born candidate of the new Republican party. That party was seen as a threat to slavery and was identified with the North. The voters also rejected Kentuckian John C. Breckinridge, candidate of the dissident southern Democrats, seen as unwilling to compromise and identified with the South. Louisville and Jefferson County saw the choice as between Stephen A. Douglas of Illinois, the regular Democrat, and John Bell of Tennessee, candidate of a coalition of old-line southern Whigs and the remnants of the Know Nothings calling themselves Constitutional Unionists. Bell's platform, silent on slavery, was a simple message: preserve the Union.

Both Douglas and Bell provided what Louisville wanted: soothing words to the North and to the South. But by the fall of 1860 it was too late for more soothing words. Only in the border areas, such as Louisville, were Bell and Douglas popular candidates. Yet it did not matter which way the border states and cities voted. The national split was wide open: the North and West voted overwhelmingly for Lincoln, the South overwhelmingly for Breckinridge. Louisville chose Bell, casting 3,823 votes for the Constitutional Unionists. Douglas, stalwart of northern Democrats and the only candidate to visit Louisville, achieved a respectable second place with 2,633 votes.

Above: Major Robert Anderson, born at Soldier's Retreat in eastern Jefferson County, was in command of Fort Sumter in Charleston harbor when it was attacked by Confederates. He was later made a brigadier general and placed in charge of raising Union troops in Kentucky.
Harper's Weekly, *January 12, 1861*

Breckinridge trailed badly, gathering a mere 854 votes, while only ninety-one voters cast ballots for Lincoln. The pattern was the same in the county precincts: Bell, 1,073; Douglas, 808; Breckinridge, 268; Lincoln, fifteen. Bell likewise carried Kentucky. Though this vote for compromise had no effect on the national outcome, it delivered a message: as Major Anderson had done, his native area had chosen the Union.

Though dismayed by Lincoln's election, the majority of local citizens did not waver in their opposition to joining the Confederacy. On February 22, 1861, an occasion was made of the "raising of the stars and stripes over our magnificent Court House" where attorney James Speed admonished the throng: "Let us...be on our guard how we rashly step off from the Constitution and from under that flag." Three weeks later a Southern Rights meeting precipitated a minor riot by Union supporters. The spontaneous formation and rapid growth of the Union Club, whose members took an oath to support the federal government, come what may, was another indication of the deep undercurrent of Union support in the city.

Louisville chose the Union, but wanted to avoid war. When Lincoln, after the fall of Fort Sumter, issued a call for 75,000 troops, the pro-Union *Democrat* sneered: "Let them go South, as many as can get there; not many will get back. The climate and General Beauregard will take care of them."

Expressing Louisville's hopes of remaining aloof, the City General Council on April 17 embarked on a remarkable course, providing $50,000 for defense of the city from North *or* South, and naming attorney Lovell H. Rousseau a brigadier general, perhaps the only municipal generalship in American history. Yet the trend of the future was clearly shown when this quickly organized Home Guard was armed with some of the controversial "Lincoln guns," sent secretly to Kentucky in May at the urgent request of Unionists. The Louisville shipment was hidden in the basement of the Court House and dispensed cautiously to trusted men. The members of the Home Guard were later mostly absorbed into Federal forces, but at the time Louisville seriously thought it could become an island of neutrality, while remaining in the Union. The State thought it could, too, and officially adopted neutrality as a policy on May 20. Some hopeful Kentuckians, such as James Guthrie, believed that the state could be "the great mediator for the restoration of peace and the preservation of our Country." Only Walter N. Haldeman, once an emancipationist, once a Know Nothing, and now a fire-eating southern Democrat, spoke enthusiastically in print of conflict. The *Courier* editor declared that Louisville was "now united as one man in the unalterable determination to meet the hordes Mr. Lincoln is about to pour down on the South [,] and drive them back at the point of the bayonet." Haldeman was one of the few who recognized that Kentucky could not remain neutral. "She will not be permitted to be so," he asserted. "Her [geographical] position forbids it."

Haldeman spoke for a minority of Louisvillians, but a vocal, influential minority. Louisville's internal cleavage generally followed economic lines. The Main Street wholesale merchant princes, whose dealings were mostly with the South, provided the chief reservoir of support for the Confederacy. The rising industrialists (some of whom still labored in their shops), blue-collar workers, small retailers, and professional men provided the larger reservoir of support for the Union. But there were Louisvillians ready to accept Haldeman's challenge; two companies of Confederate volunteers left by steamer on April 20 for New Orleans. Five days later three more companies departed for Nashville on the new L&N Railroad.

Union supporters responded with a recruiting office at Eighth and Main and a training camp in Clarksville on the Indiana side of the river. One Louisvillian recalled that "it was no uncommon sight...to see a squad of recruits for the Union service marching up one side of the street while a

THE WAR BEGUN!

FORT SUMTER ATTACKED

FULL DETAILS!

CORRESPONDENCE BETWEEN THE SECRETARY OF WAR OF THE CONFEDERATE STATES AND GEN. BEAUREGARD!

ANDERSON DEMANDED TO SURRENDER!

HIS REPLY!

INFAMOUS TREACHERY OF FOX AND LINCOLN'S ADMINISTRATION!

Effects of the Bombardment!

BREACH MADE IN FORT SUMTER!

GUNS DISABLED!

Floating Battery not Damaged!

THE REVENUE CUTTER HARRIET LAN INJURED!

REPORTED ARRIVAL OF TH FLEET!

NO LOSS OF LIFE REPORTED THUS FAR!

A TERRIBLE STORM!

BOMBARDMENT CONTINUED!

squad destined for the Confederacy was moving down the other." Yet, at the final count, Kentucky supplied far more soldiers to the Union than to the Confederate cause—approximately three to one, and the first nationally popular war song, "The Union Forever," was written by Louisvillian Will S. Hays.

The Indiana training ground was named for Louisville attorney and radical Republican Joseph Holt. His was the first Kentucky voice raised unequivocally not only for the Union, but for support of whatever measures were necessary to keep the Union intact, including armed force. Holt, who had been postmaster general in the Buchanan administration, put the issue squarely on the line in a widely heralded speech at Louisville's Masonic Temple, Fourth and Jefferson, on July 13. "There is not and there cannot be any neutral ground for loyal people between their own government and those who at the head of armies are menacing its destruction. Your inaction is not neutrality, though you may delude yourself with the belief that it is so…," he asserted.

This speech and others like it that he made across the state were powerful statements of all-out Unionism that hit their mark. In the August elections for the State General Assembly, Unionists won strong majorities in both houses. The Louisville delegation included James Speed, a champion of the Lincoln administration. This was a change from April when Louisville had elected John M Delph as mayor on a neutrality platform. (Delph, however, became a strong Unionist when hostilities broke out in Kentucky.)

Still, outsiders could see the division of opinion in the city. A correspondent for the *New York Tribune* described the Louisville he found in July: "At the breakfast table one looked up from his New York paper…to see his nearest neighbor perusing *The Charleston Mercury*. He found *The Louisville Courier* urging people to take up arms against the Government. *The Journal*, published just across the street, advised Union men to arm themselves, and advised that any of them wanting first-class revolvers could learn something to their advantage by calling upon its editor. In the telegraph office, the loyal agent of the Associated Press, who made up dispatches for the North, chatted with the Secessionist, who spiced the news for the southern palate."

The certain threat of sectional conflict caused many Louisville whites another concern: what would local blacks do? Even though the latter were only 10% of the population (and slaves only 7.5%), there was some fear of a revolt, or an increase in runaways across the river where the Fugitive Slave Act might not now be rigorously enforced. But the tight clamp placed on Negro assemblages was needless. Blacks adopted a wait-and-see attitude and obviously considered the war a white man's affair. When the Union Army later sought Negro recruits, few Kentucky free blacks came forward, although many slaves slipped away to a military career as a way to freedom.

Meanwhile, the sundered ties of commerce brought Louisville's economy to a low ebb, though there was one busy place in the spring and summer of 1861: the L&N's new depot at Ninth and Broadway. The L&N, now headed by James Guthrie, with Albert Fink as his indispensable lieutenant, was run ragged with traffic, practically all southbound. The Confederacy, stockpiling while it could, found Louisville merchants and the L&N delighted to oblige as long as possible. Traffic jams built up around the depot with "drays, black drivers with long whips, singing amidst the tumult, and laughing and pushing forward…Broadway, between Ninth and Tenth… perfectly blocked…[shipments of] bacon, coffee, pork, beef—everything possible and impossible, and unexpected—from lady's gloves to terra cotta for a church in Tennessee."

Louisville's old upriver rival, Cincinnati, fumed at this traffic, unhappy with the fact that Louisville had a railroad to the South and it did not, and unhappy with Kentucky's self-proclaimed neutrality. "Property might as well

Above: This gleaming, high-wheeled L&N passenger locomotive, Quigley, was among those captured by the Confederates when General Simon Bolivar Buckner advanced up the railroad as far as Munfordville in the fall of 1861. The L&N did not recover the Quigley until after the war, when this photograph was made in Louisville. The horns on the headlight may commemorate a speed record.
L&N Railroad

Left: Louisville Daily Courier, April 13, 1861

be consigned to Charleston, S.C., or to Richmond, Va., as to Louisville, Ky.,'' one Cincinnati newspaper curtly observed. The Treasury Department had issued an order May 2, 1861, banning such trade, but the surveyor of customs at Louisville was Walter N. Haldeman, a holdover from the Buchanan administration not yet replaced. Even more importantly, Lincoln was treating Kentucky gingerly, avoiding any action that might push it toward secession.

But finally, in September, when Confederate troops occupied Hickman and Columbus, on Kentucky's few miles of Mississippi River shore, Union troops moved into Paducah. Governor Magoffin demanded withdrawal of both forces. The Unionists, who controlled the General Assembly as a result of the August elections, quickly rejected that resolution and approved one demanding only Confederate withdrawal, then sustained it handily over Magoffin's veto. The unreal shadow world of neutrality was over on September 13, 1861. Kentucky was a Union state.

With the end of neutrality, Louisville found itself suddenly plunged into the maelstrom. In rapid-fire order General Robert Anderson (advanced in rank after Fort Sumter) moved his headquarters from Cincinnati to Louisville, the Louisville Legion at Camp Joe Holt was mustered into the Federal service, Walter Haldeman's *Courier* was suppressed as an "advocate of treason," and a Confederate army headed toward Louisville. The approaching army, commanded by General Simon Bolivar Buckner, seized Bowling Green on September 17, then sent an advance force to occupy Munfordville. In one quick move the Confederacy controlled half the L&N Railroad. There were no more trains to Nashville. Instead, northbound trains carried Confederate troops toward an alarmed Louisville. Almost overnight neutrality had turned to war for the nation's twelfth largest city.

The city moved rapidly, though, to prepare what defense it could. Mayor Delph mobilized the 2,000-man Home Guard the day Bowling Green was captured. The response was immediate, with the entire complement at the L&N depot that night, ready to move out. General William T. Sherman, Anderson's second in command, was in charge of the Guard, and Lovell Rousseau hurried the Louisville Legion, another 2,000 men, across the river from Camp Joe Holt. Louisville's streets resounded with the tramp of marching men, not on parade this time, but on the way to battle. A member of the Legion, noting his pale-faced comrades, wrote that: "This night many of us realized for the first time that the war had begun in earnest."

The Legion joined the Guard at the depot that had been swamped only a few weeks earlier with freight going south. Now it was raw recruits, men new to war and soldiering, but the only defense force available. Civilians milled about, many asking for and receiving arms to join the troops. The procession of trains rumbled southward through the night. The latest report put Buckner's forces at Lebanon Junction.

Though they went forward bravely, the Louisville troops were undoubtedly relieved to find that the enemy was not threatening the city after all. Confederates had been in Lebanon Junction, but only as a skirmishing party charged with destroying the L&N bridge over Rolling Fork. Mission accomplished, they quickly withdrew, damaging the railroad as they went. Had Buckner known the slim opposition he faced, he might well have proceeded to attack Louisville. Instead, he pulled his forces back to Bowling Green and dug in for the winter. Digging in with him was Haldeman and his *Louisville Courier.* Though Louisville's first war scare was over, its railroad was held by the enemy. For nearly five months L&N trains could operate only to Elizabethtown and Lebanon.

Buckner's feint toward Louisville alarmed not only local residents, but the Union high command as well. Louisville's strategic location demanded that it be held at all costs, and soon Federal troops began pouring into the city and Union recruiters began work in earnest. As three Pennsylvania regiments, who arrived in six steamboats, marched through the city to set up camp near the Oakland Race Course, the *Democrat* felt reassured. "The bright barrels of muskets and the gleaming spears of bayonets flashing in the sun and a whole regiment moving as one man gave us a sure faith that they were on to victory."

On and on the troops came, from Wisconsin and Indiana and Ohio and now new regiments of Kentuckians. Some were sent south toward Bowling Green in preparation for a spring offensive. Colonel Curran Pope's Fifteenth Kentucky Infantry marched to the depot shouting "Going to see Buckner; going to call on Haldeman." An Ohio officer recorded his most vivid impression of Louisville: "As we marched through the city my attention was directed to a sign bearing the inscription, in large black letters, NEGROES BOUGHT AND SOLD." The influx of soldiery rapidly turned Louisville into an armed camp. Besides the Oakland track and a large area of what is today Old Louisville, tent cities and training grounds sprang up in Portland, at Eighteenth and Broadway, and along the Frankfort and Bardstown turnpikes.

With all this activity, Louisville's stagnating economy picked up, but the economic benefits of war were not an unmixed blessing. An army in camp is always difficult to control, as Louisville soon discovered. By the beginning of 1862 there were some 80,000 Union soldiers in and around Louisville. Newspapers reported numerous instances of trouble between troopers and civilians: disturbances at the theatres, fights in bars, drunken soldiers causing trouble on the streets. When a Butchertown bartender refused to sell liquor to a cavalryman, the disgruntled soldier mounted his horse and rode into the bar, firing his pistol wildly.

But there were many places where the soldiers and their money were welcome. An almost continuous line of gambling establishments offering keno, faro, roulette, and poker games lined the north side of Jefferson from Fourth to Fifth, turned the corner on Fifth to Market, and continued on the south side of Market back to Fourth. Ladies of the evening were in abundance, too. When a New York state regiment received four months' back pay at one time, the scene at camp next morning was one of scores of soldiers returning in carriages, "being in no condition to walk," while others were

Above: Louisville Daily Democrat,
September 24, 1861

accompanied "by their frail companions."

The troop build-up meant that Louisville soon got its railroad back, however. After the Confederates suffered body blows in eastern Kentucky and western Tennessee, they hastily evacuated Bowling Green in mid-February 1862, even as Union forces under General Don Carlos Buell (who succeeded the ailing Anderson) were approaching. Buell kept going and by the end of February occupied Nashville. Haldeman and his *Courier* retreated with the Confederates. As the Louisville publisher moved with the southern troops, Prentice sneeringly referred to the *Nashville-Murfreesboro-Bowling Green-Louisville Courier.*

Louisville, meanwhile, became the great supply center for Buell and other Union forces in the western theatre. Train after train disgorged materiel at Jeffersonville for transport across the river on shuttling ferry boats. The rush of military supplies southward was matched by a different kind of northward movement: in 1862 Louisville began to witness the horror of war as the wounded—Union and Confederate—came streaming in. By early 1863 there were nineteen military hospitals in Louisville, set up in public schools, private homes, factories, even a church. Brown General Hospital rose near the present Belknap Campus of the University of Louisville, and other hospitals were established in New Albany and Jeffersonville. By early June 930 deaths had been recorded in the Louisville hospitals and Cave Hill Cemetery set aside a plot for Union soldiers who died in Kentucky. Many who survived carried war's reminders for the rest of their lives. An English visitor to Louisville in 1863 noted "that what first struck a stranger was the number of maimed men...."

Though Louisville saw its first Confederate prisoners in 1862, the year was not a good one for Federal forces. The war was going badly in Virginia; then, in August, two Southern armies, one commanded by General Edmund Kirby Smith, the other by General Braxton Bragg, moved into Kentucky.

Filling the labor quota

Construction of an elaborate system of fortifications to protect Louisville from Confederate attack was begun in the summer of 1864, long after the need had passed. Only two batteries had been equipped with artillery by the time the war ended in early April 1865. Meanwhile, the Army had used drastic measures to "recruit" labor.

"The frail sisters of easy virtue of Lafayette and Marshall streets, and their ardent admirers were surprised, dumbfounded, and completely muddled...by the sudden bursting from the clear sky of one of these military thunderbolts. Each house was, in turn, surrounded by the guards, and a thorough search of the apartments instituted....the patrols did not experience much difficulty in carrying their orders into execution, by arresting those gentlemen of free and easy habits known as the up-town 'rounders'.... They were...escorted by the 'gleaming bayonets' to the fortifications and set to work....

"The 'rounders' were not the only ones surprised....The darkeys were fully honored. They were picked up by the hundreds on the streets, and all the lazy, idle characters set to work."

Louisville Daily Journal, *August 18, 1864*

Kirby Smith's gray-clad troops bypassed Union defenses at Cumberland Gap, while Bragg's force skirted Buell's eastern flank. The Confederate objective: Louisville. General P.G.T. Beauregard offered advice for the fate of the city: "I would construct a work there for the command of the Ohio and the canal, and I would destroy the latter as soon as possible and so completely that future travelers would hardly know where it was." Meanwhile, the outflanked Buell started in pursuit of Bragg, presenting the unusual spectacle of a Union army pursuing a Confederate army northward.

While Louisville braced for attack, hoping Buell could intercept Bragg before the Confederates reached the city, Kirby Smith's Confederate force entered Lexington on September 2. The General Assembly, in session at Frankfort, immediately decamped to Louisville and resumed business in the Jefferson County Courthouse. James Guthrie at last saw his 'Folly' used for the purpose for which it was intended, though it was only for a month. Around the outskirts of the city, a swarm of troops, volunteers, and impressed labor worked feverishly to complete a ring of breastworks and entrenchments while fresh troops poured in. One newly arrived regiment found entrenchments being dug "by candlelight." Meanwhile, General William "Bull" Nelson, in charge of the defense of Louisville, had pontoon bridges built to Jeffersonville and New Albany to speed the arrival of reinforcements and supplies, and for evacuation of the city, too, if necessary.

By September 21 raiding parties of Kirby Smith's cavalry were in Shepherdsville and the Louisville wharf was a frantic scene of men, women, and children fleeing "in a panic of fright." The rest of the city "was in a howling uproar, filled with troops, teams, dust and the clatterbang of arms." Prentice predicted the attack would begin September 21 and urged *Journal* readers to "bear yourselves that not a spot or blur shall mar the glory of the issue." On Prentice's predicted day of attack (General Nelson predicted the

Above: Refugees of war, women and children who fled a Louisville threatened by Confederate attack in September 1862, camped on the Ohio River bank in Jeffersonville. With the arrival of the Union forces of General Don Carlos Buell, the refugees returned home. Frank Leslie's Illustrated Newspaper, October 18, 1862

25th), a reporter for the *Cincinnati Commercial* went south from Louisville to see for himself what was happening. With military approval, he drove out Salt River Turnpike (Dixie Highway) by horse and buggy.

Somewhere between West Point and Elizabethtown he saw a huge cloud of dust raised by an approaching army. It was, to his relief, Buell's advance guard leading ten miles of troops plus an almost equally long wagon train bringing up the rear. "They had been on the road ten days without a change of clothing," the Cincinnati reporter wrote, "traveling through a continuous volume of dust all the time. Some of them had no shoes, others no hats…they had not slept in tents for several weeks, and had been on half rations for more than a month." One of those marching men later recalled that the dust was often six to eight inches deep and that when they arrived in Louisville they were the "hungriest, raggedest, tiredest, dirtiest, lousiest and sleepiest set of men the hardships of this or any other war produced." But despite his ill-clad and hungry troops, Buell had outflanked the Confederates. Louisville had its defense force.

Bragg, instead of marching directly to Louisville, had dispersed his troops and wasted precious time installing a Confederate government in Frankfort. Buell still expected Bragg and Kirby Smith to consolidate forces, however, and attack Louisville. Certainly the signs pointed that way. Indeed, a 500-man Confederate cavalry troop swooped into the vicinity of Eighteenth and Oak on September 26. The Southerners, who could see the city's church spires across the open fields, captured some fifty Federal soldiers. The following night a heavy skirmish occurred just beyond Middletown on the Shelbyville Pike and on September 30, after Confederate and Union pickets clashed at Gilman's Point (St. Matthews), Federal troops drove a detachment of Confederates back through Middletown to Floyd's Fork. But there was no Battle of Louisville. Instead, as the Confederates fell back under Union

A black soldier's story

When word spread among Kentucky slaves that enlisting in the Union Army would bring freedom, many slipped away to recruiting offices. Elijah P. Marrs, who lived near Simpsonville in Shelby County, led a group of fellow slaves to enlist in Louisville in September 1864. The group traveled along Shelbyville Road.

"After many an adieu I formed my men in line, twenty seven in number.... Our arms consisted of twenty-six war clubs and one old rusty pistol....There was one place on our route we dreaded, and that was Middletown, through which the colored people seldom passed with safety. When we got within two miles of the place I ordered my men to circle to the left until we got past the town....

"Day was now breaking, and in one half hour we were within the lines of the Union Army, and by eight o'clock we were at the recruiting office in the city of Louisville....By twelve o'clock the owner of every man of us was in the city hunting his slaves, but we had all enlisted...."

Life and History of the Rev. Elijah P. Marrs, 1885

Right: Collection of West T. Hill, Jr.

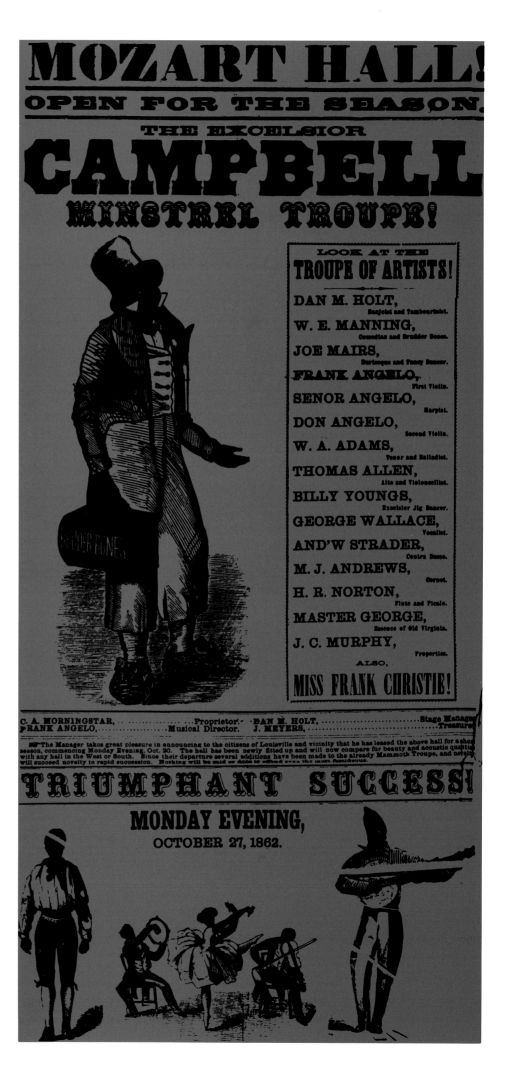

pressure, there was a Battle of Perryville on October 8, the bloodiest ever in Kentucky. The Confederate invasion of 1862 was over and Louisville was never again in serious danger.

The city was so busy preparing to defend itself that a momentous event in Washington was scarcely noticed until later. On September 22, 1862, Lincoln, under intense political pressure, issued the Emancipation Proclamation, which declared that on January 1, 1863, all slaves in any states still in rebellion would be free. Though the proclamation did not affect Kentucky, it was disturbing to many Kentucky Unionists who were also pro-slavery. "Well, the deed is done. The President is as bad as his promise," Prentice lamented in the *Journal.* Some Kentucky officers were so disturbed that they resigned their commissions, and many from northern states were also unhappy with the proclamation.

Slavery did not officially end in Kentucky until the Thirteenth Amendment to the Constitution took effect in December 1865. Yet, the institution was effectively destroyed before then by a development that tore to shreds the already-tenuous relationship between Kentucky and the Lincoln administration: the recruitment of slaves into the Union army. Since, in 1863, all slaves in Union-held territory were freed by the Emancipation Proclamation (and tended to flock to Union army camps), an obvious step was to tap this vast source of manpower. Before the year was out the recruiting of blacks had been extended to all loyal states (including Kentucky, Missouri, Maryland and Delaware), but the reaction in Kentucky was so severe that it was

Incident on Broadway

This recollection of Confederate prisoners in Louisville was written by Mrs. Francis Piper, who was 12-year-old Anna Stone when she witnessed the circa 1864 incident on Broadway, where she lived.

"...Confederate prisoners became a common sight [toward the end of the war] and a sad sight they were...thin, emaciated, half-starved....One morning going to school I ran into a large detachment of them who seemed to be worse off than they usually were....The Union soldiers had allowed them to stop and rest at the corner of Third and Broadway, where they were scattered about... most of them lying flat, and some looking ready to die....

"They were in front of one of the fine residences...where the people were probably Southern sympathizers, and as I passed two colored men in white jackets were serving hot coffee and cornbread to the men from silver trays. Some were too weary to care whether they lived or died, but others snatched the food like animals."
Louisville Times, January 17, 1957

delayed until March 1864. Despite the delay, the political storm stirred up helped put the state solidly in the Democratic party ranks for nearly a century.

By July an average of 100 slaves a day were enlisting, some by permission of their owners, some by running away. Others were drafted. Still others, unhappy with the whole affair, fled to Canada and elsewhere. In all, 24,438 Kentucky blacks eventually served in the Union army; nearly all were slaves and received their freedom. Their owners, if loyal Unionists, were entitled to $300 compensation. The Taylor Barracks, at Third and Oak in Louisville, was the induction point for Kentucky's black recruits, while the Hospital d'Afrique in New Albany cared for wounded black soldiers. Many who succumbed were buried in Louisville's Eastern Cemetery. The military service of blacks, which released the youngest and ablest from slavery, was a severe blow to the peculiar institution in Kentucky. The Thirteenth Amendment was but the *coup de grâce* to an institution in its death throes.

The recruitment of blacks also was made necessary by declining white enlistments (which resulted in a military draft), reflecting the profound war weariness seeping through the North. The demands of "Peace Democrats" for an armistice or an end to the war and the restoration of the Union "as it was" (with slavery) found fertile soil in Louisville. Unionist Thomas H. Crawford was defeated by Democrat William Kaye for mayor in the 1863 municipal elections. Two years later, Peace Democrat Philip Tomppert defeated Unionist K.P. Thixton.

Perhaps the most remarkable thing about Tomppert's election, however, was not his peace proclivities, but the fact that only a decade after the horror of Bloody Monday, Louisville had chosen a German for its highest office. The choice reveals not only war weariness, but the rapid decline of nativism, the growing strength of immigrants in the city, and their strong allegiance to the Democratic party. By 1860 German- and Irish-born citizens

Above: Actress Pauline Cushman, born in New Orleans, was recruited as a Union spy in March 1863 during an appearance at Woods' Theatre (old Mozart Hall) in Louisville. Pretending southern sympathies, she managed to gain the confidence of the Sons of Liberty and similar underground groups opposed to the war. Apparently all she found were ineffective malcontents caught up in the romance of secret midnight meetings.
Library of Congress

comprised 34% of Louisville's population. Tomppert's election demonstrated the integration of the immigrant into the mainstream of society, one of the significant changes the war brought in Louisville.

Still, disenchantment with the war and disillusionment over the issues of emancipation and enlistment of slaves were important factors in Louisville's mood in 1863 and 1864. It was a mood that alarmed unconditional Unionists and military authorities, too quick to read treason into statements of disagreement with the Lincoln administration. Louisville's important position as a supply base made the Army especially sensitive to what it was prone to consider as disloyalty. Commanders of the Kentucky Military District (General Jeremiah T. Boyle and his 1864 successor, General Stephen G. Burbridge), headquartered in Louisville, often exercised their authority capriciously, interfering with the election process, ordering arrests on slight evidence, withholding trade permits from businessmen whom they suspected of southern sympathies, and dispensing favors to friends. Such actions only widened the breach between loyal Kentuckians and the Republican administration.

To deal with military suspicions, a number of businessmen organized the Louisville Board of Trade in early 1862 as a pro-Union organization. A year later the Board (predecessor of the present Louisville Area Chamber of Commerce) affirmed its loyalty in strong terms. At the behest of Bidermann du Pont (whose family in Delaware was producing most of the powder used by Federal forces), each member was required to take an oath declaring that he would "in no way knowingly aid the Rebellion...." Federal successes in 1863 doubtless gave wavering Louisville Unionists new hope: the capture of New Orleans, then Vicksburg, which opened the Mississippi to navigation; and the halting at Gettysburg of the Confederate thrust into the North. The Confederacy was slowly being hacked to pieces and Louisville was a key point in the supply of troops and equipment for the dismemberment. When Union forces in Chattanooga found themselves in a precarious position in late September 1863, the North (which had learned to use railroads as a weapon) transferred 23,000 troops from the Army of the Potomac to the Tennessee city by way of Indianapolis and Louisville in only two weeks.

With the Mississippi River in Union hands, Louisville's river traffic began to resume southward in 1863. The fall of Vicksburg was followed shortly by a report in the Democrat that "a boat is loading for New Orleans." And Louisville received a welcome Christmas gift when a vessel arrived December 24 from the Crescent City with molasses and sugar. Sweets from the South did little, however, to soothe the disagreements in Louisville over the future conduct of the war. Local political lines had hardened by 1864 between Unconditional Unionists (unreservedly for crushing the South at any cost and for freeing the slaves) and the Union Democrats (unalterably opposed to emancipation and Negro enlistments). General Burbridge, native Kentuckian and hard-line Unionist, continued to ruffle political tempers by failing to distinguish between real enemies—freebooting guerrillas often posing as Confederates—and those Kentuckians merely weary of war. His arrest of twenty-one prominent Louisvillians, plus the chief justice of the State Court of Appeals, on treason charges, rocked the state. The guerrillas, meanwhile, made life so miserable across the state that a day without trouble was news. The Democrat reported in early 1865 that "The Nashville train arrived on time last night. All was quiet along the road."

Captured guerrillas were brought to Louisville for imprisonment and trial, and many were hanged, usually on Broadway at Fifteenth or Eighteenth streets. A few met a different fate: execution by firing squad, with four guerrillas shot for each murder of a Union man. But the selection of victims was often haphazard, with genuine Confederate prisoners sometimes mixed with guerrillas. One execution took place at Jeffersontown in the fall of 1864 after a Union soldier was found murdered on Bardstown Pike, the deed

Too incredible to be true
When the first news of Lincoln's assassination arrived by telegraph in the early hours of Saturday morning, Louisville newspapers were being put on press and were able to insert only a brief report.

"The story is too revolting, too incredible to be true....We incline to believe this must prove to be a cruel hoax."
Louisville Daily Democrat,
April 15, 1865

ascribed to the notorious band led by Sue Mundy (Jerome Clarke). One of the executed prisoners was seventy years of age, unlikely material for a hard-riding group of pillagers.

Against this background, Louisville approached the presidential election of 1864, which pitted Lincoln against General George B. McClellan, former commander of the Army of the Potomac, and a 'War Democrat'. McClellan polled 4,986 votes in the city for an easy victory. But Lincoln's 1,942 votes were an impressive advance on the ninety-one he received in 1860. Louisville, though its citizens were divided politically, still served as the great supply depot for the Union armies. "The Atlanta campaign," Sherman declared, "would simply have been impossible without the use of the railroads from Louisville...to Atlanta." By the close of the year, when Louisville attorney and strong Unionist James Speed accepted Lincoln's call to join the Cabinet as attorney general, the approaching Union victory was obvious.

On April 9, 1865, at Appomattox Court House, Virginia, the Army of Northern Virginia, commanded by General Robert E. Lee, surrendered to the Army of the Potomac, commanded by General Ulysses S. Grant. Richmond had fallen six days earlier. Lee's surrender was anti-climactic for Louisville. It had already celebrated when Richmond fell: not the fall of Richmond as much as the fact that the end of the ordeal was in sight.

The city did celebrate Lee's April 9 surrender, but not in the spontaneous carnival atmosphere that swept the North. Instead, an official day for observance was proclaimed by Mayor Kaye on April 14, five days after Lee's army laid down its arms. The day chosen was both Good Friday and the fourth anniversary of the fall of Fort Sumter. A huge parade brought out thousands of spectators during the day, while that night bonfires blazed in the streets, fireworks lighted the sky, and band music filled the air. Illuminated transparencies shone forth: one on a military headquarters building cheerfully noted "No More Draft," while a householder at Fifth and Broadway erected a huge transparency reading "The Republic Triumphs Over Traitors at Home and Abroad."

Then, the *Democrat* reported, "About 10 o'clock it commenced sprinkling and the excitement subsided, and the city became quiet." While Louisville celebrated, a grim drama was unfolding in the nation's capital. The next day Louisville flags flew at half-staff in mourning for Abraham Lincoln, assassinated at Ford's Theatre by John Wilkes Booth.

Chapter Nine

A Mania for Manufacturing

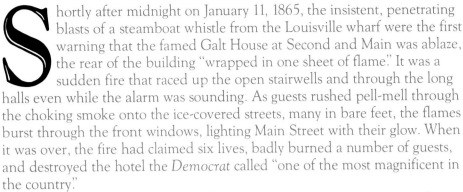

Shortly after midnight on January 11, 1865, the insistent, penetrating blasts of a steamboat whistle from the Louisville wharf were the first warning that the famed Galt House at Second and Main was ablaze, the rear of the building "wrapped in one sheet of flame." It was a sudden fire that raced up the open stairwells and through the long halls even while the alarm was sounding. As guests rushed pell-mell through the choking smoke onto the ice-covered streets, many in bare feet, the flames burst through the front windows, lighting Main Street with their glow. When it was over, the fire had claimed six lives, badly burned a number of guests, and destroyed the hotel the *Democrat* called "one of the most magnificent in the country."

The destruction of the Galt House symbolized the changes that the post-war era was to bring to Louisville as the impact of sweeping nationwide economic and social developments crumbled many of the city's hallowed institutions and ways of life, while new ones rose to take their places. The most significant change came in the sphere of transportation. Though Louisville and the river system were fixed in place, railroads were not. The city by the Falls soon discovered that it was to lose more than the Galt House: it was also to lose its near monopoly of transportation from the upper Ohio Valley to the South, especially when it failed in its attempt to prevent Cincinnati from building its own railroad across Kentucky and into Tennessee. Without the stranglehold on trade to bolster their position, Louisville's merchant princes increasingly had to share economic power and social prestige with the rising industrialists, just as earlier they had to make room for the professional men.

The mercantile community fought a rear-guard action against such developments as a "Short Line" railroad to Cincinnati and a bridge across the river at Louisville, fearing these changes would make the city a mere way station, but the merchants lost the battle. To industrialists, on the other hand, the proliferation of transportation routes was not a handicap, but an advantage: a way to ship manufactured goods in all directions and to receive raw materials. The Main Street commercial palaces and the elegant river packets were soon to be obscured by clanging factories and rumbling freight trains. As industry grew, so did the army of blue-collar workers, and the labor union at last came to be a force that could make an impact in Louisville.

Though this changing economic emphasis was basic, it was but one of the changes that made post-war Louisville different from the ante-bellum city. The end of slavery brought thousands of blacks flocking from the Kentucky countryside to Louisville for whatever opportunities an urban environment might provide in their new freedom. Foreign immigrants, no longer seen as a threat but rather an asset, found opportunities widening. The most remarkable influx, perhaps, was a host of former Confederate officers taking advantage of the opportunities in a thriving commercial center undamaged by the war, not under military government, and in which they found a ready welcome not likely to be tendered in a hostile North. Too lean in the pocket at first to invest in merchandising and manufacturing, these cavaliers of the "Lost Cause" went mostly into law, insurance, real estate, sales, and similar professions. Walter N. Haldeman, too, returned after his war-time peregrinations behind Confederate lines. His *Courier* resumed publication in Louisville on December 4, 1865, and quickly outdistanced both the *Journal* and the *Democrat*.

The impact of the ex-Confederates was out of all proportion to their numbers. Louisville's gradual loss of enthusiasm for the war continued to be a potent factor in the city during the post-war years. In addition, the bitterest memories were kept alive by the continued military presence. Louisville was headquarters for the Military Division of the South until the withdrawal of troops from the southern states in the late 1870s. The romanticizing of the South as victim began early, with former Confederates accorded the halo of

Who made how much?

The first federal income tax was imposed during the Civil War to help pay the enormous costs of that conflict. The tax (10% on all income over $5,000) was continued for a few years after the war, with taxable incomes listed in the newspapers for all the world to read! Here are a few Louisville incomes from 1867. The figures include income from all sources.

John Bull, patent medicine manufacturer, $155,625.
Benjamin F. Avery, plow manufacturer, $67,321.
James Guthrie, L&N president, $55,644.
M. Kean, Louisville Hotel proprietor, $33,616.
William B. Belknap, hardware wholesaler, $31,127.
Bidermann du Pont, paper manufacturer, $28,985.
Joshua F. Speed, real estate, $25,899.
James C. Ford, retired merchant, $24,336.
Adolph Brandeis, grain dealer, $22,360.
Henry W. Whitestone, architect, $14,625.
Archibald P. Cochran, foundry, $12,377.
Albert Fink, L&N general manager, $12,254.
Benjamin H. Bristow, attorney, $10,625.
David Frantz, tannery, $8,120.
Vene P. Armstrong, meat packer, $6,380.
Delos T. Bligh, police detective, $5,150.
William H. Galt, physician, $5,106.
Gideon Shryock, architect, $5,030.
Louisville Daily Journal, May 11, 1868

Post-war Louisville

A roving journalist found his ideal of Louisville as a place of quiet luxury rudely shattered.

"Thus Louisville…turns out to be in fact only a rival of Pittsburg. Masses of smoke, belched from numberless chimneys, keep the place in a perpetual fog, and, descending in showers of soot, produce a monotone of color not cheering to the sight….Louisville is very thriving, and its population rapidly increasing. Property is held high and house rents are more exorbitant than in New York."
Harper's Weekly, May 5, 1866

defenders of a just cause. And, certainly, a pro-southern stance had definite advantages in mending the broken threads of southern trade. Louisville, seeking a regional identity, found the South most suited to its needs. When Robert E. Lee died in 1870 more than 250 of the city's business establishments closed in respect and prominent citizens led a large procession honoring the revered military commander.

Yet, as always, Louisville remained a city of diverse currents and was impossible to characterize easily. Despite its overtures to what has been called neo-Confederatism, it was also home to a small, but persistent, core of Republican strength. When the *Louisville Commercial* entered the journalistic arena at the end of 1869 as the organ of moderate Republicanism, it took note in its first issue of local feelings. "Prophecies of evil to our undertaking say that the rebel sentiment of Louisville is so bitter, that she is so dependent on Southern trade, and has done so well by being so pronounced in her Southern sympathies, that she won't patronize a Republican newspaper." The *Commercial*, in fact, though never achieving financial strength, survived until the end of 1902 as an ably-edited opposition voice. Nor did the city's pro-southern stance prevent war-time opponents from joining forces in commercial ventures. Former Confederate General Edmund Kirby Smith of Florida, for instance, was associated with former Union General Jeremiah T. Boyle of Danville, Kentucky, in the Southern Telegraph Company.

In addition to the contingent of ex-Confederates, a number of arden Unionists also made Louisville their new home: attorneys Benjamin Helm Bristow and John Marshall Harlan, political careerist Eli H. Murray, and the banker brothers George W. and William F. Norton. Most of these newcomers, however, departed for more promising careers elsewhere, the Nortons being a notable exception. Bristow, one of the founders of the *Commercial*, became secretary of the treasury, as had James Guthrie before him. Harlan was named to the Supreme Court, and Murray was appointed territorial governor of Utah. Most of the ex-Confederates stayed. They included such familiar Louisville names as John B. Castleman, Bennett H. Young, Basil Duke, and J.J.B. Hilliard. The arrival of former Unionists and Confederates also had non-political dimensions, reflecting the continuing attraction of urban Louisville and its opportunities. During the first half of the Nineteenth Century most of the city's leaders were from elsewhere—men such as Guthrie, the Shreves, Prentice, Haldeman, probably most of the leading wholesale merchants and manufacturers.

These social and economic developments occurred in a city that was changing physically as well, and expanding rapidly into the thinly settled areas surrounding the old core. A large slice of territory on the west and south was annexed in 1868, increasing the size of the city from 8.2 to 12.3 square miles. The most significant factor in the spread of the city, aside from increasing population pressure, was the network of street railways that began to thread the thoroughfares and reach out beyond the edge of the old "walking city."

The new street railways and their gaudily painted mule-drawn cars were tied to the rise of manufacturing, as another new publication, the weekly *Louisville Industrial and Commercial Gazette*, recognized. The new journal, itself symptomatic of the feverish interest in industry that was apparent from the very close of the war, noted that street railways did more than spell the end to "omnibuses with their rattling, rumbling motion and always 'room for one more.'" They also provided the necessary transportation for workers who would have to live on the outskirts of the city where new housing could be built inexpensively. "If we would have *cheap* labor, we must have *cheap* living," the *Gazette* admonished. "No city can…push forward her mechanical and manufacturing interests without providing ample and cheap accommodations for the operatives upon whom we are

Right: Rails smoothed rough paving for the streetcar and permitted mules to haul heavier loads faster than was possible with the old omnibuses. Though this Twenty-seventh and Chestnut scene dates from the 1890s, it is typical of the whole mule-car era. Louisville's blacks won an early civil rights victory in 1871 when protests against segregated car seating (black men were not even allowed on the Market Street line's cars) ended in Federal District Court, which ruled against the railway companies.
Kentucky Railway Museum

Below right: 'Shotgun' cottages, one room wide and three to four rooms deep, proliferated in Louisville in the years after the Civil War, coinciding with expanding industrialism and the rise of the blue-collar worker. These now vanished houses at 3605 and 3607 West Market Street are of the 'humpback' variety, with a second bedroom over the kitchen. There is no evidence that humpbacks carried a legally mandated lower tax rate, as local legend holds. Recent research suggests the shotgun house form originated in Africa and was brought from the West Indies to New Orleans by blacks, then spread upriver. The Dahomey word "to-gun," a house or place of assembly, is also suspiciously close to "shotgun."
Preservation Alliance

mainly dependent for our resources." With the development of street railways came the rise of the "shotgun" cottage, a housing type that Louisville had borrowed from New Orleans sometime before the war. As street railways and blue-collar workers proliferated in post-war Louisville, so did the simple shotgun cottages. Each on its own narrow lot, the shotguns gave working families a privacy unknown in older industrial cities while providing the inexpensive housing a developing industrial economy demanded.

The first of the new street railways actually began running before the end of the war. General Boyle, whose activities as military commander of Kentucky raised such a furor that he was relieved of his duties in January 1864, immediately turned his attention to business interests. The first was the Louisville City Railway, which he headed and which secured a City franchise to operate streetcar lines on Main and other streets. The work of building the Main Street route between Twelfth and Wenzel began in April 1864. Soon "all was bustle and commotion, the air resounded with the sound of shovels and pickaxes wielded by sturdy arms," but cars did not start running until November.

At Twelfth Street the City Railway connected with the old Louisville & Portland, whose Main Street omnibuses were some of those displaced. Boyle and his associates, however, wanted not only the Main Street traffic, but the through travel to Portland as well—a traffic still heavy because of the steamboat transfer. They secured a franchise for their own parallel route on Portland Avenue (the old company's line was on Bank Street), making a

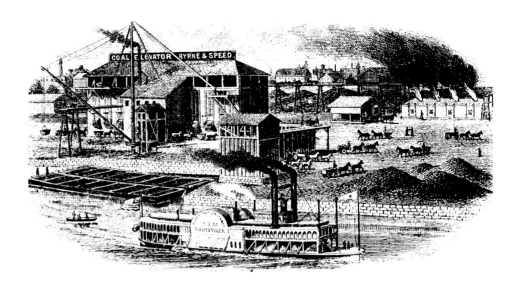

RAY, VARBLE & CO.,

Proprietors CHAMPION SAW-MILL,

stretch of nearly five miles from Wenzel to the Portland wharf. Other lines followed quickly: on Preston to the Lion Garden at St. Catherine, on Second to Breckinridge, and on Broadway to Cave Hill Cemetery.

Despite the complaints of some citizens that the car rails were a hazard to carriages and wagons, Louisville residents obviously welcomed the new transportation, which met a real need. Two other companies soon were organized and the *Democrat* enthusiastically called street railways "the great improvement of our city." The Citizens Passenger Railway operated cars on Market between Twentieth and Woodland Garden (at the east end of Market Street), while the Central Passenger Railroad built lines on Fourth to Oak, and on Walnut between Eighteenth and Baxter. These lines, all running by the summer of 1866, reached out into developing territory. Extensions continued apace, including the remarkable Beargrass line, whose cars rolled alongside Bardstown Turnpike to Doup's Point, then along the Taylorsville Turnpike to the vicinity of present-day Bowman Field, ending at "Mrs. Smyser's hotel," apparently a retreat from the city's summer heat. By the end of the 1870s there were fifty miles of street railway carrying about eight million passengers a year.

Like the steam railroads, the street railways became consumers of locally manufactured products, as well as manufacturers in their own right, building many of their cars. This small boost to the city's industrial output must have pleased the drum-beaters of manufacturing. No sooner had the war ended than Louisville developed what can only be described as a mania for manufacturing, though the results did not quite match the propaganda barrage. Scarcely a month after Lee's surrender, the *Journal* predicted that "in the transition state through which we are now passing, a general reorganization of industry must take place [nationally]." Louisville must extend its vision, the *Journal* advised "beyond the circumscribed lines of past commerce, manufacturing, and agricultural operations, and project a future which will be commensurate with our natural resources and advantages." Other local publications, regardless of political leanings, joined in the general chorus. "No city can be a great metropolis without the mechanic," the *Democrat* asserted. The *Commercial* observed that "Louisville aspires, and hopes to be one of these days a manufacturing town, capable of competing with such centers as Cincinnati and St. Louis."

These were remarkable pronouncements in a city that had grown to importance on mercantile trade. Wholesaling and distribution continued, in fact, for many years as the chief determiner of Louisville's attitudes and largely shaped its pro-southern stance, as well as its reactions to external threats that endangered its near-monopoly of transportation to the South.

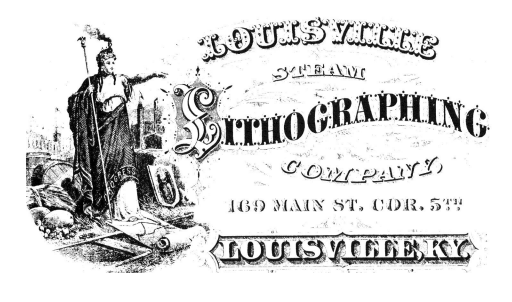

Right: Louisville, emerging unscathed from a Civil War that was profitable for its merchants, manufacturers, and the L&N Railroad, entered the new era confidently. Here "Progress" points the way to the city's future. With a smoking locomotive for a crown, the new City Hall and Industrial Exposition in the background, tobacco and other Kentucky agricultural produce surrounding her, and a railroad map spread at her feet, she symbolizes Louisville's post-war mood: a sense of exalted community. Smith's Louisville Commercial and Statistical Directory, 1875-76

An old drover
When cattle and hogs were driven to the Louisville market on foot, the stock drover was a familiar sight in the city. A newspaper reporter in 1894 interviewed John T. Ewing, an old drover.

"In those days when there were no railroads...the big droves of cattle had to be driven into Louisville over bad roads and great distances....The men in charge of the herds nearly always walked the entire distance, and Mr. Ewing often brought a herd of as many as 150 cattle from Washington County to Louisville without any help, but that of a dog.... Many a time he slept night after night in the open air with the herd around him and only the dog to watch.

"There was danger in this, too, for the country he traveled through was very wild in many places...and there were men in it ready to cut his throat when he returned with the price of the drove in his pocket...for live stock brought high prices..."
Louisville Commercial, September 16, 1894

But the city was adding the string of manufacturing to its bow as a way of maintaining its position in the changed post-war world.

Yet a gulf divided the merchants and manufacturers on the transportation issue. Though both groups had a common interest in improved access to markets, there was a point where they parted company. As long as new transportation lines did not threaten Louisville's position as a trans-shipment center, the mercantile community would favor them. Thus a railroad westward to St. Louis could receive united support. The argument that "Southern Illinois and Southern Indiana are holding out their hands to us and urging us to establish direct commercial relations by means of this road" produced results. The City of Louisville provided financial aid for the "Air Line," which promised trade not only toward St. Louis, but "the great Northwest" beyond. (Today the route is part of the Southern Railway.) Likewise a railroad west to Paducah (now part of the Illinois Central Gulf Railroad) was supported by both merchants and industrialists. This line promised to open western Kentucky coal fields for the benefit of Louisville manufacturers and, at the same time, counter the projected rail lines from Owensboro and Evansville south to Nashville. Improvement of navigation of the Kentucky River also was non-controversial and, in 1870, $150,000 in City funds was provided to aid this endeavor.

But two important post-war transportation projects revealed the mercantile fear that Louisville would become a way station. One was the Ohio River bridge to Indiana, the other the Short Line railroad to Cincinnati. Both bore, not surprisingly, the stamp of James Guthrie, and both were part of his posthumous legacy to the city in which he had been such a significant figure. Though his 1830s bridge project had been doomed by economic factors, the bulldog-like Guthrie never abandoned the idea. In 1850, the same year the L&N Railroad was founded, he secured a charter for the Louisville Bridge Company and renewed it during the Civil War.

Finally, with the end of that conflict, he set the project into motion. With assistance from the L&N, construction began in 1867 on what was at that time the longest iron bridge in the United States. The structure left the Louisville shore at Fourteenth Street, crossed the remains of Corn Island (cut away by years of quarrying), and reached the Hoosier side at Clarksville. Designed by the redoubtable Albert Fink, the bridge utilized his own unusual truss design.

But the bridge's admirable qualities were of little interest to the Louisville mercantile community. The Louisville Board of Trade, alarmed at the prospect of goods rumbling right through Louisville, declared that the bridge would make Louisville "simply a way station." Board President Vene P. (Venerando Politza) Armstrong argued that the bridge would benefit only

the L&N Railroad. The controversy was a replay of the canal debate of a half-century earlier and ended the same way. The bridge was dedicated February 18, 1870, amid great fanfare and with Kentucky Governor John W. Stevenson and Kentucky and Indiana legislators as guests on a special train. Some of those invited declined to ride, however, being "timid about crossing the bridge."

The other controversial project, the railroad to Cincinnati, opened nearly a year before the bridge. Though the Short Line to Cincinnati was built by the little Louisville & Frankfort Railroad, diverging from its main line at LaGrange, the construction actually was forced by Guthrie and the L&N. Louisville merchants saw it as giving Cincinnati equal advantages with Louisville in the competition for southern markets. Guthrie, however, saw it as a necessary adjunct to the L&N and had threatened that the L&N would build it if the Louisville & Frankfort did not. The railroad, now come of age, found that by serving Louisville interests only, it damaged its own traffic and profit potential.

But in the gloom over the Short Line, mercantile interests found a gleam of hope. The new route did not have a track connection with the L&N. The Louisville & Frankfort, now renamed the Louisville, Cincinnati & Lexington (LC&L), still rattled down Jefferson Street to halt at Brook. The mercantile strategy was clear: prevent a connection and force continued trans-shipment of Cincinnati freight. Any other course, said the *Journal*, was "suicidal." The impasse over joining the tracks was finally settled by a curious — and expensive — compromise. The Board of Trade recommended in the summer of 1868 that the connection be permitted by the City, *provided* that the track gauge of the LC&L be changed so that cars could not be run through. This was tantamount to no connection at all, though it permitted car-to-car freight transfer without an expensive wagon haul. When the LC&L balked at the cost involved, the City agreed to pay three-fifths while the L&N, happy to have the dispute resolved in some fashion, agreed to pay the rest.

The result was a bill for more than $178,000 to pay for a barrier to Cincinnati freight. Choosing a route for the connection also proved to be controversial, but finally a track swinging around the eastern edge of the city and past the House of Refuge was agreed upon. It connected with the L&N at what was to become South Louisville, where Churchill Downs was opened in 1875. After all this bickering and expense, cars were run through Louisville, though to do so required a change of trucks under each car — a costly nuisance.

The merchants' emphasis on southern trade dictated their provincial view of transportation facilities. Yet, they probably had little choice. National trade patterns were shifting east-west as railroads leaped beyond the Mississippi River and pushed westward from Chicago and St. Louis. The opening of the transcontinental railroad to California in 1869 accelerated this flow, which bypassed the Ohio and lower Mississippi valleys. It meant Louisville could develop little in the way of mercantile trade anywhere but in its traditional southern sphere. Cincinnati felt the same pressure (though less acutely) and the two cities were soon locked in a bitter struggle for the southern markets.

Louisville industrialists, on the other hand, sought a wider market. By 1872 the Louisville Cement Company was shipping a daily average of five carloads to Chicago, and Louisville woolens found a ready market in St. Louis. A decade later Dennis Long & Company was sending its cast-iron pipe eastward to Pennsylvania and westward to the Pacific coast. Bremaker-Moore Paper Company found outlets for its products "all over the United States." The mercantile community retained its old prestige, but manufacturing provided the new muscle for the city's economy, utilizing large forces of workers ranging from laborers to highly skilled mechanics. Though Louisville lagged behind such formidable rivals as Cincinnati, Chicago, and St. Louis, it

began making giant strides in manufacturing. Industrial employment climbed from 7,396 in 1860 to 10,813 in 1870, and 17,448 in 1880, an increase of 61% in the latter decade alone. The value of industrial output increased steadily from $14.2 million in 1860 to $18.5 million in 1870 and $35.4 million in 1880. The near doubling during the 1870s far outpaced national growth, which recorded a mere 26% increase of industrial output. Louisville's showing was all the more remarkable since the Panic of 1873 left the national economy in a shambles during most of this period.

No wonder that a writer in 1875, praising the future promise of the "little forest of smokestacks that ornaments our city," wagged a finger at Main Street: "By mere trading among ourselves the community can never be enriched…the secret of substantial and steady growth is found in workshops teeming with mechanics and laborers who are earning money from those living in distant parts of the country." Nor is it any wonder that the number of manufacturing establishments spiraled upward from 436 in 1860 to 1,108 in 1880, while capital invested jumped from $5 million to $21.6 million.

The manufacture of steam engines and boilers was an easy leader in Louisville's immediate post-war economy, employing 2,236 workers in 1870. Other metal-working industries, including agricultural implements, and machinery and castings of various kinds, added another 2,228 workers, for a total of 4,574. Furniture making and woodworking were important in the economy, too. Other industries that were distinctly small scale in comparison included tobacco processing, distilling, leather working, and manufacture of clothing. But Louisville's real industrial strength lay in diversity; from one bagging plant (140 employees) to three woolen mills (123 employees).

A highly visible proof of the rising importance of manufacturing, the Louisville Industrial Exposition, opened September 3, 1872, in a specially constructed building on the northeast corner of Fourth Street and Chestnut. Sponsored by a private group, the Industrial Exposition provided a showcase for the city's manufacturers to display their wares to potential buyers—and an admiring public—in a big annual event. "The manufactures of the city have grown and increased in the years since the war to an extent of which few people are aware," the *Commercial* declared.

That newspaper, which originally suggested the project, was ecstatic at the opening. When the gas lights were turned on the newspaper called them the "energizing light of a new era," found the sound of the working machinery "an audible asservation of limitless power," and said "the ancient quiet of Fourth Street was disturbed and banished." Directors of the Exposition Company were largely the city's industrialists: furniture maker J.H. Wramplemeier; foundrymen Charles S. Snead and George Ainslie; paper maker and railroad promoter Bidermann du Pont; and railroad financier H. Victor Newcomb, son of the L&N's new president, Horatio D. Newcomb.

The Exposition was headed by John T. Moore, whose career exemplifies the shift from mercantile pursuits to manufacturing. Born in Jeffersontown, Moore had come to Louisville as a young man to clerk in wholesale houses, succumbed to "California fever" in 1849 and went to seek his fortune in the gold fields. He made money in California—as a retail merchant—and returned to Louisville in 1855 to enter the wholesale grocery trade. When the Civil War disrupted that business, he joined a new partnership, Bremaker, Moore & Company, that hedged its bets by launching out in two directions at once—wholesaling groceries throughout Kentucky and Indiana, and manufacturing book paper for Louisville's busy book-publishing trade. By the mid-1870s the firm had a second mill at Wawasee, Indiana, for newsprint.

In addition to working machinery and displays of local products, the annual expositions offered other attractions. Band concerts livened the scene at night, providing "music, full, gushing, delicious." An art gallery displayed works by popular artists of this opening period of High Victorian culture, including works by Louisville's resident artists, most still remembered at least locally. The names included German-born Carl Brenner and Nicola Marschall. Stuffed animals educated 1874 visitors to the wonders of natural history, while a huge aquarium installed the same year was something of a disaster. When the glass broke, pouring ankle-deep water into the hall, startled visitors scurried for a dry spot. The Egyptian mummy was undamaged, however. Not all the commercial displays were of Louisville's mechanical marvels. One year an exhibit displayed the steps in processing Kentucky tobacco from field to consumer products. That made the *Commercial* wonder why the meat packers did not show off their products, especially the hams for which Louisville was noted.

Many of the visitors to the annual expositions came from Jeffersonville and New Albany. Travel between the two Indiana communities and Louisville was much quicker after the Ohio River bridge opened and the JM&I (Jeffersonville, Madison & Indianapolis) Railroad started running the "Dinky" trains on frequent schedules to Louisville's new Bridge Depot at Fourteenth and Main. Both of Louisville's north shore neighbors were experiencing the same industrial growth as Louisville. The three Falls Cities (the phrase became current in the 1870s) were recognizing, sometimes reluctantly, the economic unity that had been obscured by pre-war rivalries. Even before the bridge was opened in 1870, Louisville newspapers began carrying daily columns of news from the two Indiana cities.

The expansive, prosperous post-war years were reflected not only in Louisville's changing economy, but also in a building boom that changed the look of the community, creating a cityscape in the business center that was largely intact until recent years. Only five months after Lee's surrender, the *Democrat* observed that "Every carpenter, brick layer, and plasterer in the city is kept busy." The newspapers, too, were kept busy chronicling the demise of venerable landmarks, all replaced by larger, more impressive structures. With their stone fronts and elaborate detail, the new buildings were concrete examples of what has been called the Gilded Age; symbols, too, of the quickening pace of trade and industry and of Louisville's spurt of growth.

A new Galt House, larger, handsomer, and infinitely more luxurious than its predecessor, rose at First and Main in 1869. Behind its Renaissance Revival facade visitors to Louisville—including such distinguished personages

as Grand Duke Alexis of Russia and Emperor Dom Pedro II of Brazil—found accommodations far more sumptuous than those that had pleased Charles Dickens thirty years earlier. A block westward, at Second and Main, the burned-out site of the old Galt House became in 1877 the location of another Renaissance Revival building, the new headquarters of the L&N Railroad. Though the L&N has long since departed, the building's stately facade still proclaims the Nineteenth Century victory of rail over river.

One more block westward, at Third and Main, foundryman James S. Lithgow completed his own visible symbol of success in 1873, the five-story Lithgow Building. It not only housed offices of its owner's manufacturing enterprise, but offered rental space to other successful businessmen. It was one of Louisville's first distinguished office structures, and, along with the L&N Building, a precursor of the need for large amounts of office space made necessary by the administration of large enterprises. All three buildings were designed by Henry Whitestone, though the Lithgow Building's High Victorian style was radically different from the architect's usual work.

Almost all center-city streets were changed—some transformed—by new construction. The buildings of Louisville's construction boom of the 1830s had displayed elegance as a contrast to frontier simplicity. The buildings of the post-war boom displayed amassed wealth. A sampling of noteworthy structures includes Weisiger Hall, a Mansard-roofed French confection of about 1868 on Fourth between Liberty and Walnut; the 1874 Tyler Block on Jefferson between Third and Fourth; the 1876 Courier-Journal Building at Fourth and Liberty; the 1878 Carter Dry Goods Company building (now the Museum of Natural History) on Main between Seventh and Eighth; the 1870 expansion of the old Marine Hospital on Chestnut into City Hospital; and numerous churches. Fourth Street, beginning to make inroads on Market as the fashionable shopping thoroughfare, was also the axis around which many of the new churches were built: First Christian at Fourth and Walnut, Warren Memorial Presbyterian at Fourth and Broadway, the Church of the Messiah (now First Unitarian) at Fourth and York, and Calvary Episcopal on Fourth south of York.

Not all the new religious edifices were along Fourth. When the

Opposite far left: A leading Louisville wholesaler, Carter Dry Goods Company built this forthright commercial structure at 731 West Main in 1878, and expanded it later. It now houses the Museum of Natural History and Science.
Louisville, Kentucky: The Falls City, 1904

Opposite left: The original Louisville Marine Hospital of the 1820s became the central section of the enlarged Louisville City Hospital, opened in February 1870. One of the institution's functions, caring for ill and injured rivermen, had been taken over by the United States Marine Hospital, opened in Portland about 1851. City Hospital was replaced by a new structure on the same Chestnut and Preston site in 1914.
Filson Club

Opposite bottom: Louisville's first public library was launched in the early 1870s through a grandiose scheme that only the Gilded Age could have conceived. With over $400,000 raised through a State-sanctioned lottery, the Public Library of Kentucky took over Weisiger Hall on Fourth Street and then re-named it Library Hall. The overly ambitious plans called for an art gallery, natural history museum, lectures, and various 'academies,' as well as a library. Initiated by Reuben T. Durrett and his law partner, former Governor Thomas E. Bramlette, the proposed intellectual center never lived up to its promises, prompting questions about disposition of the lottery funds. Bankrupt by 1878, the library was taken over by the Polytechnic Society of Kentucky, which became the nucleus of the Louisville Free Public Library.
German & Brothers Louisville City Directory, 1869-70

Louisville Theatre at Fourth and Liberty burned in 1866, the fire also destroyed the adjacent Jewish Synagogue of Adath Israel on Fourth. It was replaced by the large brick Temple Adath Israel completed in 1868 on the southeast corner of Sixth and Broadway. This new structure, costing over $144,000, was a visible symbol of the success of Louisville's relatively recent and relatively small Jewish community. Most of the community's Jewish population was German, part of the tide of immigration of the 1850s, though a handful of English-born Jews had arrived earlier. But even in 1869, after the new Temple was completed, membership in the congregation was less than 200, practically all in mercantile trade or the professions.

Since Louisville liked to go to the theatre almost as much as it liked to go to church, the destruction of the Louisville Theatre, the city's finest, called for its quick rebuilding as the Louisville Opera House. When it, in turn, gave way to the Courier-Journal Building, actor Bernard "Barney" Macauley filled the breach in 1873 with a new building on Walnut east of Fourth Street which became the best-known and longest-remembered of all in the city's long list of theatres that followed the pioneer venture of 1808.

But the most dramatic example of the sense of exalted community that was infusing post-war Louisville was the new City Hall, a massive limestone building on the northwest corner of Sixth and Jefferson dedicated July 4, 1873. Its tall clock tower, restless wall surfaces, and sheer size proclaimed it an important public building in a city moving confidently into a restless new era. Architect John Andrewartha called its design "Renaissance of the present age," boldly putting a decorative band of tobacco plants around the second story; carved heads of cattle, hogs, horses, and corn and wheat projected over the windows. These forthright representations of the agricultural portion of Louisville's mercantile trade represented a tough post-war realism, a striking contrast to the studied repose of the neighboring Court House on its green lawn.

The sweeping changes in the heart of the city were matched by new rings of growth around the core, areas where carpenters, bricklayers, and plasterers also were busy transforming open spaces into extensions of the urban fabric. Population growth was part of the reason—by 1870 the city had passed the 100,000 mark—but the expansion of the built-up area outstripped the growth in numbers. The change was in scale: instead of the dense, shoulder-to-shoulder construction in the old city, the new areas were marked by individual houses set apart from their neighbors. A luxury only the wealthy had been able to afford earlier, it was made possible by the new street railways. As the city grew, distinct neighborhoods emerged, areas distinguished by an internal unity: income level, occupation, ethnic background, or perhaps only geographic location.

Like many post-war trends this was an acceleration of earlier development. Portland, annexed permanently in 1852, retained its sense of separate identity. Ill-fated Shippingport, doomed by the canal around the Falls and by rival Portland, was a depressed area (perhaps Louisville's first) long before the Civil War. The community was kept alive mainly by dusty cement mills that utilized the limestone rock at the Falls of the Ohio as their raw material.

While Shippingport languished, Portland found itself tied closer to Louisville as the first wave of post-war expansion moved primarily westward. "A few years ago Portland was considered a good way from Louisville," the *Commercial* observed on the first day of 1874. Pointing out that the old Western Cemetery at Fifteenth Street had recently been on the edge of the city, the newspaper added that "now it is entirely surrounded with residences, and, looking westward, as far as the eye can reach rows of houses are to be seen." The annexation of 1868 had added the area roughly between Eighteenth and Twenty-eighth streets to the city and by early 1870 plans were in the making to extend Broadway from Eighteenth westward to the river, widening the old Dunkirk Road to transform it into a street.

The most ambitious of the westward developments was Parkland, south of Broadway and west of the City limits. Still "covered in many places with shrubbery and noble forest trees," this rural tract of 342 acres was subdivided into 1,072 lots and launched with a widely advertised auction conducted by Morris, Southwick & Company on July 10, 1871. Hopes of speculative profits raised interest to such a fever pitch that some businesses, including the tobacco warehouses, closed to permit proprietors and employees alike to go to the sale. Attendance was estimated at more than 2,000 and the *Commercial* noted that "The Parkland sale and Robinson's circus absorbed the people yesterday." To make Parkland accessible, the development company contracted with the Central Passenger Railway to extend its Walnut Street track to Twenty-eighth and south along that street. This new line prompted the owners of Elliott's Woods, along Walnut west of Eighteenth, to subdivide their property and hold an auction on July 13. Louisville's West End began to take shape.

In the east, the Point, between Beargrass Creek and the river, had fallen to a lower estate from its early history as a secluded retreat of fine homes. Its social decline was undoubtedly related to the upriver expansion of shipyards and sawmills, with an accompanying spread of modest housing southward to the creek. This development earned the Point the jocular title of "the Creek Nation" even before the Civil War.

The Point's former role of sylvan retreat for the wealthy moved upstream beyond the new Water Works to the rocky bluffs overlooking the Ohio. Typical of this development was the purchase of the Berry Hill estate in 1868 by wealthy meat packer James C. McFerran. The house at Berry Hill had been built shortly after 1800 by Virginian planter James Smalley Bate. McFerran established a trotting-horse farm and named it Glenview, a name that has outlived the horse farm. Another who made the move to this area was James Callahan, who purchased the old Rock Hill estate. Callahan demonstrated the essentially urban character of these new country dwellers by also maintaining his city house at Eighth and Broadway. As the area along River Road to Harrods Creek, and even beyond, was turned into a quiltwork of country estates of affluent urban families, the need developed for convenient transportation to the city. To solve the problem a number of estate-owners in 1870 organized the Louisville, Harrods Creek & Westport Railroad with Callahan as president. By 1877 the little line (it was not only short, but of narrow gauge) stretched its rails some twelve miles from the riverfront at

Right: Woodland Garden, at the east end of Market Street next to Bourbon Stock Yards, was a favorite retreat of Louisville's German citizens, many of whom lived in nearby Butchertown. During the 1850s it represented foreign decadence to 'Americans,' who professed shock that such gardens dispensed beer, cigars, and music on Sunday afternoons. It is shown here in an illustration from the New York Daily Graphic *of April 29, 1875, during the time when Henry Watterson found it a delightful spot.*

"In those days popular music here was known only among the Germans and those few Americans who loved music enough to seek it in the open air. The two public gardens, Woodland...and the Lion [at Preston and Kentucky] were...as typical gardens as any to be found in the Fatherland....simple, peaceful, virtuous Sunday afternoons under the trees, with good music and good beer and good sausage and good cheese and a pretzel...."
Louisville Anzeiger, March 1, 1898

Left: Temple Adath Israel, completed in 1868 on the southeast corner of Sixth and Broadway, was one of the city's most imposing religious edifices. After completion of a new Temple at 834 South Third in 1906, the old structure became Methodist Temple in 1907 and was demolished in 1942.
Potter Collection,
U of L Photographic Archives

Opposite far left: The restless wall surfaces and prominent corner tower of Louisville's 1873 City Hall are a reminder of the restless and expansive new era that followed the Civil War.
Harper's Weekly, April 5, 1890

Opposite bottom: The Episcopal Christ Church Cathedral is Louisville's oldest church building. Completed in 1824 as Christ Church, it was enlarged at various times and acquired its present facade in 1870-72 to a design by architect William H. Redin. Christ Church was made a cathedral in 1894.
Potter Collection,
U of L Photographic Archives

First Street to end in an open field in a locality known as Sand Hill—today's Prospect. Other affluent Louisvillians escaped the city by moving eastward to the Crescent Hill area or beyond to Anchorage or Pewee Valley, all along the line of the railroad to Lexington, which became Louisville's equivalent of Philadelphia's Main Line.

In the eastern end of the city itself, the focus of activity shifted from the Point to Butchertown. This area had grown up before the war along the Louisville entrance of the turnpike from Frankfort and Lexington (now Story Avenue), the route along which cattle and hogs were driven from the Bluegrass region to the Louisville market. Butchering and the related leather tanning and soapmaking trades, banned at an early date from the core of the city, found this area suited to their needs. Even before the war the neighborhood's economic base had been diversified by the Louisville Glass Works. The post-war years brought a wave of development: Louisville's largest woolen mill, a chair factory, breweries, and a distillery.

As an area in which many of the industrial operations were small scale with the proprietors living nearby, and where "master" butchers often worked right where they lived, Butchertown developed a definite work-a-day, *petit bourgeois* character. This was leavened by the presence of a working class employed in the larger industries. Shotgun cottages of blue-collar workers rose next to the more substantial dwellings of small proprietors. They all lived on equitable terms with the "death squeals of assassinated porkers" and the grease from the packing houses that flowed into Beargrass Creek in such quantities that some residents collected it, apparently to make soap or lard.

As the entry point for the majority of slaughter animals reaching Louisville (though they came over every turnpike entering the city), Butchertown as early as the 1830s became the principal stock market of Louisville, with activities centered around the Bourbon House, an inn at Cabel and Story that provided holding pens for stock. But when the railroad from Lexington took most Bluegrass stock off the turnpike and put it on rails, the Bourbon House was in the wrong location. In 1869 the new Bourbon Stock Yards opened at the east end of Market Street and next to the railroad, its site ever since.

A neighborhood not too distant from Butchertown in miles, but vastly different in lifestyle was taking form slowly in the 1870s. The area southeast of the city core was called the Highlands as early as 1831 because it was so much higher than the city below it. But not until after the Civil War did real-

estate developers begin to turn this attractive, undulating landscape into home sites. On the map the new development had the prosaic name of Henning & Speed's Highland Addition, not a name to win the race for permanence. It was still the Highlands, a name that was to become real-estate magic in time. The developers were Joshua F. Speed, Abraham Lincoln's old friend from Springfield, Illinois, days, and James W. Henning. They purchased 134 acres in 1869 from George Douglass and laid out their subdivision the following year with New Broadway (Cherokee Road) as its backbone thoroughfare.

When Henning's daughter married ex-Confederate J.J.B. Hilliard, their gift from the bride's father was a new and spacious two-story brick home at the corner of Cherokee and Grinstead Drive where it still stands among the trees. Henning and Speed, whose subdivision extended only to Patterson Avenue, had planted the seed for the Highlands, but it was relatively slow in germinating. The area's genteel flavor was tinged with a rural aspect for many years. Not until the 1890s, after the creation of Cherokee Park, did intensive development begin.

Some neighborhoods reflected their ethnic majority by their names. Germantown had won its distinctive name by 1865. Growing up along Shelby Street well south of Broadway, Germantown has maintained its strong self-identity through all the years of urbanization that have followed the days when it was devoted mostly to small dairy farms. Numbers of Irish, meanwhile, seeking regular wages, found employment on the L&N Railroad; first in its construction, later in its operation. They created their own enclave of Limerick near the L&N yards and shops. Seventh Street, the old Oakland Turnpike, became the main thoroughfare through this neighborhood, which grew up south of Kentucky Street. At the south end of Limerick the former Oakland Race Course, which breathed its last as a track in the middle 1850s and served as a war-time military camp, turned into a rude amalgam of the poorest of blacks and the cast-offs of white society. Though it was the setting for Alice Hegan Rice's popular 1901 novel, Mrs. *Wiggs of the Cabbage Patch,* the post-war press described events there as occurring "on the Oakland."

Germantown and Limerick clearly reflected their ethnic composition through their names, but the California area demonstrates the sometimes murky origin of neighborhood designations. Louisville oral tradition holds that the locale received its name during the California gold rush, perhaps because it was so far west — in the neighborhood of Fifteenth Street. But development must have been sparse. During the war years it was described as a "secluded, marshy, and muddy part of Louisville." By 1870 California was a working-class neighborhood filled with shotgun cottages and a mixed black and white population with no apparent ethnic concentration. In time, however, California became all black as Louisville developed segregated housing patterns. As early as 1870 the California Colored School was in operation at Fifteenth and Prentice.

Louisville's black population, slowly declining before the war, took a sudden jump upward in the immediate post-war years, more than doubling by 1870 over 1860, as former slaves flocked to the urban center. The influx began even before Kentucky slaves were freed by the Thirteenth Amendment in December 1865. The war was hardly over when the *Democrat* in early May reported an "accumulation of negroes in this city." Disturbed local officials complained to General John M. Palmer, who had succeeded General Stephen G. Burbridge as commander of the Kentucky Military District in February. Palmer later recalled that the mayor and other officials "expressed apprehensions of pestilence from [the blacks'] crowded state and asked me to cooperate with them in ridding the city of this evil." His solution was not what was expected. Instead of sending the slaves back to their masters, he issued

passes to them; more than 5,000 crossed the river to Indiana and points north. Their places were soon taken, however, by new waves of former slaves.

Absorbing the flood of newcomers into the city's population was not simple, but it was eased for the former slaves by the Freedmen's Bureau, a federal agency set up to help in the transition to free status. A Freedmen's and Refugees' Home was set up at Eighteenth and Broadway to provide temporary housing and the Army's Crittenden General Hospital at Fourteenth and Broadway was turned over to the Bureau to provide medical care for the ill. By September 1865 a branch of the Freedmen's Savings and Trust Company, sponsored by the Bureau, was opened on Walnut near Third as part of an effort to encourage thrift. The Louisville branch was one of the most successful in the nation. By the end of 1869 its 1,074 depositors had total deposits of over $647,000.

It was both a difficult and hopeful time for the former slaves facing a white world that largely believed they were incapable of ordering their own lives. Some freedmen with special skills or unusual drive made a successful adjustment, as the impressive bank figures show. (Some of the depositors, however, had likely been free before the war.) By 1874 there was a black newspaper, the *Weekly Planet;* some blacks owned restaurants catering to a white clientele; others operated blacksmith and wagon-building shops. The hauling business was especially popular and by 1874 there were 150 draymen with their own wagons and teams, while another eight to ten were "boss" draymen owning several wagons.

Even so, in black Louisville barbering continued as a high-prestige occupation (because of contact with influential whites), and janitors and messengers were felt to occupy "positions of trust" and hence prestige. Yet most blacks eked out a marginal existence as day laborers, while others found bar rooms and gambling dens more congenial. The *Commercial* observed that "The white community looks lightly on the good conduct of the many, while it judges harshly the bad conduct of the few."

As Louisville's Negro population soared, reaching nearly 15,000 by 1870, compared to 6,820 in 1860, black neighborhoods began to develop. Though many of the former Louisville slaves doubtless continued to live in quarters provided by their former owners, and were thus dispersed through the city, the newcomers had no such option. While blacks at first appear to have lived in the same blocks as lower-income whites in the older parts of the city, subtle segregation patterns had appeared by 1870. Blacks were usually concentrated in one or two tenements in any block, whites in the rest. The pattern gradually evolved into heavy concentrations of blacks on both the east and west sides of the old central core, particularly south of Broadway. Thus California on the west and Smoketown on the east were essentially all-black neighborhoods before the end of the century.

Though California was once racially mixed, Smoketown appears to have developed from its beginning as a predominantly black community centered along Jackson Street. As early as 1866 freedmen began leasing lots from the white owners of this yet-undeveloped area and building frame shotgun cottages. "The houses were not the finest, but furnished a neat appearance....The war was over and everyone was *free and equal*," Louisville black historian Henry Clay Weeden recalled. But he recorded the sad sequel. When land leases expired during a depressed economic period, many home-owners were unable to renew and lost their total investment. "Our people were in a worse condition than before," Weeden wrote.

But there were victories for Louisville blacks, including the establishment of schools supported by local taxes to replace those set up by the Freedmen's Bureau and the American Missionary Society. The location of the new schools indicates the neighborhoods of growing black concentration. The first was the Central Colored School (later Mary D. Hill School) at Sixth and Kentucky, dedicated in October 1873. The choir of the First African Baptist Church opened the proceedings with the carefully chosen hymn, "I Have Waited Patiently." Horace Morris, cashier of the Freedmen's Bank and chairman of the Colored Board of Visitors, which was to oversee the new schools, noted that "This is the first building erected out of public funds for the education of colored children in Kentucky." He slyly added that "I guess we will have to get used to such things and act like 'white folks.'" The Eastern Colored School was completed in Smoketown in 1874 and the Western Colored School in California in 1875.

Amidst all this urban ferment still another neighborhood was taking shape, one that would outpace all the others in prestige until it had to share honors with the Highlands after the turn of the century. Today it is called Old Louisville, a recent name. In its early days it was simply the "Southern extension," or "the southern part of the city." It was annexed to Louisville in 1868 in the same sweeping move that had extended the line westward. The corporate boundary was moved southward from Kentucky Street to the vicinity of Magnolia, with a long finger extending along Third and Fourth streets to take in the House of Refuge grounds. Only a year later architect Gideon Shryock (still practicing his profession, though long eclipsed by later arrivals) called the annexed area "a growing and beautiful suburban locality."

By 1874 the *Commercial* could assert that "South of Broadway we have a new city." It had not been long since "there were but few houses on the other side of Broadway; when ducks and snipe were hunted...and game could be found anywhere beyond where College Street has been made." Now, the *Commercial* proudly observed, "the ponds have been filled up, the woods cut down, and in their stead magnificent residences are found." A handful of those magnificent residences remain from that first surge into Old Louisville. One is the home erected about 1867 on the northwest corner of Third and Ormsby by Vene P. Armstrong, at the same time he was opposing the construction of the Ohio River bridge. He built the stone-fronted residence after his marriage to the famed and much-married Louisville belle, Sallie Ward. He was her third husband and was to be succeeded by a fourth.

Another early residence still standing is that erected by the Rev. Stuart Robinson, pastor of the prestigious Second Presbyterian Church, in 1871 on the northeast corner of Fourth and Magnolia. Robinson, whose Confederate sympathies forced him to seek refuge in Canada during part of the war, built the house only a year or so after he had erected another imposing home across Fourth Street in what is today Central Park. He sold the earlier house to Alfred Victor du Pont in the fall of 1871, though the new bachelor owner never lived there. Rather, his brother Bidermann, who had a large family, moved in. Ever alert to financial opportunities, the du Ponts immediately turned the tract into money-making Central Park, even though Bidermann and his family lived in the midst of it. Balloon ascensions, fireworks displays,

Below: Any Louisville restaurant with claims to prestige employed black waiters after the war, as before. This is a waiter at the Galt House.
The Great South, 1875

Above: The parlor of the 1868 Brennan House at 631 South Fifth Street reveals the opulence of Louisville's post-Civil War years. Built by Francis S.J. Ronald, partner in a Main Street tobacco warehouse, the house was sold in 1885 to Thomas Brennan, agricultural implement manufacturer. It is now owned by The Filson Club as a house museum. Filson Club

Right: Built about 1869-70 by the Rev. Stuart Robinson, prominent Presbyterian minister, this house was sold in 1871 to the du Ponts, who turned the surrounding seventeen acres into Central Park. Though it was the scene of band concerts, fireworks displays, balloon ascensions, and other attractions, Bidermann du Pont and his large family lived in the house in the midst of the busy events. The Parks Board purchased Central Park in 1904 and the old home was demolished soon after. Collection of J. Van Dyke Norman, Jr.

Cave Hill and the Daisy Field

In the 1930s jeweler William Kendrick set down his recollections of the Louisville of his youth. This is his remembrance of the East Broadway hill rising from Beargrass Creek to the Cave Hill Cemetery entrance as it was about 1870.

"In the days referred to this hill...was a thickly wooded tract known as 'Preston's Woods.' Through the center a deep cut was made, with clay-bank sides [for] a real country dirt road, just wide enough for the passing of two vehicles....This road led to the entrance of Cave Hill and on to the country beyond. A plain board fence, with large swinging gates, marked the separation of the cemetery from the road....What is now our beautiful Highland district...was...mostly farm lands, cornfields and truck garden patches....

"We pass around the side of Cave Hill on what is now Cherokee Road, up to and out the present Grinstead Drive [Daisy Lane]...the road leading to a large open field...the 'Daisy Field,' reaching down nearly to where the present golf links are in [Cherokee Park]...where the ground was white with these flowers."
Reminiscences of Old Louisville, 1937

band concerts, and other attractions lured the public there. The du Ponts also gained control of the Central Passenger Railroad, with its streetcar line out Fourth, and extended the track from Oak to Magnolia to make their venture more accessible.

There were also other diversions to lure the public to Old Louisville. One was base ball, spelled as two words in those early days. The game, played at first by gentlemen amateurs, had made its appearance in Louisville by 1860. The ballground in the early post-war years was near Fourth and Ormsby where the clubs, apparently already organized into a local league, attracted small crowds and occasional newspaper notice. The sport's rising popularity can be gauged by increasing newspaper attention and, by 1875, a new ball park in the vicinity of present St. James Court. The game had also become professional and soon became more than slightly tainted.

In 1877 the Louisville Grays, a member team of the new National League, turned an unpromising season start into league leadership by August. The *Commercial* predicted Louisville would win the league pennant, remarking, however, that "the game of ball is very uncertain." The remark proved more than accurate as the Grays posted a seven-game losing streak against Boston and Hartford. It was discovered that four team members had been paid by gamblers to lose the games deliberately. All four were banned from professional baseball for life. The Gilded Age, Louisville was learning, had a seamy side.

While baseball began to win the affection of Louisvillians, the old love affair with Thoroughbred racing was in temporary eclipse. The Woodlawn Association track, which succeeded the moribund Oakland Race Course in 1858, itself closed about 1870 because of "financial troubles, coupled with a lack of concord." The financial troubles were related to the upheavals of the Civil War. With the disruption of the plantation labor system—slavery— many of the gentlemen owners who raced Thoroughbreds more for sport than money could no longer afford such a luxury. "The demand for thoroughbreds was confined to a few rich men in the East," one account reported. In the whole nation only six tracks were operating, including the Kentucky Association track at Lexington. Many Bluegrass breeders, facing declining demand, were considering dropping out of the business, or turning to trotting horses. At this critical juncture Colonel Meriwether Lewis Clark was dispatched in 1872 by the Thoroughbred breeders to England, where racing was in a healthy state. His mission was to study the English (and French) methods as a possible solution to Kentucky's problems.

His report was encouraging: copy the English system of racing horses by class and age so that they are equally matched. Most importantly, however, set the stakes high enough to make it worthwhile to own and race Thoroughbreds. Clark's suggestions were in line with the new post-war economic wave. Racing could no longer survive as the sport of a disappearing landed gentry. It had to become professional and profit making. The next step was to organize a track where the new principles could be put to work.

The result was Churchill Downs, organized in 1874 as the Louisville Jockey Club. The name harked back to the days of exclusive membership, but the rules, the stakes, even the names of the races were straight from England. The Kentucky Derby, which received nationwide publicity, was the showpiece of the new approach: a race for three-year-olds only with a purse that was phenomenal for the times: $1,000 added to the entry and other fees. By contrast, the Phoenix Hotel Stakes in Lexington had only $250 added. The new track was built some distance south of the new City limits amid "green fields and woodlands" on 100-plus acres of land leased from Clark's uncles, John and Henry Churchill.

On opening day, May 17, 1875, a crowd of 10,000 assembled, probably the largest ever for the opening of a new track or the first running of a new

Above: Racing enthusiasts paid 50 cents for tickets like this to travel to Churchill Downs on the Fourth Street mule cars of the Central Passenger Railroad. The cars operated only to Magnolia Street except during spring and fall race meets at the track. The L&N also operated special trains to South Louisville when Churchill Downs was open.
Author's collection

Right: The original grandstand of the Louisville Jockey Club (soon familiarly known as Churchill Downs) was on the east side of the track so that the afternoon sun shone in spectators' eyes. This 1875 structure was replaced in 1895 by the present grandstand on the west side.
Frank Leslie's Popular Monthly, November, 1885

stakes race. The Derby, with fifteen starters, began its long tradition when surprise winner Aristides, piloted by black jockey Oliver Lewis, set a new time record. It was an auspicious first day for the track that set American racing on a different course.

The track with its lively throngs was a bright spot in Louisville's development, but a different side of the post-war years was reflected in the House of Refuge, a mile or so north of Churchill Downs and just inside the far-southern tip of the city. Two buildings completed on the eve of the war—just in time to become Park Barracks—were quickly returned to their intended purpose of reclaiming delinquent and homeless boys. With widespread juvenile delinquency one of war's bitter legacies to the city, the *Democrat* welcomed the new institution. "Louisville," the newspaper lamented in 1865, "contains...probably more children running at large and going the broad road to destruction than any other city in the Union." One gang of young boys, aged nine to fourteen, had earned the name "Forty Thieves" because of their "heavy robberies."

These street-wise youngsters often began hard drinking at an early age and the populace at large found liquor conveniently available in almost any part of the city. The *Commercial* in 1878 estimated that there were at least 5,000 retail liquor outlets, including drug stores, corner groceries, confectioneries, and ice cream parlors. These were in addition to that ubiquitous Nineteenth Century institution, the saloon. Louisville counted nearly 400, ranging from "elegantly furnished rooms with mirrors reaching from floor to ceiling, to the dirty little hole down in O'Neal's alley, dignified with the name 'bar room.'"

The habitués of O'Neal's Alley, near the riverfront, were frequently in trouble with the law, but the kind of patrons likely to be found in the elegant establishments were not always pillars of Victorian rectitude. The peculations of Robert Atwood, a prominent businessman and partner in a successful insurance agency, stunned the city in 1872 and cost trusting business acquaintances some $500,000 in money loaned to him. Atwood, caught up in the acquisitive fevers of the Gilded Age, speculated in cotton, pork, whiskey, and gold, aspiring to "a Fiske or Vanderbilt fortune." He even forged the signature of his father-in-law, well-known physician Dr. Lewis Rogers, to checks. The would-be millionaire was sentenced to twenty years in the State

Top: Though the Louisville & Port-
land Canal became more an obstacle
than an aid to navigation within a few
years of its 1830 opening, efforts to
bypass the old three-step lock with a
larger, two-step design did not begin
until 1862. By 1865 wartime inflation
had sapped the canal company's
resources and work ceased. (The federal
government owned the majority of stock
after 1855, but expended no funds on
the waterway.) Under pressure from
river interests, Congress appropriated
money to complete the lock—opened in
1872—plus additional funds that year to
widen the canal itself.
Filson Club

Bottom: In 1874 the United States
gained outright ownership of the canal,
shown here at its upper end, and elim-
inated all tolls in 1880. Ironically, these
moves came as river traffic entered a
long period of decline.
Frank Leslie's Illustrated Newspaper,
March 22, 1873

Penitentiary, and the *Commercial* hoped the episode would teach bankers
and businessmen that old-fashioned ante-bellum trust was no longer in style.
The sad affair, the newspaper concluded, was "one of the penalties of
growing greatness."

Politics began to take on an unsavory aspect, as well, bubbling up in
1865 with the revelation that a member of the General Council had accepted
a $5,000 bribe for a favorable vote on a street railway franchise on Market
Street. Councilman N.S. Glore, owner of a Jefferson Street saloon, had been
bribed by Isham Henderson, president of the Louisville & Portland Railroad
and a part owner of Prentice's *Journal*. Other councilmen said that they, too,
had been offered money for a favorable vote. Not surprisingly, the *Journal*
backed Henderson, while the *Democrat* strongly opposed his proposal.
Recently-elected Mayor Philip Tomppert also opposed Henderson's bid, not
only because of the bribery issue, but because the line would interfere with
the City's market houses on Market Street and because it did not extend into
Butchertown. Despite the Mayor's reasoned arguments, the City legislators
approved the franchise, then passed it over his veto. Even so, Tomppert
refused to sign it.

Events then took an even stranger turn. The General Council, with
Glore voting, impeached the mayor on a charge of neglect of duty, and found
him guilty by a vote of ten to two. Only after the mayor was thus deposed
did the legislators impeach and then expel Glore. Tomppert was later vindi-
cated by the State Court of Appeals, which ordered him reinstated in 1867.
(James Lithgow served as mayor in the interim.) In retrospect, the incident
can be seen as a disturbing harbinger of the future course of local politics.
The corruption that blemished the later Nineteenth and early Twentieth
centuries was an indirect legacy of the Civil War, which created one-party
politics in Louisville and Jefferson County. The political process became

Above: Mary Anderson launched her stage career at Macauley's Theatre in Louisville in 1875, playing Juliet in "Romeo and Juliet." In her autobiography, A Few Memories, she recalled that exciting night.

"I became feverishly anxious to begin. It was hard to stand still while waiting for the word. At last it came: 'What, lady-bird! God forbid! where's this girl? what, Juliet!' and in a flash I was on the stage, conscious only of a wall of yellow light before me, and a burst of prolonged applause. Curiosity had crowded the house. 'Why, it's little Mamie Anderson. How strange! it's only a few months since I saw her rolling a hoop!' etc., were some of the many remarks which, I was afterwards told, ran through the audience."
Portrait, Filson Club

Above right: Commodities were traded in the Exchange Room at the Board of Trade Building, Third and Main streets. Foundry-owner James S. Lithgow completed the imposing structure in 1873, then lost it almost immediately as a result of the financial panic of that year.
Frank Leslie's Illustrated Newspaper, June 5, 1880

primarily a changing of the palace guard, a struggle among factions within the Democratic party. It was too tempting and too easy for many office holders to regard their positions as a way to receive valuable favors in return for value given.

In this feverish, sometimes shady, speculative milieu, Louisville only reflected the national mood. And nationally there was a price to pay. The Panic of 1873 came like a thunderclap from an almost cloudless sky. Precipitated by the failure of the important—and overextended—private banking house of Jay Cooke & Company in the fall of 1873, the panic was no quick ripple. It was the severest and longest depression the nation had yet known: four years of economic lull, widespread unemployment, falling wages and prices, and bankruptcy of many business houses that had been thriving enterprises. James Lithgow was forced to sell his just-completed new office building at Third and Main at a sacrifice price. In 1879 it would become the Board of Trade Building.

But the hard times fell most severely on the blue-collar workers, and particularly those thrifty freedmen who lost most of their savings when the Freedmen's Savings and Trust Company went under in the general crash. By early 1874 the Workingmen's Association was organizing groups in each of the city's wards to make collections for a relief fund for laborers and mechanics. Newspapers through the next few years made frequent references to charity fund raising, and to efforts of churches to aid the needy. The City also frequently gave aid, usually coal by the bushel, providing a way for councilmen and aldermen to entrench their political power by judicious distribution.

Economic distress undoubtedly increased class consciousness in Louisville's labor force and paved the way for the upsurge of trade unionism that marked the 1880s. But during the depression years it was mainly a matter of grimly holding on. An explosive outburst and an election for State

legislators in 1877, however, revealed the resentment bubbling just beneath
the surface, even among the employed, who found wages dropping faster
than prices.

Like the depression itself, the 1877 riot was part of a national pattern.
Louisville's experience was, in fact, minor compared to violence elsewhere.
Allen Pinkerton, the era's most noted private investigator, called the Louisville disturbances "a tempest in a teapot." The nationwide rash of strikes and
violence, mainly among railroad workers, started in the East after a 10% pay
cut that followed a series of earlier cuts. The L&N had followed the example
of the eastern roads with a wage reduction on July 1. Employees grumbled,
but little else. Then news burst from eastern cities of the bitter reaction of rail
workers there, culminating in a full-scale confrontation on July 21 between
strikers and militia in Pittsburgh that left twenty persons dead. With ex-
quisite bad timing the Short Line announced a pay cut for August 1, then
hastily rescinded it when workers threatened a strike. That encouraged L&N
workers to demand restoration of their pay, and it was quickly granted.

But by July 24 the general excitement spilled over to workers on sewer
construction projects in Louisville. The laborers, mostly black, were persuaded by roving groups of fellow workers to strike for $1.50 a day. As the
group grew larger it set out for Crescent Hill, successfully stopping construction of the water company's new reservoir. That night an aimless group of
some 2,000 gathered in front of the Court House and soon a call went up for
Mayor Charles D. Jacob, perhaps the most popular chief executive in the
city's history. (He served four separate terms in office.) Wealthy, Harvard-
educated, old family, he was described by Pinkerton as a "gentleman of ...
culture, whose life of elegant ease hardly fitted him for a rough grapple with
a turbulent mob." Jacob came over from the new City Hall, but was shouted
down. Then an ominous new cry went up: "Let's go to the Nashville depot."
A crowd of perhaps 600 answered the call.

Down Jefferson and south on Seventh, still a street of many well-to-do
householders, went the mob, shattering gas lamps, then windows. At the
L&N station not a window was spared; even wooden sashes were smashed.
The arrival of police sent the vandals howling back east on Broadway, accompanied by the continual crash of broken glass. The remnant of the mob was
routed by police fire as it approached the Short Line depot at Brook and
Jefferson. Young Louis D. Brandeis, just graduated from Harvard Law School
and destined to become the first Jewish justice of the United States Supreme
Court, returned home from a party to find the front window smashed in the
family home on Walnut near First.

Soon Brandeis was among the 700 citizen-volunteers, many veterans
of the recent war, who patrolled the streets to keep order. His parents were

relieved, he recalled later, when he "turned in his munitions unused and himself unharmed." Though there was no more mob action, the rest of the week brought a rash of strikes among industrial workers. The *Courier-Journal* took a decided employer stance, but the Republican *Commercial*, defending the right to strike while condemning violence, recognized the rising importance of labor. "There has always been a labor question," the newspaper declared, "with which the great parties of the country have co-quetted with discreet non-committalism, but…a non-committal policy will no longer answer."

Louisville's economic establishment soon received another rude shock. On July 30 local workers formed a unit of the national Workingmen's Party of the United States and nominated candidates from their own ranks for Louis-ville's seven State legislative posts to be filled on August 6, scarcely a week later. Amazingly, they elected five out of the seven with an aggregate majority of 4,000 votes. The *Commercial* gleefully billed it as a Democratic defeat, noting that the workers usually voted for that party. Rubbing salt into Dem-ocratic wounds, the newspaper added: "The workingmen did not bribe voters because they had no money."

By 1878 the depression was all but over and a new decade was fast approaching that was to be filled with Nineteenth Century inventiveness. The end of the 1870s gave a forecast of the future. At the Louisville Industrial Exposition of 1877 the exhibits included Alexander Graham Bell's newly invented telephone. In 1879 the telephone entered Louisville's daily life when the American District Telegraph Company opened the city's first exchange on February 1 with about 200 subscribers and wires draped informally over rooftops. The somewhat-overwhelmed *Commercial* could only exclaim "Wonders never cease." Before the year was over the telephone company was reorganized with James Breckinridge Speed, nephew of James and Joshua Speed, as president. Speed already was president of the Louisville Cement Company, which turned out its product by water power from the Falls at the old Tarascon Mill in Shippingport. He was to become an even more impor-tant figure in Louisville business during the next twenty years.

The electric light made a tentative bow in 1878 when primitive, sput-tering, arc lights (a giant spark between two carbon electrodes) were installed in William C. Kelly's axe factory on Portland Avenue and in James Lithgow's Eagle Foundry at Main and Clay. Within five years the city would be the site of a showcase display of Thomas Edison's new incandescent bulb. The world was beginning to look much brighter as Louisville approached the beginning of its second century.

Chapter Ten

A Solid Victorian City

On May 1, 1880, Louisville took a quick backward glance at its first century, then plunged into plans for the future. The city celebrated its centennial with an afternoon band concert at the Zoological Gardens (occupying part of the Churchill Downs acreage), and a lengthy address that night on the community's history by attorney Reuben T. Durrett. A special guest at Durrett's discourse at Library Hall was James Harrison, the oldest person born and living in Louisville. He had come into the world in 1799 at the southwest corner of Sixth and Main in the third brick house erected in the pioneer community. But the honors of the occasion went to Durrett, who had already achieved a reputation as the foremost expert on Louisville's past. He became the moving spirit in the founding of The Filson Club in 1884 as a center of research and repository for Louisville and Kentucky historical materials.

Whatever interest younger Louisvillians took in the city's past, however, was overshadowed by their involvement in its future. The community was growing, but the slower pace—22.8% during the 1870s compared to 48.1% during the 1860s—was a signal that Louisville was reaching maturity. The 1880 population of 123,758 put the city sixteenth in size rank among American urban centers, down from fourteenth in 1870. No longer in the race for supremacy in the Ohio Valley or the Midwest, Louisville had passed the sometimes-frenzied years of rapid growth and was settling down to enjoy its achievements.

In 1880 *Frank Leslie's Illustrated Newspaper* called Louisville "one of the four great cities of the West [along with Chicago, St. Louis, and Cincinnati] which chiefly control the collection and distribution of produce of the soil and the mine, and the counter-movement of merchandise from the East [Coast] and from foreign countries." Despite the magazine's use of the term "West" (a habit the Louisville press itself continued), the city's chief avenue of trade remained southward, a market for which it had to exert extra efforts now that Cincinnati had completed its own railroad into that region. The rising generation of Louisville leaders could take pride in the past, but now it was necessary to maintain the status which the city had achieved. The *Commercial* declared that Louisville had advanced "so far that she must keep on or be trod down and run over."

The effort that made the greatest impression on the community memory was the Southern Exposition launched in 1883 and continued annually for five years. It remains Louisville's single most ambitious promotional effort, one that attracted national attention and brought President Chester A. Arthur to the opening ceremonies. The Exposition, financed entirely by local private capital, supported *Leslie's* 1880 assertion that "there are evidences that a more ambitious and progressive spirit is pervading the community." Growth in the past had come generally without effort. The 1880s marked the period when successful local development would require continuous planning, not the spurts of reaction to specific problems that had marked earlier years.

Construction of the L&N Railroad had been the result of reaction to a specific problem. Now, as the 1880s opened, a series of spectacular events not only gave the city a stronger penetration into the South, but also revealed national dynamics at work that took control of the railroad away from Louisville's Main Street and City Hall. A sudden burst of activity in 1880 transformed the L&N from what was still primarily Louisville's own line into one of the major rail systems of the nation. This expansion, which pushed the L&N southward to New Orleans and westward to St. Louis, was engineered by Victor Newcomb, son of Horatio D. Newcomb, one of Louisville's early New England-born merchants and the man who followed James Guthrie as L&N president in 1868.

In a series of breathtaking tactical and financial moves that riveted the attention of Wall Street, Newcomb, during the early months of 1880, acquired

a string of mostly down-at-the-heels roads extending south to Mobile and New Orleans, with another line flung to Pensacola. He then turned his attention to Georgia, outwitting his rivals to gain control of the route between Chattanooga and Atlanta, with alliances beyond Atlanta that provided another outlet to the sea at Savannah.

But the Louisville press wondered aloud what the quick transformation of the L&N into 'Newcomb's Octopus' meant for the Falls City. Part of the answer was that Louisville's southern connections were now secure. At the same time the sudden expansion spelled the end of Louisville control. New York financial circles, impressed by the strides made by the 'New South,' were especially interested in what was now that region's most important railroad. Infusions of eastern capital diluted Louisville ownership and influence. The City, facing the need for an enormous amount of street paving and sewer construction to keep pace with its expanded territory, sold its L&N stock on a rising market, realizing about $1.6 million on the original $500,000 investment, while the number of Louisville directors on the L&N board dwindled to token representation. Victor Newcomb moved to New York, where he became an important figure in financial circles.

The shift of L&N control was symptomatic of emerging national patterns in which Louisville would have to shape its new directions. The rise of New York as the nation's financial powerhouse, plus the growth of the West, which catapulted Chicago and St. Louis far ahead of the once-larger Ohio Valley cities, dictated that Louisville's future lay in cultivating its strong regional position. Although Louisville had to surrender its rank as one of the nation's largest urban centers, it expanded its strong manufacturing and mercantile economy, replacing lost industries with others. Woodworking, for instance, emerged as a dominant activity, while leather tanning grew in importance.

Louisville had, in fact, reached a comfortable and prosperous plateau that permitted more attention to civic housekeeping and such urban amenities as parks, expanded educational facilities, the arts, and organized charity, developments supported by a growing managerial class. This well-to-do group, finding the 'Southern extension' and the Highlands suited to its aspirations for the good life, filled the vacant spaces with substantial housing in the new architectural fashions. Louisville became a solid Victorian city, but knew that holding its position required high visibility in an increasingly competitive national economy. It was a need that gave rise to the Southern Exposition.

As the *Commercial* had been the chief journalistic voice urging the annual Industrial Expositions that began in 1872, so the *Courier-Journal* was a moving force behind the Southern Exposition. The new effort, far larger and more comprehensive than its predecessors, compared favorably in size with international world fairs. The seed for the Exposition was planted by Boston financier-writer Edward Atkinson, who had noted the South's rapid recovery from the war. In a letter to the *Courier-Journal* in the summer of 1880 (immediately after the L&N's whirlwind march to New Orleans), Atkinson suggested that Louisville sponsor a cotton exposition, and editor Henry Watterson took up the cause. 'Marse Henry', who had been a lukewarm Confederate, then a leader in urging the South to accept the fact that it had lost the battle to maintain a planter aristocracy, found Atkinson's idea in line with his own thinking.

While Louisville pondered, Atlanta moved, opening its Cotton Exposition in 1881. That in itself was another symptom of Louisville's changing competitive milieu, but it resulted in a more important project than first suggested. Instead of merely a cotton exposition, Louisville put together an industrial and mercantile show covering forty-five acres, larger than any previous American exhibition except the Centennial Exposition at Philadelphia

VIEW FROM THE PARK.

in 1876. The site chosen was the vacant land immediately south of the
du Pont's Central Park, where the huge main building was erected between
Fourth and Sixth streets. Central Park became a promenade, picnic ground,
and site of an art gallery "filled with the best American and foreign pictures,"
mostly from eastern collectors, including August Belmont, J.P. Morgan, and
former Louisvillian Victor Newcomb. Music, too, was an important part of
the Exposition, which boasted an immense pipe organ and symphonic concerts directed by well-known conductors, including young Walter Damrosch
of the Metropolitan Opera.

When the Exposition was opened by President Arthur on August 1,
1883, it was a proud moment for the city. "Louisville scarcely recognizes
herself—there is something electric in the atmosphere," the *Courier-Journal*
exulted. In words that probably came from Watterson's pen, the newspaper
added that the Exposition's "influence will be felt for years in cutting new
channels for commerce, in opening new avenues of industries, and in fur-
nishing us new sources of wealth and power."

At the Exposition visitors saw the varied products and attractions of
the Southland and other regions as well; they saw operating machinery and
floral displays; and they wandered through the field of growing cotton
stretching southward beyond the main building, listened to concerts, and
looked at the displays of art. But the most astonishing sight at the Exposition
came each night when the lights were turned on: not glaringly bright arc
lights of the type that were already in some Louisville stores, but the soft
glow of Thomas Edison's newly invented incandescent light.

Packaged in a small glass bulb, the incandescent lamp allowed small
units of light to be scattered evenly about, providing far better illumination
than the extremely bright arc light. The use of the new technology was both
a daring and shrewd move on the part of the Exposition managers, who
signed the $100,000 contract only a month before the opening. It was daring
because it was the largest installation yet made: 4,600 lamps. That was
more than all the incandescent lamps in New York City, where the pioneer
installation had been made less than a year earlier. It was shrewd because the
lighting itself was an attraction.

Crowds gathered in the evening to wait for the lights to come on,
enthralled as the "amber glow began to seep through the dusk, brightening,
brightening until what had been familiar corridors of the big, barn-like building became…aisles of blinding light, touched with gold." The Exposition
was the first large space lighted by incandescence and many electrical
pioneers felt that the Louisville success did more to stimulate the growth of
interior electric lighting than any other Edison plant.

The lighting was not the only example of the coming electric age and
of Edison's inventiveness. An electric railway carried visitors on a narrow
track circling Central Park, even plunging through a contrived tunnel lighted
by incandescent bulbs. The railway, the *Commercial* reported, was "a thing
people cannot understand, and it is an object of curiosity that is only partially
satisfied by taking a ride on it." It was a precursor of the electric trolleys that
were to appear on Louisville streets six years later.

When the Exposition ended its 100-day run on November 10, nearly a
million visitors had passed through the turnstiles, a large number of them
editors and other special guests from southern states as well as those north of
the Ohio River. The *Commercial* urged that the Exposition be continued.
"Louisville has felt in every artery of her commercial and social existence the
advantage of one season's use of that building," the newspaper asserted,
adding that "We will have to do something next year." The directors agreed.
The Exposition continued another four years, attracting crowds and exhibits,
pleasing local residents, and stimulating the economy.

By 1887, final year of the exhibition, the *Courier-Journal*, surveying

Right: Typical of the impressive residences in Old Louisville built for the city's growing managerial class was this one at 1440 St. James Court, occupied by the Bannen Coleman family. Mr. Coleman was secretary of the Central Coal & Iron Company, controlled by the du Pont family, which opened coal mines in western Kentucky near Central City. Mrs. Coleman was the daughter of Bidermann du Pont.
Filson Club

The tobacco and whiskey trade
"There is only one important trade in which Louisville takes precedence over all other cities, either of America or Europe. The quantity of leaf-tobacco sold there annually is greater than in New York, Baltimore, Richmond, Cincinnati, or any other market. The sales after good crop years run from 60,000 to 70,000 hogsheads per annum, and the hogshead is also heavier in weight than in any other important market....

"Of Bourbon whisky, otherwise known as fine Kentucky whisky, Louisville claims to be headquarters. The largest distilling interest in the state is owned by Louisville houses, and the major part of the whole Kentucky product is handled here."
Frank Leslie's Illustrated Newspaper, *June 5, 1880*

the city's progress since the beginning of the decade, pridefully called Louisville "A New Gotham," and catalogued $10 million in building construction slated for the year. The Exposition itself, located in relatively open territory in 1883, was surrounded in 1887 by new housing in the stylish Queen Anne and Richardsonian Romanesque forms. During 1885 alone, 260 residences were built in the Old Louisville neighborhood. (In 1890 the Exposition site was turned into St. James and Belgravia courts.) By 1887 Louisville was served by ninety-four miles of street railways, more than double any other city its size, the Board of Trade boasted, while passengers totaled nearly nineteen million annually. With these evidences of growth all around, Louisville tended to overestimate its population, claiming nearly 196,000 in 1887. The 1890 census found only 161,129 and placed Louisville twentieth in urban size rank. Still, the population showed a 30% increase over 1880, an eminently satisfactory figure and a higher growth rate than in the depressed 1870s. These were good years for the Falls City, supported by a stable manufacturing and commercial base created by local entrepreneurs.

The city was the world's largest tobacco market, edging out New Orleans during the post-war years. The rise was based largely on burley, a crop that replaced stock farming. The 65,281 hogsheads sold in 1880 in Louisville's thirteen warehouses climbed to 144,612 in fifteen warehouses in 1890. The city had also become an important tobacco-products manufacturing center with sixteen plants, and seventy-nine smaller firms making cigars. Distilling, a part of the city's economy since pioneer days, became big business in the final years of the century. In 1887 Bourbon shipments totaled 119,637 barrels. By the middle 1890s Louisville counted nineteen distilleries, plus handling the output of Nelson, Daviess, Anderson, and other counties.

Though the nation saw Louisville principally in terms of tobacco and Bourbon, the city's prosperity rested on a diversified base. Dennis Long & Company had become the nation's largest producer of cast-iron pipe, while

B.F. Avery & Sons was the world's largest producer of plows. Three other agricultural implement manufacturers added their output for an 1886 total of 190,000 plows, more than double the 1880 figure. Jeans cloth, once produced as work clothing for southern slaves, now found a larger market among industrial workers. By 1890 Louisville was the world's largest producer, turning out some eight million yards annually of the coarse but durable material.

Though it was eclipsed by Chicago in the meat-packing business, Louisville actually increased its production to keep pace with an expanded home and regional market. New technology was at work in this old trade as refrigeration permitted packing houses to work in the summer as well as winter. The related leather-tanning industry became a $2.5-million annual business with sixteen tanneries. Woodworking, a factor from the earliest days, grew to large dimensions as Kentucky's own forest resources were exploited to replace dwindling supplies from Michigan and other traditional lumbering areas. C.C. Mengel, Jr. & Brothers, founded in 1887, was shipping lumber abroad by 1891 and eventually owned its own fleet of ocean vessels. Louisville's transportation facilities and the availability of Kentucky hardwoods attracted woodworking industries from other cities.

Cement making, which had sustained Shippingport, spurted after the Civil War. Most production, however, moved across the Ohio River to Clark County, Indiana, where the same limestone strata forming the Falls of the Ohio could easily be reached by shallow quarrying. By the end of the century Clark County's thirty mills made it one of the nation's most important cement producing areas. The two giants of the industry were the Louisville Cement Company, headed by James B. Speed, and the Union Cement & Lime Company, headed by Dexter Belknap.

Enjoying its prosperity, Louisville turned also to a greater enjoyment of life. The arts received a wave of support that would have pleased early chroniclers Dr. Henry McMurtrie and Benjamin Casseday, who found the

Above: The huge rambling Auditorium at Fourth and Hill, seating 3,000, was erected of material salvaged from the nearby Southern Exposition building. Built by William F. Norton, Jr., the Auditorium was joined at the rear by his outdoor Amphitheatre.
Collection of Anna Lee Deerr

Below: Chewing gum was given to the world in 1873 by Louisville druggist John Colgan. His Taffy Tolu was flavored with an aromatic extract called tolu imported from South America. By the 1890s he had a number of local competitors, the most successful of which was the Kis-Me Gum Company.
Kentucky of Today, 1896

city's single-minded attachment to business its chief fault. The Southern Exposition undoubtedly helped generate a wider Louisville audience for serious music by giving its special cachet to works by Beethoven, Wagner, Mendelssohn, Verdi, Rossini, Bellini, and numerous lesser-known composers. Certainly the fact that a cornetist named Liberati was paid $250 a week by the Exposition "for blowing his horn" must have created a new respect for musicians among the thousands who attended the concerts.

Though Nineteenth Century Louisville's musical tastes probably were best served by the sentimental creations of that prolific local songwriter, Will S. Hays ("Mollie Darling," "Wait for the Wagon," and at least 348 others), it was not unacquainted with work of a higher caliber. Following Anton Philip Heinrich's pioneering concerts of 1819-1820, interest in serious music was sustained by amateur groups. The short-lived St. Cecilia Society of 1822 was apparently the first. The community's musical life took an upward turn with the arrival of large groups of German immigrants, who organized many singing groups. The most important was the Liederkranz (Wreath of Song) of 1848. The following year the Mozart Society was organized and presented concerts in Mozart Hall, center of the city's musical life until the Society was disbanded during the Civil War.

The German influence was felt even more strongly after the war when the Louisville Philharmonic Society was organized in 1866 with the ambitious hope of attracting a large audience for a series of symphonic concerts each year. The Society's orchestra (amateur musicians all) was conducted by Louis H. Hast, a native of Bavaria, who became the city's outstanding musical figure until his death in 1890. Despite Hast's best efforts, the Philharmonic was not a financial success. Classical and serious music remained the province of a coterie of devotees, though opera apparently was relatively popular. This

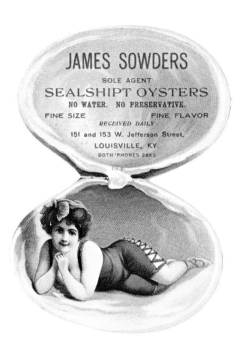

Above: James Sowders used risqué art to attract customers to his oyster house on Jefferson Street. Folded shut the advertising piece simulated an oyster shell.
Filson Club

Right: Transportation was very much the theme of the cover of this 1887 promotional volume published by the Board of Trade. The view of the upper end of the Portland Canal shows downtown Louisville in the background. On Shippingport Island at left limestone is quarried for making cement.
Author's collection

Below right: This fanciful heading adorned Macauley's Theatre programs throughout the 1880s. John T. Macauley had taken over management of the playhouse founded by his brother, Bernard.

Above: Aurelius O. Revenaugh, who came to Louisville in 1886, painted "The Newsboy" (above), selling The Courier-Journal on a winter's day. The work is owned by the Speed Art Museum. Louisville native Patty Thum displayed a tinge of Impressionism in her Old Louisville scene (right). The view is of St. Paul's Episcopal Church (now the Gospel Assembly) at Fourth and Magnolia as seen from Central Park. The work is owned by Dr. William F. Furnish.

may reflect opera's theatrics and also the affinity for opera in the city's large German community as well as among its handful of Italians.

It was in this milieu that the Southern Exposition introduced Louisville audiences to their first sustained exposure to symphonic and light classical music. When the Exposition closed, one Louisvillian decided his city was ready for more such music. He called himself Daniel Quilp (a repulsive character in Dicken's *Old Curiosity Shop*) in his role as impresario, but otherwise was William F. Norton, Jr., who in 1886 inherited the estate of his banker father. Devoted to music and the theatre, he utilized salvaged material from the Exposition building to erect the rambling Auditorium, seating over 3,000, at the southwest corner of Fourth and Hill in 1889. Soon after, he added the Amphitheatre, the site of spectacular fireworks displays ("The Last Days of Pompeii," "The Burning of Moscow," and similar extravaganzas), bicycle races, and other outdoor events. For the next fifteen years the Amphitheatre-Auditorium (it burned in 1904) brought outstanding music, musicians, and singers to Louisville: the New York and Boston symphonies, the Metropolitan Opera, Edward Strauss's orchestra from Vienna, and regular seasons of summer opera, including much Gilbert and Sullivan.

One Louisville girl of the period remembers the thrill of attending the summer opera, joining expectant throngs "walking out Third or Fourth streets in the soft summer evenings, the girls in their ruffled organdy dresses, with yards of satin ribbon edging the ruffles, and floating on top of the world." The Auditorium was the home of drama, as well, and the great names of the late Nineteenth Century stage appeared there: Ellen Terry, Sarah Bernhardt, Lillian Russell, Nat Goodwin, Edwin Booth, and Lawrence Barrett among a long list. None were new to Louisville, where the theatrical scene was more active than ever as audiences grew larger. Macauley's, always the city's leading theatre, presented everything from Shakespeare to Buffalo Bill. In 1883 Macauley's hosted the American premiere of Henrik Ibsen's then-controversial masterpiece, "A Doll's House" (retitled "Thora"), with Helena Modjeska in the title role. It was the theatre where Mary Anderson made her infrequent Louisville appearances after her triumphs in England.

Numerous other theatres shared patronage with Macauley's. The Masonic Temple at Fourth and Jefferson included an auditorium where Oscar Wilde lectured in 1882 and Mark Twain in 1885. Liederkranz Hall, built by the Liederkranz Society, was used frequently by touring opera companies and especially by German-language theatrical troupes, while other

A Louisville ragtime pioneer

Ragtime, the predecessor of jazz, burst upon America as the Nineteenth Century drew to a close. Though it originated among black pianists, the first ragtime hit was improbably written by a white Louisville musician.

"If one took the date of copyright or of publication as the criterion, then precedence in the ragtime field would go to a white musician named Ben R. Harney...whose celebrated hit tune, "You've Been a Good Old Wagon but You've Done Broke Down," was published in Louisville in January, 1895. The following year it was brought out by Witmark in New York....Another famous early ragtime hit of his was Mr. Johnson (Turn Me Loose), published in 1896."
America's Music 1955

The eccentric Daniel Quilp

William F. Norton, Jr., whose mother regarded the theatre as "the vestibule of hell," became Daniel Quilp when attending to affairs of his Auditorium-Amphitheatre at Fourth and Hill. Edmund Rucker, who served as press agent for the theatrical venture, recalled Norton's eccentric double personality.

"Daniel Quilp could promote stage entertainment, could even drink and shoot dice – but William F. Norton's life remained austere....When he drank champagne while attending to the business of the Auditorium, he let no man address him as Norton....'The name is Quilp – Daniel Quilp,' he would bark....

"When some stellar attraction....was not patronized he was furious [and] began referring to Louisville as 'Deadville' or 'the graveyard'....Later he hit upon a happier title, 'Calamity Gulch,' and it remained his designation until his death."
Courier-Journal Magazine, June 13, 1965

Opposite bottom: Irish-born 'Madame' Glover, one of Louisville's leading dressmakers of the late Nineteenth Century, designed this 1880s example of women's high fashion. Her chief rival was 'Madame' Grunder, born in Holland.
Louisville Museum of Natural History and Science

theatres came and went. But the longest-lived was the Buckingham, owned by brothers John and James Whallen, powers in the Democratic party. The 'Buck', which in 1881 became the first Louisville theatre equipped with arc lights, presented a vastly different fare from Macauley's. Vaudeville and burlesque were the Buck's stock in trade. John Whallen, gearing his presentations to the working man, declared in 1882 that "Louisville has gotten to the point where it will support...Macauley's and a theatre like ours, run in a genteel, decent manner at cheap prices." Not all Louisvillians agreed that the Buck was run in a genteel manner, nor that cheap prices were its chief attraction.

In 1894 the Whallens, longing perhaps for acceptance in higher social circles, opened the lavish new Grand Opera House on the north side of Jefferson between Second and Third, a block east of the Buckingham. This was apparently not a new building, but an extensively remodeled structure built to house The Fair, Louisville's first reasonable approximation of a department store. With the Whallens among the principal owners, The Fair opened in 1885. This "vast bazaar" offered "everything one would wish to buy in a day's shopping," except clothing. But it was not a financial success, and in late 1888 the store disposed of its stock in a giant liquidation sale. Neither did the Grand Opera House fulfill the Whallens' hopes, and in 1898 it became the new location of the Buckingham, taking over the repertoire as well as the name of the older venture.

In addition to the increasing audience for music and theatrical fare of all kinds, the visual arts also gained a wider interest in the final years of the Nineteenth Century. Though Audubon found little encouragement as a resident portrait painter during his second brief sojourn in Louisville during the 1820s, the city later supported a small group of artists who made the community their permanent home. Best known were two German-born painters: Carl Brenner, who arrived in 1854, and Nicola Marschall, an 1873 newcomer by way of Alabama. Brenner was famed for his landscapes, especially those picturing the beech trees that grew in profusion around Louisville. Marschall, credited with designing the Confederate flag, was a portraitist, as was Aurelius O. Revenaugh, a Michigan native, who came to the city in 1886.

This exclusively male world of art began to change during the 1880s and 1890s as a handful of Louisville women took an active professional role, seeking training (which most of their male counterparts lacked), and putting their artistic abilities on the market. The first was painter Patty Thum, a student of Thomas Eakins, whose work was shown at the Southern Exposition. Following her came sculptress Enid Yandell, a woman of independent mind who flew in the face of family opposition when she chose a career outside the home, and especially when she went to Paris to study with Auguste Rodin. There may have been grudging acceptance of her course when she was chosen, at age twenty-two, as one of the two women to work on the exterior decoration of the Women's Building at Chicago's Columbian Exhibition of 1893. Miss Yandell later executed the Daniel Boone statue and Hogan's Fountain, both in Cherokee Park, and the figures for Louisville's Confederate Monument.

Louisville's widening interest in the arts included literature and produced several writers who achieved at least modest national reputations. Heading the list was poet Madison J. Cawein, whose stress on nature echoed the theme of Brenner's paintings. Victorian romanticism permeated Cawein's verse, from his first published volume (*Blooms of the Berry*, 1887) to his final works completed shortly before his early death in 1914. Louisville's black community also produced an important literary figure whose first works appeared before the end of the century. Joseph Seamon Cotter, born in Nelson County in 1861, was brought by his family to Louisville as part of the post-Civil War black surge to urban centers. He became an educator, teaching first at the Western Colored School in the California neighborhood, and in 1895 produced his initial volume of poetry, *A Rhyming*, followed in

127

1898 by *Links of Friendship*. Cotter's work made use with equal facility of both Negro dialect and the sometimes overblown allusions and deliberate archaisms that characterized much Nineteenth Century verse. Louisville's literary stirring also produced an impressive but unsuccessful attempt to establish a regional journal of literature and comment in 1892. The *Southern Magazine*, modeled on *Harper's Monthly* and similar national publications, provided an outlet for artists and illustrators from throughout the South, though Louisvillians were disproportionately represented. Although the magazine ceased publication in 1895 (a victim, perhaps, of the economic disturbance of the middle 1890s), the city's literary ferment continued into the early years of the Twentieth Century.

The interest in art and literature paralleled the development of organized ways of dispensing help to those at the bottom layers of society, and reflected in different form the same humanistic concerns. Charity, public and private, was not new, but in the 1880s it began to assume a different dimension and a glimmering recognition that poverty might grow from social conditions and not always from personal fault. Significantly, the movement arose after the Panic of 1873 demonstrated what a prolonged depression could do to the fabric of an industrial city like Louisville.

It was a city where, at the upper levels, "Family counted and money was important...," but where a large segment of the population depended upon industrial wages. Though skilled workers could afford shotgun cottages, an army of unskilled laborers, poor blacks, destitute elderly, and new immigrants (including Lebanese and Italians) could find housing only in older buildings near the central core. Once occupied largely by the earlier German and Irish immigrants, these now shabby structures became crowded tenements, and many an old mansion suffered the same fate as the affluent moved to newly fashionable areas.

The appalling need for help brought in its wake the need to avoid duplication of effort, and in 1883 the Charity Organization Society was founded. It was not designed to provide financial aid, but to investigate those who applied for help from churches, ethnic charitable societies, private individuals, and the like. Though a chief aim was to prevent "imposters" from exploiting charity, the Society also adopted a new approach: counsel to those in need to help them develop "habits of providence and self dependence." This program was carried out by "friendly visitors" from the "educated and well-to-do class, especially the women of the city, who...can impart to the cheerless tenement a little of their own happiness." Despite this naive approach, with its heavy overtones of *noblesse oblige*, it was a forward step that attempted to recognize "the self-respect of the recipient" of aid. It was the reflection in Louisville of a nationwide trend that led eventually to social work as a specialized helping profession.

corruption in every canvass. Money has been spent freely and the purchasable element has increased year by year." The police, who held their posts by political favor, campaigned openly for particular candidates and often enforced 'discipline' at the polls. The *Courier-Journal* charged the police force was "a mere political machine," little interested in enforcing the law. "The ladies of Louisville might carry their purses in their boots," the newspaper advised, "until we get a first-class police force."

Hovering in the background and prime target of the reformers were the Whallen brothers, who manipulated elections, political appointments, and the police from their headquarters in the Buckingham Theatre. John came to Louisville in 1871 from Newport, Kentucky, where he had been a policeman, and opened a saloon on Green Street between Fourth and Fifth. He reportedly introduced the five-cent schooner of beer to Louisville, a move that won him both affection and patronage. His brother, James, joined him in 1880 as a partner in the new Buckingham enterprise on Jefferson Street. Neither Whallen ever ran for elective office, nor is the full extent of their 'business' operations known, but a corps of friendly policemen was helpful.

John and James formed a powerful team: John the visible, outgoing 'Duke of Buckingham;' James the behind-the-scenes strategist. Their strength lay in their humble Irish origins that gave them rapport with the working men, and their straightforward, no-nonsense approach to winning elections. "I reckon I have bought as many votes in my time as any man...," James once admitted. "It has been recognized in this city for years that it is impossible to win elections without money." The Whallens also formed on-again, off-again alliances with powerful individuals, including Walter N. Haldeman of the *Courier-Journal*, and Aaron Kohn, a Jewish attorney.

This naked quest for political power (not always confined to the Whallens), stirred the same progressive impulses that led to establishment of the Southern Exposition and dictated attempts to reform the political process. Since the Democrats were dominant, the battle was fought within that party. The first move was an effort to insulate the police from politics. A bill approved by the State legislature in early 1882 removed the police from the control of the mayor and Council, substituting an independent board, and also specifically prohibited police from engaging in political activities. Two years later reform groups backed a successful move for adoption of a voter registration law. Speaking from obvious experience, Baxter asserted that elections cost candidates "a great deal of money," and added that had a registration law been adopted twenty years earlier, he himself would "now be worth $50,000."

But voter registration, though it eliminated much fictitious and multiple voting, did not solve the basic problem of vote buying. As long as voting was verbal, with tally clerks recording the expressed choices, the buyers of votes could easily check the performance of the 'bummers' who accepted

money. The system invited bribery of tally clerks, as well. Finally the issue came to a head in 1887 when Republicans put forth their first candidate for mayor. He was Samuel L. Avery, son of Benjamin F. Avery, founder of the agricultural implement works that was one of Louisville's most important industries.

The Republicans had reason for hope. The party had been slowly increasing its strength in Louisville, proving especially attractive to many merchants and industrialists as it shed its early image of uncompromising defender of black civil rights. As in the rest of the nation, Republicanism began to be seen, instead, as representative of business interests. Even so, black voters still pinned their hopes on the party, giving it a needed reservoir of strength. The Democratic party, meanwhile, racked by the issue of municipal reform, entered the 1887 contest hopelessly split. Jacob sought the office a third time, but was opposed by Democratic County Judge William B. Hoke, the Whallens' candidate. Even with this division in the ranks, Jacob's great popularity carried the day. His 11,339 votes outnumbered the combined total of Avery's 5,987 and Hoke's miniscule 3,326.

The outcome demonstrated that Whallen vote-buying did not always produce the desired results, especially in the face of militant reformers. As a result of the work of sharp-eyed watchers at strategic polls, vote bribers were arrested "by the wagon load," including an alderman and a councilman. So heavy was the vote buying among blacks that Avery, who confidently expected 95% of the total Negro vote, received only 15%.

The furor over such blatant bribery led to the crowning achievement of the reform impulse: the adoption of the Australian, or secret, ballot in 1888. Though it had long been advocated nationally, Louisville became the pioneer in adopting the printed ballot, which the voter filled out in secret to be deposited in a locked ballot box. It was not a cure-all, as later ballot-box stuffing proved, but it was a giant step forward. The secret ballot made it impossible, the *Courier-Journal* noted, for the vote-buyer to know his purchases were effective.

Meanwhile, the Republican party continued to gather strength, profiting especially from the economic depression that began in 1893 during the administration of Democratic President Grover Cleveland. In 1894 a Republican congressman was elected from Louisville and the following year a statewide tide put William O. Bradley in the Governor's Mansion as Kentucky's first Republican chief executive. Louisville voters not only joined the move to Bradley, but also gave Republicans control of the City's Board of Aldermen and Common Council. The latter vote, midway in the term of Democratic Mayor Henry S. Tyler, was achieved despite Tyler's brisk efficiency in office and his moves to introduce 'business-like' methods in government. The days when Democratic candidates would automatically be elected in Louisville were over.

Right: The Louisville Female College (certainly a misnomer given the age of the students) was on the west side of Fourth Street between Broadway and York. This photograph was made about 1888.
Collection of Mrs. Marshall Seibel

Below: This election campaign card dates from Democrat Henry S. Tyler's initial and successful bid for office in 1890.
Filson Club

1890. December Election. 1890.

Henry S. Tyler

—→ FOR ←—

MAYOR.

The year 1895 was thus a watershed in Louisville and Kentucky politics as a disbelieving Democratic party nursed the wounds of its first major defeats since the Civil War. But Louisville Democrats had not seen the end of their troubles. In January 1896 Mayor Tyler's sudden death in mid-term left the vacancy to be filled by the Republican-controlled Common Council, which chose George D. Todd as the city's first Republican chief executive. Yet, the Republicans were not without their own internal problems. For one, the party was finding its black constituents becoming restive, seeking a greater share of power now that Republicanism was beginning to win victories.

Though the party relied on black votes, it was reluctant to sponsor black candidates. In the summer of 1895 the attempt by Negro Republicans in Louisville's Sixth State Legislative District (coinciding with the Tenth Ward) to nominate black attorney Nathaniel R. Harper as candidate for the State House of Representatives was thwarted by the City-County Republican Committee. In the Democratic camp, disorganized by defeat and the death of Tyler, the reform movement lost its momentum. That left the door open for John Whallen to take control and choose Charles P. Weaver, former alderman and now postmaster, as the Democratic standard-bearer.

With these new political alignments, Louisville approached the first mayoral contest to pit a Republican candidate directly against a Democrat. Republican Todd faced Weaver and the wily 'Duke of Buckingham' in November 1897. It was a Democratic victory, though Weaver's margin was but a modest 2,728 votes over Todd in a total turnout of nearly 40,000. The *honest* figure more likely gave the Democrats at most 1,000 votes over the Republicans. The Republican *Commercial* headlined the result "The Rankest Fraud in the History of the City," charging that the polls were "under the domination of pool-room sharks, detectives, firemen and police," that polling places were changed without notice, opened late, and that most blacks (especially in the Ninth and Tenth wards) were prevented from voting by various stratagems. Even the *Courier-Journal*, a faithful Weaver supporter, was forced to acknowledge the drastic drop in black votes, but explained it as a Negro rebuke to the Republicans for snubbing Harper in 1895.

Yet, analysis of the returns indicates that the Democrats would have carried the election (by a razor-thin edge) even without Whallen's manipulations. With Weaver's move into City Hall, most of the work of the reformers was undone and the Whallen machine found ways to circumvent such annoyances as voter registration and the secret ballot. Reform was an issue that would have to be taken up again in the new century.

Despite the seesaw battle between reformers and political 'ringsters' that marked the final decades of the Nineteenth Century, real progress was made in Louisville's municipal housekeeping and in vastly improved public facilities, including such basics as sewers and street paving.

But the most notable achievement was the creation of an extensive system of public parks. Though a handful of citizens advocated parks even before the Civil War, the idea failed to secure popular support in a city where the open countryside was only a brisk walk away. As urban growth swallowed up the close-in open spaces in the post-war years, however, and industrial pollution blackened the atmosphere, interest in parks grew.

The drive to reserve unspoiled open space got under way in earnest in 1887 when the Salmagundi Club, a men's "social and literary organization whose membership commanded the highest respect and confidence," launched a campaign for a system of parks, enlisting the support of the business community. The project moved quickly, receiving State legislative approval for an independent Board of Park Commissioners in 1890. Though the Commission was empowered to pick the park sites, Jacob, a man who "equated his opinion with the public good," had on his own initiative purchased the southern (Iroquois) park acreage in 1889. It was a move that caused controversy.

Jacob used his own funds to acquire the 313-acre tract four miles south of the City limits. He was then reimbursed for his $98,000 expenditure by the City treasurer without the approval of the City Council. Ignoring criticism, Jacob plunged ahead on plans for a boulevard (Southern Parkway) to the park. It would be, he asserted, comparable to the Champs-Elysées in Paris, and he convinced the Council to approve the project. Property owners along the route donated land for what first was called Grand Boulevard.

To connect the boulevard with Third Street required a right-of-way through the grounds of the School of Reform, a project for which the Council appropriated $17,000. Though Jacob's single-handed approach to the parks issue roused the ire of Salmagundians, his Grand Boulevard became the model for the system of broad thoroughfares intended to link all the parks. They are today's Southern, Eastern, and Western parkways.

Above: One of Louisville's pioneer trolley cars of 1889 pauses in the end-of-the-line carbarn at Baxter and Highland avenues for the photographer. The young man at the controls is giving lessons in operating the new electrical marvel to veteran mule-car drivers, round-shouldered from years of handling reins. The coming of the electric streetcar triggered an explosive outward growth of Louisville's urban area.
Author's collection

The trolley car arrives
"The Green-street electric railway was formally opened yesterday afternoon.... The start [from Fourth and Liberty] was made promptly and the cars were whirled rapidly up Green street....The sidewalks all along Green street and Baxter avenue were crowded with people anxious to see the first car pass, and all along the route people were at their windows on the lookout. As the cars came rapidly by, sparks were thrown out on all sides from under the wheels, and especially the much-abused but hardy little street-car mules on Baxter avenue were badly frightened."
Courier-Journal, June 14, 1889

Inheriting the mayor's purchase (first called Jacob's Park), the commissioners proceeded to pick the sites for two other large parks, one on the eastern, the other on the western fringe of the city. The first acreage for Cherokee Park in the East End was purchased in the spring of 1891 and for Shawnee Park in the West End a year later. Underscoring the desire to create excellent parks was the happy choice of the office of Frederick Law Olmsted, the nation's finest landscape architects, to design the road systems and planting patterns.

The new parks were an instant success, largely because of a technological development unforeseen when the promotional campaign was launched in 1887. As wooded, rural retreats, they were necessarily some distance from the built-up portions of the city. Even Cherokee and Shawnee parks were outside the City limits when they were established. (Though these two were taken into the corporate boundaries in 1895, Iroquois Park was not within the City until 1922.) Yet even distant Iroquois was made easily accessible by 1892.

The unforeseen factor was the electric trolley car, which proved to be a far more potent force in bursting the bounds of the old city than the mule-car had been. Louisville's first, somewhat experimental, line was opened on Green Street and out Baxter Avenue to Highland Avenue on June 13, 1889, quickly demonstrating its superiority over the older form of transit. The electric lines required a large initial capital investment, however, which was the principal factor in the 1890 merger of all local lines into the Louisville Railway Company. The new company (direct predecessor of the Transit Authority of River City) quickly set about converting the major routes to electric operation.

The first was the Fourth Street line, traversing the rapidly growing Old

Above: Pewee Valley was a favorite place for well-to-do Louisvillians to escape summer's heat during the non-air-conditioned Nineteenth Century. This 1895 group at "The Locust" included the families of William E. Grinstead and Dr. Robert Vaughan, along with their "help." The head of the household usually spent the week in the city, joining his family on weekends.
Collection of Julia Vaughan

Right: This mule-drawn Central Passenger Railroad car stands at a nearly abandoned Portland wharf about 1888, the weeds attesting to the decline of steamboating and the end of the Portland-New Albany ferry, doomed when the K&I Bridge (background) opened in 1886. An open summer-car of the rival Louisville City Railway is partially hidden at right. In 1890 the two companies were merged and the electric trolley came to Portland, but not to the old wharf.
Author's collection

Louisville area and beyond to Churchill Downs, where trolley cars began operation in early 1891. The simultaneous arrival of the electric streetcar and the parks dovetailed unexpectedly to create the most intensive speculative boom in real estate yet witnessed in Louisville, overshadowing the westward move of twenty years earlier. By the spring of 1891 the newspapers were filled almost daily with advertisements extolling the unparalleled virtues of the Highlands near Cherokee Park and the great stretch of level country southward to Iroquois Park. Old estates and farms suddenly bloomed with surveyors' stakes marking out subdivision lots. The Eastern Land Company proclaimed that its new subdivision reached Willow Avenue, "The Gateway to the New Eastern Park," but the greatest flurry of activity was southward. Here the electric trolley first showed its capacity to translate population growth into a leapfrogging urban expansion impossible before.

To the races
"The crowds going out on the electric cars to the races yesterday afternoon were a sight to see. Although the cars ran at frequent intervals, three in a train, men and boys hung on by their eyelids, so to say, and by the time they reached Jefferson, going south, they were generally so crowded that no more could be accommodated."
Louisville Post, May 14, 1891

The South End had an early advantage over the Highlands. "We Have the Electric Car" was the theme of advertisements of such outside-the-city developments as Oakdale, Beechmont, and Jacob's Addition. The aggressiveness of the numerous South End developers, plus the potential travel to Iroquois Park, combined to put two electric lines in operation by July 1892. The opening of Southern Parkway the following year increased the development fever.

Notwithstanding an earlier start and hopes of promoters (particularly for Beechmont), these South End developments did not in the long run match the Highlands in prestige. Cherokee Park got its trolley line in the summer of 1893, a route extending out Bardstown Road and terminating at Willow and Cherokee Parkway. From that time the Highlands began a rapid rise, attracting the same managerial and professional class that was moving into Old Louisville. The trolley car also ushered in an era of transport democracy, serving all income levels and all neighborhoods before the advent of the automobile.

Despite this explosive outward growth during the final decades of the Nineteenth Century, with development running ahead of the extension of the City boundary, Louisville's central core continued as the undisputed heart of what was becoming a metropolitan area. The electric trolley lines guaranteed that this would be so, forming fixed channels of communication from all outlying points to the core, unlike the automobile that was to corrode and then dissolve fixed bonds by its all-direction mobility. The core was, in fact, strengthened because of its role as the central point for transit lines, and development continued steadily even as the streetcar suburbs began their mushrooming growth.

Downtown church spires suddenly had to share skyline space with a

new generation of office buildings that towered above even the tallest older structures. Most notable was the Columbia (originally Commerce) Building rising ten massive stories on the northwest corner of Fourth and Main and opened January 1, 1890. It was not only Louisville's tallest building for a decade, but another indication of the drive to maintain visibility. A project of the Commercial Club (formed in 1887 by young businessmen who found the Board of Trade too staid in promoting Louisville), the Columbia Building was erected to attract notice and to give downtown a contemporary image.

Designed in the new round-arched Romanesque style made popular by architect Henry H. Richardson, it was a solid, pressed-brick building on a red stone foundation, and somewhat severe for Louisville tastes. "It is entirely and painfully devoid of any of the graceful ornamentation of modern architecture," the *Post* complained in a critical judgment that falls strangely on the ears of a later generation. The Columbia was followed by numerous other buildings in the Richardsonian Romanesque form, including the 1893 Louisville Medical College at First and Chestnut, the most successful of the numerous private medical schools that had sprung up to compete with the University of Louisville's Medical Department.

In addition to numerous medical schools, Louisville also became home to two theological seminaries, both of which chose downtown locations. The Presbyterian Theological Seminary had its beginning in 1893 and ten years later occupied its newly built Gothic quadrangle (now Jefferson Community College) at First and Broadway. The Southern Baptist Theological Seminary had moved to Louisville in 1877 from Greenville, South Carolina, seeking a larger urban area. It proved a propitious move, bringing increasing enrollment and, in 1887, generous endowments that permitted construction of a distinguished complex of buildings at Fifth and Broadway.

With the rapid shift of the urban core to largely commercial uses, the

Above: The Board of Trade acquired the Lithgow Building at Third and Main as its new home in 1879. The Louisville telephone exchange occupied the top floor soon after, sending out a veritable maze of wires from the roof. The building, the city's finest office structure when it was built in 1873, was demolished by the Urban Renewal Agency in 1975. Louisville Anzeiger, March 1, 1898

Above right: Norton Hall, facing Broadway between Fourth and Fifth, was the principal building of Southern Baptist Theological Seminary in its former downtown location. The hall, built about 1890 with funding from Louisville's Norton family, housed classrooms and administrative offices. The site was later occupied by the Greyhound Bus Depot. Caufield & Shook Collection, U of L Photographic Archives

Right: Louisville's dusty streets of the 1890s were wetted down by sprinkling carts during the summer, but along the new electric trolley lines this 2,000-gallon wonder performed the job much more efficiently. The sprinkler was invented by Louisvillian John R. Gathright and marketed throughout the nation by the United Tramway Sprinkler Company. Street Railway Journal, February, 1892

affluent abandoned their mansions on Walnut, Chestnut, and even Broadway, giving rise to an entirely new building type for Louisville: the apartment house. The first of this new breed, the elegant Rossmore (now the Berkeley Hotel), made its debut in 1894 on Fourth just north of Broadway. The apartments (five rooms plus bath) were designed for the well-to-do who wished to live close to the city's active center. Each floor provided private rooms at the rear for family servants. Technologically, however, one of the most significant aspects of the Rossmore's design was the use of gas for heating.

Until the 1890s all gas used in Louisville was extracted from coal at the Gas Works on Jackson Street near the river. The limited supply was used primarily, if not exclusively, for lighting. The discovery of natural gas in nearby Meade County in the late 1880s suddenly made seemingly unlimited quantities available to Louisville consumers at a lower price. The first well, drilled near Brandenburg in 1887 by the Union Gas Company, was such a novelty that river boats took excursionists to see the burning gas flaming forty feet into the air. The abundance of gas may have delayed the spread of residential electric lighting in Louisville. Most homes built during the 1890s, and even later, used gas lighting and most also had gas-burning fireplaces for heating.

Despite this natural gas bonanza, the brilliance of 2,000-candlepower electric arc lights made them the logical choice for street illumination, and Louisville began replacing the gas lamps that had been a source of swelling civic pride fifty years earlier. The Louisville Gas Company (owned partly by the City) was well aware of the trend toward electricity. Moving adroitly, the company in 1890 acquired a controlling interest in the tiny Louisville Electric Lighting Company, then erected the city's first large-scale electric generating station in 1891. By the end of 1893 arc lights outnumbered gas lights on Louisville streets by 875 to 301.

Above: The opening of the Kentucky &
Indiana Railroad Bridge in late 1886
spelled the end of the ferry service between Louisville and New Albany.
Sometime before that date the spick-
and-span Music waited for passengers at
the rocky Portland wharf. She later became an excursion boat, carrying pic-
nickers to Sugar Grove below New
Albany and Fern Grove (later Rose
Island) above Jeffersonville.
Lin Caufield

Above right: A day at the wharf about
1890 found only two steamers in port,
where once there would have been a
dozen or more. The small sternwheeler
Lancaster would take freight and passengers to Frankfort and other Kentucky
River landings. The large sidewheeler
New South, built in 1887 at the Howard
Shipyards in Jeffersonville, was preparing to depart for Cincinnati.
U of L Photographic Archives

These far-reaching internal changes in the urban area were matched by
an array of external developments that would have occupied center stage in
an earlier day, but now had to share a larger and more active Louisville scene.
The first Ohio River bridge, completed in 1870, had been a major and controversial development. The construction of two additional ones before the
end of the century was seen as only fulfilling normal expectations, given the
proliferation of the city's railroad network. The first of the new bridges was
the Kentucky and Indiana (K&I), spanning the river between Portland and
New Albany. Proposed in 1880 by a group of Louisville and New Albany
entrepreneurs headed by ex-Confederate Bennett H. Young, the bridge was
opened October 16, 1886, challenging the Fourteenth Street bridge's monopoly of cross-river rail traffic, and also providing a vehicular roadway.

Construction of the second of the new bridges, this one linking Louisville and Jeffersonville, started on the Indiana side in the fall of 1889, but the
bad luck that was to plague the project began almost immediately with the
death of sixteen workers in two accidents in early 1890. Work proceeded —
though fitfully — and by 1893 the last of the great iron spans was being
erected. Then, on December 15 of that year, fate struck an even crueler blow
when a sudden heavy gust of wind knocked a partially completed span off
the piers and dropped it into the river. Later that day the completed adjacent
span, damaged when the first fell, also collapsed. The death toll reached
twenty-one in the accident called the most serious of its kind American
bridge building had yet experienced. By the time of this tragedy the project
had been taken over by the Cleveland, Cincinnati, Chicago & St. Louis
Railway (Big Four), which planned to extend a line to Louisville. The collapse delayed completion of the bridge by a year or more, but in August 1895
the work was finished. Three bridges now spanned the river at the Falls of
the Ohio.

Above: The Ohio River embraces Louisville, sweeping around the city in a wide arc in this 1890 view. The Pennsylvania or Fourteenth Street bridge crosses in the foreground, the Kentucky and Indiana bridge between Portland and New Albany in the background. The partial dam was built in the early 1880s to divert additional water into the Portland Canal.
Harper's Weekly, April 5, 1890

By the time the Big Four Bridge was completed, its tracks touching down in Louisville along the waterfront near Preston Street, there were already other rails with which it connected. The annoying tracks along Jefferson Street had been removed finally in 1881, relocated on the old filled-in bed of Beargrass Creek. And there was a line of elevated trackage along the wharf, completed in 1884. Valuable for freight transfer, the elevated track also provided the route into downtown Louisville for the 'Daisy' passenger trains from New Albany via the K&I Bridge.

In addition to new traffic routes, railroad expansion also brought Louisville two new passenger stations, impressive gateways to the city and additions to downtown's inventory of contemporary, Romanesque-style buildings. The L&N erected Union Station at Tenth and Broadway, while the Chesapeake & Ohio (an 1880s newcomer) built Central Station at the foot of Seventh Street along the new riverfront track and almost on the very spot occupied by Fort Nelson a century earlier.

Union Station was by far the more elegant of the two, its rusticated stone walls crowned with towers and turrets and pierced by two huge circular stained-glass windows. Polished brass and marble fixtures in the waiting room reflected the gentle light filtering through a stained-glass skylight. Opened in September 1891, Union Station at last provided L&N passengers a Louisville entry worthy of both the city and the railroad.

The Chesapeake & Ohio's red-brick station, boasting a single tall corner tower and completed a few months before the L&N's, was a replacement for an earlier and smaller depot that vanished in a hail of falling bricks and timber on March 27, 1890, during the most destructive tornado Louisville had yet known. The death toll reached nearly 100 and the property damage $2 million when the "whirling tiger of the air" cut a swath through the city from Parkland on the west to the Water Works on the east. Yet the

Above: Union Station at Tenth and Broadway, completed by the Louisville & Nashville Railroad in 1891, shared business with other railroad stations at Fourteenth and Main, Seventh and the river, and First and the river. None, however, could match its Romanesque Revival magnificence, nor its huge stained-glass windows. Today the building is headquarters for Transit Authority of River City.
Author's collection

city politely refused all outside offers of aid, mustering its own resources to aid tornado victims and to clean up the wreckage. The refusal of help was likely motivated by the same sense of community self-reliance that created the Southern Exposition and reform politics. The new Seventh Street station, rising larger and handsomer out of the rubble of its predecessor, was one example of Louisville's rapid recovery. All along the tornado's path new structures quickly replaced the old. Within a year, scarcely a sign of the disaster remained.

As the Nineteenth Century ran out its final few years, Louisville initiated a series of annexation moves that gathered into its corporate fold much of the new development that had sprung up around the city. The expanded boundaries included Clifton, Crescent Hill, Cherokee Park and the Highlands neighborhood surrounding it, South Louisville (the area adjacent to Churchill Downs), the West End to Thirty-second Street (plus a finger extending to and enveloping Shawnee Park), and once-distant Parkland. With its new acquisitions, Louisville ended the century with a population of 204,000, a figure that revealed the accelerating rate of urban growth. It had taken ninety years for the City by the Falls to pass the 100,000 population mark, but only thirty years to double that.

For the first time a significant part of the new growth had spilled beyond the corporate limits, indicating the way that new transportation patterns were changing the form of the urban area. It was an early signal that in the future the population within the City limits would no longer be an accurate index of what constituted an urban area. Some of the areas annexed were also small incorporated cities in their own right (Clifton, Crescent Hill, South Louisville, Parkland), another signal of future developments beyond the boundaries of the 'mother city'.

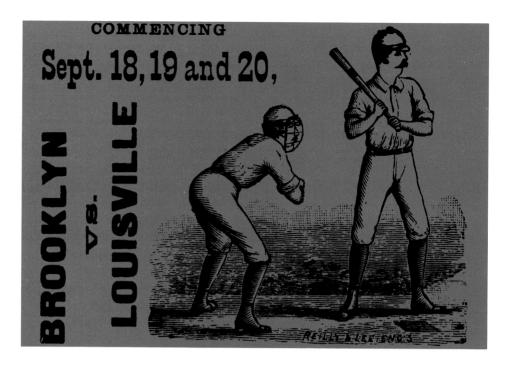

Above: Hero of the old Eclipse Park at Twenty-eighth and Elliott, Lewis Rogers 'Pete' Browning was the star slugger of the Louisville Eclipses of the American Association. (The Association was a major league from 1882 to 1891.) When 18-year-old John Hillerich made Browning a bat in 1884, the Hillerich & Bradsby woodworking firm was set on a new direction. Browning, fired from the Louisville club in 1889 because of drinking problems, recovered and went on to play with Cleveland and Pittsburgh until 1894.
Hillerich & Bradsby Collection, U of L Photographic Archives

Above right: By the early 1880s Louisville's professional baseball was played at Eclipse Park, Twenty-eighth and Elliott, now the site of a public playground. In 1893 a new park was built a few blocks south at Twenty-eighth and Broadway. This advertisement appeared in a Macauley's Theatre program of 1888.

These last years of the old century were filled with other indicators of the new one. Women were taking an active role not only in art, charitable enterprises, and educational ventures, but also in fields of gainful employment that had been the exclusive preserve of men. As early as 1882 the L&N Railroad employed its first woman, young Miss Sallie Curtis Murphy, who became a secretary in the Second and Main headquarters. The following year the Southern Exposition employed "young ladies in the executive department." They may have been 'typewriters', the name applied to the young women who wielded these new office machines. Other women moved into more demanding work. By 1888 the Bremaker-Moore Paper Company employed a "female chemist who was an expert in her profession and gave entire satisfaction in her work." And the *Louisville Times*, the afternoon newspaper Walter N. Haldeman launched in 1884, soon employed Elvira Sydnor Miller as the city's first woman reporter.

Baseball emerged as the national sport in fact, if not yet in name. By the end of the century Louisville's ball park had migrated to Twenty-eighth and Broadway, with a grandstand in place of bleachers. As the masses turned to baseball, the classes found tennis and golf more appealing, organizing the Louisville Tennis Club in the 1880s and the Louisville Golf Club about 1893. Yet horse racing remained the city's first love and in 1895 Churchill Downs built a new grandstand with twin spires that were destined to become one of the nation's best-known symbols of Louisville.

In 1899 a social harbinger of the future appeared. The Louisville Country Club, complete with swimming pool, opened near River Road at Pipe Line Lane (Zorn Avenue) on the rocky bluff above the golf club. The swimming pool was ready-made: the original reservoir of the Louisville Water Company, long since supplanted by the Crescent Hill Reservoir. In April 1899 the last ten gas street lights were turned off, replaced by electricity. Louisville was ready for the Twentieth Century.

Chapter 11

A City in Search of the Twentieth Century

The first automobile
"Mr. John E. Roche, president of the Louisville Carriage Company [later Louisville Taxicab & Transfer Company] was the first resident of Louisville to own an automobile. His first automobile was propelled by steam, and he used it for nearly a year, when he decided to exchange it for a machine run by electricity. This is the machine he now has, and he declares that it is a source of great satisfaction to him, both in the way of pleasure and convenience."
Courier-Journal, June 8, 1902

The new century seemed to start off well for Louisville and Jefferson County. With economic skies clear and sunny, employment at a high level, and the technological advances of the Nineteenth Century abundantly in evidence, the *Courier-Journal* struck a note of optimism on January 1, 1901: "So, as the bells which rang out the old century still sound in our ears, let us thrill... with exultation in the race which we know [mankind] is to run in the century that is to come." The Twentieth Century was only four days old when James Ross Todd announced plans for the city's second ten-story office building, to be erected on the northeast corner of Fourth and Market. Before 1901 was over, the last of the streetcar mules—on the Crescent Hill route—were put out to pasture when the electric cars took over. Even rising food prices had a bright side: they were blamed on full employment and resulting high demand.

The Nineteenth Century, convinced by its own experience that 'progress' was inevitable, welcomed the Twentieth Century as a newer and brighter version of what had gone before. By 1902 some thirty-six automobiles contested with horse-drawn vehicles for Louisville street space; and the city was introduced to the thrills of auto racing (at Churchill Downs) in 1903. A year later Louisville's first motion picture theatre, a 'nickelodeon' appropriately named Dreamland, opened on Market near Fifth. In 1906 Louisvillians saw their first airship: a gasoline-engined, sausage-shaped, gas-filled bag that attracted crowds to Fontaine Ferry Park. That same year the police force acquired two automobiles as better suited than horses to "pursue criminals." In 1910 the "Wright aeroplane" took to the skies (but not very high) at Churchill Downs, with daring aeronaut Glenn Curtiss at the controls. The Twentieth Century was revealing its surprises, one by one.

But, as Louisville was to discover, not all the surprises were pleasant. The solid Victorian city, comfortable and rather smug, seemed to mistake the outer apparel of the new century—splendid new hotels, office buildings, theatres, apartment houses, a new public library, growing suburbs—for the century's essence. It took some time for the power structure even to admit that something had gone amiss. But the census of 1910 shocked the city into a realization of deep-seated trouble. Since 1900 Louisville's population had increased only 9.4%—an increase in numbers of a mere 19,197. It was the lowest growth rate in the city's 130-year history. Clearly something was wrong. Mayor William O. Head provided the initial response: the figures were incorrect.

"I am positive that Louisville has a population greater than 223,928," he asserted. "I am heartily in favor of retaking the census....I am confident that 25,000 to 30,000 names would be added." The agitation impelled one of the local census enumerators to describe his experience: "I found in my precinct...many vacant houses, empty lots and factories," he wrote to the *Courier-Journal*. The figures on manufacturing employment corroborated his observations. The total of industrial wage earners was only 28,716, lower than the 29,926 of 1900.

The population figures of Jefferson County outside Louisville revealed one of the factors in the city's slowing growth rate. In the county, population had increased 13,000, or 42.4%, a startling contrast to previous decades. From 1890 to 1900, for example, county population was static, showing a gain of only 349. The trend toward leapfrogging growth beyond the City boundaries that had begun in the 1890s had been obscured by the annexations of that decade. But the city had not expanded since absorbing South Louisville in 1898 and a part of Crescent Hill in 1900.

Manufacturing, too, was spreading beyond Louisville, especially to Highland Park, the incorporated community that stretched along the L&N tracks south of the larger city. Highland Park and nearby Oakdale, another incorporated community, boasted 4,000 residents between them. Also included in the overall county growth figures were the returns from various

When motoring was an adventure
*"Never before in the history of Louisville
have so many extended tours been taken
by automobile drivers, as in the present
season. When the automobile first became popular in this city a few years
ago, very few drivers ventured further
than the nearby country towns in Jefferson county, but, like the sailors of the
Middle Ages, they gradually widened the
scope of their tours until at the present
time Louisville motorists have made trips
over the entire Eastern section of the
United States, embracing a territory extending from the Gulf of Mexico to the
snow-covered hills of Northern Canada."*
Courier-Journal, October 2, 1910

unincorporated suburban residential developments such as Beechmont and
Jacob's Addition. Other developments were on the way, such as Audubon
Park of 1912.

Another significant factor contributing to growth beyond the city was
the system of electric railways extending like fingers from downtown Louisville to Orell, Okolona, Fern Creek, Jeffersontown, Middletown (and beyond
to Shelbyville), Anchorage (and beyond to LaGrange), and Prospect. Built
between 1901 and 1910, at a time when the automobile was still more toy than
transportation (there were perhaps 600 in the city and county by 1909) and
most roads were bottomless pits in wet weather, these electric interurban
lines opened large new areas of the county to development. Each route, with
its 'country cars' skimming through the rural landscape, became a corridor of
nascent urbanization. Many middle-class city residents now took up the pleasures of country living, commuting to the city on the frequent electric cars.

One of the more distinguished of these passengers was *Courier-
Journal* editor Henry Watterson, who had purchased in 1894 near Jeffersontown a country estate he named Mansfield. When the electric cars reached
Jeffersontown in 1904, Watterson became a regular patron. With the outward
migration, the city's share of the total Jefferson County population fell from
88% in 1900 to 85.2% in 1910. The Falls region was tending to become a
metropolitan area, a concept difficult for either Louisville or the Census
Bureau to recognize in 1910, especially since the 39,000 residents in the county
outside Louisville were no match for the city's 224,000.

And despite the outward movement of urban residents, the county
remained overwhelmingly rural. It boasted the nation's largest onion farm
near Doup's Point on the Bardstown Road. Kentucky agricultural exhibitors
at the St. Louis World's Fair of 1904 included L.L. Dorsey, Anchorage, who
displayed Morgan horses, while H.F. Hartsfield, Prospect, and W.F. Mills,
South Park, entered Jefferson County corn. The most exciting event in Fern
Creek was the Jefferson County Fair, held every September, where farmers
vied for blue ribbons for their produce.

The unsettling 1910 census news came hard on the heels of other
internal prolems centered around political corruption so brazen that the
Kentucky Court of Appeals declared the 1905 municipal election fraudulent.
In a sweeping indictment of the Whallen machine's tactics, the Court turned
out of office every candidate who had been elected to City and County posts.
This political earthquake caused a former mayor to commit suicide; brought
new names to the fore, including suave young attorney Robert Worth Bingham; and was a prelude to the shift of Democratic Louisville to a Republican stronghold.

The 1905 election and its aftermath had its roots in Louisville's bizarre late
Nineteenth Century politics, which were not changed by the mere arrival

Crescent Hill's life line
The mule-drawn streetcar out Frankfort Avenue to Crescent Hill began operation in 1883. When the mule car was replaced by electric trolleys in 1901, its demise brought a rush of memories.

"It was when the present asphalted Frankfort avenue was then hot, dusty Shelbyville Pike, when everybody in Crescent Hill knew everybody else, and the appearance of a stranger was a conversation-making event, that the mule car line flourished. The mule car was the round-up place of Crescent Hill news. The men discussed politics at leisure on the 7:30 car; the women settled vexing social problems, arranged church socials and swapped cook stoves [sic] at 10 o'clock and on the noon run, while at 8 o'clock in the morning and at 2 o'clock in the afternoon the time was given over to the [school] children."
Courier-Journal, *October 27, 1901*

of a new century. The 1897 municipal election, entrenching the Democratic machine in power, was one potent factor coloring the political process in Louisville and Jefferson County. Perhaps equally important were the sensational events of January 1900 in Frankfort, when William A. Goebel, Democratic aspirant in the disputed 1899 gubernatorial election, was mortally wounded on the street by a hidden rifleman. Goebel lived long enough to be declared governor by the Democratic-controlled legislature (and thus to be succeeded by his running mate, J.C.W. Beckham). Republican William S. Taylor (who had actually polled 2,000 more votes than Goebel and had been inaugurated earlier) was accused of participation in the assassination plot. He fled the state and took up residence in Indiana.

One of the complications following Goebel's murder was a hostility between Democrats and Republicans that went far beyond normal party differences. In Louisville the hostility ruptured the cooperation between Republicans and independent Democrats that had won earlier victories against 'Boss' Whallen.

When Democrat Charles F. Grainger was elected mayor in 1901 as a respectable 'front man', the center of Louisville political power remained the Buckingham Theatre. At the Court House, where Charles A. Wilson occupied the office of County Judge with the blessing of the Whallens, a monumental statue of Thomas Jefferson was dedicated November 10, 1901, only four days after the election. The sculpture was a gift of brothers Isaac and Bernard Bernheim, Jewish German immigrants, who had prospered in the wholesale liquor trade and revered Jefferson as the one "who had done more than any other one man to make this country free...." The irony apparently was lost on Louisville.

Or, perhaps it was not. Reform was again showing itself, spurred by the tide of Progressivism—the middle-class enthusiasm for social and economic reform—sweeping the nation at large. Louisville was only one of a long list of American cities suffering political corruption and boss rule. The attempts to 'clean up' these cities merged with a nationwide suspicion of the growing power of large corporations, trusts, and 'interests', which were perceived as allied with urban political machines.

The assassinated William Goebel, with his attacks upon corporations (especially the L&N Railroad), his call for increased support to education, his friendship for labor, his refusal to use race as an issue (unusual among Democrats, he sought black votes), and his general antipathy to the Kentucky Establishment, was cast in the Progressive mold. It was not accidental that one of Goebel's bitter opponents in the Democratic party was John Whallen. The charges of duplicity between corporations and urban political machines was a familiar one in Louisville, where Whallen often was castigated as the "handmaiden of the L&N," and of the large distillers, as well.

By 1905, when Louisville and Jefferson County were again to elect a

A ride out West Market

Shortly after the turn of the century, much of the West End was still rural, as this description of a trolley ride on West Market Street shows. The trip was probably taken in one of the open-sided summer cars.

"For several miles toward the western end of the line the cars go whizzing past pleasant little farms, with the corn now waving in the breeze, with the cows standing knee-deep in clover and with the fresh, cool air from the river blowing in the faces of the excursionists.

"Fountain [sic] Ferry Park is the Mecca of many who take the Market-street car in the late afternoon and evening, Western [Shawnee] for those who go west during the day...."

"The people in the western part of Louisville find much of their delight in spending a day now and then at the park....Fish camps are sprinkled on the far limits of the park, and are peopled by those who know the joys of the outdoor life offered by the big reservation."
Courier-Journal, July 27, 1902

mayor and County judge, plus the usual assortment of lesser officials, the reform forces had mended their differences and were ready to challenge the machine. This fusion of independent Democrats and Republicans had its origin in the newly formed City Club, and received significant support from the Louisville Ministerial Association. Many Protestant ministers had long used their pulpits to excoriate gambling, prostitution, and saloons, which they associated with corrupt politics and lax law enforcement. Under the collective name Fusionist, the reform elements agreed on a slate of local candidates, with attorney J.T. O'Neal for mayor. The Fusionist leaders included an impressive array of business and professional men: ex-Confederate Basil W. Duke, Thomas W. Bullitt, William Marshall Bullitt, William R. Belknap, Richard Knott, Helm Bruce, William Heyburn, Augustus E. Willson, the Rev. E.L. Powell of the First Christian Church, Episcopal Bishop Charles E. Woodcock, and the Rev. Edgar Y. Mullins, president of the Southern Baptist Theological Seminary.

The machine prepared for battle in its usual heavy-handed way, unable to comprehend the depth of righteous outrage it faced. The incidents of intimidation that marked the November 5 election were preceded by others during the October voter registration. The most brutal incident was the assault by a policeman on Fusionist Arthur D. Allen, auditor of Belknap Hardware & Manufacturing Company. Knocked unconscious, Allen was arrested and dumped unattended in a jail cell. William R. Belknap's efforts to have Allen released or transferred to a hospital were rebuffed.

On election eve the bronze statue of Thomas Jefferson in front of the Court House witnessed one of the more raucous political assemblies in Louisville's history as the machine used every trick of disruption and intimidation at its command to break up a Fusionist rally. As the estimated crowd of 10,000 gathered to hear Fusionist candidates berate the Democrats, police with notebooks circulated through the throng, ostensibly taking names. A sudden avalanche of clanging trolley cars imperiously demanded the right of way through Jefferson Street, bell-ringing fire engines converged upon the Court House, and a crowd of machine cohorts added to the uproar with a barrage of catcalls from the windows of the Court House and City Hall. Despite the din, one Fusionist speaker after another thundered away at the machine.

Election day proved the Fusionists deadly accurate in their predictions of fraud. But probably even they had underestimated its unprecedented scale. The machine, fearful it would be doomed by anything approaching an honest election, outdid itself. In some precincts, if the official records were to be believed, the voters were so methodical that they presented themselves in exact alphabetical sequence. Ballot boxes were stuffed, stolen, or 'lost'. Many polls opened late, Fusionist precinct officers were threatened, voters intimidated, and election certificates forged. Even more astonishing was the

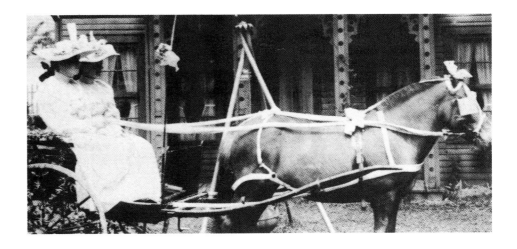

careless way in which the machine failed to disguise its crimes. Accustomed to arbitrary use of power and contemptuous of its Fusionist opponents, the machine did not vary its methods in the 1905 voting; it merely used them on a larger scale. The certified election results came as no real surprise. Paul C. Barth, Democratic candidate for mayor, moved into City Hall with a 4,826-vote lead over O'Neal.

There was, no doubt, much self-congratulation at the 'Buck' over the success of the election tactics. But the contest was not over. Fusionist leaders, stung by the defeat, determined to contest the vote results. With financial backing from a wide segment of the business community, and editorial support from the *Evening Post* and the Republican *Louisville Herald* (successor to the *Commercial*), a Committee of One Hundred was formed to press charges of election fraud. Attorneys William Marshall Bullitt, Helm Bruce, and Alexander G. Barret prepared the voluminous evidence for presentation to Jefferson Circuit Court. A year was required just to take depositions and not until December 1906 was the evidence presented in court. On March 23, 1907, the chancellors (Shackleford Miller and Samuel Kirby), although they conceded fraud, held that it did not affect the election result.

The reformers were not ready to surrender, however. The decision was immediately appealed and, with unaccustomed speed, the Kentucky Court of Appeals heard the case in April and delivered its four-to-two decision in May. The announcement was political dynamite. The election of November 1905 was declared invalid and *all* elected Democratic office-holders in both Louisville and Jefferson County were removed from office. Mayor Paul Barth, County Judge Charles Wilson, members of the City Council, the County sheriff, and on down the line—all were out. Never had the Whallen machine suffered such a humiliating defeat. Now it was up to Governor Beckham to replace the deposed politicos. His choice of mayor surprised everyone. It was Robert Worth Bingham, described by Henry Watterson as "an unorthodox Democrat."

Bingham, a native of North Carolina and educated at the University of Virginia, moved to Louisville, attended the University of Louisville Law School, and entered private practice. He had held only one public office— County attorney—when he was appointed mayor. Why did Governor Beckham choose this man? The rising tide of Prohibition sentiment in Kentucky probably played a major role in Bingham's selection. Though Prohibition, because of the bad name it received in practice, may "seem like a historical detour…an extraneous imposition on the main course of history," it was in the early Twentieth Century associated with reform and Progressivism. Certainly the male world of the saloon was seen as a divisive influence on family life. Saloons also were centers of strength for urban political machines, serving as command posts in the field.

"What happened! With a boldness un-paralleled even in the history of Louisville, hired robbers, the commonest type of manhood, went into your polling places, stole from the law's receptacle the ballots you had cast, and carried them away as so much junk."
Louisville Herald, *November 8, 1905*

Below: The traditional custom of having the highest local government official toss out the first ball to open each baseball season was faithfully observed in Louisville. Here Mayor William O. Head performs the ritual in 1912 at Eclipse Park, Seventh and Kentucky. Spectators arriving on Fourth Street trolleys reached the park through an alley shortcut still known as Baseball Alley.
Potter Collection,
U of L Photographic Archives

As County attorney, Bingham had made determined efforts to enforce the State law prohibiting Sunday opening, which saloons in Louisville and Jefferson County blithely and safely ignored. Though his efforts were blocked by the courts, his stand had won him the backing of Protestant ministers who fulminated against the practice. Too, many Louisvillians who had no sympathy with temperance found it difficult to condone the flouting of the State law. Bingham took office on Saturday, June 29, 1907. The following day thirsty Louisvillians could not find a single saloon open. Nor did they ever open on Sunday again.

Bingham was to serve only four months as mayor. (A special municipal election was set for November 1907 to choose permanent successors to the ousted Democratic officeholders.) Yet, in his brief tenure (July-October), he brought to Louisville the full scope of the Progressive doctrine of reform. His shake-up of the police started at the top, with Chief Sebastian Gunther replaced by J.H. Haager. His newly-appointed Board of Public Safety reduced most police officers in rank. Nearly fifty patrolmen and officers resigned after William Marshall Bullitt lodged charges against them of participating in election frauds.

The newly-appointed sheriff, Alexander Scott Bullitt, followed Bingham's lead by enforcing Sunday closing in the county, including the bars at popular Fontaine Ferry Park and its new rival, White City. (Both were in areas not annexed by Louisville until 1912.) In the city, Chief Haager vigorously attacked prostitution with periodic raids in the Green Street 'red light' district. Even the city's barbershops were closed on Sunday, though Bingham was unable to carry out the ministers' requests to close the theatres on that day.

As part of his busy few months in office, Bingham continued to investigate past political sins. The discovery that former Mayor Barth had retained a fine saddle horse, purchased with City funds, was aired at great length in the reform press. For Barth, described by the sympathetic *Courier-Journal* as a "sensitive man," the strain proved more than he could bear. On August 21, 1907, he took his own life in his Main Street office. The bullet that killed Barth also killed Bingham's chances for election to the post he held temporarily. By then the Republicans had already decided not to participate in a Fusionist ticket in November (perhaps because they felt the state ticket in this gubernatorial election year would be enhanced by a local slate), and Bingham, with no large base of support within a Democratic party still controlled by the machine, was unable to secure that party's nomination. But the Bingham administration, as its last act, assured a scrupulously fair election. On November 5, 1907, Louisville voters chose James F. Grinstead as the city's second Republican mayor by a comfortable 4,700-vote majority. Former Fusionist Augustus E. Willson became Kentucky's second Republican governor.

The Republican withdrawal from cooperation with independent Democrats signaled the end of inter-party reform politics in Louisville. The Grinstead administration, though honest, did not attempt any major changes, but did launch an investigation of slum housing. The Whallen machine nursed its wounds and waited for 1909. (Grinstead served only two years, completing Barth's term.) The Democrats, meanwhile, had picked an issue calculated to divert attention from vote fraud at the same time that it provided a weapon to undermine Republican gains. The issue was simple: blatant racism. It also was successful.

By 1910 Louisville's blacks numbered slightly over 40,000, or 18% of the population, compared to 15,000, or 14.8%, in 1870, five years after the end of slavery. As the black population increased, Negro neighborhoods grew in area, although low incomes and informal segregation policies prevented the kind of scattering that marked white housing patterns. The black neighborhoods, instead, simply pressed against and gradually took over portions of older white neighborhoods. By 1910 the black ghettoes had pushed north of

Right: Without access to public parks, black youngsters depended upon white philanthropy for a few small play plots, such as this one on Roselane near Hancock in Smoketown. It was a project of the Presbyterian Committee on Colored Evangelization, headed by the Rev. John Little. The narrow space was located between Hancock Street Presbyterian Church at right and a saloon at left. The site is now within the Sheppard Square public housing project.
U of L Historic Archives

Below: When Walter N. Haldeman (pictured here), a towering figure in Louisville journalism and politics since the 1840s died in 1902, his son Bruce became president of the corporation which published the Courier-Journal *and* Times. *Bruce, together with his brother, William, who edited the* Times, *used the newspapers to implement the Democratic party's use of racism to win the 1909 local elections.*
History of the Ohio Falls Cities and Their Counties, 1882

Broadway on both the east and west sides of the central business district. The Negro community had also developed its own social strata, the top level being educators, ministers, attorneys, and physicians, who generally chose the area west of downtown to live. Here they occupied the larger houses on Walnut and Chestnut streets that had once been the homes of well-to-do whites.

Despite its growth in numbers and the relative success of a few blacks, Louisville's Negro community was afforded fewer opportunities in the Twentieth Century than it had enjoyed previously. This tightening of the color line was part of a nationwide trend. The gains made after the Civil War had been diminished by the Supreme Court decision in 1883, wiping out most provisions of the Civil Rights Act of 1875, and by the 1896 "separate but equal" doctrine. (In Kentucky, railroad cars were legally segregated in 1891, while the Day Law of 1904 imposed legal segregation in higher educational facilities.) These retrogressive steps helped create a movement for race pride and civic betterment among urban blacks throughout the South. The first Louisville expression of this movement was the Negro Outlook Committee formed in the early 1900s. In one of its early successes, it forced removal of a police patrolman for being "too free with the use of the billet." This rather tame militancy of an awakening black consciousness provided the background for the racist campaign of John Whallen's handpicked 1909 candidate for mayor, tobacco-warehouse owner William O. Head.

Ironically, this tactic came at a time when Louisville's black population growth was slowing even more than that of the white majority. From 1900 to 1910 the black increase was only 3.5% (during the next ten years, the black population would show an actual decrease). But, playing on white fears of Negro 'domination', the Haldeman papers served up stories designed to alarm white voters. "Negroes Swarm Registration...Encouraged by Hope of Dominating City," read a typical headline. The Grinstead administration, like its

Above: Merchant tailor and Whallen protegé Matt J. Winn was a member of the group that purchased financially troubled Churchill Downs in 1902. Though he is remembered today as the man who made the Kentucky Derby the nation's premier Thoroughbred race, he was noted earlier as the father of a large number of daughters.
Kentuckians as We See Them: By Louisville Newspaper Cartoonists, 1905

Matt Winn and the Derby
The group that purchased Churchill Downs in 1902 made Matt Winn general manager. In 1903 the track showed a profit. Winn then set about promoting the Derby through publicity and by luring the best Thoroughbreds.

"In the years before America entered World War I, the Derby was blessed by …events that greatly enhanced its image: Donerail won the 1913 Derby, paying a record $182.90 for a $2 bet; Old Rosebud broke the track record in winning the 1914 Derby; and Harry Payne Whitney's Regret became the first (and only) filly to win the Derby in 1915.

"Winn made certain that these events received maximum coverage, especially Whitney's statement that 'this is the greatest race in America at the present time, and I don't care whether she [Regret] ever starts again….'

"From then on, the Derby's prestige, purse and crowds grew steadily, thanks to Winn's constant prodding. He established his off-season headquarters in New York City, all the better to chum around with Damon Runyon, Grantland Rice, Bill Corum and the other sportswriters whose bylines were known from coast to coast."
Courier-Journal, July 19, 1976

predecessor, insured an honest election and was defeated by over 2,000 votes. Robert W. Bingham, the unorthodox Democrat, viewed the election as the return to power of "the old corrupt and vicious Democratic ring."

With the Whallens back in power and race as a continuing issue, the Democrats also won the 1913 election, which pitted the machine against the forces of reform in a new and unexpected alliance, the Progressive or 'Bull Moose' party. This political meteor summed up in itself the middle-class fear of what it saw as a threat to individual enterprise. Progressivism distrusted big corporations and 'big' politics (exemplified in the political machine) as corrosive of individual freedom and its counterpart, the competitive system. The new party took form in 1912 when Theodore Roosevelt bolted the Republican party, creating the Progressive party as the vehicle for his own candidacy. Drawing Republican strength, the new political grouping was a major factor in the Democratic victory that put Woodrow Wilson in the White House in 1912.

Still a potent force in 1913, the party in Louisville reawakened the moral fervor that had animated the Fusionists in 1905. With self-made small businessman Wood F. Axton, head of Axton-Fisher Tobacco Company, as candidate for mayor, the Progressives soaked up Republican votes like a sponge. Axton, a personal friend of Roosevelt and Kentucky state chairman for his 1912 presidential bid, attacked the Whallen machine as the "invisible government" and the incarnation of all evil. Fearing monopolies, the Progressives had attacked the formation of the Louisville Gas & Electric Company earlier in 1913 (a merger of two rival electric power companies and two rival gas companies) as a concrete example of threat to competition. The merger, they charged, was made with the connivance of the Democratic administration, thus demonstrating the connection between urban machines and big corporations. Even the *Herald* deserted the Republican standard to back the Progressives and the party's platform, one plank of which called for "the saving and improvement of the riverfront for the use of the people…." It was a moral crusade that made a remarkable showing. Axton received 20,399 votes to Democrat Dr. John Buschemeyer's 24,944. Republican George T. Wood mustered only 1,388 votes, revealing plainly whence came the Progressive strength—and where it would return.

Buschemeyer's administration proved to be the low point in black-white relations in Louisville, with the passage in 1914 of the City's first attempt to legalize what had been informal (and, hence, incomplete) residential segregation of the races. Designed to stop "the gradual influx of the negro into blocks or squares where none but whites reside," the ordinance forbade blacks from occupying housing in any predominantly white block. In an apparent bow to "separate but equal," it also forbade the reverse. Despite the efforts of black leaders such as William H. Steward, Dr. Charles H. Parrish, C.B. Allen, and Albert E. Meyzeek, the ordinance was passed unanimously by both the Board of Aldermen and the City Council and signed by Mayor Buschemeyer on May 11, 1914. The Republican *Herald* attempted to ignore the issue while the *Courier-Journal* remained neutral, though the *Times* (edited by Walter N. Haldeman's son, William) and the *Evening Post* supported the law.

Black leaders were not to let the ordinance go unchallenged, however. The first consequence of the new law was the formation of the Louisville chapter of the National Association for the Advancement of Colored People (NAACP). The new group moved quickly to set up a test case with the cooperation of a friendly white real estate agent, Charles Buchanan, who also opposed the ordinance. Black editor William Warley purchased from Buchanan a lot in Portland with the stated purpose of erecting a house in a predominantly white block. Buchanan then filed suit in Jefferson Circuit Court, charging Warley had violated the law. This was an unanticipated test of the ordinance by a white man.

After the legislation was upheld by both the Jefferson Circuit Court
(December 24, 1914) and the Kentucky Court of Appeals (June 18, 1915), the
case was taken by the NAACP to the United States Supreme Court. On
November 5, 1917, the Supreme Court in a unanimous decision declared the
ordinance unconstitutional because it interfered with property rights. Inter-
estingly, the newest member of this court was former Louisvillian Louis D.
Brandeis. Nominated by President Woodrow Wilson in 1916, Brandeis had
been confirmed despite stiff opposition based on his Jewish background and
his reputation as a zealous reformer. With the overturn of the ordinance,
Louisville's black community, with the aid of the NAACP, had won a victory
with nationwide implications. The decision was later cited as a precedent in
overturning housing segregation ordinances in other cities.

Shortly after he became the City's chief executive in 1909, Mayor William
O. Head was the principal speaker at a meeting of the Associated Charities of
Louisville, successor to the Charity Organization of the 1880's. "It is the city
which has created the greatest problems of the world today, and it is the city
which must answer the needs for which it is responsible," he declared, sounding suspiciously like a Progressive. "In the country it may be possible for a
family to remain a separate entity," he continued, "but not in the city. We are
inter-dependent on each other."

The words seem a mockery in light of his party's divisive use of racism.
Nevertheless, Head addressed a real issue the city faced, and one that
affected black residents most: slum housing. The departure from center city
of both the wealthy and the middle-class opened the way for older housing
stock to be converted to tenements crowded with those at the bottom of the
social heap. It was not an overnight phenomenon. It had proceeded far
enough in some areas by the 1880's (East Jefferson Street, for example) to
spur the founding of missions and the first kindergartens. By 1900 one-third
of Louisville families lived in tenements. The early social workers (including
the volunteer women from 'better families') who dealt with the problem
came to realize that social uplift could make little headway until the physical
conditions of life were improved.

It was first-hand contact with living conditions among low-income
Louisvillians that prompted Alice Hegan to write her first and phenomenally
successful novel, Mrs. Wiggs of the Cabbage Patch, published in 1901. She
had, she said, "discovered the proletariat" through her service as a volunteer
worker at a mission Sunday School and was captivated by the "romance
about them." In 1917 Alice Hegan (by then married to poet Cale Young Rice)
produced Calvary Alley, frank "propaganda...written at fever heat," to call
attention to the evils of slum housing. The difference between city and far
suburb (or, at least, the way the difference was perceived) was pointed out by
another local novelist, Annie Fellows Johnston. In contrast to Mrs. Wiggs, an

Right: The original Kentucky & Indiana Railroad Bridge between Portland and New Albany was replaced by the present span in 1912. Here a Monon Railroad passenger train enters Louisville on the old 1886 bridge while the replacement span is under construction alongside. The Pennsylvania Railroad also replaced the Fourteenth Street bridge of 1870, Louisville's first river crossing, in 1916-18.
Author's collection

Below: The heart of downtown moved south during the early years of the Twentieth Century. This 1910 view, seen as if from "a balloon over the Mary Anderson Theatre," shows each building in the area, which was alive with people at night. A count made one evening between 5 p.m. and 11 p.m. showed 13,559 pedestrians in the block between Walnut and Chestnut, another 6,397 in street-cars, and 930 in other vehicles.
Chained Lightning, March 10, 1910

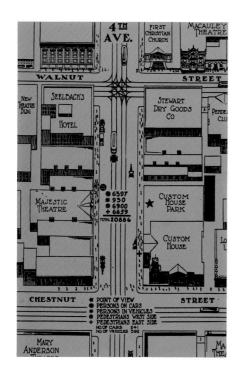

adult woman whose wisdom was gained from a hard urban life, Mrs. Johnston produced *The Little Colonel*, young, fresh, and sweet, living in wondrous, secluded Pewee Valley (called Lloydsboro Valley). The *Little Colonel* series were among the first (perhaps *the* first) novels devoted to upper-income suburban life as opposed to the old duality of city and farm.

By the time *Calvary Alley* appeared, the tenement situation in Louisville had already been called forcefully to public attention. In 1908 Associated Charities enlisted the aid of the elite Woman's Club of Louisville (formed in 1890 as a social activist group) to investigate slum housing. Concluding, after a preliminary study, that nothing could be done without stricter municipal regulations, the two groups convinced Mayor James F. Grinstead of the need. As a result, the Tenement House Commission was formed in early 1909 and prepared a report before the end of the year. Janet Kemp of Boston, commissioned to make the survey, found Louisville's tenements far different from the massive, purpose-built structures to which she was accustomed.

Commenting on the rows of old two- and three-story brick dwellings on East Jefferson, she said that "it is hard to realize they are tenements." Yet these buildings housed up to eight families where once Louisville's pre-Civil War German immigrants lived one family to a house. West of the central business district, where Irish immigrants once held sway, the name of Bug Alley, north of Main Street, "graphically suggests the local conditions and standards," she reported.

Lack of adequate water (often one hydrant in a courtyard was the single supply), "overflowing" open privies, entire families crowded into "one gloomy room," prostitution, drugs, pigs and poultry, all combined to reproduce on a small scale the tenements of the large East Coast cities. Miss Kemp found the tenement population to be a varied lot: blacks and native-born

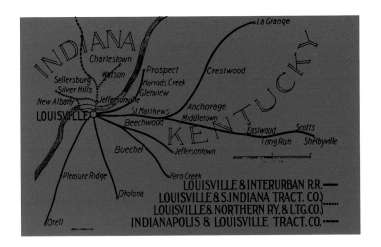

whites, plus recent immigrants from Ireland, Germany, and Russia. Along Brook Street between Main and Walnut was a "Syrian [Lebanese] Colony." The worst housing was occupied by blacks, some of it built as tenements. The 'Tin House' east of downtown contained thirty-seven rooms and housed thirty-one black families, even with two rooms vacant. One group missing from the tenements, Miss Kemp found, was "the aristocracy of labor—the specialized and well-paid mechanic or artisan...." The Nineteenth Century shotgun cottage had provided alternate housing for them. Though Grinstead was defeated in his 1909 re-election bid before action could be taken on the report, the Tenement House Commission's proposed model housing law was approved by the State legislature in 1910 during Mayor Head's administration and incorporated into the City Charter. Slum housing remained dismal at best, but a remedy had been supplied for the worst abuses.

The changing economic environment of the new century also brought change to Louisville's industrial scene. The rise of the large corporation that attempted to dominate production in a given field actually started in the Nineteenth Century. Louisville's first experience with the new order came in 1891 in the important tobacco products industry. A year earlier North Carolina native James Buchanan Duke had formed the American Tobacco Company with the intention of absorbing as many of the important tobacco manufacturers as possible. That included the Louisville firm of Pfingst, Doerhoefer & Company, producer of plug chewing tobacco, acquired in early 1891 for $1.8 million. The long-established Southwestern Agricultural Works, controlled by the Brennan family, was taken over in 1900 by the American Seeding Machine Company. By 1906 Dennis Long & Company was linked with former competitors as part of the multiplant United States Cast Iron Pipe & Foundry Company.

Nabbing errant motorists
"Following the recommendation of [Police Chief] Col. H. Watson Lindsay, your Board recently purchased two motorcycles for use by plain clothes men in the apprehension of 'speeders.' So satisfactory has been the results of the use of these, that a marked improvement in handling automobiles and motorcycles in public streets has been noted by many of our citizens."
City of Louisville Annual Reports for 1913

Such industrial concentration, allowing the stabilization of profits through reduction of competition, worked only when the stronger producers in any given field were involved. Smaller firms, whose output was of little concern to the new giants, were left to fend for themselves. Many long-established, locally owned Louisville industries found it impossible to survive under the new conditions. Papermaking and leather tanning, for instance, disappeared from the local scene. In at least one case, however, the situation was reversed. The Ahrens & Ott Manufacturing Company, founded in 1885 by Theodore Ahrens, Sr., and Henry Ott to produce plumbing fittings (including enamel-ware basins and bathtubs in 1893), took the lead in forming the new Standard Sanitary Manufacturing Company of 1900. Ahrens, an 1858 German immigrant to Louisville, served as president of the new company, which consolidated nine other plumbing fixture manufacturers in various parts of the country with the Louisville firm. Economic changes also brought new kinds of industry to Louisville, each newcomer usually a plant of an out-of-town corporation. With the market for automobiles constantly increasing, the Ford Motor Company (which had been piecing together about twelve Model T's a day in a small shop at Third and Breckinridge) in 1914 purchased a plot of ground at Third and Eastern Parkway. Here it erected a large, three-story automobile assembly plant, opened in 1916.

The preoccupation with politics, reform, and urban problems that marked the early years of the Twentieth Century tend to obscure the physical advances of the period. Even 'machine' politics, seen as the great evil by its contemporary critics, carried out projects of lasting value to the city. The Louisville Free Public Library, successor to the old Polytechnic Society of the 1870s, moved in July 1908 into an imposing new building, facing York between Third and Fourth streets. It was built with a $250,000 gift from the Andrew Carnegie Foundation and $60,000 in City funds to acquire and clear the site. The occasional success of the black community's demands for better civic services was also demonstrated in 1908 when the new building of the Western Colored Library at Tenth and Chestnut was completed. It replaced a make-shift facility opened in 1906, the first public library south of the Ohio River for blacks.

Public health, always a concern to the middle class of the Progressive Era, made a giant advance with the completion of the Louisville Water Company's Crescent Hill filtration plant in 1909 that finally eliminated the Ohio River mud, a colorful ingredient of the city's water ever since the utility began service in 1860. Because of the sediment, many Louisvillians did not use the water for drinking, but only for bathing, indoor toilets, laundry, and lawn sprinkling. (Public bath houses were provided for low-income individuals.) After the city was provided with "the luxury of a supply of perfectly clear, wholesome water," usage leaped upward, increasing by more than 395

Above: Driving was an adventure when these two unidentified Louisville women set out in an early-model Ford equipped with acetylene lights and a bulb horn, but sans windshield. The determined driver wears a duster to protect her clothing from the hazards of unpaved roads.
Filson Club

Above right: The Ford Motor Company assembly plant, opened January 2, 1916, at Third and Eastern Parkway, was an example of a trend toward straight-forward functionalism in industrial structures that forecasted similar simplification in other building types. Purchased by Reynolds Metals Company, the plant turned out aluminum airplane parts during World War II. Reynolds later gave the building to the University of Louisville.
Caufield & Shook Collection,
U of L Photographic Archives

Next page: This remarkable view westward along Market Street as seen from the tower in the former Louisville Trust Company Building at Fifth Street was painted about 1910 by Michael Reichert, who evidently executed it to advertise his skills. The new fifteen-story Lincoln Savings Bank Building, then Louisville's tallest, dominates the scene at Fourth and Market, flanked by the 1901 Todd Building. The familiar Levy Brothers clothing store is at Third; beyond at Second is the clock tower of the German Insurance Bank (which later became Liberty National Bank & Trust Company). Louisville's first high-rise, the ten-story Columbia Building erected in 1888-89, thrusts up at left from Fourth and Main. In the distance a train crosses the Big Four Bridge and beyond lies Butchertown.

million gallons annually from 1909 to 1915. At the same time the old corner pumps, which the citizens of the 1850s insisted on retaining, were finally removed as health hazards. By 1913 the City Health Department reported that typhoid fever was decreasing because of water filtration and the reduction in the number of pumps.

Health concerns also led to the building of a new City Hospital to replace the antiquated structure dating from 1870 (and incorporating the original Louisville Marine Hospital of the 1820s). The new building, opened in 1914 on the Chestnut Street site of the original, was termed the "Million Dollar Hospital." Part of the reason for the high cost was revealed by architect Dennis X. Murphy (who had taken over the office of Henry Whitestone). He noted that because of the "color problem" practically all facilities had to be duplicated.

Another public facility demanding attention during the years before World War I was the University of Louisville. After the brave start during the 1830s, the University had become a municipal orphan. With no City funding, the medical and law schools functioned, in fact, as private institutions without endowment and dependent entirely upon tuition fees. Though curriculum improvements kept the schools somewhat abreast of current higher education practice, neither fulfilled the high hopes of their founding days. The Law Department depended upon prominent Louisville attorneys to conduct classes, while the Medical Department suffered from the competition of numerous private schools of varying quality that sprang up in the city. (These institutions also made it difficult for the Medical Department to raise its academic standards, since it would lose even more students to the competing schools.)

But, with the stiffening of national standards for accreditation which threatened the standing of all the local schools, a solution was imperative. Finally, in 1906, negotiations began for the merger of three medical schools with the University of Louisville. Though this was a tremendous advance, it solved only part of the problem. The new standards required pre-medical training in chemistry, biology, and other sciences for would-be physicians. With no academic unit, the University was unable to provide such instruction. So it was that early in 1907 the trustees authorized establishment of an Academic Department (today's College of Arts & Sciences). Still without municipal funding (despite broad hints from the trustees), the Academic Department relied on private funds solicited in the community and on a part-time faculty. This Founders' Fund was barely sufficient to keep the department afloat.

While the University struggled with its academic and financial problems, a bombshell—the Flexner report—was exploded that turned out to be the impetus required to start the institution on a stable course. Abraham Flexner, born in Louisville in 1866, was a product of the intellectual interests

Above: The Seelbach Hotel, opened in 1905, was a significant factor in transforming Fourth and Walnut into the crossroads of downtown Louisville. This photograph of about 1925 shows the corner altered by the display windows of a Walgreen drugstore. The Seelbach boasted the city's first roof garden while its basement Rathskeller was finished in tiles from the famed Rookwood Pottery of Cincinnati.
Author's collection

Right: This was the new 1911 quarters at 554 South Fourth of Jennie Benedict's famous confectionery, which had been located a block farther north since 1900. The soda fountain and tea room (at rear) were favorite relaxation spots for downtown shoppers. Miss Benedict created a favorite Louisville sandwich filling called benedictine: cream cheese with green coloring and a cool cucumber flavor.
Potter Collection,
U of L Photographic Archives

that abounded in the city's Jewish community. Educated at Johns Hopkins University, young Flexner began teaching at Male High School in 1886, later opening his own private school. When he joined the Carnegie Foundation for the Advancement of Teaching in 1908, his first assignment was to prepare a study of deficiencies of medical education in the United States. His report, which spared no institution, was published in 1910. It marked a turning point in the schooling of American physicians.

One of the schools feeling the sting of Flexner's lash was his hometown's University of Louisville. Pointing out that the private medical schools so recently absorbed had been "money-making in spirit and object," he found that little had been done to upgrade standards. Some students were admitted who had less than two years of high school. The new Academic Department, with its part-time staff and lack of proper funding, was dismissed by Flexner as perhaps a "people's institute," but certainly not the academic department of a university. The University's basic problem, of course, was lack of funding, a shortcoming that Flexner's report forced the municipality finally to face. Under the administration of Mayor Head, annual appropriations were begun and in 1914 the University's newly elected president, Arthur Y. Ford, became the first to spend sufficient time at the task to warrant a salary. With renewed attention to Louisville's academic stepchild came renewed hopes for a major university. The planning that began before World War I would bear fruit in the 1920s.

While government struggled with accumulated urban problems, private investment continued to change the face of the city. In downtown Louisville, the heart of a metropolitan complex that now included New Albany and Jeffersonville firmly in its orbit, office buildings climbed higher as rising land values dictated more intensive use of space. The Lincoln Savings Bank

The Flexner Report
"The University of Louisville has a large scattered plant, unequal to the strain which numbers put upon it. In the old days, Louisville, with a half dozen regular schools, was a popular medical center, to which crude boys thronged from planta-tions. The schools offered little beyond didactic teaching. Now they have been arithmetically added together; the result-ing school is indeed superior on the lab-oratory side to any of its component parts; but…classes are unmanageably huge; the laboratories overcrowded and undermanned; clinical facilities, meagre at best…."
Medical Education in the United States and Canada, 1910

Building of 1907, on the northwest corner of Fourth and Market, reached upward fifteen stories; five years later the Starks Building, replacing the First Christian Church on the northeast corner of Fourth and Walnut, rose sixteen stories; in 1913 a new record of nineteen stories was set by the Kentucky Mutual Home Life Building on the northeast corner of Fifth and Jefferson. Accompanying the upward reach was a commercial movement southward on Fourth Street, which emerged as the dominant shopping thoroughfare, to the dismay of Market Street merchants.

Most imposing of the new Fourth Street structures was the Seelbach Hotel, opened in 1905 on the southwest corner of Fourth and Walnut. Erected by brothers Louis and Otto Seelbach, it replaced their original Seelbach Hotel at Sixth and Main (which they renamed Old Inn). The Seelbachs were members of the German immigrant community that proved so valuable to Louisville and their hostelry brought a new standard of hotel-keeping to the city. Lavish in its appointments (it boasted the city's first roof garden) and located in the new direction of commercial growth, the Seelbach was an immediate success. It was, in fact, one magnet that helped make Fourth and Walnut the new 'crossroads' and busiest intersection in down-town Louisville. (Stewart's built its new department store across from the Seelbach in 1907.)

Apartment buildings, pioneered by the Rossmore in 1894, also became a familiar part of the city scene. By 1912 Louisville counted 138, most in or near downtown, and ranging from modest 'bachelor' quarters to the luxurious Weissinger-Gaulbert complex at Third and Broadway. The L&N Railroad, too, added to the city's heightening skyline with its new Ninth and Broadway office building, a modern, steel-framed substitute for Whitestone's elegant Second and Main building of 1877.

New theatres, too, were part of the urban changes. The Schubert

Above: The five-cent admission charged by such early motion-picture theatres as the Star at 226 South Fourth, gave rise to the name 'nickelodeon.'
Caufield & Shook Collection,
U of L Photographic Archives

Charming, carefree Louisville
Elliot Paul, probably best known for his post-World War II novel The Last Time I Saw Paris, *spent part of his teen years (1909-10) in Louisville. For the young Bostonian, away from home for the first time and imbued with youth's unfolding awareness, Louisville always remained a special memory.*

"Louisville, before the World Wars, was one of the most charming and carefree communities, north or south, in this country or abroad....

"[Newcomers] soon learned they were in a city where personal eccentricities were accepted as normal, but civic, quasi-public and other institutions conformed to no rigid pattern and displayed, along with their charming informality, an originality that was characteristic. For instance, because of the indolent ineptness and gentlemanly corruption of the city government, Louisville had two rival telephone systems [merged in 1925], both flourishing and as inextricably tangled as two daddylonglegs in one demitasse....

"Many people in Louisville then had views about the right or wrong of the situation and more than once I noticed that hostesses deftly changed the subject when guests brought up the question, in order not to probe old scars or start sleeping dogs barking."
My Old Kentucky Home, *1949*

Masonic Theatre (later the Strand) opened in the new Masonic Building, on Chestnut between Third and Fourth. The new building replaced the venerable (1852) Masonic Temple at Fourth and Jefferson, destroyed by fire in 1903. The old Liederkranz Hall at 123 West Market was transformed into the Hopkins Theatre, while the Mary Anderson, named for Louisville's own contribution to the international stage, came on the scene in 1907. Because the 'movie' was still in its early crude stage, a kind of cheap novelty fit only for the nickelodeon, all of these playhouses were designed for live actors on stage. But that was soon to change (largely through the work of moviemaker and former Louisvillian David Wark Griffith), and in 1909 the Hopkins switched to motion pictures and claimed to be the largest cinema in the United States. The new medium scored an even greater triumph in 1912 when the Majestic, Louisville's first elegant theatre built expressly for motion pictures, opened on Fourth Street near Chestnut. By 1913 the Mary Anderson admitted the motion picture, and the Schubert Masonic and others soon followed, usually alternating a movie-vaudeville mix with legitimate live drama. Even Macauley's capitulated, but only for occasional outstanding films such as D.W. Griffith's "Birth of a Nation" in 1916 and "Intolerance" in 1917.

While Louisville basked in its changing Twentieth Century cityscape, it also watched many Nineteenth Century institutions and personages fade from view. On December 3, 1913, John Whallen, who had run the Democratic machine and the Buckingham Theatre with an iron hand for over thirty years, died less than a month after his final political victory: Dr. John H. Buschemeyer's win over Progressive Wood F. Axton. It was a timely death that spared the old warhorse the shock of witnessing the long string of Republican victories that followed 1917. With John's death, his brother Jim seemed to lose interest in continuing the Whallen tradition. Michael ('Mickey') Brennan, party stalwart and 'Portland Irish', soon emerged as the new Democratic chief. In 1917 Jim sold the 'Buck', and the new owners renamed it the Savoy. Other familiar names vanished, too. By the time the Whallens faded from view, the du Ponts were a community memory. Bachelor Alfred Victor ('Uncle Fred') du Pont had died in 1893 shortly after the opening of DuPont Manual Training High School, his gift to Louisville. Soon after, when Bidermann du Pont retired to his native Wilmington, a move was initiated to acquire Central Park for public use. A City bond issue permitted purchase of the seventeen-acre tract in 1904.

Other hallowed Louisville locales did not fare so well as Central Park. The wharf, once the veritable heartbeat of Louisville commerce, still welcomed a few steamboats to its granite-paved expanse, but they were mere remnants of the vast traffic that had once kept the riverfront in a perpetual uproar. Passengers and freight now went by railroad, with but few crumbs left for the steamers. There were only two departures and arrivals daily of the veteran Louisville & Cincinnati Packet Company, plus the Louisville & Henderson Packet Company's downriver traffic. These two routes survived mainly to serve the tiny river hamlets the railroads bypassed. But even this trade was precarious. On December 31, 1906, the Henderson line carried its last mail. "In the last few years rural [postal] routes have been established to reach most of the small river towns," the *Courier-Journal* noted. The Cincinnati packets had lost their mail contract even earlier. The transshipment trade around the Falls had ended with the opening of the enlarged Portland Canal in the 1870s. What through freight was left (half of it coal) sailed past Louisville in barge tows. By 1917, with the sudden ending of the coal trade, Ohio River tonnage reached its lowest point since the end of the Civil War.

In the summer months excursion steamers still livened the wharf, drumming up trade with calliope concerts, while the Jeffersonville ferry created a flurry of activity with each arrival and departure. Yet even the ferry

service was in financial trouble by early 1907, a little over a year after electric trolleys began operation across the Big Four Bridge to the Indiana city. Up on Main Street, the now somewhat shopworn Galt House of 1869, built near the river on the reasonable premise that the packets would always supply guests for the high-ceilinged rooms, was threatening to close by 1911. It was rescued by Jacob Greenberg, who attempted to breathe new life into the beloved Louisville institution, but First and Main was no longer the proper location for a quality hotel. In 1919 the Galt House locked its doors.

While many vestiges of the colorful Nineteenth Century were passing away to a new life as part of Louisville's collective memory, the city's business community wrestled with the new problems of the Twentieth Century. The shock of the 1910 census figures produced a slow realization that, indeed, something was wrong. The Louisville of the 1880s had learned that the days of automatic growth and prosperity born of the river monopoly had vanished. The Louisville of 1910 had painfully to relearn that lesson. When it did, the business community initiated action to come to grips with the problem. The Louisville Convention & Publicity League was formed in 1910 as one way to promote the city. In 1916 an even more positive step was taken by the

Right: The latest in early Twentieth-Century kitchen design was provided in the prestigious Weissinger-Gaulbert Apartments at Third and Broadway. Though spartan and poorly lighted by today's standards, the kitchens provided such features as gas ranges, hand-operated meat grinders, and (not shown) separate entrances for grocery deliveries and fans to carry away heat and cooking odors. The most-appreciated feature, however, was the automatic, ice-making refrigerator placed in the large walk-in pantry.
The Weissinger-Gaulbert Apartments, 1912

Jazz as it was
Whether jazz came 'up the river from New Orleans' or by a more devious route, it had arrived in Louisville by 1909 when Elliot Paul discovered it in its primeval lair, a 'sporting house' at Seventh and Market. "Whatever else I remember about Louisville, my most poignant recollections have to do with hearing…jazz," he wrote. It was piano jazz, played by a black musician….

"The devil knows what Al was thinking about when he was playing. His finely shaped expressive eyes had a far-away look, and often he would moan an obligatto….In contemplative movements, he spun thin wires of tone, a treble and a bass that formed a moving outline, and at times called for a middle voice that formed a blue chord, or a square major equally surprising. The tune he had chosen…he called the 'Black Snake Blues'.…Asked later to repeat a few measures, he would repeat others just as good. He never grasped the fact that 'classical' musicians played a piece the same way, over and over again, as far as the notes were concerned."
My Old Kentucky Home, 1949

Louisville Board of Trade: the launching of the Million Dollar Factory Fund. The concept took form quietly about 1913, grew in stature as it was discussed by business leaders, then burst forth with evangelistic fervor in July 1916. (Significantly, that was the same month the rather staid Board of Trade began publication of its *Board of Trade Journal*.)

The goal was to raise $1 million to expand the city's industrial base through aid to new manufacturers, as well as to help existing plants expand production and market outreach. The Factory Fund was a frank recognition of the "sluggishness that exists in Louisville's industrial progress." In a whirlwind eleven-day campaign ending July 28 the goal was reached. The volunteer fund raisers "seemed to be obsessed with the feeling that the future of the city was in their hands," the *Board of Trade Journal* reported. The contributions were made as purchases of stock in the non-profit Louisville Industrial Foundation, which was formally organized in December 1916. The Foundation was set up not only to make medium-term loans to promising industrial firms that might have difficulty securing bank credit, but also to inventory Louisville's industrial resources and serve as a point of current information on land and plant availability, utility services, transportation, and all the specific information that large industries were beginning to demand in making site choices.

Louisville now for the first time possessed a professional organization to promote the city industrially and to lure new plants and jobs. It was a giant step forward in the search for the Twentieth Century. Only two months after the Foundation was formed, it announced that through its efforts three Virginia brothers, owners of a small cleaning-powder manufacturing firm, were moving operations to Louisville and would occupy a vacant factory. The company was the Reynolds Corporation. Within a few years the little manufacturer was expanding mightily as the aluminum-producing Reynolds Metals Corporation.

But while Louisville mended its economic fences, it suddenly faced a new and totally different situation. The three Reynolds brothers had scarcely announced plans to move to Louisville when a different kind of news pre-empted attention. The United States entered World War I. Neither the nation nor Louisville would ever be quite the same again.

Chapter Twelve

"To Hell With the Hohenzollerns and the Hapsburgs"

Cornstalks into Camp Taylor
"Six months ago Jefferson County, Kentucky, contained within its borders the largest city in the state. Today it embraces the two largest and most important communities in Kentucky. One is Louisville and the other is Camp Zachary Taylor, one of the sixteen cantonments erected for the instruction of the nation's selected army.

"Of the two it is easily conceivable that Camp Zachary Taylor is the most important....It sprang out of the most arable soil in the vicinity of Louisville.... But today the cornstalks that waved over the hundreds of acres have been replaced by so many rifles..."
Camp Zachary Taylor Souvenir, *1918*

ntil 1917 only two American wars had profoundly affected Louisville: the American Revolution of its founding days and the soul-searing trauma of the Civil War. Other conflicts created excitement—the War of 1812, the Mexican War, the Spanish-American War—but their impact at the Falls of the Ohio was minimal. Now a European war came alive in Louisville with an outpouring of emotional involvement unknown since the dark days of the 1860s. The enthusiasm for war and the suspicion and sometimes outright hostility directed at Louisville's citizens of German descent would have surprised the city of 1912 could it have seen five years into the future.

In that earlier year Louisville and Jefferson County gave most of their votes to Democratic presidential candidate Woodrow Wilson, though Theodore Roosevelt, the Republican-turned-Progressive, ran a strong second. Between them, they captured 90% of the vote. Both men, moreover, were cast in the mold of the Progressive Era: both spokesmen of its optimism, of its belief that right-mindedness could solve all social and economic problems, and of its tacit assumption that right-mindedness resided principally in white, Anglo-Saxon, Protestant, middle-class America.

There were dissenters, of course. The conservatives (and the blacks) stayed with Republican William Howard Taft, who received 6.7% of the Louisville-Jefferson County vote in his bid for a second term. The more radical—2.9%—cast ballots for militant labor leader and Socialist presidential candidate Eugene V. Debs.

But the war that engulfed Europe in August 1914 was a deep shock to this hopeful America that wanted to believe in a world improving day-by-day as a result of enlightened attitudes. The guns of August mocked all such hopes. Soon divided American opinion mirrored the divisions within Europe.

In Louisville, although the tide of German and Irish immigrants of the 1850s had long been absorbed into the wider community life, both groups retained a strong sense of cultural identity, reinforced by ties of overseas kinship. Immigration into Louisville dropped sharply after the Civil War, but enough German and Irish newcomers arrived to freshen and help keep old ethnic loyalties alive. These loyalties tended to create pro-German sympathies among German-Americans and to reinforce anti-English feelings among Irish-Americans—attitudes that ran head-on into Watterson's own personal declaration of war against Germany and the Central Powers in 1914. Initially sharing the general American dismay at the idea of a European war, the 74-year-old Watterson within a month swung round to a bellicose anti-German position, to which German- and Irish-Americans quickly responded. The war of words began in Louisville on September 3, 1914, when Watterson first used the phrase that became a later American rallying cry: "To Hell with the Hohenzollerns and the Hapsburgs." The protests of some religious leaders against what they considered its profanity only stiffened Watterson's back; he used the phrase over and over.

This, coupled with Watterson's barbs against the German-Americans (whom he previously held in high esteem), led the Louisville German-American Alliance to a vigorous protest, backed by the Republican *Herald* and the *Kentucky Irish-American*. The *Herald* called Watterson's stand unfair, narrow-minded, and malicious. The *Irish-American* castigated the veteran editor for his "vile abuse" of both German- and Irish-Americans.

Watterson also found opposition within the *Courier-Journal*. Bruce Haldeman, who had become president of the company upon the death of his father, Walter N. Haldeman, in 1902, was disturbed at the result of German-American reaction to Watterson's belligerence: lost advertising and lost circulation. When Isaac Wolf Bernheim, who had presented Thomas Jefferson's statue to the community, complained about the newspaper's editorial stand, Bruce Haldeman forwarded the complaint to Watterson with a note. "Enclosed you will find a letter from one of your liquor friends, Mr. I.W.

Bernheim. I am not surprised....I sincerely trust you will suppress your inclination to indulge in any more abuse of the Germans."

Meanwhile, American public opinion generally was swinging to the side of England and France, although not toward participation in the war. Wilson, re-elected in 1916 on the slogan "He kept us out of the war," carried Louisville and Jefferson County with 28,840 votes, the slimmest of pluralities. Republican Charles Evans Hughes won 28,386 votes, and the Socialists, ideologically opposed to a capitalist war, tallied 1,193 votes, or 2% of the total. But by April 1917, only five months after the election, the United States was at war, ostensibly because of German submarine warfare and disregard of American rights. Yet, in a broader sense America's entry into the conflict can be interpreted as the ultimate—and, as it proved, fatal—crusade of the Progressive Era with the German Kaiser cast in the role of the last and most powerful political boss, whose overthrow would make things once more right throughout the world.

The war came closer in May when a German submarine torpedoed the four-masted sailing vessel *Dirigo*, owned by the Louisville wood products firm of C.C. Mengel & Brother, as it was on its way to Africa for a cargo of hardwoods. Then in early June came the news that the efforts of the Board of Trade to secure one of the new military training camps for Louisville had been successful. The city's location and transportation facilities made it the logical choice to assemble drafted and enlisted men from Kentucky, Indiana, and Illinois. Before the end of June, Camp Zachary Taylor (named for the Virginia-born president whose early years were spent in Jefferson County) began rising south of the new Audubon Park suburban development.

The military installation brought not only a boost to the Louisville-area economy, but some significant social changes, including the end of a Louisville institution hallowed by time, if by nothing else. The red light district, the Victorian way of handling prostitution by segregating it, came to an end at midnight, August 31, 1917. The Army, fearing that 'sporting houses' would interfere with its task of quickly turning raw recruits into soldiers, insisted that the district (centered on West Green street) be closed before Camp Taylor opened. The military camp received its first drafted men on September 5. By the end of November 28,000 recruits were learning the trade of war, while new arrivals came in by the trainload.

Louisville's enthusiasm for the great crusade for democracy grew by the week. Even the Socialists divided on the issue (as they did nationally), to Watterson's delight. When Charles S. Dobbs, "for a good many years banner bearer and perennial candidate of the local Socialists," left the party, then joined the Army as an artillery officer, he won Watterson's editorial praise. "The Socialists who continue agitation," the editor asserted, "prove their insincerity by their unwillingness to work for the betterment of mankind."

Above: For many a desk-bound man, the war offered an exciting change. Courier-Journal, August 28, 1917

The day of the military draft
"Among all the red letter days in history, yesterday will remain forever as the day the war came home to everybody.... War, the great leveller, made itself felt among high and low. The selective draft, the blind lottery, swung with a blind force and a fine, fateful impartiality which fell upon bootblacks and million-aires alike....

"William O. Seelbach, assistant man-ager of the Seelbach Hotel, was called to the colors. Louis Mahan, colored bell-boy at the Seelbach, was called....

"One man...stood at the corner of Third and Green streets and threw a large crowd into hysterics by shouting, 'God help the Germans—they've done drawed me.'"
Courier-Journal, July 21, 1917

Socialism also was suspect because so many German immigrants brought the ideology with them. Henry Fischer was one example. He had arrived in Louisville about 1892 from Germany and started a small wholesale meat firm in 1899, delivering his products himself in a horse-drawn wagon. By 1917 his Fischer Packing Company in Butchertown had become a well-known Louis-ville firm, its success based largely on the smoke-flavored, boneless, cooked ham he had perfected in 1909. But business success had not altered his political belief. He remained a member of the Socialist Labor Party, making no secret of his position: the war was a "capitalist scheme" for international markets and territorial expansion on the part of both sides.

In the upwelling of nationalist feelings that accompanied the war, such outspoken dissent made Fischer suspect, even a candidate for deportation. But his ideology, which insured good wages and good working conditions in his plant, also earned him friends among organized labor. When federal agents began investigating Fischer, two Louisville labor leaders intervened in his behalf. Patrick E. Gorman, president of the Louisville Trades and Labor Assembly, and Peter Campbell, secretary of the Kentucky State Federation of Labor, pleaded Fischer's case with American Federation of Labor President Samuel Gompers, whose influence apparently was successful. The investiga-tion was dropped.

Still, Henry Watterson worried in print about a possible uprising of German-American "Kaiserists," and Police Chief Ludlow F. Petty alluded darkly to certain unspecified events, which he attributed to "the hand of the

It was Camp Zachary Taylor
The Army followed Henry Watterson's suggestion in the Courier-Journal that its new Louisville training center be named Camp Zachary Taylor. Thereafter Watterson insisted that the newspaper use the full name of the camp, as Managing Editor Arthur Krock recalled.

"One day Mr. Watterson came down to his office and sent for the managing editor. 'I see the War Department,' he said, 'has adopted the Courier-Journal's suggestion to name our camp for Old Rough and Ready. If you ever let it get in the paper as Camp Taylor, I'll have your hide, hair and horns.' And on the one or two occasions when the slip was made, Marse Henry would put a huge ring around the passage and urge the managing editor to burn or slay the office wight that had thus offended."
Editorials of Henry Watterson, 1923

Hun." The greatest German threat Louisville and Jefferson County faced, however, proved to be only the "old Breckinridge place" on Taylorsville Road. It was owned by a genuine German baron serving as an officer in the Kaiser's military forces. Young Baron Konrad von Zedwitz, who had never been in Louisville nor in the United States, had become owner of the nearly 600 acres of farmland in a roundabout way through pioneer surveyor and settler John Floyd. After Floyd's death in a 1783 Indian ambush, his widow had married Alexander Breckinridge. In a later generation Mary Breckinridge Caldwell married the Baron von Zedwitz. In June 1918 their son, the young Baron von Zedwitz, turned twenty-one and inherited the Breckinridge estate, plus a considerable amount of downtown property. (Both his father and mother were dead.) The federal Alien Property Office, which kept track of such matters, immediately seized the "vast Boche estate." (In the early 1920s the seized farmland was turned into Seneca Park and Bowman Field.)

Some visible evidences of the strong role German immigrants had played in Louisville's development were scrubbed out. The German Security Bank became simply the Security Bank; the German Insurance Bank, the Liberty Insurance Bank; and the German Insurance Company, the Liberty Insurance Company. The financial institutions noted that "The time has passed when 'America' will be known as a nation composed of all nationalities. We are 'Americans' to the core...."

Louisvillians, meanwhile, contributed to the Red Cross, subscribed to Liberty loans (over $7 million in the first; $17 million in the fourth and final drive), bought war stamps, cultivated Liberty gardens, and faced manpower shortages. In the spring of 1918 Jefferson County farmers, blessed with a record wheat crop of some 16,000 acres, vainly sought help in the vast harvesting job. But overriding all other concerns was the anxious waiting for word of sons and husbands overseas. Sometimes the news was grim. In October 1918, less than a month before the Armistice that ended the fighting, editor Henry Watterson received word that his grandson and namesake, Henry Watterson, III, had been killed in action. Altogether, 350 local soldiers and three nurses died overseas.

That toll was miniscule, however, compared to the military deaths in Jefferson County itself. The first local hint of the ravaging Spanish influenza that swept across the nation in the fall of 1918 came in the form of rumors in September that the virulent 'flu' had broken out at Camp Taylor. The rumors appeared in print on September 20, but military authorities did not confirm them until five days later. By then it was obvious that the military post, housing nearly 60,000 recruits and veterans returned from France, faced a major epidemic. (The veterans were the likely source of the virus.) By the end of the first week in October fifteen barracks had been converted to hospital use. As the death toll reached thirty, forty, or more each day, Army

Above: Troop trains bound for East Coast ports of embarkation were a common sight in Louisville during the war years. In this 1918 scene at Union Station, Red Cross workers provide impromptu refreshments to soldiers on their way to do battle with the German Kaiser's military forces.
CSX Transportation

trucks "piled high with coffins" made frequent somber journeys to the railroad stations. Altogether, over 11,000 soldiers became ill and 1,500 died, a toll equal to the worst months on French battlefields.

At the height of the epidemic, military authorities asked Louisville physicians to "lend a hand," but their services also were urgently needed by the civilian population falling victim to the virus. In early October theatres, schools, and churches were closed, and all large gatherings discouraged. Though the influenza in Louisville was much less severe than in Camp Taylor, it was frightening enough. During October alone 6,415 cases were reported. Total civilian influenza deaths in Jefferson County during 1918 reached 879 (compared to forty-one in 1917), and deaths from tuberculosis and pneumonia also increased, probably as a result of flu attacks.

Meanwhile, the German government, facing internal revolt, plus a Western Front crumbling under Allied assaults, proposed an armistice while negotiations went forward toward a peace treaty. When the news was flashed across the United States in the early hours of Monday, November 11, all influenza precautions were forgotten. (Fortunately, the epidemic was on the wane.) Downtown Louisville streets became a bedlam of happy, flag-waving, singing, noisy crowds and impromptu parades. The *Courier-Journal* said it "exceeded any other exhibition of patriotism ever seen in Louisville."

The Louisville of 1918 that cheered the end of the bloodiest and costliest war the world had yet seen was a changed city from the one that had read with shock of the German invasion of Belgium in 1914. Its emotion spent, Louisville before long would wonder whether the sacrifice and fervor, the rows of crosses in Flanders and Cave Hill, had accomplished their purpose. A change in mood that has been described as the end of innocence seeped slowly through the United States, a mood that would set the dominant tone

Rather an understatement
"Louisville may expect important effects in its development in the future from the growing use of the automobile."
Board of Trade Journal, *October 1916*

of the 1920s, a mood to which Louisville was not immune. There were other changes, too, that gave a glimpse into the coming decade.

Automobiles had become so common that it was necessary to limit parking on downtown streets to sixty minutes. On York Street across from the Public Library an automobile 'service station' provided an off-the-street facility for dispensing gasoline. Muddy Eighteenth Street Road had become paved, two-lane Dixie Highway. The highway passed by a second new military post, Camp Henry Knox, in nearby Hardin County, set up for artillery practice. The government did not dispose of this property, as it did Camp Taylor. There were new industries (twenty in 1918 alone) that the energetic Louisville Industrial Foundation lured to the city. The Reynolds Corporation switched from producing cleaning powder to aluminum foil. As the industrial base broadened, labor unions grew stronger. And when the war ended there was a Republican mayor in City Hall and a new hand at the helm of the *Courier-Journal* and *Louisville Times.*

The election of Republican George Weissinger Smith as mayor in November 1917, only six months after American entry into the war, was perhaps a hint that, despite the outpouring of patriotic sentiment, many Louisvillians retained deep-seated reservations about the war. The Republicans, however, campaigned on the theme of corruption, charging that the Whallen machine openly protected gambling and prostitution. Paradoxically, it may have been the presence of Camp Taylor that gave the issue a special edge. When the Army demanded that the red light district be closed, one military officer asserted that in forty years of service he had "never seen a city anywhere in the world where vice is more open than it is in your city."

The glare of the spotlight on Green Street in the wake of the closing of the brothels created a demand by many residents and businesses along the street that its name be changed. (Only a short stretch had been in the red-light district, but the publicity affected the whole length of the thoroughfare.) The *Herald* aided the cause by asking readers to suggest a new name. Entries included Reformed, Pershing, and Liberty. The new Republican City Council responded on April 5, 1918, by choosing Liberty. At the same time the stretch east of Preston was renamed Fehr, honoring the brewery at Preston and Green.

While Louisville reacted with varied emotions to the war, the dynasty that had dominated Louisville journalism for a half century came to an end in 1918, itself a victim of internal tensions created both by the war and the spreading movement to prohibit liquor. The bond between Watterson and Bruce Haldeman, never very strong (Haldeman was twenty-two years' Watterson's junior), was weakened almost to the breaking point by disagreements between them over Watterson's editorial thrusts at the German-Americans.

The final break came, however, not on the issue of war, but prohibi-

tion, and actually began as a dispute between Bruce and his older brother, William, who edited the *Times*. Both Haldeman brothers, as well as Watterson, were strongly opposed to prohibition; the dispute between Bruce and William concerned editorial strategy for opposing its statewide adoption. Kentucky had already (in 1906) so strengthened its local-option law that it was impossible for part of a county to remain 'wet;' by 1915, 102 counties had banned liquor. Dry forces now were attempting to get a statewide law. When the Haldeman brothers disagreed in late 1916 on opposition tactics, Watterson's attempts at peace-making only created such a gulf between himself and Bruce that the venerable editor announced he would retire.

But it was not to be—not yet, though Watterson was now seventy-seven. Urged by William Haldeman and attorney Bennett H. Young, the other principals in the corporation, to remain as editor, Watterson was plunged squarely into a nasty fight for control that ended in the Kentucky Court of Appeals, where Bruce Haldeman lost. Watterson was elected president of the corporation, a post whose duties he did not relish. In addition, neither he nor William Haldeman (now sixty-one) had suitable heirs to serve as successors in editing and managing the two newspapers. Within a year both were anxious to find a buyer for the property.

That buyer was at hand: Robert Worth Bingham, whose brief tenure as mayor was followed by appointment to the bench of Jefferson Circuit Court in 1910 by Republican Governor Augustus E. Willson. Though Bingham had declined the suggestions of friends that he run for mayor in 1913 and 1917, he maintained a deep interest in Louisville and Kentucky political affairs. Ownership of the *Courier-Journal*, read throughout Kentucky, would enable him to exert a powerful political influence. Moreover, he had inherited $5 million from his second wife, Mary Lily Flagler Bingham, who died in 1917. On August 6, 1918, Bingham, now one of the wealthiest

Above: The aftermath of war: Cave Hill Cemetery on Memorial Day 1920.
Caufield & Shook Collection,
U of L Photographic Archives

men in Kentucky, became owner of the newspaper made famous by Watterson and with roots back to George D. Prentice. Bingham realized, as Bruce Haldeman had not, that Watterson's name was an important asset. The new owner suggested that the old journalist continue to contribute editorials on any subject he saw fit. Watterson gratefully accepted, choosing for himself the title "Editor Emeritus." At seventy-nine he still had something to say.

It was soon painfully apparent, however, that what he had to say did not coincide with what Robert Worth Bingham had to say about the League of Nations. Bingham's pre-war reform and progressive tendencies made him a supporter of the Wilsonian idealism embodied in the League. Watterson opposed the League. For some weeks the *Courier-Journal* presented the curious spectacle of editorials on both sides of the League issue. It could not continue, of course, and when it was suggested to Watterson that other topics might be more suitable for his pen, he finally cut all ties with his beloved newspaper in early 1919.

It was an anti-climatic end to an illustrious journalistic career. Yet, in a curious way, Watterson's isolationism (rooted in the deep past), paralleled the new American mood of wispy disillusionment. Watterson lived long enough (until December 1921) to see his editorial stand become majority opinion, but it put him in unfamiliar company. The vote that swept Republican Warren G. Harding into the White House in 1920 was a vote for "normalcy" and for rejection of American membership in the League. Louisville and Jefferson County voted enthusiastically for the new order. Unlike the post-Civil War years when Louisville avoided the American mainstream in an attempt to find a regional identity with the South, the city now agreed with the majority opinion that "The business of America is business." In the shocks of World War I and its aftermath, Louisville found the Twentieth Century. The search was over.

Chapter Thirteen

The 1920s: Everything Seemed Possible

Each time the auctioneer's hammer came down, another piece of Camp Zachary Taylor passed into private hands. With the war almost three years past this spring of 1921, the nearly 3,000 acres were sold in bits and pieces, the buildings one by one. Some of the smaller structures were carted away intact, the larger ones torn down for their lumber. The thought perhaps did not strike many Louisvillians, but the dismantling of this tangible reminder of the great conflict was paralleled by the simultaneous dismantling and transformation of much of the pre-war ethos. The Louisville of the 1920s faced a different world than the one left behind in 1914, and faced it with a vastly different set of expectations and attitudes.

A certain springy and perhaps naive sauciness had vanished through the years of war. The emphasis on Americanism and the desire to be free of European entanglements contributed their share to the paranoid fear that radical elements threatened the United States. In one of thirty-three simultaneous 1920 Palmer raids (set in motion by Attorney General A. Mitchell Palmer) across the nation, ten federal agents with drawn revolvers swept into Louisville's Socialist headquarters—Karl Marx Hall—on Jefferson Street. But they found no dangerous foreign Communists; only eighteen American Socialists. All were released after questioning.

Nevertheless, the raid—unthinkable before the war—highlighted the changes in mood that followed the conflict. A few months earlier famed German violinist Fritz Kreisler canceled a Louisville appearance when the *Courier-Journal* and the American Legion opposed it. Perhaps it was this mood that led Isaac Wolfe Bernheim in 1922 to present Louisville a statue (placed at the Public Library) of Abraham Lincoln, the president who wanted to heal wounds once the Civil War was over. In this time of confusing turmoil, the urban middle class, the progressive movement's greatest reservoir of strength, largely abandoned its concern with correcting social ills and settled down to enjoy prosperity. The old belief in action to solve social problems was turned on its head in the pervasive slogan of the 1920s: "Don't be a knocker; be a booster." In 1913 Progressive mayoral candidate Wood F. Axton had received 43% of the local vote. In 1924 Progressive presidential candidate Robert M. 'Fighting Bob' LaFollette could muster only 0.3%. The easy local victor was Republican Calvin Coolidge with 52.4% of the total.

Though it declined precipitously, progressivism left numerous national legacies, including direct election of senators, votes for women—and Prohibition. Banning the production and sale of alcoholic beverages was seen by most progressives as a forward step in the continued improvement of mankind, and they allied themselves with churchmen and temperance groups to achieve the goal. On January 16, 1920, the nation went officially dry, but had, in fact, entered that thirsty state July 1, 1919, as the result of an act passed during the war to conserve grain. Prohibition—the most sweeping economic and social change to which Louisville had to adjust after the war—meant more than closing the twelve breweries and upwards of thirty distilleries in the city and county; it also affected many other jobs, especially among cooperages, printing plants, and railroads. There was an estimated loss of 6,000 to 8,000 jobs in the Louisville area alone. The Louisville-based Kentucky Distilleries & Warehouse Company, a giant of the industry, sought to enjoin enforcement of the National Prohibition (Volstead) Act. But the Supreme Court turned down attorney William Marshall Bullitt's arguments, as well as those of numerous other challengers from across the nation, on June 7, 1920.

Once the legality of Prohibition was settled by the court decision, federal enforcement officials announced they would make Louisville "whiskey proof," a goal that was never reached despite vigorous enforcement. Frequent raids (eighty-three in one week alone) turned up stills in private homes, watered whiskey at newsstands, bottled beer, moonshine, and expensive imported liquors in various unlikely places. Most of the old familiar

Louisville brewing and distilling names vanished, but a few found strategies for survival. Oertel's Brewing Company developed a "cereal beverage" brewed with the legal limit of 0.5% alcohol and advertised it as a drink that provided "a pleasant memory." (Of real beer, no doubt.) Brown-Forman Distillers took advantage of a provision in the Volstead Act that permitted sale of whiskey on hand for medicinal purposes. Owsley Brown, son of Brown-Forman founder George Garvin Brown, secured one of only ten permits issued for such sales. The operation was successful enough that he later bought Bourbon stocks from former competitors to replenish his dwindling supply.

Medicinal sales enabled Brown-Forman and a handful of other distillers to ride out the thirteen-year drought, but such sales did not replace the jobs lost through Prohibition. Yet Louisville overcame this bad start to the decade and surged ahead during the 1920s, sharing the wave of prosperity that bathed the nation in a frenzy of growth enshrined in legend as the 'Roaring Twenties.' New and expanding industries provided the economic underpinning; industrial employment climbed from 29,902 in 1919 to 36,860 at the end of the decade. The consumption of electric power rose from 91.5 million kilowatt hours in 1920 to 297.6 million in 1930.

The automobile came into its own in the 1920s, clogging downtown streets as the number of registered motor vehicles in Jefferson County more than doubled, totaling 54,524 by 1930. With the automobile age came the first highway bridge across the Ohio and a new kind of suburb that dispensed with the rail-bound trolley car. Above all, the city expanded, resuming the kind of large-scale annexation not seen since the 1890s. As a result, Louisville's population grew magnificently: 31% during the decade, rising from 234,891 in 1920 to 307,745 in 1930. It was the kind of antidote the city needed after the disturbing years of war and a depressed growth rate of only 4.9% during that period. That low growth—an increase of only 10,963 between 1910 and 1920—was related to failure to annex the thriving developments beyond the City boundaries, and to the lure of well-paying war industries to the north, which drained away many workers, especially blacks. Louisville's black population, in fact, actually declined during the war decade, from 40,522 in 1910 to 40,087 in 1920.

The sudden reversal of this static economy during the 1920s produced a decade comparable only to the spurts of growth that marked the 1830s and the decade after the Civil War. The first sign of the superlatives that were to mark the period (and proof that the motion picture had fully come of age) was the Rialto Theatre on Fourth Street. A neighbor of the older Mary Anderson, the Rialto opened in the spring of 1921 as Louisville's first movie palace. Seating 3,500, boasting chandeliers of Czechoslovakian crystal, decorative wall tiles from the famed Rookwood Pottery in Cincinnati, a $30,000 pipe organ, a proscenium-arched stage for vaudeville, a grand staircase of marble, and other touches of elegance, the Rialto was undoubtedly the finest—certainly at $1 million the costliest—theatre in the city. The Macauley's Gilded Age splendor paled in comparison. The Rialto was not only an impressive theatre, but the signal that Fourth Street's burgeoning commercial development would push from Chestnut south to Broadway.

Less than three years later, in October 1923, the fifteen-story Brown Hotel opened at Fourth and Broadway, its 700 rooms making it the largest hostelry in the city. Its tone was set when David Lloyd-George, Britain's wartime prime minister, signed the register book as the first guest. With its spacious lobby, four restaurants, and numerous meeting rooms, this project of lumberman J. Graham Brown overshadowed the Seelbach. It became, in fact, the chief symbol of Louisville's self-confident image of itself in this brash new age of jazz, flappers, illegal 'hooch,' a soaring stock market, and seemingly limitless opportunities. As early as 1923 the *Herald* could pridefully announce

Below: The only legal alcoholic beverage during the years of Prohibition was a weak "near-beer" with only 0.5% alcohol. Nevertheless, it permitted some breweries to survive the dry spell. Oertel's called its product "Double Dark," and used advertising art to picture it as a substitute for liquor among the affluent. Courier-Journal, *June 2, 1920*

Top right: The $1-million Rialto Theatre, built in 1921 on the Fourth Street site of the antebellum Kaye home, was Louisville's most elaborate motion picture palace throughout most of the decade. This view looks north past the earlier Mary Anderson Theatre, the columned Post Office and Custom House at Chestnut, and the Seelbach Hotel at Walnut.
Author's collection

Bottom right: Loew's State Theatre of 1928, almost directly across the street from the Rialto, eclipsed its rival in both cost ($2.5 million) and grandeur. In contrast to the classic marble interior of the Rialto, Loew's exuded 'atmosphere.' This view of the lobby entrance, with the stairway at the right leading to the mezzanine and balconies, was the bedazzled moviegoer's first hint of the even greater opulence that lay beyond. The whole theatre was turned into an opulent stage setting where the real world was excluded.
Caufield & Shook Collection,
U of L Photographic Archives

Purple prose in St. Matthews
"The Pathway of Progress points eastwardly from the congested center of the crowded City. The thousands toiling at the treadmill of Trade turn their eyes to the rising sun and see a vision of green grass and shady trees, where children play; and there is escape from the dirt and din of downtown crowded apartments.

"Such is charming Chenoweth Place in St. Matthews...a spot for flower bordered lawns and growing gardens... but within fifteen minutes of the heart of the City."
Advertising brochure, about 1928

175

Above: James Graham Brown, born in 1881 in Madison, Indiana, upriver from Louisville, came to the larger city around the turn of the century and, in 1903, opened a lumber business with his older brother, Martin. From then on, Graham Brown was identified with the city by the Falls. As the lumber operations expanded (logging vast tracts of southern timber), Brown turned his attention to investment and building in Louisville. He also used his wealth to benefit his adopted city in other ways, aiding the University of Louisville and making possible the building of the Red Cross Blood Bank and the Zoological Garden, among many other civic endeavors. At his death in 1969, he left almost his entire estate of nearly $100 million to the James Graham Brown Foundation, which continues its founder's philanthropy.
Louisville Free Public Library

that expenditures planned for new downtown buildings totaled $15 million. Nor did the pace slacken. In 1927 *Forbes* magazine surveyed Louisville and found that "There is an awful lot of riveting." As the city shed its old orientation as an outpost of the Confederacy, the *Times* declared that Louisville was "now a typical American city."

As in earlier periods of rapid development, old landmarks fell before the onslaughts of the new builders. Solger's Confectionery, dispensing superb delicacies since the 1870s, made way for the Brown Hotel. Macauley's Theatre, which had maintained itself as Louisville's premier playhouse since its opening day in 1873, vanished in 1925 to make way for an expansion of the Starks Building. On Main Street, the Galt House, standing forlorn since its 1919 closing, was mercifully dispatched in 1921, replaced by the massive new headquarters and wholesale warehouse of Belknap Hardware & Manufacturing Company.

The loss of Macauley's inspired J. Graham Brown, Louisville's outstanding builder of the decade, to provide a replacement. No sooner was the impending demise of the venerable Macauley's announced than Brown changed the plan of his new Brown Medical Building (next to his Brown Hotel) to include the Brown Theatre. Seating 1,500, the Brown was opened October 5, 1925, for stage productions only. Mary Anderson, in retirement in England, sent a letter of congratulation, recalling that it had been a half-century since she made her debut at Macauley's at the age of seventeen. Though new construction peppered the entire downtown area, most was on the southern fringe, especially around the "magic corner" of Fourth and Broadway. J. Graham Brown moved again in 1926 with plans for the Martin Brown Building (now Commonwealth Building) on the northwest corner of that intersection. The following year William R. Heyburn, president of Belknap Hardware & Manufacturing Company, began construction of his seventeen-story Heyburn Building on the southeast corner.

The building boom produced not only a lot of riveting on Fourth Street, but a quantum leap in traffic, not the best of conditions for patients in ancient St. Joseph's Infirmary, which had occupied a site midway between Chestnut and Broadway since the 1850s. This, plus the fact that the old building was far too small for the demands of an increasing patient load and modern medical technology, prompted the Sisters of Charity of Nazareth to replace the old institution with an immense new St. Joseph's on Eastern Parkway at Preston Street. Opened in 1926 with 325 rooms, it was the city's largest and finest hospital. The sale of the Fourth Street property was a case history of the decade's hyperactive real-estate market. In 1924 the Sisters were offered $650,000 for the old site. Advised by a real-estate expert to wait, the Sisters sold the site two years later for $1.25 million.

Replacing old St. Joseph's was the city's newest theatre—the apex of the motion-picture palace in Louisville. Loew's State was not simply a theatre: it was an adventure. The Fourth Street exterior, based loosely on Spanish Baroque design, was intriguing, but only a hint of the 'atmospheric' fantasy land inside. Statuary and castles stood silhouetted against a magical orange and blue glow; overhead the ceiling was transformed into a moonlit night sky with scudding clouds, twinkling stars, and even flying birds. The Rialto had cost $1 million at the beginning of the decade; Loew's cost $2.5 million. When it opened on September 1, 1928, Loew's opulent unreality matched the unreality of the decade's financial euphoria.

The automobiles that thronged downtown streets descended daily on the central core from the far reaches of the city and beyond. As the streetcar had earlier shaped the urban area, the automobile now began slowly to impose its own logic of development. In 1920 the trolleys had carried eighty million passengers; by 1925 that total declined by nearly eleven million fares. Yet there were more people downtown than ever before. A large number obvi-

ously arrived by the motor cars that searched for parking spaces and waited impatiently at intersections where traffic police attempted to avert total chaos. But the 1920s were not prescient enough to see that every new car on the streets was a sign of future trouble for downtown (and for the public transit that had built it). The motor cars, which could go anywhere, came downtown simply because the stores, the best restaurants, the first-run movies, and the offices were there.

The Louisville Railway Company saw the problem as involving chiefly the numerous 'jitney' buses that began siphoning away passengers as early as 1915. The elimination of this haphazard competition (accomplished by a new franchise in 1928), plus bus routes to subdivisions in areas not served directly by streetcars, would solve the problem, transit officials thought. The company put its first buses into service in 1923. In an optimistic 1924 assessment, the company declared that "The increasing difficulties in finding suitable parking space...together with cost of operation, we believe, are gradually discouraging the use of automobiles by private owners." Yet, inexplicably, it seemed, the new bus routes carried few passengers. Traffic on some short trolley routes, such as Brook, Seventh, and Fifteenth streets, serving only the inner-city, dropped drastically during the 1920s, an indicator of population decline in the older sections. Between 1910 and 1930 nearly the entire area bounded by the Ohio River and Broadway, and Tenth and Wenzel streets lost well over 25% of its population, and the loss also extended south of Broadway to Kentucky Street.

Out on the city's fringes, where the population was increasing and where most of the downtown-bound automobiles began and ended their daily jaunts, development during the 1920s matched the downtown pace. Institutions other than St. Joseph's Infirmary also found it desirable to move outward, including the Southern Baptist Theological Seminary. By the early

Listening to the radio
Radio introduced a new element into home entertainment in the 1920s. WHAS, Louisville's first radio station, began broadcasting July 18, 1922. This sampling of programs on the station's sixth anniversary reveals that news had not yet become a staple electronic item. Broadcasting did not begin until noon. Except for two National Broadcasting Company programs, the Philco Hour at 7 p.m. and the National Light Opera Company at 8:30 p.m., all programming was local.

"12   P.M.— Kentucky Hotel
                 Orchestra.
"12:25 P.M.— Brown Hotel Orchestra.
"12:50 P.M.— Livestock quotations
                 from…Bourbon
                 Stockyards.
"1   P.M.— Weather forecasts; river
                 stages; police bulletins.
"1:07 P.M.— Selected Courier-Journal,
                 Louisville Times editorials.
"1:25 P.M.— Instrumental Quartette….
"2   P.M.— Organ recital…Christ
                 Church Cathedral
                 organ.
"2:30 P.M.— Closing New York Stock
                 Exchange quotations….
"2:45 P.M.— Louis Mathieu, pianist.
"3   P.M.— Saw solos: William W.
                 Francisco.
                 [Music dominated the
                 programming until]
"11:30 P.M.— Playette: Marion Wells
                 and Lester Vail of the
                 Brown Players, with
                 orchestra background."

Courier-Journal, July 18, 1928

1920s it was the world's largest seminary, with an average enrollment of 421, and cramped for space at Fifth and Broadway. In 1921 an old Lexington Road estate, the Beeches, was purchased; by 1926 the Seminary's new $3-million home, built in the popular Georgian Revival style, was completed on its sweeping campus. Not far to the east, in the St. Matthews area, potato-raising was still the chief activity. But to the south, on the old von Zedwitz estate along Taylorsville Road, a new sound could be heard.

In 1919 Louisville aviation enthusiast A.H. Bowman leased from the federal government fifty acres of the seized property, cut the weeds, erected a rather ramshackle wooden hangar, and called the site an airport. Daring Louisvillians took short flights in Bowman's second-hand Canadian JN-4 ('Jenny'). But Bowman, who operated a local hauling company, was not at the controls. The man who brought the air age permanently to Louisville never learned to fly. Bowman's belief in aviation was rewarded in 1922 when the Army took over his lease, then in 1923 named the 'airdrome' Bowman Field. As the possibilities of commercial aviation became apparent, the Board of Trade pushed for municipal ownership of the field, a goal accomplished in 1927. In that year voter approval of a parks bond issue provided funds for purchase of the entire von Zedwitz property for $750,000. The major portion of the purchase became Seneca Park, the rest Bowman Field. In 1928 the Louisville & Jefferson County Air Board was created to administer the airport.

Even before the Air Board was created, an attempt had been made to provide commercial air service. The open-cockpit biplanes that Cincinnati's Embry-Riddle Company operated between Cleveland and Louisville could carry two passengers or 600 pounds of freight on each flight. The service was started with suitable ceremony when the company's entire fleet of six planes arrived in Louisville from Cincinnati on May 18, 1927, after a flight of two hours and twenty-five minutes. But despite the enthusiastic hopes of aviation boosters, the service to Cleveland proved premature. Four months later the planes stopped flying; only 109 passengers and 360 pounds of freight had been carried in that time.

Pioneer aviation, plagued by lack of financing and small-capacity planes, needed an assured cargo to make service feasible. There was only one source for such a dependable load: a contract to carry mail. The United States Post Office Department had been experimenting with such service (at extra charge) for some years and by the middle 1920s was ready to award contracts for a network reaching important cities. Continental Air Lines (predecessor of American Airlines) won the contract for the Cleveland-Louisville link and began service August 1, 1928. The following year a passenger terminal and paved runways were completed at Bowman Field.

The wood, wire, and fabric planes that attracted crowds of Sunday watchers to Bowman Field (park benches were installed to accommodate

How to get to Anchorage

Early automobile owners found pleasure trips marred not only by bad roads, but by lack of direction signs. The Louisville Automobile Club helped solve the problem with booklets containing precise directions to certain points. All mileages are from Fourth and Broadway. We pick up the directions at Grinstead Drive and Lexington Road, mile 3.8.

" 3.8 *End of road [Grinstead Drive] at large brick storehouse. Turn right up-grade.*

" 4.9 *Avoid road [Stilz Avenue] to left.*

" 5.1 *Pass Sacred Heart Academy on left.*

" 6.2 *Cross trolley and turn right along same.*

" 6.3 **St. Matthews.** *Bank on left. Straight through.*

" 8.2 *Turn left [onto Lyndon Lane] with double line of trolley.*

" 9.3 **Lyndon.** *Station on right. Straight through.*

" 9.7 *End of road at R.R. Turn right, shortly crossing same.*

"10.4 *Ky. Military Institute on left.*

"12.8 **Lakeland.** *Station on right. Straight through along R.R.*

"13.2 *X. R.R.*

"13.3 *Go under R.R. bridge.*

"13.6 **Anchorage."**

Automobile Tour Book, 1921

them) trailed clouds of glamour each time they lifted into the sky. But another form of transportation, more mundane, was far more important at the time. The intercity motor bus came onto the scene almost unannounced, but by 1925 fourteen different lines operated between Louisville and such points as Lexington, Indianapolis, Evansville, and Nashville. That year a long-distance bus service was inaugurated between Louisville and Jacksonville, Florida: it operated weekly, carried twenty passengers, and took four days (with stops overnight). J. Graham Brown noted these still-crude vehicles lumbering noisily through the streets to four separate bus stations that could be consolidated. In mid-1925 his Brown Hotel became the single station.

Brown's sense that intercity bus transportation would increase in importance was quickly borne out. By 1928 buses made 104 arrivals and departures daily from Louisville, more than could be comfortably accommodated at curbside in front of the Brown Hotel. Brown himself, however, had already moved to solve this problem by leasing the vacated site of the Southern Baptist Theological Seminary and building a station there. On April 11, 1928, his Louisville Union Bus Depot opened. On part of the site he erected the Brown Garage, recognizing the fact that many hotel patrons were arriving by automobile.

Despite planes, buses, and automobiles, the passenger train remained the conveyance of first choice all through the 1920s, though the spread of paved highways cut into the passenger total. In contrast to the 104 buses arriving and departing daily, the passenger train figure was 114, each train equivalent to many buses. For long-distance travel, the passenger train reigned supreme and was more luxurious than ever. In 1921 the L&N had inaugurated the *Pan American* from Cincinnati to New Orleans as the flagship of its fleet, and in 1925 upgraded it to an all-Pullman train. Leaving Louisville at a half hour past noon each day, the *Pan* put its passengers into New Orleans at 9 o'clock the next morning. On the way they enjoyed such luxuries as valet and maid service, showers, and club car equipped for radio reception.

Though the motor truck began making its first tentative appearance in intercity freight service, the railroad also remained the premier freight carrier of the nation. The L&N's system-wide freight tonnage rose from forty-seven million tons in 1920 to 63.8 million tons in 1928. To expedite this increasing volume new facilities were required, including a giant switching yard in Louisville, built on the extreme western acreage of former Camp Zachary Taylor. Officially it was called Mapother Yard (to honor recently deceased L&N president Wible L. Mapother), but was universally known as Strawberry, a reminder of what had been the chief farming activity in the vicinity. The need for the new facility reflected Louisville's expanding industrial output.

From 1923 to 1927 alone the city gained 153 new manufacturing plants, many through the efforts of the Louisville Industrial Foundation. As in

Top right: In 1925 Ford Motor Company replaced its Third and Eastern Parkway assembly plant with this new facility at 140 South Western Parkway and stretching back to the Ohio River. The new plant still produced Henry Ford's ubiquitous Model T in its first years, then switched to the replacement Model A.
Louisville Area Chamber of Commerce

Bottom right: Foundry workers preparing molds for casting stopped work in October 1920 to pose for this photograph. The scene may be at the Vogt Brothers Manufacturing Company at Fourteenth and Main.
Caufield & Shook Collection,
U of L Photographic Archives

Below: The Kentucky Wagon Manufacturing Company, whose sprawling factory complex was almost directly across the street from the Ford Motor Company assembly plant at Third and Eastern Parkway, also manufactured automobiles for a few years. The Dixie Flyer, made from about 1916 to 1924, was a four-cylinder car that sold for about $1,000. Earlier the firm had manufactured a battery-powered truck called the Urban Electric.
Doe-Anderson Advertising Agency

earlier periods, the new industries were a diversified group, ranging from the manufacture of scales for food markets to trailers for the new trucking industry. Furniture manufacturing continued to be important, but woodworking also moved into new fields. The Wood-Mosaic Company produced fine hardwood and inlaid flooring, while the Mengel Body Company employed more than 1,000 workers turning out the components for automobile bodies, still at the time framed of wood.

The automobile was also responsible for other new industries. As early as 1919 two gasoline refineries were in operation along the river near South Western Parkway. The Aetna Oil Company and the locally owned Stoll Oil Company each processed about 500 barrels of Kentucky-produced crude oil each day, receiving the petroleum by barge. In that same year Standard Oil Company completed a refinery capable of processing 2,000 barrels each day. In early 1925 the Ford Motor Company opened a new plant at 1400 South Western Parkway, replacing the plant at Third and Eastern Parkway, erected only a decade earlier.

Local inventiveness was the basis of several important Louisville industries founded during the 1920s, including American Air Filter (AAF) and the Girdler Corporation. AAF's roots date to about 1921 when William M. Reed sought a way to keep dust from settling on newly painted cars in his automobile repair shop. The filters he developed found a local market and led him to form Reed Air Filter Company, which combined with four other small manufacturers to form AAF in 1925 with Reed as president. The Louisville-headquartered company soon fabricated more sophisticated systems for industrial dust control, ventilating, and air handling, becoming a world leader in design and production of such devices.

The Girdler Corporation, formed at the very end of the decade in June 1929, gathered under one umbrella the results of research and develop-

The automobile suburb

In 1929 the developers of a new subdivision west of Bardstown Road near Doup's Point published a promotional brochure, Homelawn In "The Highlands." *The copy stressed the new mobility of the automobile era.*

"'We have room here for a sun room and a sleeping porch!'

"'And the vegetable garden can be right back here!'

"'Can I feed the chickens, Daddy?'

"'Can I plant any flowers I want to, Mother?'

"Mr. and Mrs. Brown, two modern and intelligent young people, have just bought a fine large home site on the edge of town and are planning the home they're going to build....

"The Browns are typical of an American family that has fallen in step with the Own Your Own Home Movement and the pronounced trend toward building in the suburbs and on the edge of town in this day of good roads and almost universal ownership of automobiles."

ment of earlier years. Founder Walter H. Girdler was not an inventor, but an entrepreneur with an eye for promising technological developments. He had formed Tube Turns, Inc., as licensee for a European-designed method of making curved pipe fittings that could be welded in place. He also had formed another company that sponsored successful research for extracting helium from natural gas and became the only commercial producer of the rare gaseous element. The Girdler Corporation also took over the manufacture of the Votator, a product of Louisville inventor Clarence W. Vogt. The Votator, designed initially to make ice cream, also found wide application throughout the food processing industry.

By the time the post-war industrial expansion was in full surge, the City had completed the largest single expansion of territory in its history. In 1922 Louisville annexed some eleven square miles of territory and added about 40,000 residents. The move insured that the lion's share of industrial growth and residential construction during the decade was within the City boundaries. The newly added territory extended from the Lexington Road area on the east to the Ohio River on the west. But the greatest increase of population came from the old South End streetcar suburbs. Churchill Downs and Iroquois Park were both now within the city. Newly enlarged, the City set to work on other pressing municipal matters, including planning and zoning.

Louisville, like other American cities during the Nineteenth Century, simply grew. Despite sporadic attempts to segregate some less desirable activities (for example, the early exclusion of butchering and leather tanning from the heart of the community), there was no attempt to designate specific uses for privately owned land. Industries, residences, stores, and other uses built up in a patchwork pattern, especially in the older parts of the city. The move for more orderly urban development in Louisville was spearheaded by architect

Right: Though Fourth and Broadway was "the magic corner," Fourth and Walnut was the busiest. This parade of automobiles kept the traffic officer at the intersection busy throughout the day. Signals had not yet been installed to control the constant flow of vehicles and pedestrians. The view, made about 1925, looks north toward Liberty.
Caufield & Shook Collection,
U of L Photographic Archives

A catalogue of discrimination

The Commission on Interracial Coopera-tion, founded after World War I with support from both southern whites and blacks, sought to develop better rela-tions between the races while carefully avoiding attacks on segregation. The Commission's Kentucky branch, based in Louisville, was headed by James Bond, a native black Kentuckian and 1892 graduate of Berea. In the following letter to the editor he catalogued dis-criminatory practices in Louisville in the 1920s.

"For instance, there is the University of Louisville, for the maintenance of which negroes are taxed without any provision for the higher education of negroes by the city; the unsatisfactory arrangement at the City Hospital; the unjust distribution of public funds as applied to swimming pools and play-grounds for colored children; the con-stant complaint and protest at the treat-ment of colored people by the Louisville police and the neglect on the part of the police of sections wholly occupied by negroes; in the failure of the city to make provision for a colored physician and colored nurses in the Waverly Hill Tuberculosis Sanitorium, etc....

"Everybody knows, of course, that the money for these interracial adjustments can be found."
Courier-Journal, *May 11, 1924*

James C. Murphy, who began his campaign in 1901 with the Engineers & Architects Club as his forum. Support grew all through the pre-war years, in-cluding backing from such influential groups as the Women's City Club and the Louisville Real Estate Board.

The concept of planning and zoning was congenial to the pre-war Progressive Era, based as it was on two important tenets of progressivism: scientific management and replacement of *laissez-faire* by the use of govern-ment power to achieve what were regarded as socially desirable ends. The fact that the move toward planning and zoning continued strongly into the post-war decade argues that, although the moral fervor of progressivism had evaporated in the heat of war, some of its goals had not. Under the Republi-can administrations that controlled Louisville during the 1920s the City sought planning and zoning authority from the State. The first act, adopted by the General Assembly in 1922, was "worthless" in the view of Mayor Huston Quin, since it authorized an advisory commission only. Quin refused to appoint commission members and the law was repealed. Attempts to secure stronger legislation failed in the 1924 General Assembly and again in 1926 and 1928.

Meanwhile, the proliferating automobile made more urgent than ever the need for a city development plan, plus zoning restrictions. Long lines of impatient motorists waiting for passing trains underscored the need for a comprehensive plan to eliminate street-level railroad crossings, while the incursion of gasoline stations into residential areas caused laments from homeowners. Irritated by the failure of the General Assembly to act, the City moved on its own, establishing a Planning Commission with zoning powers in 1927. James C. Murphy, who had pioneered the concept, was fittingly named its first chairman. Though without the broad powers sought from the State (the City could only attempt to maintain existing usages), the new

Commission won some local victories. Its legal authority was upheld by the courts after it halted construction in 1927 of a gasoline station at Third and Woodlawn in Beechmont.

Success in gaining broad planning and zoning powers from the State was finally achieved in 1930, a year after the City had contracted with the St. Louis city-planning firm of Harland Bartholomew & Associates to develop a comprehensive planning blueprint. Not surprisingly, the first priority was streets and traffic flow. But there were larger goals. The *Herald-Post* summed them up: the plan would be the first step of the "hope to rebuild the city." To the 1920s, everything seemed possible.

While some Louisvillians dreamed of a city rebuilt, others dreamed of a university to match. By 1920 enrollment in the University of Louisville's College of Arts & Sciences had reached 615, proof of the demand for higher education, a demand exceeding the limited facilities of the old Miller mansion on Broadway. The University had no building funds, but did own a campus site in the Highlands, a 1916 gift of the Belknap family. Optimistic hopes of building a modern educational plant were dashed, however, when a $1-million bond issue was turned down by voters in 1920. The voting pattern showed clearly what had happened. Blacks refused to tax themselves to build a university they could not attend and those votes made the crucial difference.

The rejection of the bond issue demonstrated not only the political power that blacks could wield, but also the vulnerability of a municipal university prevented both by State law and white community sentiment from admitting black students. Casting about for a solution, University trustees seized an opportunity in 1924 to purchase the grounds of the Industrial School of Reform, which had moved from Third Street to a new location at

Above: The elegance of the Gilded Age was preserved when Nazareth College (now Spalding University) was opened in 1920 in the former Tompkins/Buchanan mansion of 1871 at 851 South Fourth Street. This is a view of the drawing room used by the Catholic women's college for dances and receptions. Spalding is now a coeducational institution.
Louisville Free Public Library

Above right: This group of women was attending class at Central Colored High School in July 1920. They may have been school teachers attending summer sessions to increase classroom skills.
Caufield & Shook Collection,
U of L Photographic Archives

Ormsby Village in eastern Jefferson County. To finance the purchase, the University sold the Highlands property for $95,000 (it had cost the Belknaps $35,000), and was forced to borrow another $150,000. But the new site, named Belknap Campus to commemorate the Belknap gift, came equipped with buildings that could be adapted to educational use. A gift in 1925 from the son and daughter of James Breckinridge Speed was utilized to found the Speed Scientific School.

The move to Belknap Campus in 1925 coincided with a second drive for passage of a $1-million University bond issue. This time City officials and University trustees, to forestall the fate of the 1920 effort, conferred with black leaders before the proposal was announced publicly. It was agreed that $100,000 would be set aside to provide higher-education facilities for blacks. On November 4, 1925, the bond issue was approved overwhelmingly. Improvements at Belknap Campus began almost immediately and a new Administration Building, modeled on the University of Virginia Library designed by Thomas Jefferson, was completed in 1928.

Not until 1931, however, was the black college opened, after the project was actively pursued by Dr. Raymond A. Kent, who became University of Louisville president in 1929. The question of location, one of the problems that had delayed establishment, finally was solved in an unexpected way when the Simmons University campus became available. Simmons, founded in 1879 by the General Association of Colored Baptists in Kentucky as State University, served as an important institution of higher education for blacks from all parts of Kentucky. It was later renamed Simmons to honor Dr. W.J. Simmons, who began his long tenure as president in 1880. In the middle-1920s the school, then headed by Dr. Charles H. Parrish, Sr., began an over-ambitious building program on the Seventh and Kentucky streets campus. The resulting financial difficulty prompted the institution's trustees

Above: The dedication of the Municipal Bridge across the Ohio River at Second Street on October 31, 1929, brought out a huge crowd.
Caufield & Shook Collection,
U of L Photographic Archives

Top right: Mayor William B. Harrison, who arranged the financing plan for the bridge, views the completed span from one of the ferry boats it replaced.
Courier-Journal, October 20, 1929

Bottom right: Before the bridge was built, vehicular traffic crowded onto the ferries, as in this 1921 scene. The last ferry trip was made on December 31, 1929.
Caufield & Shook Collection,
U of L Photographic Archives

to sell most of the campus property in 1930 to the University of Louisville, which transformed it into Louisville Municipal College.

Developments in higher education were not confined to the University of Louisville. Nazareth (now Spalding) College, a Catholic institution for women, opened in 1920 in the former Tompkins/Buchanan mansion at 851 South Fourth near Breckinridge. Founded by the Sisters of Charity of Nazareth, the college was that religious order's recognition of the changing role of women. With the goal of preparing women for "participation in social, public, and political life," it enrolled seven students in its first class. By the 1925-26 school year enrollment had reached 160.

The Ohio River, where Louisville had its beginnings, loomed importantly in public projects, too. As cross-river automobile traffic to Jeffersonville soared, the slow and inconvenient ferry service became a bottleneck and, to Louisville 'boosters,' an anachronism of another era. In the automotive age they wanted their city to be on the main line of highway communication. Just as in the railroad age, that meant a bridge. (Cross-river rail traffic also increased, requiring replacement of the original Fourteenth Street Bridge in 1916-18 and of the Big Four Bridge in 1928-29.)

The first move for a vehicular bridge, spearheaded by Board of Trade President Frederic M. Sackett (later a United States senator), began in 1923. The Board's Bridge Committee initiated engineering studies and presented a highly favorable report to Mayor Quin on January 1, 1924. At the same time public sentiment for a new span was building because of the "high" 30-cent toll charged on the K&I Bridge. Though Quin and the City Council enthusiastically endorsed the idea, the knotty question of money was of concern to many Louisville taxpayers. The initial proposal for a free bridge, financed by a bond issue to be paid through taxes, was rejected in 1926. A revised pro-

Above: The Falls of the Ohio were transformed into a bare expanse of rock when the new dam and hydroelectric plant were completed in 1927. The course of the Indiana Chute is marked by a pool of still water. When the river was high, however, the rushing water topped the dam and flowed its old accustomed route.
Louisville Gas & Electric Company

Louisville: Gateway to the North
"Louisville, when she started her boosting, employed the slogan 'Gateway to the South.' She still employs it, but more and more she is now using 'Premier Industrial Location' instead.

"For Louisville, still sentimentally attached to the South, has discovered that modern industry…is not a matter of geography.…

"A gateway, moreover, can not be open in the one direction without being open in the other. Louisville is finding herself equally a gateway to the North, and her prosperity is all tied up with prosperity in every other section."
Forbes, August 15, 1927

posal, calling for bridge tolls to aid in retiring the bond issue, was defeated in 1927.

Finally, the impasse was solved during the administration of Mayor William B. Harrison by a new departure in financing public projects. A securities firm agreed to purchase the $5 million in bonds, which would not be an obligation of the City, but depend entirely on tolls for repayment. Construction of the bridge, which crossed the river at Second Street, began in June 1928 and was completed in less than a year and a half. On opening day, November 1, 1929, the *Times* counted traffic during the first hour and reported that seventy-two cars had paid the 35-cent toll.

To Louisville of 1929 that was a remarkable total, enough to bring an end to the ferry service. On December 31, 1929, the last of what the company proudly called its "big steel steamers" came to the Louisville wharf and put out its fires, a casualty of the automobile age. The trolley to Jeffersonville followed suit.

The Louisville Municipal Bridge was a notable achievement, but the Ohio River it crossed was the scene of even more remarkable engineering changes. By 1929 the long-range plan to create a year-round minimum river depth of nine feet had been completed. Designed to make the river navigable in all seasons, the minimum depth was achieved through a series of dams and locks the entire length of the waterway from Pittsburgh to Cairo.

The canalization of a river with declining traffic had not met with universal approval when it was authorized by Congress in 1910. But navigation improvement was seen as a test case: the Ohio had more traffic potential than any other navigable stream. The future of waterways improvement elsewhere would hinge on the success of the Ohio River project. A key element and the first work undertaken was a dam at the Falls of the Ohio that would raise the river level sufficiently to create a nine-foot minimum depth upstream to Madison, Indiana. Completed about 1912, it replaced the timber-crib dam built part way across the river in 1881 to divert more water into the Portland Canal. As the navigation improvement proceeded, the Army Engineer Corps concluded that increasing the height of the Falls dam by six feet would not only obviate the need for a dam at Madison, but also provide sufficient 'head' in the river to permit the Falls to be harnessed for electric power generation. The Corps, sounding out interest in such a hydroelectric project, found both the Louisville Gas & Electric Company and the City of Louisville eager to participate.

The serious intent of the administrations of Mayor George W. Smith and his successor, Huston Quin, in asserting the City's right to build and operate the proposed hydroelectric plant is additional evidence that the ideas of the Progressive Era did not vanish entirely with the advent of the 1920s. Armed with the report of its consultant, retired Engineer Corps General W.L. Sibert (former Corps' Louisville district engineer), the City pressed for the construction license in the 1923 hearing before the Federal Power Commission. But, because the financing required would have exceeded the City's financial capacity, the Commission awarded the right to Louisville Gas & Electric Company. Construction of the new dam and the generating plant proceeded together. Hydroelectric power production began on October 10, 1927. The Falls of the Ohio were tamed at last.

Even before the final lock and dam in the navigation system was completed in 1929, river traffic began to climb upward as proponents of canalization had predicted. From the Twentieth Century low of 4.6 million tons in 1917, cargo reached eight million tons in the 1924-25 fiscal year, then doubled in 1925-26. But it was a different kind of traffic than the packets had carried. Steel, coal, sand, gravel, and petroleum became the staples of the river's resurgence. "Barge fleets are succeeding the packets on the inland streams," the *Board of Trade Journal* noted in 1926, the same year that the Louisville-based American Barge Lines began operation with fifty steel barges and three

Above: Shelby Park pool was a favorite place to cool off in summer. This group of swimmers tried the water in June 1920.
Caufield & Shook Collection, U of L Photographic Archives

Top right: These excursionists, just arrived at Rose Island on the steamer America, will spend the day at the recreation park on the Indiana shore at Fourteen Mile Creek. The flood of 1937 wrecked the resort; three years later it was purchased by the federal government as part of the acreage of the Indiana Ordnance Works, which produced smokeless-powder during World War II.
Caufield & Shook Collection, U of L Photographic Archives

Bottom right: Gertrude Ellis and her all-girl orchestra entertained patrons at Fontaine Ferry Park. The group is pictured in the park's bandstand in July 1925.
Caufield & Shook Collection, U of L Photographic Archives

diesel-powered towboats. The change in river traffic was underscored four years later when the Louisville & Cincinnati Packet Company, tracing its ancestry to 1818 and the very beginnings of the steamboat era, went bankrupt.

Though the packet boats fell onto hard times, the excursion boats still carried full loads. The steamer America made regular trips to Rose Island, upriver on the Indiana shore at Fourteen Mile Creek. Not an island at all, it was old Fern Grove, transformed by entrepreneur David B.G. Rose from a tranquil Nineteenth Century picnic spot to a 1920s recreation area, complete with swimming pool, dance pavilion, a 'zoo', and even summer cottages rented to urbanites seeking escape from the city's heat. Another recreation spot, Fontaine Ferry Park in Louisville's West End, fairly pulsed with happy summer crowds come to ride the amusement devices, picnic under the trees, and enjoy band concerts.

Louisville's army of baseball enthusiasts flocked to the new Parkway Field on Eastern Parkway at Brook Street, opened May 1, 1923. With a huge steel-framed grandstand that could seat some 18,000 spectators at Louisville Colonels' games, Parkway Field replaced old Eclipse Park at Seventh and Kentucky, destroyed by a spectacular fire in the fall of 1922. Not everybody went to the baseball games, but there were few who did not attend the movies. Though neighborhood theatres were scattered about the city, the big attractions came downtown. A 1923 attraction was "My Old Kentucky Home," using actual scenes of the 1922 Kentucky Derby as the high point. In 1927 the first sound motion picture arrived. This initial Vitaphone production, shown at the Strand, though only a variety program on film, was a foretaste of what was to come. Home entertainment was available, too, through the magic of radio. WHAS went on the air (only a few hours each day) on

The journalistic wars
"The career of Mr. Brown's newspaper …was startling. There were fantastic circulation drives, alley fights between the minions of Mr. Bingham and Mr. Brown; the Herald-Post's *city room is recalled as a madhouse. The paper imported an Indian brave, Chief Thunderwater, who was received by a police band….The Bingham papers exposed Chief Thunderwater and showed him a fraud. At once the chief sued for half a million dollars….At the trial, the Bingham people hotly denied any intention of discrediting Mr. Brown's paper. Their sole intention, said one, was to 'always try in a decent journalistic way to do what we can honestly to promote our own business.'"*
Harper's Monthly Magazine, September 1937

July 18, 1922, as the "radiophone" of the *Courier-Journal* and *Times.*

One of Louisville's favorite recreations, however, came under attack in the 1920s. The throngs of eager horseplayers who descended upon Churchill Downs and other Kentucky tracks faced the prospect that racing might vanish and heard predictions that the venerated Kentucky Derby itself might be moved to Chicago. The anti-race-track-gambling movement whose principal spokesman regarded the Derby as "a saturnalia of vice" had a short career, but it created internal dissentions in both the Democratic and Republican parties and changed Louisville journalism. The movement, which dominated Kentucky politics at mid-decade, originated in the Louisville Churchmen's Federation and enlisted many of the city's pre-war political reformers.

The Churchmen's Federation (predecessor of the Louisville Area Council of Churches) was formed in 1910 as "essentially the secular and political arm of Louisville Protestant churches." Helm Bruce and many other leaders of the 1905 Fusionist campaign against the Whallen machine dominated the Federation's membership. The anti-gambling campaign, launched about 1920, also gained the support of such prominent Louisvillians as William R. Heyburn, Robert Worth Bingham, petroleum refiner C.C. Stoll, and Patrick H. Callahan, president of Louisville Varnish Company. As a Catholic Prohibitionist, Callahan was probably the most unusual backer of the crusade. Many other Prohibitionists also joined the effort, now that their goal of outlawing liquor had been achieved.

Seeking support of Protestant ministers throughout Kentucky, the Federation was so successful that it launched the Kentucky Anti-Race-Track-Gambling Commission to press the issue. Though urban reformers originated the anti-gambling crusade, urban political figures, such as Louisvillian James B. Brown, generally took an opposite stance. Remembered most for his banking and financial activities, Brown also was an important figure in the Democratic party, with his roots in the old Whallen machine. Elected City tax receiver in 1901, he became cashier of the First National Bank in 1906 through Whallen's influence and two years later was president.

Brown's mastery of the intricacies of finance made for a further meteoric rise. By 1919, as head of the National Bank of Kentucky, the largest financial institution south of the Ohio River, Brown dominated Kentucky banking. True to his Whallen heritage, he had opposed Prohibition and was now allied with the Democratic wing that opposed the anti-gambling crusade. (Matt J. Winn, who managed Churchill Downs and is generally credited with making the Derby a national event, also was a Whallen protegé.) Thus, by 1923, the year that the gambling issue first entered statewide politics, Brown and Bingham, probably the two richest men in Kentucky, were on opposite sides within the Democratic party. When the Bingham-backed candidate, young Alben Barkley from Paducah, lost his primary election bid to become

The voting population is doubled
On November 2, 1920, women voted for the first time in a national election. This is the story of one woman's experience.

"I knew that if I did not vote as they did, they would tease me for the next four years. I just could not stand that'.

"Miss Inez Mounch is a teacher in the Eastern Departmental School. She approached the polls near the Cherokee Theatre. Several women attempted to persuade her to vote 'their way'.

"She couldn't decide how to vote, she said. She voted.

"'Well, it went for Harding', she explained.

"'Are you satisfied?' she was asked.

"'No, I'm not', she answered.

"'Would you have been satisfied if you voted for Cox?'

"'No', she answered. 'I am not satisfied at all'."
Courier-Journal, November 3, 1920

the Democratic gubernatorial candidate, the gulf between Bingham and Brown widened. When the Brown-backed candidate, William J. Fields, was elected governor, Bingham's newspapers began a sniping campaign that continued through Fields' four years in office. Brown retaliated by purchasing the *Louisville Post* and the *Louisville Herald*, merging them in 1925 as the *Herald-Post*. The move not only gave Brown a journalistic voice, but left Louisville without a Republican newspaper for the first time since 1869.

The anti-gambling issue finally was settled in the 1927 governor's race. Democratic candidate J.C.W. Beckham (who had named Bingham mayor in 1907) enthusiastically endorsed the crusade. The Brown faction was so dismayed that it supported Republican Flem Sampson. Though Sampson carefully avoided the gambling issue, it was well understood that he opposed the anti-gambling crusaders. The election results also demonstrated that the majority of Kentuckians opposed the crusade, despite its moral and religious overtones. Ticket scratching on an unprecedented scale put every Democrat into office except Beckham, who lost to Sampson by over 32,000 votes. To the *Nashville Tennessean* the outcome indicated that "evidently a majority of the voters in Kentucky prefer the Derby to the Democratic party."

Many Kentuckians also preferred alcohol to Prohibition, and found numerous ways to quench their thirst. In addition to the 'speakeasies', liquor was available in many long-established private clubs. The prestigious Pendennis Club, which moved into its elegant new Georgian building in 1930, was visited that year by federal Prohibition-enforcement officers. "I never saw so many different kinds of drinks in my life," one astonished officer declared. Alcohol could also be obtained by private arrangement. "The Watterson Hotel had a famous bell-captain," one Louisvillian recalled. "You could make a rendezvous and he'd take you up in an elevator and stop between floors. He had fine whiskey...you could get a pint of Old Sunnybrook for $7. The story was that thieves dug under the Old Sunnybrook Distillery at Twenty-eighth and Broadway and tunnelled out the whiskey."

The failure of Prohibition to accomplish its goal of making Louisville "whiskey-proof" was not the only failure of the 1920s. Signs of over-expansion and of cracks in the glittering facade were not difficult to find, though the booster mentality and seemingly endless credit and constantly rising profits tended to prevent a realistic assessment.

In 1923 a local group headed by book dealer W.K. Stewart announced plans to build the 430-room, $3-million Kentucky Hotel at Fifth and Walnut, eliciting grumbles from J. Graham Brown, whose hotel was still under construction. Funding for the Kentucky Hotel came from local stock sales and a bond issue handled by Caldwell & Company, Nashville securities dealers who were to play a prominent role in Louisville's most shocking experience of the Depression of the 1930s. The eighteen-story hotel was opened in 1925;

189

Right: Running into the ditch was one of the hazards of driving an automobile in the 1920s on narrow roads designed for horse-drawn vehicles. The Louisville Automobile Club, however, was prepared to dispatch help twenty-four hours a day. Caufield & Shook Collection, U of L Photograhic Archives

Below: Gambling was in Jim Brown's blood long before his spectacular—and losing—game of chance with the assets of the old (1834) and trusted National Bank of Kentucky. This pre-war cartoon depicted his favorite recreation. Kentuckians as We See Them: By Louisville Newspaper Cartoonists, 1905

The eccentric Jim Brown

"Known for his nocturnal business hours, Brown typically operated from the chair of a vice-president at one of his bank's branch offices, where it was not uncommon for business associates, whether from Louisville, Washington or New York, to have to wait until well after midnight to confer with Brown.

"When he was not gambling with his despositors' money, Brown would some- times entertain from 50 to 60 friends at the Gorge Inn at French Lick, Ind., where he would cover the gambling losses of all his guests. But Brown's ulti- mate eccentricity was his enchantment with revolving doors—a passion so strong that he frequently paid doormen at the Brown or Seelbach to turn the doors just so he could watch them spin!" Louisville Magazine, January 1979

less than a year later it was in financial trouble and in 1927 was sold at a commissioner's sale for only $506,000.

Louisville Elks and Shriners, making no small plans, both embarked on ambitious projects to build new clubhouses. The Elks were first, announc- ing in 1921 their intention of erecting at Third and Chestnut "the greatest Elks home in America." The eight-story building, billed as an athletic club available to the whole community, was opened in 1924. It contained a gym- nasium, running track, swimming pool, bowling lanes, 1,500-seat auditorium, and 184 guest rooms. Less than two years after opening, it was in dire finan- cial straits and in 1927 went into receivership. "The venture, it seems, was too pretentious," the *Herald-Post* observed. The building, sold at a loss in 1928, became the Henry Clay Hotel.

The Shriners, inspired perhaps by the Elks, announced plans in 1922 for a spacious, seven-story Kosair Temple on Broadway near Floyd. Offering the same kinds of facilities as the Elks Home, it suffered the same fate. In 1929 the $1.25 million building was sold at foreclosure for $481,000 and transformed into the unsuccessful Fort Nelson Hotel. Rescue came in 1934 when the federal Farm Credit Administration purchased it to house the local Federal Land Banks. There were other signs of trouble, as well. Between 1923 and 1928 industrial employment actually declined by 3,500 despite new industries and expansions of existing plants. A Board of Trade economic sur- vey found that 1928 had been "spotty," while many clients of the Louisville Industrial Foundation sought financial assistance to stabilize credit. In the first quarter of 1929 construction outlays declined 25.7% from the first quarter of 1928.

The most ominous signs, however, were not visible to the Louisville public at large. The National Bank of Kentucky, that seeming Gibraltar of the financial world, was pursuing an erratic course under the domination of James B. Brown, who, after 1921, was both president and board chairman. The lending policies were so lax that federal bank examiners by 1925 began warning the institution's directors that they should exercise some control over Brown's one-man rule. Not only was the bank making loans beyond its lend- ing limit, but many of the loans were, at the least, unbusinesslike. As a result, by 1926 more than $4 million in loans was being repaid very slowly. By 1929 that figure had increased another $1 million.

One of the recipients of these loans was the Kentucky Wagon Manu- facturing Company, a large and once-prosperous industrial enterprise that found the market for its products shrinking rapidly. The company's earlier modest successes in producing electric trucks and the Dixie Flyer automobile led to a grandiose scheme in 1922 to make the company a principal unit in a vast automobile-manufacturing enterprise with plants in several cities. The plan never materialized. The ultimate cost of the loans to the bank was $3 million. Brown also arranged continuing loans to a Louisiana lumber mill and

The war—ten years later

"In company with almost the entire world, we are observing the tenth anniversary of Armistice Day. Time, the great healer, has erased the hatreds and softened the pain of those terrible days of 1918....With friend and foe alike, we rejoice that peace and prosperity have bloomed out of the shambles of yesterday."
Mayor William B. Harrison
November 10, 1928

a New Jersey tire manufacturer, though both companies posted consistent losses. A Louisville brokerage firm, which handled Brown's personal speculative investments, had special borrowing privileges. Personal friends of Brown had no difficulty in obtaining unsecured loans.

Despite these and numerous other instances of reckless squandering of the bank's funds, the directors took no action to control their errant president and chairman, even though prodded frequently by federal examiners. Actually, the directors were so impressed with Brown's legendary business acumen that they were unwilling to rein him in. Assets had climbed from $37.1 million in 1921 to $53.2 million by the end of 1926. They included, of course, all the slow-pay and unsecured loans. The fact was that it was only the expansive financial climate of the time that permitted Brown to operate as long as he did. He did add solid assets, however, in 1927 when the National Bank of Kentucky affiliated with Louisville Trust Company.

The directors, meanwhile, annoyed at the constant criticism from the federal examiners, decided in 1929 to denationalize the bank and operate under the Kentucky charter of Louisville Trust, withdrawing from the Federal Reserve System and rejoining as a state bank. A problem immediately developed. The Federal Reserve Bank of St. Louis advised the directors that National Bank of Kentucky could not withdraw until it had repaid some $8 million. Further, it could not rejoin unless it eliminated $4 million in doubtful loans from its claimed assets. Since the bank could meet neither of these requirements, a different strategy was developed: the formation of BancoKentucky Company.

BancoKentucky, chartered in Delaware in July 1929, had one principal object in view: to sell its stock to raise cash to replace the doubtful assets of National Bank of Kentucky. BancoKentucky, in turn, would absorb these assets. The value of BancoKentucky's stock would come from the fact that the corporation was a holding company controlling both National Bank of Kentucky and Louisville Trust. The new holding company was announced to the world with suitable fanfare in the *Herald-Post* (which itself had accumulated losses of $5 million since Brown formed it) on July 20, 1929.

It is interesting to speculate how much longer Brown could have continued to inflate balloons. As it turned out, however, he had little time left. On October 29, 1929, after days of nervous performance, the stock market took a dizzying plunge. The great Depression of the 1930s had begun.

Chapter Fourteen

What Happened to Prosperity?

lthough the stock-market crash was front-page news, it was not recognized immediately for what it portended: a collapse of the American economy worse than any that had gone before. Many observers, in fact, regarded the events beginning October 29 as a healthy corrective to an overheated market. Louisville's *Civic Opinion*, for instance, welcomed Wall Street's debacle as an end to the wild speculation that had become the market's hallmark. The mass media and business and government spokesmen assured the nation that all would be righted in 1930.

Middle- and upper-class Louisville investors gave proof of their faith by heavy purchases of stock in James B. Brown's BancoKentucky Corporation, which became a favorite local speculation. Those who needed funds to purchase the stock found Brown's National Bank of Kentucky eager to serve. In early April 1930 BancoKentucky advanced from $20 to $25 per share in one week. Even Wall Street stocks began a hopeful recovery and soon billboards appeared across the nation asking "Wasn't the Depression terrible?"

But the nation's economic foundations were eroding. Buried away in the Louisville statistics of the *Board of Trade Journal* were some disquieting figures. Construction, not yet mechanized and consequently a major source of employment, was down 50% in March 1930 from the same month a year earlier. Industrial production and retail sales both showed significant declines. A special federal census revealed that unemployment on April 1 was 13,314, nearly 9% of the labor force. As 1930 ground along its weary way, there was more and more evidence that prosperity was not just around the corner. The brief revival of the stock market topped out in May, and Jim Brown found the market for BancoKentucky stock vanishing, too. By late October shares dropped to $12.50 each. With industrial production falling and unemployment increasing, the situation in Louisville by fall was so serious that the City launched a pitifully inadequate program of aid, attempting to hire as many of the unemployed as possible for odd jobs three days a week at thirty cents an hour. More than 11,000 registered for work, but jobs were provided for less than 1,000 at first. By the fall of 1932 that figure had reached 2,200. The registration figure did not shed light on the number of workers on short hours as factories cut production. Blacks, mainly in marginal jobs, were hardest hit, with a jobless rate estimated at 12.1% by the end of 1930.

In the midst of this general gloom an even greater shock rocked the city on November 17. On that Monday morning the National Bank of Kentucky did not open. A notice on the door stated it had been closed by order of the directors (who had finally asserted their control too late to save the bank). A similar notice appeared at Louisville Trust Company. At the Security Bank, a smaller financial institution that had come under BancoKentucky control, depositors rushed to remove their savings. Though the bank was probably sound, the withdrawals caused it to collapse. As James B. Brown's shaky financial empire came tumbling down, it also forced the closure of the Bank of St. Helens and two black institutions: First Standard and American Mutual Savings banks. All had used National of Kentucky as their depository.

The failure of National Bank of Kentucky, a shocking surprise to Louisville at large, had been anticipated by the more sophisticated members of the financial community, who had been watching Brown's maneuvers with extra interest after the formation of BancoKentucky. That interest was heightened in June 1930 when BancoKentucky, with great fanfare, announced its merger with Nashville-based Caldwell & Company. Headed by Rogers C. Caldwell, Brown's Nashville counterpart in speculative financial ventures, the firm was the best known securities dealer and investment banking house in the South and already had strong Louisville connections through its control of Inter-Southern Life Insurance Company. Brown's *Herald-Post* proclaimed

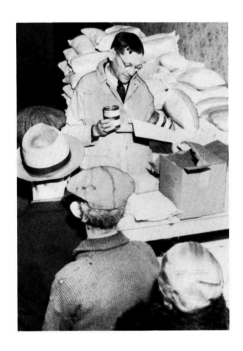

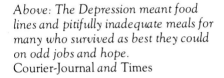
Above: The Depression meant food lines and pitifully inadequate meals for many who survived as best they could on odd jobs and hope.
Courier-Journal *and* Times

that the merger had created "by far the largest and most important financial structure ever built in the Middle Western or Southern States and one that will undoubtedly stand out in the future as one of America's greatest financial ventures."

Conservative Louisville business elements suspected the hyperbole for what it was: pure bluff. Caldwell and Brown each tried to hoodwink the other. The merger was nothing more than a desperate gamble by each side to save itself through the supposed assets of the other. Brown proved the more gullible. Though his empire was tottering, Caldwell's was insolvent. Instead of bolstering BancoKentucky, the merger hastened its demise. Now holding half of Caldwell's worthless stock, Brown used $2.4 million of National Bank of Kentucky's dwindling resources in what proved a futile attempt to shore up the Nashville firm.

Brown's bank also was losing the deposits of knowledgeable Louis-villians and corporations, including Standard Oil (Kentucky) and the L&N Railroad, which began quietly withdrawing funds after the announcement of the Caldwell merger. When the true condition of Caldwell & Company became public knowledge on November 6, five months after the merger, the withdrawals from National Bank of Kentucky skyrocketed: $8.8 million by Saturday, November 15. At the close of that business day the bank held only $17,000 in cash. The following day the bank's directors agreed there was no viable alternative but to suspend operation. It was one of the largest bank failures in a decade that was to record hundreds of others nationwide.

The collapse of National Bank of Kentucky, and of BancoKentucky that followed soon after, spread the economic catastrophe from blue-collar ranks into middle- and upper-income levels. Those who purchased Banco-Kentucky stock at up to $30 a share earlier in the year saw their investments wiped out. But that was not all. After lengthy court litigation, it was ruled that BancoKentucky stockholders were liable for losses by depositors in the banks the holding company controlled. Borrowers who had taken advantage of National Bank of Kentucky's liberal lending policies found that what once seemed their good fortune now came to haunt them as the bank's receiver pressed for quick repayment. Mortgage foreclosures and bankruptcies prolif-erated among these hard-pressed borrowers. In early December James B. Brown, once the symbol of unbridled speculative hopes, himself filed for bankruptcy. Robert Worth Bingham must have taken a certain grim satisfac-tion in his rival's spectacular fall. In any event, the *Courier-Journal* publisher enhanced his own reputation by announcing that he would aid the Christ-

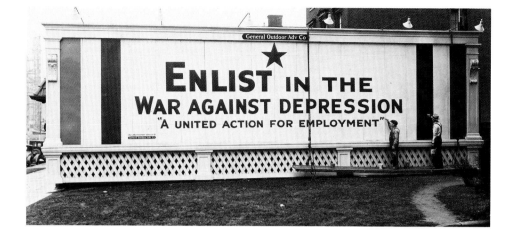

**Graham Brown's
Depression discouragement**
*"It is doubtful if the full despair of the
Great Depression can be grasped by
anyone who didn't experience it at a
reasonably mature age,"* Dorothy Park
Clark observed in her biography of
James Graham Brown. *The drastic
retrenchment in business activity
threatened even Brown's empire. The
demand for lumber fell precipitously
and the S.W. Straus & Company
banking interests in Chicago were
threatening to foreclose the mortgage
on the Brown Hotel. Mrs. Clark, whose
husband, Edward Clark, was secretary
of the various Brown enterprises, recounted one of the few moments of discouragement in Graham Brown's life.*

*"Edward Clark ['Click'] well remem-
bers one evening when Mr. Brown, after
having had to let so many employees go,
and...to cut salaries and wages...stood
silently at a window in his office looking
out into the darkness, his fingers drumming on the sill.*

*"Finally he said, without turning
around, 'Everything's about done for,
Click. I don't see any way out.'*

*"Click tried to murmur something
encouraging, but Mr. Brown shook his
head [and] said, 'I can parcel out what
little comes in to keep myself and the
few of you still with me afloat as long as
I've got anything to parcel.'"*
"Louisville's Invisible Benefactor:" The
Life Story of James Graham Brown, *1978*

mas Club savers in Brown's bank by personally paying half of all such accounts. Bingham's action helped bring a glimmer of cheer into an otherwise
somber 1930 Christmas, a season in which bell-ringing Santa Clauses on
street corners were joined by needy men selling apples at five cents each.
Two days after Christmas, Brown's *Herald-Post* followed its owner into bankruptcy court.

While the pyrotechnics of the greatest financial disaster in Louisville's history filled the newspapers, the city's economy creaked along at an ever-
slowing pace. Though it seemed the situation could not possibly worsen,
1931 proved even more dismal than 1930. Declines were registered in construction expenditures, railroad carloadings, the number of registered motor
vehicles, and even the number of telephones. Bank deposits showed a sharp
25% drop from 1930. There were a few bright spots: Southern Bell Telephone Company began construction of a ten-story headquarters building at
Sixth and Chestnut; work began on the block-long, $3-million Post Office
and Custom House on Broadway between Sixth and Seventh (replacing the
1893 structure at Fourth and Chestnut); and Louisville Trust Company,
freed from the clutches of Jim Brown and BancoKentucky, reopened on a
sound basis.

Brown's *Herald-Post*, sold at a receiver's sale in October 1931 to New
Yorker John B. Gallagher, received an infusion of new money in May 1933
when industrialist Walter Girdler invested heavily in the enterprise. Despite
the newspaper's new editorial brightness, it could not survive the fierce competition of Bingham's *Courier-Journal* and *Times*, and ceased publication
October 30, 1936. Louisville joined the growing ranks of cities with a single
newspaper ownership.

The slough of despond deepened even more in 1932 when Louisville's
unemployment rate reached an estimated 23.5% among whites and 37.2%
among blacks, while practically all those working suffered deep wage cuts.
Construction expenditures that year fell a sickening 62.9% below 1929, while
retail sales were down 60% from that last year of prosperity. Some relief was
afforded property owners by a cut in City taxes and the Board of Trade
urged a "special effort to foster those lines of enterprise which are more or
less depression-proof." Fortunately, Louisville already had some depression-
proof industries. The Kentucky Macaroni Company continued more or less
normal production, probably because the price of its product fit Depression-
era food budgets. Demand also was high for inexpensive clothing, a boon to
such industries as Enro Shirt Company. But the city's star performer was the
tobacco industry.

In 1932 Louisville's three producers turned out eleven billion cigarettes, three times the 1931 volume. Production continued upward in 1933. A
nervous America, calming its jittery nerves with tobacco, could afford ten-

cent packs of cigarettes. Louisville produced 85% of these inexpensive panaceas and could scarcely keep up with demand. Brown & Williamson Tobacco Corporation, a 1929 newcomer to the city, reported in 1934 that it had "been able to operate at capacity or near-capacity through these treacherous years of depression." The company's employment averaged 3,000 throughout the decade. Axton-Fisher Tobacco Company launched construction of a seven-story addition in 1932 and increased its employment to 1,500. Business maverick Wood F. Axton, who retained the progressive faith that had led him to seek the mayor's office in 1913, declared at the new plant dedication that America's principal problem was that not enough of its wealth was shared with the producers and consumers. "If there are any pay raises in this factory, they will start at the bottom and not at the top," he added. He practiced what he preached, reducing his own salary to $10,000 annually to become the "lowest-paid president of the largest independent tobacco company in America."

Not many industrialists locally or across the nation agreed with Axton's philosophy, but it struck a responsive chord among those Louisvillians— blue-collar and white-collar workers alike—who were using up what resources they had, struggling to survive on the few jobs City relief provided, or on charity. The ineffectual efforts of the administration of President Herbert Hoover to deal with the national crisis paved the way for a resurgence of the Democratic party. A nation despairing of the future turned to Franklin D. Roosevelt in the presidential election of November 1932. Louisville, which had given Hoover 60% of its vote when he ran against Democrat Al Smith in 1928, reversed itself in 1932. Though Roosevelt gained only 51.3% of the local vote, it marked the beginning of the change of party fortunes. In 1936, when Roosevelt was reelected for a second term, 60.2% of Louisville voters cast ballots for him.

While the nation waited impatiently for the jauntily optimistic Roosevelt to take office on March 4, 1933, the 'lame-duck' Hoover administration glumly watched economic conditions worsen. One estimate put the number of unemployed Louisvillians in 1933 at over 35,000. Across the nation panicky depositors began removing such large sums from banks that many states ordered all financial institutions closed to prevent a complete collapse of the banking system. On March 1 Kentucky followed suit; by March 4, the day of Roosevelt's inauguration, every bank in the nation was closed. The new president's quick actions (he called Congress into special session on Sunday, the day after his inauguration), brought a surge of hope to a ravaged nation. By March 12 the banks were reopening.

And by early April the breweries were turning out real beer once more. The new Congress had quickly amended the Volstead Act to permit beer to be brewed with an alcoholic content of 3.2%. Louisville, issuing beer licenses again after a thirteen-year lapse, sold the first to Police Captain James

A Depression-era speakeasy
William Lucas, who joined Brown-Forman Distillers in 1935 after the repeal of Prohibition and later became president of the company, recalled the dry era during the early 1930s.

"On Preston between Walnut and Liberty there was an alley between two large buildings. Down that alley you'd come to a small door with a white door-knob. Open that door and you'd find a modern nightclub downstairs, selling all kinds of liquor by the drink. It was called 'Abe's White Doorknob.' Abe was a Harvard graduate with a Ph. D., but …he could make a lot more money at this than at whatever else was available."
Louisville Magazine, January 1979

B. Cunningham. His establishment at Fifth and Breckinridge had gained a reputation during the 1920's as being well supplied with what the law prohibited. Cunningham and 324 other license holders began dispensing beer on 'Foamy Friday', April 6, 1933.

Though Roosevelt's program was designed to stimulate the business system through the active intervention of the federal government, business was generally wary of the new administration and its New Deal, considering many of its measures an unwarranted interference with business decisions. In Louisville, however, the early emergency measures found support not only from Wood F. Axton, but from Louisville Varnish Company president Patrick H. Callahan, who constantly scolded his fellow businessmen for their opposition. Callahan, who had instituted employee profit-sharing in his plant, remained a staunch New Deal supporter even when Roosevelt sought an unprecedented third term. In 1939 he supplied his salesmen with calling cards reading, only half in jest, "Give me an order or I will vote for him again." The more usual business attitude toward Roosevelt was represented by Louisville-area native Tom M. Girdler, president of Republic Steel Corporation, who gained national prominence for his denunciations of the New Deal.

While many businessmen fumed about Roosevelt, a significant number of black voters began a switch to the Democratic banner, a shift that accelerated as New Deal social and economic policies gradually alleviated some of the worst effects of the Negro's exclusion from the American mainstream. The beginning of this shift in Louisville, however, was not related to the New Deal, but rather to black discontent with the long-standing failure of the Republican party to grant a share of power. As early as 1921, following success in the fight against the residential segregation ordinance, serious attempts were made by the new militant leaders to build a more sophisticated political

awareness within the black community. In that year the newly formed Independent Lincoln party put forward the first slate of black candidates for City offices and three State legislative seats.

Unlike earlier black leaders, whom they were challenging, the new group had no ties to influential whites. They included funeral-home owner A.D. Porter, candidate for mayor; publisher William Warley, candidate for magistrate; publisher I. Willis Cole, candidate for State senator; and Wilson Lovett and W.W. Wilson, candidates for State representatives, plus candidates for the City Council and a number of other posts. The Democratic party, elated at the threat to the Republican vote, provided financial assistance to the dissident group, while Republican boss Chesley Searcy organized a campaign of threats and intimidation. Wilson Lovett, head of First Standard Bank and an active Lincoln party member, recalled those tactics.

"Ches. Searcy admitted to me that the campaign cost them (the Republicans) $200,000. He bought up the underworld and most of the preachers. We were rotten-egged and stoned with absolutely no protection from the police....Most of us were jeered on the streets as 'nigger' Democrats." Porter's Funeral Home and Warley's newspaper plant were vandalized and the First Standard Bank was threatened. The Lincoln party polled only 274 votes, but the National Association for the Advancement of Colored People charged that ten times that many were "thrown in the river."

Not until the decade of the 1930s, with its shifting political alignments, were the two major parties willing to sponsor black candidates—and then only in areas with a heavy black vote. The issue was reopened by 1930 Louisville newcomer C. Eubank Tucker, one of a group of young black leaders who came to the fore during the Depression years. Others included educator Lyman T. Johnson, attorney Charles W. Anderson, and publisher Frank Stanley, Sr., founder of the *Louisville Defender*. Tucker was both an attorney

Above: With the repeal of Prohibition, distilling began again in Louisville at the end of 1933. This scene is the warehouse of the Frankfort Distillery Company on Dixie Highway in 1936. The many new distilleries established within a few years of repeal included the world's largest, the plant of Joseph E. Seagram & Sons, which was opened on Seventh Street Road in 1937.
Caufield & Shook Collection,
U of L Photographic Archives

Above right: Steamboat excursions were one way to forget Depression blues. The Idlewild, *today's* Belle of Louisville, *took on a full load of excursionists from a flimsy dock at Fontaine Ferry Park for a downriver trip. The shallow water near shore served as a satisfactory, if muddy, swimming area.*
Caufield & Shook Collection,
U of L Photographic Archives

and a bishop of the AME Zion Church. When the Republican party rebuffed his efforts to secure backing for a black candidate, Tucker himself became a State representative candidate in the November 1933 election as an independent with Democratic backing. Such support was not difficult to secure, since Democratic candidates usually fared poorly in the Republican-dominated district west of downtown.

Though Tucker was defeated by his white Republican opponent, his energetic campaign attracted enough black votes to the overall Democratic ticket to be a significant factor in the election of attorney Neville Miller as mayor and the end of Republican domination of City Hall that had begun in World War I. Without the votes generated by Tucker, Miller's relatively slim margin of 3,171 in a total vote of 128,475 would have been razor-thin at best. The victorious Democrats, in a shift from the party's older attitudes, rewarded black supporters with several mid-level governmental appointments. In 1935, when Democrats chose Tucker to run again for the State representative post, Republicans responded by choosing Charles W. Anderson, who easily defeated Tucker. Anderson was the first Negro to serve in the Kentucky General Assembly and was re-elected for six consecutive terms.

On November 7, 1933, Louisvillians not only returned the Democratic party to power (a position it would hold for thirty years), but expressed their overwhelmingly negative opinion of Prohibition. Increasing national dissatisfaction with the 'noble experiment' prompted the Democratic party to include repeal of the Eighteenth Amendment in its 1932 platform. But even before Roosevelt's inauguration, the expiring Congress voted in February 1933 to submit repeal to the nation. Many states had already voted their approval by the time the issue was on the Kentucky ballot in November. By a lopsided vote of 61,040 to 7,151 Louisvillians joined the statewide rejection of

Right: Radio station WAVE began regular broadcasting on December 30, 1933, with studios on the top floor of the Brown Hotel. The station, headed by George W. Norton, Jr., succeeded WLAP, which had a checkered career after its July 4, 1929, opening. This early mobile broadcasting unit was photographed at Bowman Field in June 1937.
Caufield & Shook Collection,
U of L Photographic Archives

Below right: Stock-car races were a feature of the State Fairs held at the old West End fairgrounds. This group of open top cars stirred up the dust at the 1931 fair.
Caufield & Shook Collection,
U of L Photographic Archives

WAVE goes on the air

Prohibition. By December the necessary two-thirds of the states had voted wet.

The few Louisville distilleries still intact, including Bernheim Distilling Company (now Schenley Distillers) at Seventeenth and Breckinridge, and Stitzel Distillery in Butchertown, had anticipated the result and were ready for immediate production. So was Brown-Forman Distillers, which launched construction of a new distillery in the summer of 1933, completing it in time to begin mashing operations on November 11. Each new opening helped reduce Louisville's unemployment. Brown-Forman, for instance hired 1,000 women to operate the bottling line. Other new distilleries also were built, with the Shively area a favored location.

Prosperity still was not just around the corner—unemployment remained abnormally high all through the 1930s—but the low point of the Depression was past. By the end of 1933 the city's economic statistics started a slow upward climb that continued, with minor fluctuations, during the rest of the decade. The number of telephone, gas, and electric customers, which had been declining, rose by the end of 1933. The *Board of Trade Journal* noted optimistically of the year that "One of the most heartening developments has been ...the revival of our former great distilling, brewing and cooperage industries," adding that twenty-five new plants of all types were established during 1933, increasing employment by 3,659. By the fall of 1934 the *Journal* reported that all 'For Rent' signs had vanished from downtown Fourth Street between Main and Broadway. In 1935 Joseph E. Seagram & Sons selected Louisville as the site of the world's largest distillery, a $4.5-million dollar plant to be erected on forty-seven acres along Seventh Street Road. Completed by early 1937, the plant was thrown open for public tours on Derby weekend. Seagram followed this with the announcement of a bottling plant employing 1,000. And by summer of 1937 Louisville had achieved a mild boom compared with the dark days of late 1932 and early 1933.

Above: Boating became a common sight on downtown Fourth Street during the record January 1937 flood. The view looks south toward Broadway.
Caufield & Shook Collection,
U of L Photographic Archives

The great flood of 1937
On January 6, 1937, scarcely a week into the year when Louisville's economic recovery would become apparent, it began to rain. Nearly an inch fell that day. Three days later the rains began in earnest up and down the Ohio Valley: mere showers one day, torrential downpours the next. The sun vanished behind lowering clouds; the rain-soaked earth yielded water from the lightest footfall like a squeezed sponge. Nearly half the rainfall for a full year fell during that one month.

By January 13 the river had risen three feet; by January 20, eighteen feet. By then marooned families in the Point were being rescued by boat. As the waters continued to climb upward it was obvious that the city faced a major disaster. Louisville had known extraordinary floods before, beginning in the spring of 1779, but never one like 1937. One staff member of the Army Corps of Engineers, not an organization known for imaginative prose, called the flood a "calamitous inundation of almost Biblical proportions." On January 22 some West End residents began leaving the area ahead of the rising water. On January 23 the rise reached thirty feet, equaling the 1884 flood, highest ever recorded. On January 24 the river had risen another three feet; electric power failed and tap water was available only two hours each day. Mayor Neville Miller ordered the evacuation of all residents west of Fifteenth Street.

When WHAS and WAVE were finally forced off the air by lack of power, after broadcasting information and calls for help around the clock, the city depended exclusively upon the Courier-Journal and Times, which had moved to printing facilities in Shelbyville and Lexington. The flood crested on January 27 at nearly eleven feet over the 1884 record; then began a slow and grudging retreat. Three-quarters of the city had been inundated; 250,000 residents affected. The muddy water left a bedraggled community that counted ninety flood-related deaths, nearly $50 million in property damage, and a giant clean-up job. Many houses were beyond repair. Most shotgun cottages in areas near the river had been lifted off their foundations, tossed about, and deposited every way but right side up.

Yet Louisville recovered quickly, with over 1,300 homeowners and small businesses aided by more than $1.2 million in loans from the Federal Disaster Loan Corporation. Though the river was not back to normal until mid-February, the clean-up work was already under way, including WPA workers scraping tons of mud from streets and sidewalks. By the first Saturday in May the crowds thronging into the city for the sixty-third running of the Kentucky Derby found few reminders of the greatest flood known in the Ohio Valley.

By 1937 there was a revived interest in unionism among unorganized blue-collar workers, although the nationwide upheavals of the decade (mostly in communities dominated by a single industry) had little effect in Louisville. One local worker described the city as "...an open shop town. Labor's been dead, just no nerve at all...." But Congressional approval of the Wagner Act, upheld by the Supreme Court in April 1937, gave unions stronger bargaining power. Two months later, in the first Louisville election supervised by the new National Labor Relations Board, employees of the Hart Manufacturing Company chose an American Federation of Labor union over a company union. From then on there were slow but sure gains by Louisville unions.

Though the nationwide demand for cigarettes and the repeal of Prohibition were important to Louisville's reviving business scene, other factors were involved, as well. The area's traditionally diversified industrial base provided a valuable cushion, since the Depression had varying effects on different industries. Architect James C. Murphy, who headed the Board of Trade's Welfare Endorsement Committee, noted in 1933 that "The situation in Louisville is not nearly as acute as is true of a number of other communities whose business and industry are not diversified." The continuing promotional efforts of the Louisville Industrial Foundation, headed after 1933 by former Mayor William Harrison, also brought a few new small plants to Louisville each year even in the worst of times. It is difficult to assess the precise impact of these factors, and probably impossible to determine the effects of New Deal 'pump priming'. But the Public Works Administration (PWA), designed to increase demand for industrial products by helping fund public construction projects, and the later Works Projects Administration (WPA), frankly designed to provide jobs for the unemployed, put many Louisvillians to work. Moreover, these agencies left a progeny of useful projects, including the Fiscal Court Building, the University of Louisville School of Law building on Belknap Campus, the Iroquois Branch Library in Beechmont, the Iroquois Amphitheatre in Iroquois Park, and a long list of street paving and sewer construction projects.

The federal programs eventually superseded the City's own workrelief effort, inherited by Neville Miller, who picked Dr. Kenneth P. Vinsel of the University of Louisville faculty to administer it. Many of the City projects had been of a distinctly 'make-work' character (such as a rock garden on the Court House lawn). Vinsel in 1934 transferred 632 men from work relief to direct relief payments (financed in part by federal funds) because of lack of worthwhile projects. At that time 2,700 men were on work relief. By the end of 1934 Vinsel reported 5,000 families on direct relief. When PWA took over the job-providing function in 1935, the Municipal Relief Bureau became the Municipal Bureau of Social Services, providing emergency relief, and Vinsel returned to the University.

Throughout the Depression the profound hope that the economy would soon rebound pervaded American society. This attitude prompted the *Courier-Journal* in 1938 to score the Municipal Bureau of Social Services for conducting operations on a "hopeful month-to-month basis," rather than recognizing that chronic unemployment would not vanish overnight. The newspaper also observed that it was unrealistic to expect that the physically handicapped would "return to the discreetly anonymous fold of the private charitable institution." Although no figures for 1938 Louisville-area unemployment are available, 6,000 persons were on WPA jobs.

The fact is that, despite improvements, the American economy in 1938 still was performing far below capacity and seemed to many observers likely to continue this pattern. But the newspaper editorialist did not recognize that the relief programs also were part of a more subtle and more profound shift occurring in the relationship between local governments and Washington. The federal measures to deal with the depressed economy were

Celebrating Derby Eve, 1939
"As heretofore, Derby Day started the night before and continued up to post time.
 "Crowds of visitors, looking sophisticated and well-groomed, mixed with hometowners 'on the loose' in the downtown throng that turned Louisville into a great street fair during the night. Hundreds reveled in night club entertainment, danced in hotel dining rooms and/or attended many a private-room party."
Louisville Times, May 6 1939

the precursors of a continuously widening federal role, especially as a funding source in the nation's city halls, court houses, and state capitols. The federal aid in building the Portland Canal a century earlier had been a special case; such aid would henceforth be the norm. Washington, however, would now specify the kinds of projects for which the funding could be used. The advent of public housing was a striking example of this new flow of federal aid. The community concern before World War I about slum housing, a concern first roused by the Woman's Club, abated during the 1920s along with the progressivism that had prompted it. The only local legislation on the subject during that decade was a watered-down housing code adopted in 1923. The code's chief merit was that it applied to all housing and not tenements only, as had the pre-war legislation. But the reform impulse, rekindled nationally by the Depression and given form by the New Deal, turned again to the issue of housing for the one-third of a nation that Roosevelt declared was "ill-housed, ill-clad, ill-nourished."

When PWA's emergency housing program was launched in June 1933, Mayor Harrison immediately initiated a study of housing needs, enlisting the cooperation of the Board of Trade and the Real Estate Board. Mayor Neville Miller's administration, building on the study, focused on the blighted area encompassed by Walnut, Liberty, Shelby, and Clay streets east of the central business district. Though demolition bids for part of the thirty-acre area that was to become the Clarksdale housing project were in hand by the end of that year, the project was delayed by a successful suit by a few property owners, who contended that the use of the governmental power of eminent domain to acquire land for housing was unconstitutional. This court decision temporarily changed the course of Louisville's public-housing program, which now moved to build its first projects on vacant land. College Court (taking its name from adjacent Louisville Municipal College) was erected at Seventh and Kentucky on the site of the former Eclipse Ball Park. LaSalle Place was constructed at Seventh and Algonquin Parkway. In keeping with Louisville's unofficial segregation policies, the former was for blacks, the latter for whites. Both projects were dedicated in early 1938. That same year the original project east of downtown was revived (under new federal legislation), along with another west of downtown for blacks. These two, Clarksdale and Beecher Terrace, which combined slum clearance with construction of low-cost housing, were completed in 1940. Altogether the four projects provided 1,930 units of public housing, managed by the Municipal Housing Commission.

With the economic underpinnings of distilling and tobacco, federal works programs, and the gradual improvement of business generally, all was not gloom in Louisville during the Depression years. There were, in fact, numerous positive developments. Though air service remained more an adjunct than an essential part of the area's transportation network, American Airways

Right: Louisville's air service, provided by American Airlines, continued to expand during the 1930s and planes grew larger during the decade. This is a 1935 scene at Bowman Field.
Louisville Free Public Library

Below right: In 1937 J. Graham Brown's bus station at Fifth and Broadway was replaced by this structure in Art Deco style erected by Southeastern Greyhound Lines. The building's glazed-tile walls in shades of blue and gray matched the colors of Greyhound buses. The station was replaced by a new and larger $1.7-million facility at Seventh and Walnut in 1970.
Caufield & Shook Collection,
U of L Photographic Archives

Below: Robert Whitney's arrival from Chicago in 1937 as the first paid conductor of the Louisville Civic Orchestra marked the beginning of the transition of the unpaid musical group to the nationally known Louisville Orchestra of today. Whitney served as conductor for nearly thirty years and also became dean of the University of Louisville School of Music.
Courier-Journal *and* Times

expanded service to Nashville, Atlanta, and Fort Worth and inaugurated direct service to New York. Another new transportation form, the motor truck, negligible during the 1920s, expanded during the 1930s along with the network of paved roads. The Cincinnati & Louisville Delivery Company, established in 1928, received a competitor when the Denny Motor Transfer Company began daily service between the two cities in July 1930. Denny previously had established service to Indianapolis by way of Bedford and Bloomington. A few years later the first daily truck service between Louisville and Chicago was established by Edward Buhner. In 1937 Buhner's operation became the Louisville-based Silver Fleet Motor Express.

The decade also witnessed a musical renaissance with the establishment at last of a permanent symphonic orchestra in Louisville. The 1931 transformation of the Young Men's Hebrew Association Symphony Orchestra into the Louisville Civic Orchestra gave the musical group, organized in 1926, a broader base of community support. Even though the orchestra members still were unpaid, their number was increased from fifty to sixty-five and a vigorous campaign of ticket sales launched. By 1937 funding was sufficient to secure a paid professional conductor, Robert Whitney, to succeed the retiring Joseph Horvath, who had headed the orchestra since its founding. Whitney, who came from Chicago, also had to rely on a teaching position at the University of Louisville School of Music to supplement his income, but his arrival marked a turning point for serious music in Louisville. Soon distinguished guest artists became a regular feature of the orchestra's programs. The 1939-40 season, for example, opened with pianist Eugene List as special guest. To mark its increasing community stature, the organization changed its name in 1942 to the Louisville Philharmonic Orchestra.

The Kentucky Derby Festival, first held in 1935, also helped banish Depression blues. Capitalizing on the national renown that the Derby had

Above: The anti-Semitic outrages of the Nazi regime caused thousands of German and Austrian Jews to flee their native lands. Many sought refuge in the United States, where their coming immeasurably enriched American cultural and scientific life. In Louisville the newcomers received English lessons at the Young Men's Hebrew Association at Second and Jacob.
U of L Historic Archives

Above right: Louisville's cultural life made forward strides during the 1930s, despite a depressed economy. One factor responsible was the Memorial Auditorium, commemorating Louisville's World War I dead, which opened in 1929 at Fourth and Kentucky. It provided an impressive, though acoustically defective, setting for visiting stage stars, orchestras, and soloists. George Gershwin, for instance, appeared in February 1934. In this photograph pianist José Iturbi plays to a full house in March 1938.
Caufield & Shook Collection,
U of L Photographic Archives

Below: Louisville's electric interurban cars ran out their last miles during the 1930s, unable to survive the twin disasters of Depression and the automobile. In the autumn of its years an almost-empty Prospect car crosses Harrod's Creek. The concrete-arch bridge in the background carried River Road across the stream.
Author's collection

achieved under the direction of Matt J. Winn, the Festival included a parade, fireworks, a regatta along the downtown riverfront, and a concert by the Civic Orchestra. The Festival recognized the fact that the Derby had become a very special Louisville event, apart from its wider reputation. Downtown Fourth Street on Derby eve was thronged with merrymakers, street musicians, and impromptu dancers. The art of making music from a jug was demonstrated by black musical groups, which usually included at least one virtuoso on this unlikely instrument. Though it was necessary to suspend the Festival during the war years of the 1940s, a Louisville tradition had been established.

Some older Louisville traditions and institutions vanished, however, during the 1930s. The *Louisville Anzeiger*, founded in 1849 during the high tide of German immigration, published its last issue on March 1, 1938, the day of its eighty-ninth anniversary. It was the victim both of the Depression and a younger generation that no longer read the ancestral language. The Brook Street car line, the original inspiration for Fontaine Fox's "Toonerville Trolley," ended its career in June 1930, a victim not of hard times but of the master plan of city planners Harland Bartholomew & Associates. The little-patronized trolley, it was decreed, interfered with automobile traffic. The electric interurban lines, radiating like spokes into the countryside surrounding Louisville, also disappeared one by one, victims of the Depression and ridership lost to the automobile. The Prospect line, originally the 1870s narrow gauge to Sand Hill, was the last; its final car arrived at the Jefferson Street interurban station on the night of October 31, 1935. Four years later to the day, the last car on the intercity route to Indianapolis pulled out of the same station and Louisville's electric interurban days came to an end.

The decade, too, was nearing its end, but on a far more positive note than that of the ill-fated interurban railways. Though it had been a difficult ten years, Jefferson County showed an overall population increase of more than 30,000 for a growth rate of 8.4%. The statistics show that the Depression did not halt the spillover of population beyond the city boundaries. While the city increased its population 11,332 (to reach 319,077), the areas outside Louisville experienced an increase of 18,710, (to reach 66,315). In 1930 Louisville was home to 86.7% of the Jefferson County's total population; in 1940 the figure had slipped to 82.8%. The automobile was quietly about its work of

Above: Harold 'Peewee' Reese was at the beginning of his baseball career in 1938, when he started as a shortstop with the former Louisville Colonels of the American Association. He participated in the 1939 season when the Colonels won the Little World Series and in 1940 was sold to the Brooklyn Dodgers, where he hit 126 home runs in a career that extended to 1959. Reese set a number of baseball milestones, played in eight all-star games, became a sportscaster, and in 1971 joined the Hillerich & Bradsby Company, promoting Louisville Slugger bats.
Potter Collection,
U of L Photographic Archives

Above right: The George Rogers Clark Bridge of 1929 remained the principal motor vehicle entrance to Louisville from the north for over thirty years. This view of the river crossing and the downtown waterfront dates from the early 1950s.
Louisville Chamber of Commerce

changing the relationship between city and county. The 1940 census figures also revealed the improvement of the economy. Unemployment was down to 11.5%. WPA and PWA were still at work at decade's end, but new developments would soon not only bring the emergency work programs to a halt, but result in a manpower shortage.

Once again a European war was quickening the nation's and Louisville's economy and enlisting American sympathies for England and France. Throughout the early 1930s the United States had watched with some detachment the continuing Japanese aggression in Asia and the rise of Fascism in Italy and Germany. The nation was concerned with solving its own economic and social problems and still in the mood of isolationism that followed World War I. But the outbreak of war in Europe and the fall of France brought about a rapid shift in opinion. Polls in July 1940 showed 59% of the American public preferred keeping out of war to aiding England. By January, 68% preferred aiding England even at the risk of war. In March 1941 Congressional approval of the Lend-Lease Act expanded the American supply of goods and arms flowing across the Atlantic.

The shift in American opinion was hastened by the Committee to Defend America by Aiding the Allies formed in June 1940. One of the original members was Herbert Agar, who had assumed charge of the *Courier-Journal* editorial page in October 1939. During his previous four years as associate editor, he had been largely responsible for the liberal reputation which the *Courier-Journal* had acquired. Meanwhile, the economic stimulation of aid to England was quickly felt by Louisville industries. When Reynolds Metals Company purchased the former Ford Motor Company plant at Third and Eastern Parkway in early 1940 as part of a large expansion of its Louisville operations, the *Board of Trade Journal* called it the "outstanding industrial development in Louisville in the past ten years." R.S. Reynolds, president of the aluminum manufacturer, recalling how Louisville Industrial Foundation aid had made possible the move of the firm to the city in 1917, noted simply that "Louisville is my good luck town."

In 1937 *Harper's Monthly Magazine* in an article that elicited many angry local retorts, had called Louisville "an American museum piece." But by 1940 the floodgates were ready to open, releasing the single most concentrated wave of economic development in the city's history.

Chapter Fifteen

World War II: An Industrial Revolution

favorite guessing game in the three Falls Cities in early 1940 involved the options taken on 6,000 acres of prime Indiana farm land near the small Clark County community of Charlestown (population: 750). Since the options were held by a real estate agent from Wilmington, Delaware, the most plausible guess was that the giant E.I. du Pont de Nemours & Company was to build a plant. A further supposition was that Du Pont would produce the heralded synthetic fabric, nylon, which it planned to begin marketing during the year. Du Pont, however, refused comment.

Meanwhile, there was other significant news to absorb. In February, William S. Speed and his sister, Mrs. Frederic Speed Sackett, donors of the 1925 fund to establish Speed Scientific School, made an additional gift of $130,000 to the University of Louisville to construct a new building for the engineering school. In Georgian Revival style, the building was to be constructed south of Eastern Parkway, the first expansion of Belknap Campus beyond its original boundary.

Transportation made news, too, in 1940. The number of passengers using Louisville's air service doubled over 1939, reaching 40,000. Eastern Air Lines, as well as pioneer American Airlines, now served Bowman Field. Both used Douglas DC-3 planes carrying twenty-one passengers. Eastern, which operated the Louisville-Chicago route, received authority in December to begin a Louisville-St. Louis flight. By then Bowman Field had taken on an additional role as an Army Air Corps training base. The coming of the Air Corps—announced in August—was part of the nation's defense preparedness that began with the outbreak of war in Europe. Commercial planes shared the field with the Air Corps, but the City-County Air Board began an immediate search for a site for a second field to handle student and private flights. The choice was made in the fall: 571 acres that had been owned by Nineteenth-Century L&N Railroad President E.D. Standiford. Near Preston Street Road and Audubon Park, the new field was first designated simply Municipal Airport Number Two. Funds to purchase the land were borrowed from the Louisville Industrial Foundation, while the WPA allotted $270,850 for work on the site, among the last WPA projects in Louisville.

At the same time that the late Dr. Standiford's land was being cast for a role in aviation, the L&N Railroad he once headed was monitoring the performance of its first diesel locomotives—two lowly switching engines—that went about their duties in the East Louisville Yards. In December the L&N became an essential link in the route of the city's first streamlined train, the *South Wind*, operating between Chicago and Miami. Spectators gathered along the L&N tracks to see the streamliner hurry along to make the twenty-six-hour schedule from Louisville to its Florida destination.

While these developments were taking place, the Falls Cities learned the meaning of the land options near Charlestown. Du Pont was, indeed, involved, but not to make nylon. Instead, the *Courier-Journal* reported on July 13, the $30-million plant would produce smokeless powder for artillery use. It would employ 4,000 and "dwarf any similar factory in existence." The reason for the huge acreage now became clear. Powder-making is risky business, with the ever-present danger of explosions. The plant, owned by the federal government and operated by Du Pont, would triple American smokeless powder output. The news followed closely the humiliating defeat of the French by German armies and the hasty evacuation of British troops through the port of Dunkerque.

With these disheartening developments, which left only Britain and the British fleet between the United States and German might, the powder plant (officially the Indiana Ordnance Works) represented more than welcome industrial development. It was also a concrete example of American willingness to supply the tools of war to an embattled Britain, suffering massive air raids almost daily and bracing for an expected German invasion.

Above: World War II made Louisville the world's largest producer of synthetic rubber. A worker at the Du Pont plant samples liquid neoprene for analysis.
Louisville Magazine

But employment was uppermost in the minds of many Falls Cities residents. Kentucky Federation of Labor Secretary Edward H. Weyler noted that the 4,000 construction jobs at the plant would "take up the slack" following completion of major projects in Louisville: public housing and elevation of Pennsylvania Railroad tracks along Fourteenth Street and L&N tracks in the eastern section of the city along Beargrass Creek. (The early predictions of employment at Charlestown were wildly short of the mark. A year later nearly 32,000 workers converged on the site each day.)

The economic consequences of the powder plant, however, could not be divorced from military reality. On the very July day that the project was announced, news also came from Washington that 50,000 National Guardsmen would be called to service for a year of intensive training. The order affected Louisville's 149th Infantry, which left for its tour of duty six months later. The Army had previously announced its intention to create a mechanized cavalry modeled on the German 'Panzer' units, which had easily sliced through the supposedly impregnable French defense works, the Maginot Line. One division of this new Armored Force was to be headquartered and trained at Fort Knox (the name was changed from Camp Knox in 1932). In July it was announced that the post, which had gained nationwide fame in the mid-1930s as the site of the nation's Gold Depository, would be enlarged by 20,000 acres.

It was also in July that Roosevelt sent his "total defense" message to Congress, asking $4.8 billion to strengthen the nation's defense capabilities, including defense-manufacturing facilities. The Louisville area, basking in the glow of an upsurge in its economy quite independently of the powder plant, little realized the enormous industrial expansion that lay ahead as a result of Roosevelt's proposals. In September Congress approved the Selective Service Act, the first peacetime draft in American history. Fort Knox received its initial contingent of draftees in November, the first of thousands who would carry away memories of the military post and of weekend leaves in Louisville. The same month Roosevelt was returned to office. The controversy over the unprecedented third term was obviously of little concern to voters in Louisville and Jefferson County, who cast nearly 59% of their ballots for Roosevelt.

The first hint that the powder plant was only the beginning of a series of cascading announcements of industrial expansions that were to transform the Louisville area's economy came late in 1940. The city learned that it had been selected as the site for a Naval gun plant and that a facility to prepare powder charges for artillery—each measured charge placed in a separate bag—would be constructed adjacent to the Du Pont plant at Charlestown. The 'bag plant' (or Hoosier Ordnance Works) was a federal project, turned over to Goodyear Tire & Rubber Company for operation. The Naval Ordnance Plant, constructed adjacent to the L&N's Strawberry Yards, was a $26-million project eventually employing 4,000 persons. It also was built by the federal government and operated by Westinghouse Electric & Manufacturing Company.

Construction of these two projects had not yet begun when a series of rapid-fire developments in early 1941 set the stage to make Louisville the world's largest producer of synthetic rubber. Rumors of the first of a series of such plants was confirmed in January by the Louisville Industrial Foundation, which reported that it was a national defense project and that Sheffield, Alabama, was also under consideration as a site. In February it was announced that National Carbide Company would construct a plant southwest of Louisville in the Bell's Lane area to make acetylene and that Louisville Gas & Electric Company would build a large generating station along the river at Paddy's Run in the same area.

In March, Louisville was chosen as the location of the synthetic-rubber plant. Operated by Du Pont, it would produce that company's own formulation called neoprene, of which acetylene was an essential ingredient. Two

Brandeis: The final journey home
At Justice Brandeis' death in October 1941 his ashes, at his request, were buried under the entrance portico of the U of L Law School. At a memorial service a month later in Temple B'rith Sholem, Rabbi Joseph Rauch, president of the University Board of Trustees, recalled a 1926 conference with Brandeis to discuss the future course of the institution of higher education.
"He visualized a progressive and expanding university and he was convinced that the ideal of the American way of life could be best democratized through such institutions as ours. From now on we who are concerned with the university must be guided by the spirit of this man. His life work constituted a bill of rights for education in a democracy."
Courier-Journal, November 7, 1941

months later Louisville learned that a second synthetic-rubber plant would be established by B.F. Goodrich Company. In September came news of a third, a project of the National Synthetic Rubber Company, which had originally considered Akron for the plant location. The bustling industrial area soon was given a name in the Louisville tradition that had coined Butchertown and Germantown. The recent farmland was henceforth called Rubbertown. The development of the rubber plants was not, oddly, a response to a possible Japanese threat to natural rubber supplies from Malaysia, but to rising industrial demands for the synthetic product as a result of the defense program. Yet Rubbertown proved to be more crucial to the nation than was ever envisioned at the beginning of the year.

The radio reports that flooded into American homes on the quiet, early-winter Sunday of December 7, 1941, created momentary disbelief, then shock, then anger. American interest, fixed on the struggle in Europe, had tended to ignore the mounting problems of an aggressive Japan. But the news of the massive air attack on the naval base at Pearl Harbor immediately crystallized the issue of war or peace. Isolationists, who had argued that Roosevelt's defense program and aid to Britain created the danger of war, were suddenly silenced. Kentucky native Arthur Krock, one-time managing editor of the Courier-Journal and in 1941 Washington bureau chief of the New York Times, noted immediately after the event that the Pearl Harbor attack created instant national unity: "You could almost hear it click into place...."

The massive industrial development around Louisville that had been generated by the national defense program made the area a vital part of the American role as the arsenal of democracy. Even by the spring of 1941, when construction at Rubbertown had barely begun, Louisville-area defense employment was estimated at 38,000, while other industrial employment had increased 18% over the spring of 1940. As 1942 opened, the Courier-Journal commented that the city was "the biggest, busiest industrial community it has been in 163 years," and that because of the influx of new workers (most from rural Kentucky), housing was "bursting out at the seams." Yet there was more development to come. In April 1942 the Army announced that the $318-million Nichols General Hospital would be erected on a 120-acre site at Berry Boulevard and Manslick Road. By fall some 150 temporary buildings had been erected and the institution's 1,000 beds made it Louisville's largest hospital. At the same time the Army built the huge Louisville Medical Depot on a 575-acre site south of Louisville along the L&N Railroad and National Turnpike. (Today the depot is the Louisville Industrial Center.)

The Rubbertown industrial complex also grew larger during 1942. With the advent of war, the federal government moved to quadruple output by purchasing the plants, expanding them, and then leasing the facilities to the original owners. The increased output was possible largely because of

Future considerations
"What is to happen when the war is
over? Can the powder plant and the
naval gun plant and the other war materials plants be readily converted? If so,
will there be industrial tenants willing to
convert them?"
Courier-Journal, January 1, 1942

Louisville's distilleries, which turned to wartime production of industrial
alcohol, an essential raw material for butadiene, which, in turn, was used for
the type of synthetic rubber produced by Goodrich and National Synthetic
Rubber. The butadiene plant erected by the federal government in 1942
was operated by Carbide & Carbon Chemical Corporation. By the peak
wartime-production year of 1944 the Rubbertown plants produced 195,000
tons of synthetic rubber.

While Rubbertown was growing, another large and unusual new
industry took shape at Standiford Field: a plant to manufacture cargo planes
largely of wood. Louisville was chosen to produce this venture in plane
design because of its established woodworking industry and because the
second airport (named Standiford Field in July 1941) provided an ideal site.
Built by the federal government and operated by Curtiss-Wright Corporation,
the $12-million factory assembled a few of the wooden C-76 Caravans, using
components manufactured by the Mengel Company. But the first of the
planes crashed in southern Jefferson County on a test flight in May 1943,
killing its three-man crew. Shortly thereafter, the C-76 contract was canceled
and the plant turned instead to production of the conventional C-46 cargo
planes. Both Reynolds Metals and American Air Filter manufactured components for this model. The Curtiss-Wright plant not only added to the city's
industrial base, but provided an unexpected bonus in aviation development.
The Army in 1943 agreed to lease Standiford Field and construct four full-
sized runways to better handle the plane factory's output than did the two
short runways built by WPA.

Still another wartime industry came in early 1942 when the Navy
purchased the Howard Ship Yards in Jeffersonville, which during its long
career had built many of the packets that are still famed in river lore. The
Yards had struggled uncertainly through the Depression, building a boat now

and then and turning out its last in 1940. The Navy contracted operation of the facility to the adjoining Jeffersonville Boat & Machine Company, which was already building submarine chasers. Soon the combined operation produced scores of ungainly craft, including LST's (landing ship, tanks) and LCI's (landing craft, infantry). Taken down the Ohio and eventually to distant beaches along the Normandy coast and on remote, tiny islands in the Pacific, they disgorged men and tanks when the invasion of enemy-held territory began.

Other long-established non-defense industries also turned their energies to war production. Ford Motor Company assembly lines turned out nearly 100,000 military Jeeps. Tube Turns and Henry Vogt Machine Company made artillery-shell parts, and most of the city's woodworking industry produced glider parts. Hillerich & Bradsby switched from baseball bats to gunstocks. Hardly a single Louisville industry, in fact, was not touched by war's demands, while the burgeoning work force sent Louisville transit records spiraling upward from fifty-nine million passengers in pre-war 1940 to ninety-two million in 1942. With rubber-tired transit and automobile use restricted, travel to Churchill Downs resulted in a series of "Streetcar Derbys." The tremendous influx of war workers (defense employment in the Louisville area reached 80,000 at its 1944 peak) strained not only the transit system, but housing as well. Two public-housing projects, in the planning stage when the nation was plunged into war, were built as housing for defense workers instead. The two projects, Sheppard Square along Preston Street south of Broadway in the old Smoketown neighborhood, and Parkway Place at Eleventh and Hill, were not utilized for their original purpose until after the war.

But most of the war-induced population increase was absorbed into older housing that was turned into multiple-unit dwellings with the assistance

of federal low-interest loans. This approach, actively encouraged by the Federal Housing Administration as a contribution to winning the war, affected the Old Louisville area particularly. Here were hundreds of large, substantial Nineteenth-Century dwellings in an area that had lost its early claim as the favored residential site of the city's elite, and that was well served by public transit. The wartime conversions hastened the decline of this area in the heart of the city.

The war brought about other social changes, as well. The extraordinary demand for labor, made more acute by the loss of thousands of young men to military service, resulted in the large-scale recruitment of women—both white and black—into jobs traditionally held by men. Increased opportunities also opened for older black men into better-paying jobs. (Most young blacks were in the armed forces.) The Louisville Urban League described race relations in defense plants as excellent, but noted that previous lack of educational and union apprenticeship opportunities meant that many blacks did not possess the skills for jobs that were now opening to them.

Presiding at City Hall while World War II wrought its changes in Louisville was young Mayor Wilson W. Wyatt, who took office December 1, 1941. A successful attorney and liberal Democrat elected with an impressive 17,834-vote majority, the 36-year-old Wyatt had a political philosophy— "Local government is where democracy begins"—and a belief in planning as a crucial key to solving municipal problems. A week after he took office, as he and his family were returning from a trip to Indianapolis, they heard on their car radio the news of Pearl Harbor. The problems of war were among those the new mayor had expected he might face and he had said so in his campaign speeches.

Yet, despite the extra burdens imposed by Louisville's almost-

overnight transition to a major war-production center, Wyatt pushed through the 1942 General Assembly a series of measures to increase governmental efficiency and help prepare the city for the post-war world. One piece of legislation, which recognized the growing urbanization of the territory beyond the city boundaries, made planning and zoning a countywide function under one commission. Another legislative bill merged the City and County health departments.

Wyatt's successful program also enabled Louisville to launch urban rehabilitation programs, using municipal authority to purchase and demolish blighted buildings and to make the land available for redevelopment by private capital. The move can fairly be described as another step toward the 1920s' hope that planning could "rebuild the city." Though it was impossible to pursue the program during the war years, the authority embodied in the legislation provided the basis for Louisville's venture into large-scale urban renewal with federal aid in the 1950s. A redistricting bill also increased Louisville's voting strength in the General Assembly, with five senators instead of four, and eleven representatives instead of eight. In other actions, the Wyatt administration provided for equalization of salaries of black and white teachers and appointed blacks to some City boards and commissions. Wyatt also broke tradition by reaching into the Civil Service ranks to find his police chief. Moreover, the new chief, Arthur E. Kimberling, was a Republican. The *Courier-Journal's* City Hall reporter observed that the appointment was so unconventional that "there were those who thought they heard the old clock in the [City Hall] tower strike thirteen."

Bypassing the usual patronage pattern in selecting a police chief created a minor storm, however, compared to the one following Wyatt's proposal in early 1944 that the City purchase the Louisville Gas & Electric Company (LG&E), to add $3 to $4 million a year to City revenues. The Mayor's rationale was that the city, which had struggled through a decade of Depression on reduced revenue, needed additional income for the post-war needs that were already being recognized: a floodwall, a limited-access belt highway around the city, and slum clearance, among many others. Wyatt recognized that tax increases were unpopular on the one hand, and that an opportunity to acquire LG&E existed on the other. The Securities & Exchange Commission had ordered Standard Gas & Electric (a Pennsylvania holding company) to dispose of its control of the Louisville utility. The mayor's proposal would have placed the gas and electric utility in the same relationship to the City that the water company already occupied.

Even though Republicans had taken control of the Board of Aldermen in 1943, midway in Wyatt's term, he was able to enlist the support of Board President Arthur E. Hopkins, and later the entire Board, for his proposal. Later a Citizens' Committee, headed by Edward O. Nobbe, also supported the effort. Meanwhile, Wyatt and Hopkins conferred with federal

Right: The end of the war, clearly in sight by the summer of 1945, is evident in this photograph made on August 2 of that year. The last of 93,389 military Jeeps assembled at Ford's Louisville plant on South Western Parkway, rolls off the assembly line, followed by civilian trucks.
Courier-Journal and Times

Far right: Another result of peace was this November 1945 lineup of women waiting to buy nylon stockings in a downtown store. During the war they wore cotton or went barelegged.
Lin Caufield

Below: A happy little girl holds the Courier-Journal of August 15, 1945, proclaiming the good news.
Lin Caufield

bureaus involved and with Standard Gas & Electric. Oddly, LG&E President T. Bert Wilson did not learn of the proposal until June 1944 at a meeting of Standard directors. LG&E immediately began a vigorous counterattack, stirring spirited debate on the issue. Some opponents charged City ownership of the utility would deprive the federal government of tax revenue needed to fight the war, while the more extreme branded the proposal socialistic. Standard had its own plan for relinquishing control, involving an exchange of stock and dissolution of an intermediate holding company. The Securities & Exchange Commission ruled in favor of the Standard proposal in early 1945. The final decision, however, was not rendered until 1947, two years after Wyatt had left office.

Although Wyatt failed in his effort to achieve municipal ownership of LG&E, another of his moves looking toward post-war needs succeeded handsomely. On an October night in 1943 some 300 business and civic leaders gathered by invitation at the Pendennis Club to talk about Louisville and its future. The result was the founding of the Louisville Area Development Association (LADA), a non-partisan, private group with community-wide support to do the chief work of city planning. Wyatt has described LADA as "in effect the planning arm of local government," since the Louisville & Jefferson County Planning & Zoning Commission was swamped with zoning matters and had no staff for planning. Funding, from business and labor, was entirely private. Though Wyatt served as LADA's first president, care was taken to divorce it from any political coloration. The new organization selected Kenneth P. Vinsel, who had headed the City's welfare effort ten years earlier, as its first director. (He was, at the time, in Washington on a government war assignment.)

LADA's objectives were to correct the problems that had resulted from Louisville's past "haphazard growth," to create an "orderly framework for future growth," and to "safeguard the enormous industrial expansion" of the war years. LADA's numerous action committees, composed of a mix of business, professional, labor, and government leaders, soon were working on a variety of plans for solving problems and fostering development in numerous areas: economic growth, transportation, education, the arts, health, housing, parks and recreation, governmental reorganization, statistical research, and others. When Wyatt's term in office ended in late 1945 (coinciding closely with the end of the war), the planning for the Louisville area's post-war development was well under way.

Planners, however, like the rest of humankind, are to a large extent prisoners of their own time. Despite LADA's forward thinking—its anticipation of population growth, increased vehicular traffic, the need for additional schools, parks, and other amenities—its planning was based largely on implied assumptions. One was that the City of Louisville would continue its geographical expansion, absorbing adjacent areas as they developed the need for full urban services. Another was that the central business district would continue its traditional role as the retail-shopping heart of the expanding urban area. Yet the 1920s, the first true decade of the automobile, had given strong signals—not fully deciphered at the time—of the coming change in the relationship between the City and the areas beyond its boundaries.

The change had been delayed for fifteen years—first by the Depression, then by the war, a delay that further muffled the message. With the end of the war, the barriers to an incredible outward flow from the city were removed. Even before 1945 ended, plans were announced for a shopping center in the triangular space between Frankfort Avenue and Lexington Road in St. Matthews—then still an unincorporated community. A main theme of the history of the Louisville area since the end of World War II has been the shift in the power relationship between City Hall and Court House, and the fragmentation of urban decision-making through the rise of numerous incorporated cities throughout Jefferson County.

The post-war phenomenon of governmental fragmentation actually had its beginnings in May 1938 when the small City of Shively was created in the area previously known as St. Helens, immediately southwest of Louisville. During most of its history Jefferson County contained only three municipalities: Louisville (1780), Jeffersontown (1797), and Anchorage (1878). Other towns were absorbed by Louisville. Though suburban Strathmoor Village and Strathmoor Manor, near Bowman Field, were incorporated in 1928 and 1931, the creation of Shively marked a significant change. Incorporated at the behest of distilleries to prevent annexation by Louisville, it represented an emphasis on municipal status as a device to maintain independence rather than to provide services. Two months before Shively was incorporated, a scarcely noted bill passed the General Assembly that made it virtually impossible for a first-class city (thus, only Louisville) to annex smaller cities. Only one of Louisville's eight representatives voted against the bill, which was followed by the almost immediate formation of Shively. The lesson was not lost on other communities outside Louisville. Seneca Gardens, Mockingbird Valley, Audubon Park, and Indian Hills all adopted the same strategy by 1941. After the war, City creation assumed major proportions.

But these developments still lay in the future in 1945. In the first years after the war, Louisville was concerned with immediate problems. The first priority, both in Louisville and across the nation, was to meet the pent-up demand for housing. Harry Truman, who had succeeded to the presidency in April 1945 upon Roosevelt's death, recognized the need for action and chose Wilson Wyatt as national housing administrator, charged with expediting home construction. Meanwhile, commercial construction projects bloomed in Louisville. The *Courier-Journal* and *Times* announced construction of a new home at Sixth and Broadway that would include quarters for radio station WHAS. Stewart's, the city's most prestigious department store, planned a seven-story addition. The Sisters of Charity of Nazareth revealed plans for Our Lady of Peace Hospital on Newburg Road as a treatment center for the mentally disturbed. The Corps of Engineers turned its attention to building the floodwall, which had been planned almost while the 1937 flood waters were still receding, but was delayed by the war.

Industrially, the picture was bright. Synthetic rubber had become a staple of the American economy and Louisville retained its rank as the largest center of American production. As the government-owned plants in Rubbertown were offered for sale, they were purchased and subsequently enlarged by their wartime operators. The Rubbertown complex also attracted plastics producers, notably Stauffer and Rohm & Haas Chemical companies. The Curtiss-Wright plant was purchased from the government by International Harvester Company in 1947 and converted to produce tractors. Reynolds

1943: Thinking about the future
In a 1975 interview former Mayor Wilson W. Wyatt, Sr., recalled the mood of Louisville in 1943 and the founding of the Louisville Area Development Association, which began planning for the needs of the post-war era.

"I think the war knocked a lot of complacency out of Louisville. The Harper's *piece ["Louisville: An American Museum Piece"] made a lot of younger people think hard about the city and its future direction. The war brought prosperity and new people and new industries....It jolted us and it helped us realize our locational advantage. It helped us realize that more growth was coming, that the city—the area—was going to change. The mood of the city was essentially one of optimism on the war front and on the home front."*
Louisville Magazine, *January 1975*

Top right: The Louisville & Nashville Railroad's first main-line diesel locomotives arrived in time for yeoman service during World War II, when freight and passenger loadings far exceeded all previous records. On May 18, 1942, two of the new 2,000-horsepower locomotives prepared to depart Louisville Union Station with the Pan-American, the railroad's premier passenger train. In the post-war years the automobile and the plane spelled the doom of L&N passenger service.
L&N Railroad

Bottom right: Commercial aviation operations, transferred from Bowman to Standiford Field in 1947-48, utilized a temporary terminal reached from Preston Street until the opening of the new Lee Terminal in 1950, where this Eastern Air Lines Falcon discharged passengers in 1952. The terminal has been enlarged several times to handle a passenger load that has grown from 125,000 during 1950 to two million during 1978.
Lin Caufield

Metals, correctly anticipating a large post-war demand for aluminum products, expanded Louisville operations. For the city by the Falls, World War II had created a new industrial revolution, leaving a base of manufacturing facilities of large national corporations, where previously Ford Motor Company had been almost alone in this category.

A revolution was brewing in the city's transportation patterns as well. In early 1945, even before the end of the war, major airlines were seeking authority to establish coast-to-coast routes. Louisville emerged as a major intermediate stop in the plans of American and Trans-World airlines, while Delta proposed service to Asheville. The Air Board had decided in 1944, following studies and recommendations by LADA, that post-war commercial services would be transferred from Bowman to Standiford Field. The move was carried out in late 1947 and early 1948, but the new Lee Terminal was not completed until 1950. By that year the approximately 40,000 passengers who used air service in 1940 had increased to 125,000.

Although improved air service was an important LADA priority, the organization was even more concerned with expediting the movement of motor vehicles on the ground. The planning that proceeded during the war years resulted in what probably has been the single most significant factor in altering Louisville-area residence and travel patterns. From its own working committees and the advice of outside consultants, LADA developed a plan for two major limited-access highways: today's Watterson and North-South expressways. Conceived before the national Interstate Highway program, the two routes were planned for local traffic and were seen as strengthening the core of the city. By providing easy access to the central business district, the argument ran, the belt road plus its connecting road to the city's core would discourage commercial development on the fringes. As experience proved, the analysis was erroneous.

The Watterson Expressway, first called the Inner-Belt Highway, was to extend from Shelbyville Road east of St. Matthews to Dixie Highway at Shively. While the planners foresaw a rapid increase in traffic, they were unable to envision post-war America's 'love affair' with the automobile, or the full dimensions of suburban growth based largely on the personal transportation provided by the car. Although the Inner-Belt was projected as a limited-access road, it was to be a surface route, crossing intersecting roads at grade. Construction, aided by federal funds, began in early 1949 and the first 2.4-mile link between Bardstown Road and Breckinridge Lane opened in December of that year. It was only a two-lane road, but it marked the beginning of the expressway era in Louisville and Jefferson County. In 1950 a consultant predicted that by 1970 the newly opened stretch would carry 2,200 vehicles daily. Two years after the prediction, the volume averaged 5,200 daily.

The rapid increase in automobile ownership after the war pushed the number of motor vehicles registered in Jefferson County to almost 150,000 by 1950, compared to 89,000 in 1940. The increase continued unabated throughout the 1950s; by 1960 the figure had climbed to over 245,000. As the automobile population increased, creating an inordinate demand for parking spaces and forcing the use of parking meters, the transit system carried fewer passengers each year. The buses, which replaced the streetcars after the war, carried only seventy-four million passengers in 1949, compared to the ninety-two million handled seven years earlier. By 1950 the passenger load shrank to sixty-five million.

While expressway projects and rising automobile ownership were setting the stage for an unprecedented white middle-class flow from the city to the new suburbs, a different kind of social change was bubbling in Louisville's black ghettoes, a change that would profoundly affect the entire metropolitan area within a few years. It was part of the revolution of rising expectations stirring throughout black America, a compound of hope generated during the Roosevelt years plus the opportunities opened by the wartime labor shortage. Unlike the World War I years, when many Louisville blacks migrated north to seek war-industry jobs, the World War II industrial expansion made the city a magnet for members of the race. The black population increased from 47,200 in 1940 to 57,800 in 1950. The rising expectations were the theme of the commencement exercise of the 1944 graduating class of Central High School. The student speakers emphasized the "wider range of positions that will be opened to youths in new industries after the war and increased participation in civic enterprises." Black soldiers returned to civilian life less willing to accept segregation and the inferior status it implied.

When the Republican and Democratic parties each included a black aldermanic candidate in their slates for the 1945 City election, progress toward "increased participation in civic enterprises" seemed to be accelerating.

Although Democrat E. Leland Taylor was chosen mayor to succeed Wyatt, Republicans swept the aldermanic races. Republican Eugene S. Clayton became the first black ever to serve as alderman. Although many Louisville color barriers fell one by one during the next few years, blacks found that both militancy and legal action were still necessary strategies. As the city's black population continued to increase in the post-war period, the drive for equality of opportunity became, along with the rise of suburbia, a major factor in the Louisville area's recent history.

These two underlying themes became more visible during the administration of the man that *Harper's Magazine* called "the most remarkable mayor in the city's history." *Life*, a bit more cautious, described him simply as "a strange new mayor." He was attorney Charles P. Farnsley, who took the reins of City government in March 1948 following the mid-term death of Mayor Taylor. The choice of a successor to Taylor by the aldermen (all Democrats, following the fall 1947 election), brought party divisions to the surface immediately. The Democratic Central Committee, controlled by Mickey Brennan, chose investment broker Thomas Graham as its candidate. The opposing Taylor faction first chose attorney Eli Brown III, then switched to Farnsley after labor expressed opposition to Brown (as well as to Graham). When the vote was taken March 2, the tally was five votes for Graham, five for Farnsley. The deciding vote was thus left to Aldermanic President and Acting Mayor Dann C. Byck, Sr., who voted for Farnsley. At the general election in the fall, Farnsley was an easy victor to complete the rest of Taylor's term; then survived Brennan opposition in the Democratic primary in the spring of 1949 and was the choice of voters that fall for a full four-year term.

The new mayor developed some unusual procedures for managing City government. The first—and the one that gained most attention at home and elsewhere—was the weekly 'beef session' during which any citizen could present complaints about City services directly to the mayor. Through this first-hand contact with citizens, plus the results of door-to-door interviews by a professional opinion-survey organization, Farnsley learned which problems were of the greatest concern. Facing the same financial stringency that had prompted Wilson Wyatt to suggest purchase of LG&E, Farnsley pursued a different approach: an occupational license tax that was, in effect, a City income tax on the wages of every person who worked in Louisville and on the profits of businesses.

The idea was not original with Farnsley; it had been considered during Taylor's administration. But Farnsley immediately took up the cause. With his particular low-key flair, he won support among Louisville voters by stressing the fact that the tax would force suburbanites, who worked in the city but avoided Louisville real-estate taxes, to help bear the cost of better services. He also stressed tax benefits: an expanded street-paving program, additional

Right: Construction of the floodwall encircling Louisville, begun after World War II by the Army Engineer Corps, had been completed around Portland by late 1948. The wall separated the old wharf area at right from the historic heart of the community at left. The spire is on the Catholic church of Notre Dame du Port, known now as Our Lady's Church. The entire floodwall was completed in 1956, but during the 1970s was extended southward along the Ohio River to protect southwestern Jefferson County.
Courier-Journal *and* Times

Charlie, the innovator
"The fact is that Charles P. Farnsley is a man with a passion for city government ...a passion to make Louisville a safer, happier, more livable city.

"Charlie would keep out of a lot of trouble if he sat with his feet on the desk at City Hall all day and did nothing....Instead, he throws out energy and imagination like a pinwheel on the Fourth of July, and some of the sparks start political brush-fires he has trouble controlling....It is the simplest thing in the world to criticize a man who is doing such a job, and the hardest to suggest a genuinely better way to do it."
Courier-Journal, *January 9, 1952*

police, improved traffic flow, more playgrounds, better public-health services, and public-school buildings. His opinion poll had told him that these were citizens' priorities. He convinced the Board of Aldermen of the necessity of the tax, which became effective July 1, 1948. Political experts warned him that imposing a tax when he would face the electorate in November was a sure way to defeat. Instead, Farnsley was reelected with an 11,521-vote edge.

With the additional income—$3 million the first year—from the occupational license tax, Farnsley was able to attack each of the problems during his next five years in City Hall. He stretched City funds by doing things in unconventional ways. Instead of repaving older streets from curb to curb, he had only the driving lanes resurfaced. This "half-soling" cut costs 30% and permitted sixty miles of streets to be repaved during the first year of the tax. To help solve a manpower problem in the Police Department, Farnsley hired women to serve as school-crossing guards. The accomplishment that has meant most to Louisville since Farnsley left office, however, has been the occupational license tax itself. (In 1978 the tax, increased to 1.25% in 1956, yielded $34 million.)

Not all of Farnsley's ideas—they seemed to flow like water from a never-failing spring—met with such acceptance. One proposal during his first months in office was City purchase of the Louisville Railway Company so that its profits could be used to bolster the underfunded University of Louisville. The transit company was willing to sell; University President Dr. John W. Taylor favored the move. He noted that without World War II veterans, whose tuition was paid by the federal government, his institution would be "running on a deficit," and added that City funding now provided for only 10% of the University's annual needs. But the purchase proposal encountered stiff opposition; some opponents were persons who had backed Wyatt's earlier proposal for City purchase of LG&E. The charge of socialism was

heard. In the end the Board of Aldermen unanimously rejected purchase of the bus firm. For the University, it was just as well, since local transit profits were on a downward curve. No one, however, offered an alternative plan for solving U of L's financial problems that grew as its enrollment increased.

When Farnsley took office in 1948 Louisville's racial segregation was basically unchanged from its historic pattern. Except for the fact that public transit had been desegregated in 1871, that blacks voted without hindrance, and that they had obtained a toehold in public office, the city's racial patterns differed little from cities in the South. Those differences were significant, however, and eased the transition to a more open society. By the time Farnsley left office in late 1953, many of the old barriers had fallen. Some of the changes were the result of court decisions, some were made voluntarily, and others were initiated by the Mayor. All were related to black demands for change.

In 1948 the main branch of the Louisville Free Public Library was opened to blacks at Farnsley's urging. (The policy was extended to all branches four years later.) Also in 1948 St. Joseph Infirmary admitted its first black patient and Sts. Mary & Elizabeth Hospital soon followed suit. The most significant change, however, followed the action of the Kentucky General Assembly in 1950 in virtually repealing the Day Law, the 1904 legislative act that had prohibited integration of institutions of higher education. With this legal barrier removed, all Louisville colleges—Spalding, Ursuline, Bellarmine (founded 1950), the Presbyterian and Baptist seminaries —immediately opened their doors to black students. The University of Louisville, where the process was a bit more complex because it required phasing out Louisville Municipal College, followed in 1951. Only one faculty member—Dr. Charles H. Parrish, Jr.—was transferred from Municipal College to U of L, however.

The end of the Day Law came as the result of the renewed action in Louisville's black community for an end to color barriers. Lyman T. Johnson, a black school teacher, filed suit in federal court in 1948 seeking admission to the Graduate School of the University of Kentucky after the institution had turned down his application. The court in 1949 ruled in Johnson's favor, since neither of the state's two black institutions of higher education offered the advanced work he sought. At the same time a case involving Louisville's public golf courses was taken to federal court, which ruled in 1952 that the courses and the fishing lake be opened to all. The following year Mayor Farnsley ordered blacks admitted to Iroquois Amphitheatre for performances of *The Tall Kentuckian*, a play about Lincoln. (In 1955 Mayor Andrew Broaddus, Farnsley's successor, issued an executive order abolishing segregation in all public parks.)

The early phases of the slow erosion of Louisville's color bars did not

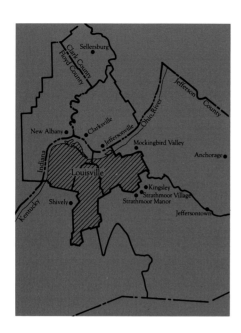

Above: By 1940 the United States Census Bureau recognized somewhat belatedly that population within city boundaries was no longer an accurate index of urban growth, but that many metropolitan districts had emerged. The Louisville district, with 434,408 residents, cut across state lines to encompass Jefferson County plus Clark and Floyd counties in Indiana. The districts are now called Standard Metropolitan Statistical Areas (SMSAs). The Louisville SMSA, enlarged in 1973 to include the Kentucky counties of Bullitt and Oldham, has reached an estimated population of nearly one million.

attract national attention, but other aspects of the Farnsley years did. There was, first, the mayor himself. Not only unconventional in his approach to government, he was also given to wearing string ties, carrying a carpetbag, defending the Confederate Monument on Third Street from those who wanted it moved as a traffic hazard, and calling upon the wisdom of Confucius. He was also interested in culture, which made him unusual among mayors. At the time he was chosen to head City government, he was not only a trustee of the University of Louisville, but also president of the Louisville Philharmonic Society. Journalistically, he was 'good copy'. But Louisville's cultural achievements during his term in office, many prompted by Farnsley himself, received as much attention as the mayor.

At Farnsley's urging, and with $50,000 in surplus tolls from the Clark Memorial Bridge, the Public Library launched new programs to serve more people, including two FM radio stations to carry educational programs for use in the schools and to broadcast serious music. The then-new television could be viewed on sets installed at all branches. Records, films, and framed art were made available to borrowers. The greatest acclaim, however, was for a new departure for the Louisville Orchestra (it dropped "Philharmonic" from its name in February 1949) in regularly commissioning new works by contemporary composers and for The Louisville Fund, founded to raise money from the whole community to support the city's arts' organizations. Both ideas were suggested by Farnsley.

The mayor also wrestled with the problem posed by the rise of small incorporated cities around Louisville's fringes. Ironically, he had been one of the Louisville representatives in the 1938 General Assembly who voted for the revision of the annexation procedure that was to cripple the City's normal expansion pattern. By 1948, however, he favored City-County consolidation and his was among the first voices raised for this solution to governmental fragmentation. He also pushed what annexation was possible, chiefly a 1950 move that added a nine-square-mile area to the southeast, including Standiford Field, the Naval Ordnance Plant, Camp Taylor, the site where the Kentucky Fair & Exposition Center was rising, and the future site of the Louisville Zoological Garden. The annexation completely surrounded Audubon Park. That same year St. Matthews became an incorporated city and the Louisville Chamber of Commerce was formed, absorbing LADA, the Board of Trade and some other groups.

While Louisville reveled in the unorthodoxy of its mayor and Jefferson County farms were being turned into suburban tracts, the post-war event that would have the greatest economic impact on the metropolitan area was being decided in New York. In 1951 the announcement was made. General Electric Company would move its entire home-appliance manufacturing operation to Louisville. Before the year was out, the buildings were rising south of Louisville near the small community of Buechel on the 1,000-acre site that would be named Appliance Park.

Chapter Sixteen

Changing of the Guard

The loss of local ownership
"The attrition of local ownership of industry here — and elsewhere — has been no economic accident.

"Inexorable forces have been at work to cause some 50 locally owned firms to pass to absentee ownership since World War II and make of Louisville a 'branch plant' city.

"The major force for merger has been the necessity to compete in a larger and increasingly national market. This means a national distribution system, national advertising, more plants, and sometimes the production of a firm's own raw material."
Louisville Times, *February 24, 1959*

General Electric's choice of the Louisville area as the single production center for its entire line of home appliances, coming on the heels of the vast manufacturing development of World War II, affirmed that the industrial revolution accompanying that conflict marked a permanent change in Louisville's industrial base. The area's industry was shifting from numerous, relatively small, locally owned enterprises to large production units owned by national corporations. But more immediately, as the area's largest industrial operation, Appliance Park meant additional employment. The 83,500 industrial workers of 1951 rose to an average of 97,500 during the latter years of the decade. Practically all of the increase was due, directly or indirectly, to General Electric. It also marked the beginning of a slow shift to what might best be described as the Louisville region. As early as 1958 more than 25% of the nearly 16,000 employees at Appliance Park arrived at work each day from outside Jefferson County. The presence of General Electric also triggered a general increase in wage rates for skilled work.

Significant as these developments were, the arrival of plants of large national corporations produced an even more basic change in the area's internal social structure. No longer did the names of individuals spring to the lips in describing the local industrial scene, but rather the names of such corporate giants as Du Pont, International Harvester, General Electric, and B.F. Goodrich. Walter Girdler's manufacturing operations became part of the Chemetron Corporation and Wood F. Axton's tobacco-processing plant was now Philip Morris. Archibald Cochran's aluminum-foil company became the Louisville operation of Anaconda Aluminum; B.F. Avery & Sons was swallowed by Minneapolis-Moline Company; the Ballard & Ballard flour milling operation was merged with Pillsbury Mills.

Louisville's new industrial revolution, like the first that followed the Civil War, was based on certain locational advantages. General Electric, for instance, determined that the city was close to the center of its market for home appliances, so that transportation costs were reduced. The Ohio River also once again assumed an important role. Now made navigable year-round, it could be used to transport steel from Pittsburgh at low cost, General Electric found, while Louisville's rail and highway connections provided the necessary network for shipping finished products. The metropolitan area, including its rural hinterlands, also insured an adequate labor supply, while electric-power costs were below the national average because of the abundant supply of Kentucky coal.

The new industrial development differed significantly from the post-Civil War pattern, however. The large corporations were geared to the national market that emerged at the end of the Nineteenth Century with the completion of the nation's rail network. Louisville's diversified but small-scale industry that looked chiefly to the South as a market suffered in the early years of the Twentieth Century from the competition of the large new corporations that integrated the functions of purchasing, manufacturing, marketing, and finance. Even though the Louisville Industrial Foundation achieved remarkable success in attracting new industry, most were small. The strata of small, diversified industry remain, however, manufacturing products that can still be marketed on a regional basis — paints and coatings, for example. But the big names in Louisville-area industry now are the national names.

Accompanying the infusion of large corporate industry was an infusion of corporate executives; managers whose ties to Louisville were forged by their corporations rather than by the lure of entrepreneurial opportunity. Though each of the corporations sent in its team of middle-level managers (who were likely to leave as they advanced up the corporate ladder), the General Electric contingent was, by far, the largest. In the first few months after the announcement of Appliance Park, the company moved 300 persons to Louisville. Eventually 500 were transferred.

Above: Ford Motor Company opened its new Grade Lane assembly plant south of Louisville in 1955, replacing the 1920s plant on South Western Parkway in the city. With five parallel assembly lines, the plant could produce five different models simultaneously. A second Ford plant, producing heavy trucks, was opened in eastern Jefferson County in 1969, an area that earlier had successfully excluded industry. The truck plant was one demonstration that the suburban areas were, in fact, an integral part of a larger urban region.
Courier-Journal *and* Times

Above right: When 1,000 acres of farm fields and pastureland near what was the small community of Buechel along two-lane Bardstown Road were transformed into General Electric Company's Appliance Park, the effect was felt throughout the Louisville area and beyond. Surveying for the giant plant, which was to become the metropolitan area's largest employer, was under way in September 1951.
Lin Caufield

Above far right: Refrigerators take shape in 1955 as they pass along the assembly line in one of the five separate manufacturing plants erected by General Electric Company at Appliance Park. Dishwashers and electric stoves are also among the appliances manufactured at the huge complex.
Lin Caufield

When George Leighton described Louisville as a "museum piece" in *Harper's* in 1937, he was not referring to the physical city as much as to the older economic patterns that it still exhibited in the new age of the national corporation. With a few notable exceptions—Ford Motor Company and some distilling and tobacco firms—industries were locally owned and managed by those who owned them. Manufacturers had first achieved a significant measure of power in Louisville during the wave of industrialization that followed the Civil War. Local entrepreneurs such as Benjamin F. Avery, Dennis Long, and Theodore Ahrens symbolized the age of individual enterprise. Engaged in competitive struggle with their counterparts who owned and managed factories in rival cities, their ties to Louisville were intensely personal and their local prestige enormous.

The new managers of the age of corporate enterprise were a different breed, playing a far different role than the old manufacturers. Though the newcomers managed vastly larger enterprises (any one of the five divisions at Appliance Park employed an average of 5,000 persons), they were overshadowed by the corporations that employed them. The corporate managers, however, made their own impact on Louisville. Well-paid and well-educated, they helped accelerate the demand for new homes in pleasant suburban settings and provided an enlarged base for support of music, theatre, and other performing arts. They helped swell passenger loadings at Standiford Field (826,335 by 1960) as they traveled on company business. They helped generate the demand to have the Eastern Time Zone moved westward to encompass Louisville, since that facilitated communication with East Coast corporate headquarters. Though there was always the annoying possibility that they might be transferred to another city, they participated in civic activities, including service on Chamber of Commerce committees.

They did not, however, erect office buildings, hotels, and theatres, establish hospitals and philanthropic institutions, endow universities, establish art museums, or place statuary in public places—activities common to the earlier generations of local wealth. (The outside corporations did, however, practice 'corporate citizenship', allocating funds to various civic activities.) With the slow erosion of the earlier group of affluent, dominant individuals whose business decisions were usually made with a Louisville bias, and who, therefore, constituted a quite visible Establishment, the base of local decision-making broadened. First through the Louisville Area Development Association and, after 1950, the Chamber of Commerce, owners and executives of smaller businesses, for example, found a medium for participation in a wide range of community planning.

Moreover, the emphasis on planning, which the Chamber inherited from LADA, was a measure of the changing milieu to which Louisville had to adapt. In this it was no different from most other urban centers. Since the most important economic decisions were made outside the city, the strategy

The power of the press
"Barry Bingham, [Sr.,] proprietor of the Courier-Journal *and* Times, *and Mark Ethridge, his publisher, have made the papers a pervasive force....It is difficult to overemphasize the influence of Bingham and Ethridge; they give daily proof of the maxim that a city is as good as its newspapers."*
Holiday, June 1957

was to attempt to influence those decisions, publicizing the Louisville area's advantages as a desirable place in which to live, as well as its advantages as a business location. In contrast, the former Board of Trade had concentrated on promoting the products of locally owned industry, on the advantages of dealing with local wholesalers, and on developing transportation routes and rates that would favor Louisville over rival cities. The new approach required planning to enhance that intangible concept, lifestyle, which loomed even larger in promotional efforts.

The role of large outside corporations in changing the character of the urban area was matched by the role of large outside governments—both State and federal, particularly the latter. Both became important funding sources for local projects. The floodwall, completed in 1956, and public housing were two important examples of federal involvement. More important than either, however, in physically reshaping the city was the advent of urban renewal—conceived initially as an effort, using local funds, to rehabilitate deteriorated housing in the central core. One of the early planning priorities of the new Chamber of Commerce, the idea was furthered by the Farnsley administration through creation of a Department of Redevelopment.

Planning went forward during 1952 and 1953 for clearance and construction of new housing in an area near Central High School (the old Medical Institute of 1837) and for developing a Medical Center in the area east of downtown around City Hospital (renamed General Hospital). The projects were passed on to the administration of Mayor Andrew Broaddus, who succeeded Farnsley in December 1953. Although Congressional legislation in 1954 made federal aid available for such projects, Broaddus' initial contacts with the federal bureaucracy were so frustrating that he tried another approach. Thomas A. Ballantine, Sr., first president of the Chamber of Commerce, recalled that the Mayor "wanted the private sector to do it all, with the City participating through strict code enforcement." However, Ballantine added, "There wasn't enough incentive for private capital to rehabilitate low-income housing, especially with the demand for new housing in the suburbs. A public-private partnership had to be established...."

The Broaddus administration finally gained federal funding in mid-1956 for two small-scale housing rehabilitation projects: one in Smoketown, the other in the West End. The Chamber of Commerce and other business groups had larger projects in mind, however, and convinced Broaddus to expand the program. In November 1957 voters approved a $5-million City bond issue for a major redevelopment effort, including the Medical Center and a proposed Civic Center west of Sixth Street. The business community's strong backing for the projects stemmed from the hope that clearing blight from the east and west sides of the retailing core would encourage private renewal efforts there. With the bond issue approved, Louisville was commit-

Above: Downtown Louisville in 1949 was yet to feel the impact of urban renewal, the North-South and Riverside expressways, and high-rise buildings clustered along a riverfront transformed by the Plaza/Belvedere. The few parking lots in evidence were to multiply during the next decade, however. The view looks north from Broadway, where the Commonwealth Building at Fourth was still the four-story Martin Brown Building.
Louisville Chamber of Commerce

Right: Fourth Street retained its role as the retailing heart of the Louisville area all through the 1950s, despite urbanization's relentless outward push. This shopping night in 1956 found sidewalks crowded. The view looks north from Fourth and Walnut. Not until the 1960s would the lights begin noticeably to dim.
Courier-Journal and Times

ted to urban renewal as a tool for reshaping large areas of the central area of the city. During the next decade the results of that commitment began to change the familiar face of downtown.

While plans for the physical restructuring were advancing, a 1954 decision of the United States Supreme Court set the stage for a social restructuring. The landmark *Brown vs. Topeka Board of Education* ruling that reversed the 1896 "separate but equal" doctrine meant the end of segregated public schools. The *Courier-Journal* immediately noted that a dissenter from the 1896 decision had been Justice John Marshall Harlan, the strong Civil War Unionist who had practiced law in Louisville following that conflict. His dissenting opinion that "Our Constitution is color blind…the destinies of the two races are indissolubly linked together…," was now recognized as the correct constitutional interpretation. Fortunately, Louisville's earlier steps toward desegregation eased the way toward coping with the Supreme Court decision.

Though school integration was not popular among most whites, the success of the earlier desegregation efforts gave reason to hope for a peaceful transition to the new order. For example, although nearly 72% of Louisvillians in a 1949 poll had opposed integration of public parks, the actual move six years later caused no problems. Nevertheless, School Superintendent Omer Carmichael, a soft-spoken Alabama native, initiated detailed planning for the process of integration, set by the School Board for the fall of 1956. The decision was made to integrate all grade levels at once, to redistrict the school system without regard to race, and to permit voluntary transfers within the capacities of the schools. This 'safety-valve' eased the process of integration for both white and black parents; of black students assigned to former white schools, transfers were requested for 45%; of white students assigned to former black schools, transfers were requested for 85%.

Though the national press had taken only casual note of the city's earlier easing of color bars, the results of Carmichael's patient, thorough preparation for school desegregation was another matter. With over 45,000 students, Louisville was among the larger school systems to integrate in 1956. Of the total student population, 27% were black, the highest in any large city initiating desegregation that year. On September 10 schools opened. Whatever the visiting reporters were expecting, they found nothing but quiet — unlike the situation in some other communities. That quiet made headlines across the nation. To its increasing reputation in the arts, Louisville added a reputation as a model in race relations. Although overshadowed by the attention on Louisville schools, the Jefferson County school system, too, made the successful step to integration at the same time. The problem was simpler in the county, however. Of 33,000 public school students in 1956, less than 3% were black. Catholic schools also integrated their classrooms.

Above: Retailing, in the form of the suburban shopping center, followed the outward flow of population, draining trade from downtown Louisville. Hikes Point in January 1957 was already home to the McMahan Shopping Center along Taylorsville Road, which runs diagonally from top left to bottom right in the photograph. Rows of new houses appear behind the shopping center, others are under construction, and a few farm structures still remain. The unwieldy, angular intersection was on the verge of becoming one of the worst traffic bottlenecks in the Louisville area. Lin Caufield

Catholic education, in addition, expanded its dimensions during the 1950s as Bellarmine College, opened in 1950 under the auspices of the Archdiocese, created a role for itself among Louisville's institutions of higher education. The new college, headed by Monsignor Alfred Horrigan, was on a wooded, hilly site between Newburg Road and Norris Place that had much earlier been the site of Preston Park Seminary. The seminary, founded by Bishop William G. McCloskey, operated from 1871 until the Bishop's death in 1909. Bellarmine College, an all-male institution in its earlier years, became co-educational when it merged with Ursuline College (founded in 1938 on Lexington Road) in 1968.

Meanwhile, in Jefferson County beyond Louisville's boundaries, the subdivisions multiplied and population continued to increase far faster than the city's. By 1960, when Louisville's population totaled 390,639 (the highest it would ever reach, but only a 5.8% increase over 1950), the county's population outside the city totaled 220,308, an almost 100% increase over 1950. Future trends were made clearer in a special federal census in 1964: Louisville's population had declined by more than 1,000 in four years; that outside the city had increased 4,000 and the number of smaller incorporated cities had reached thirty-four. Though downtown Louisville retained its position as the chief retailing center all through the 1950s, the first large suburban shopping centers were a forecast of future developments. Accompanying the population shift were signs of a disturbing antipathy between city and suburbs, both components of what was actually a single geographic and economic unit.

That antipathy was displayed forcefully in the 1956 voting on the Mallon Plan for extending Louisville's boundaries. Developed by a seven-member Local Government Improvement Committee appointed jointly by

Above: The winds of change in eastern Jefferson County are symbolized by this 1957 scene in Devondale subdivision. The 1877 residence at right, erected by Magnolia Stock Farm owner A.G. Herr, replaced a much-earlier home erected by his father, John Herr, Jr. The Herr home survived the wave of suburbanization as an artifact of an earlier age surrounded by the tokens of a newer. The name of Herr Lane, constructed in 1873, is a tangible reminder of the family that owned Devondale, now an incorporated city, for several generations. Louisville Magazine

Above right: The little that was left of Shippingport vanished in 1958, a victim of the widening of the Portland Canal. This old, gently decaying building was typical of the structures demolished. Courier-Journal *and* Times

Suburbia along Beargrass
"Oxmoor, near the junction of Route 60 and the Watterson Expressway, is the home of William Marshall Bullitt, who was Solicitor General under Taft.... Nearby stands a renovated slave hut and a log cabin.... Until recently Bullitt's fief was surrounded by open country. Now the horizon is dark with prim new developments occupied by suburbanites." Holiday, *June 1957*

Mayor Andrew Broaddus and County Judge Bertram Van Arsdale, and headed by Louisville Cement Company executive John Mallon, the plan called for merger of Louisville and its heavily developed suburban fringe. Despite the prospect of lower fire insurance and water rates, extension of sewers, and other City services, the plan was rejected by suburban voters by more than two-to-one. Louisville residents, in contrast, approved it by a 14,000-vote edge. In analyzing the opposition, the *Times* observed that "There is a general feeling that suburban life is 'different', and some residents just wanted no part of City citizenship."

The sense of residential separateness had the longest history and was strongest in the rolling country east of Louisville, where many of the city's affluent families had begun building country homes as early as the 1850s. An event in 1957 dramatized the antipathy to any development that seemed to herald an alteration of the character of this residential preserve. Reynolds Metals Company sought to build a research and development center on the old farm of Central State Hospital near Anchorage. Proposed as a distinguished example of contemporary architecture in a campus-like setting, it might have helped set the Louisville area toward developing a cluster of research facilities as sophisticated technology became more important to industry. Area residents, however, succeeded in blocking the development. Frustrated at a second site on Newburg Road, Reynolds built the research laboratory in Richmond, Virginia, where it became one of that city's showplaces. Shortly after, Reynolds also moved its marketing operations from Louisville to Richmond.

These disturbing developments were not only a shock to the business community, but also a concrete indication that the City boundary, whatever its legal meaning, was in fact a permeable membrane incapable of holding urbanistic development within Louisville. Not only shopping centers, but

227

Above: Thruston B. Morton, whose lineage includes the pioneer Clarks of the Louisville area, served as president of the family-owned Ballard & Ballard grain and flour-milling business before he entered Republican politics. Elected to the United States House of Representatives in 1946, he served three successive terms. His two Senate terms extended from 1956 to 1968. Morton was also chairman of the Republican National Committee from 1959 until 1961.
Courier-Journal *and* Times

Above right: The 1962 McAlpine Lock (at right in photograph) of the Portland Canal eliminated river traffic jams of barge tows that often were forced to wait for hours to pass through the older, small lock. The canal itself was widened to 500 feet.
Courier-Journal *and* Times

City of the Fifties
"Louisville today is bounded by history on the north, concrete on the south, smog on the west, suburban independence on the east."
Holiday, *June 1957*

office buildings, motels, and other kinds of commercial establishments, all geared to access by automobile rather than mass transit, were to follow the population spread beyond the city. Industry, too, made major moves far beyond the City limits, a trend set by General Electric. Ford Motor Company, for example, opened a new assembly plant in 1955 on Grade Lane near the L&N's Strawberry Yards.

This full-scale blooming of suburbia was spurred by the lengthening expressway network, incorporated into the new Interstate Highway system in 1957. The following year the Watterson Expressway was completed from Shelbyville Road to Dixie Highway, a concrete corridor across Louisville's southern edge. Two years later the North-South Expressway was completed to Broadway. Its southern end was already connected to the new Kentucky Turnpike to Elizabethtown. A suburban home and an automobile (preferably two or three) became the new way of life, and suburban city creation continued. (Jefferson County now contains eighty-six incorporated municipalities including Middletown, which had let its municipal status lapse, then reincorporated in 1979.)

Louisville, unable to join the outward march by annexation, turned to rebuilding itself. In the process, and to the surprise of many, it rediscovered its traditional neighborhoods. Though suburban lifestyle appealed to most, the tough old city had more vitality than its critics, and even its friends, realized.

Chapter Seventeen

New Directions: Louisville in the Post-Industrial Age

As Louisville and Jefferson County entered the 1960s, the dominant role of the manufacturing industries in the area's economy was taken for granted. The area's second industrial revolution, spawned by World War II, seemed to be a fixed fact of life that would continue indefinitely. It was a pole star to guide economic development efforts, which were concentrated on nurturing new manufacturing enterprises or attracting new ones from elsewhere. In 1963, manufacturing, with 77,536 employees (both blue- and white-collar), represented 42 percent of nonagricultural employment in city and county, up from 65,000 workers and 40 percent of the total in 1950.

This optimism in the unending bonanza of new manufacturing jobs was reinforced by the decision of Ford Motor Company to establish its heavy truck-manufacturing operations in the Louisville area. Ford's Kentucky Truck Plant, opened in 1969 in far eastern Jefferson County, was not only the largest in the world with sixty acres under roof, but added 4,350 industrial jobs. It was a triumph of the joint efforts of the Louisville Chamber of Commerce and the Louisville & Nashville Railroad in persuading the manufacturer to locate the plant here. Yet, although manufacturing jobs continued to be created by smaller enterprises, the Kentucky Truck Plant proved to be the last large-scale enterprise, signalling the end of continuously expanding industrial growth. The rising manufacturing curve that began after the Civil War, and spurted again during World War II, had reached a plateau.

Although it was not realized at the time, the Louisville area in the mid-1970s entered almost imperceptibly what has since been termed America's post-industrial age. Just as the city in the years after the Civil War was forced to shift from a mercantile to a manufacturing economy, so in the last quarter of the twentieth century it found that it had to shift to a new dominant base, moving from blue-collar to white-collar. The efforts to meet the new challenge constitute one of the basic threads in the community's history since 1975.

But in the 1960s this challenge was in the future. Another problem loomed in that decade: The effects of exuberant suburban growth on the 'mother' city. By the end of that decade Louisville had declined in population (as had most other older cities) for the first time in its history, posting a loss of nearly 30,000. The growing number of suburban shopping centers noticeably affected downtown retail trade. Even the sumptuous downtown movie palaces steadily lost ground to the twin developments of television and suburban cinemas. Nor did the growing expressway network, that now spread its fingers into the center city, reverse the decline, as early planners had predicted. As the demand for residential property in older urban neighborhoods fell, property values and tax receipts followed suit.

Office buildings that normally would have been built downtown began to spring up along the expressways instead. The unusual fifteen-story Lincoln Income Life Insurance Tower on the Watterson Expressway at Breckinridge Lane was completed in 1965. Designed by William Wesley Peters of Taliesin Associated Architects, successor to the practice of Frank Lloyd Wright, it represented the insurance company's desire to "create a famous building in Louisville." (Lincoln Income Life was absorbed by Conseco, Inc., an Indianapolis-based insurance-holding company, in 1986 and the headquarters building purchased by local investors, who renamed it Kaden Tower.) In 1965, too, the ten-story Watterson City building was erected at the Watterson Expressway/Newburg Road interchange. These were but the first ventures in the large-scale development of office complexes far beyond center city, and another indication that suburbia could not long remain merely residential. The Mall shopping center of 1963, totally enclosed and with enormous space for parking, was the first of its

Below: Industrialist Archibald P. Cochran (at left) and Thomas A. Ballantine, Sr., served as cochairmen of the 1965 Bonds for Progress Committee that mounted a successful campaign for public approval of the city bond issue to help finance the Riverfront Project. Other bond-issue projects included a new building for the Louisville Free Public Library, the University of Louisville's new medical-dental schools complex, Founders Square, and the Museum of History & Science. Cochran, named expediter of the Riverfront development in 1964 by Mayor William O. Cowger, piloted the project to success. Courier-Journal *and* Times

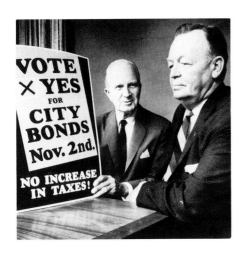

Top: The 800 Apartments, completed at Fourth and York in 1963, was Louisville's tallest building for nearly a decade. The twenty-nine story structure, designed by Louisville architect William S. Arrasmith, marked the first move of downtown highrise buildings south of Broadway.
Louisville Magazine

Bottom: The fifteen-story Kaden Tower, built in 1965 as the Lincoln Income Life Building, brought a new vertical dimension to the suburban landscape. The tower, designed by Taliesin Associated Architects, overlooked open countryside when it was built on Breckinridge Lane at the Watterson Expressway. Since then massive development, including the Paragaon Center (at left) has changed the view.
Quadrant/John Beckman

kind in this area, and a forerunner of many similar ones. This shopping center picked an interchange for its location — at Watterson Expressway/ Shelbyville Road. Large apartment buildings, once confined to the city, also began to dot the suburban landscape.

Thus, the immediate problem that demanded attention in the 1960s was not the area's underlying common economy, but, rather, the changed relationship between city and suburb. The central business district had begun to show the first symptoms of distress in the mid-1950s with slowing retail sales. The first response had been the $5-million bond issue of 1957 to renew blighted areas on the east and west sides of downtown, in the hope that this public investment would encourage private investment in a general brightening up of the retail area. The cleared areas were planned to become the Medical Center on the east and the Civic Center of new local government buildings on the west. The bond issue marked the initially reluctant entry of city government into large-scale restructuring of the built environment. The private sector at that time regarded such efforts as primarily a government function and did not participate directly.

With federal urban renewal funds now available to aid in clearance and rebuilding, the project removed block after block of deteriorated structures. The ten-square-block Medical Center became a reality (and has since been expanded), but the Civic Center never materialized. Neither city nor county government felt comfortable committing the dollars necessary to move operations to new buildings. This area was eventually developed with office structures, a Greyhound bus station, and subsidized low- and high-rise housing. But the main thrust of this first redevelopment effort — encouraging private investment in downtown — was a failure. The Chamber of Commerce recognized the problem as early as 1958 through formation of the Downtown Louisville Committee, which a year later was transformed into the independent planning organization, Louisville Central Area, Inc. (LCA), and soon authorized the first in what became a bewildering array of reports by outside consultants on ways to keep the core of the city healthy.

The first report, centered on the demand for quality apartments downtown, triggered the construction of the twenty-nine-story 800 Apartments at Fourth and York streets by Fritz Drybrough, Sr., who had also been a pioneer in developing downtown parking lots. Completed in 1963 to the design of local architect William S. Arrasmith, this was Louisville's tallest building for nearly a decade. With its liveried doorman, balconies, and blue anodized aluminum cladding, The 800 put a colorful punctuation point on the skyline, but was slow to fill. Some apartments were taken by national corporations with local operations as temporary housing for new executives transferred to the city; some were rented as office space. It took the better part of a decade to lease most of the space to residential tenants, many of them well-to-do retirees.

Meanwhile, the Medical Center was taking tangible form with new hospitals, medical office buildings, and the massive new structures of the University of Louisville medical and dental schools. (The Medical Center is now home to six hospitals, including Kosair Children's that opened in 1987.) The North-South Expressway, made part of Interstate 65, leaped north from Broadway to the John F. Kennedy Bridge (opened across the Ohio River in December 1963), clearing a wide swath in its path. Clearance for the abortive Civic Center west of downtown, which eliminated the traditional black business district along Walnut Street (renamed Muhammad Ali Boulevard in 1978), created unplanned consequences when it forced blacks westward. The movement not only accelerated white flight from the West End, but created new tensions in the black community by breaking old ties and forcing overcrowding. It seems significant that Louisville's 1968 minor version of the riots that marked many ghetto areas across

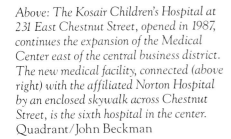

Above: The Kosair Children's Hospital at 231 East Chestnut Street, opened in 1987, continues the expansion of the Medical Center east of the central business district. The new medical facility, connected (above right) with the affiliated Norton Hospital by an enclosed skywalk across Chestnut Street, is the sixth hospital in the center.
Quadrant/John Beckman

the nation in the 1960s followed black displacement west of the central business district.

As the planning, first embodied in the 1962 LCA report *Design for Downtown*, proceeded, a new financial leadership group emerged that was destined to take a leading role in downtown redevelopment. The city's banks moved to fill the role earlier held by individual local entrepreneurs. The financial institutions, notably conservative after witnessing the financial debacle of Jim Brown's National Bank of Kentucky at the onset of the Depression of the 1930s, were perhaps propelled by circumstances (as noted below) to take a leadership role. Another factor, however, was the retirement of older bank officers to whom the flamboyant Brown was a painfully keen memory. As new hands took over management positions there was more willingness on the part of the banks to participate in downtown rebuilding.

One example was the financial participation that made possible the redevelopment of the old riverfront and wharf area, where Reynolds Metals Corporation (later joined by the General Electric Pension Fund) proposed in 1960 to construct a complex of high-rise office buildings and apartment towers surrounding a marina. The redevelopment of the historic riverfront area where Louisville had its beginnings had been suggested as early as 1930 by the St. Louis planning firm of Harland Bartholomew & Associates, consultants to the Planning Commission. The proposal was shelved during the years of the Depression and World War II. Now with a full-fledged Urban Renewal Agency (Mayor Broaddus's successors were not averse to dealing with the federal bureaucracy to secure redevelopment funding), the riverfront proposal was revived.

Reynolds Metals, intrigued by the potential profit in downtown redevelopment nationwide as federal funds fueled urban renewal, and by the emerging planning philosophy that espoused downtown living, envisioned up to 1,000 apartment units in the 'Rivergate' project. The site, to extend along Main Street and the riverfront from Third to Sixth streets, was also to include office towers and a motel. It was an exciting prospect, with the international planning firm of Doxiadis & Associates of Athens called in as chief designer. The project was predicated upon city participation in acquiring land through the urban renewal process. As it turned out, the project was never built, but precipitated a crisis that proved the catalyst

Above: The Riverfront Plaza/Belvedere and its complex of new buildings, completed in 1973, brought new life to the Main Street and riverfront area that in the nineteenth century had been the pulsing heart of Louisville's commercial activity. Although many of the city's fine Victorian buildings were demolished for the project, it was a potent factor in generating interest in the private restoration of the adjacent West Main Street Historic District.
Quadrant/John Beckman

Below: Builder-developer Al J. Schneider, whose Galt House made the Riverfront development possible, carries on the tradition of earlier Louisville entrepreneurs, such as James Graham Brown. Here Schneider inspects the Portland Federal Savings & Loan Association (now The Cumberland) Building going up on the southwest corner of Second and Broadway in 1966, which he built as a joint venture with the financial institution. In the background is the Holiday Inn of 1960 (originally Stouffer's Louisville Inn), Schneider's initial downtown venture.
Courier-Journal *and* Times

not only for large-scale renewal and renovation in the heart of the central business district, but also for the public/private partnership that was to become a hallmark of center city redevelopment.

Federal approval for the urban renewal funding was not received until 1963, and as the rather cumbersome process of land acquisition began, technical problems emerged. This was the renewal agency's first venture into an area of higher-priced real estate where many of the buildings, although aging, were generally sound and well maintained. Disputes over property valuation were frequent and the acquisition process went slowly. Another problem was the decision by the state to route a segment of the Interstate Highway System along the riverfront, which forced a design revision. Then in 1967, Reynolds — discouraged by what it saw as the spotty record of similar projects in other cities — precipitously withdrew. That left the city in a quandary, with much property acquired, demolition begun, but no developer.

After the initial shock, urban renewal planners, building on the Doxiadis design, revised the plan with underground parking topped by a public open space, the Plaza/Belvedere, plus a major hotel as the anchor to encourage office-building construction. Proposals for the hotel were solicited nationwide, but there was not a single response. It took local builder/developer Al J. Schneider, whose first downtown ventures had been on Broadway, to sense the possibilities, including the expressway exit nearby at Third Street. He agreed in 1968 to build a hotel — choosing the name Galt House to recall the city's earlier famed hostelry — if construction of the 1,600-car garage and Plaza/Belvedere were assured. The result, through solution of some financial problems, was the beginning of the public/private partnership that was to undertake a massive renewal of center city. Ironically, in 1969 the head of the Center City Committee, a consortium of public and private interests set up to formulate an overall plan for downtown redevelopment, could bemoan "the absence of a coalition of enlightened public and private leadership." It was taking shape even as he spoke.

The city agreed to build the underground garage, issuing bonds to cover the bulk of the $13.5-million cost. But because of the then seven percent interest rate set by state law on government bonds, it was feared the issue would be difficult to market. To assure that construction would not be delayed, thus jeopardizing the hotel project, Louisville's five largest banks cooperatively loaned the city $7.5 million and persuaded a New York bank to purchase $2.5 million in tax-anticipation notes. The city provided the remaining $3.5 million in cash. The funding also included costs of the Plaza/Belvedere and rebuilding the wharf to provide docking for the county-owned sternwheel steamer *Belle of Louisville*, and other visiting passenger vessels. Meanwhile, Schneider was engaged in lengthy negotiations in a tight money market for permanent construction financing for the somewhat speculative twenty-three-story hotel. He had to meet a December 24, 1969, deadline, expiration date of the contractor's bid on the garage. Foundation work on the hotel and garage had to proceed simultaneously, since the hotel was to lease air rights from the city. Moreover, the hotel was essential to the viability of the garage. Again, the local banks, joined by six savings-and-loan associations, came to the rescue with an interim construction loan. In short, the Riverfront Project was the catalyst for the beginning of the public/private partnership that proved to be the mechanism needed for the transformation of center city.

The banks' most visible contribution to downtown redevelopment, however, was the series of new office towers they erected. Liberty National Bank and Trust Company's new headquarters, opened at 416 West Jefferson Street in 1960, anticipated the wave of construction by the financial institutions. The five-story building with its glass-curtain wall was Louisville's introduction to contemporary architectural trends. Bank of Louisville's 1967 eleven-story headquarters at Fifth and Broadway, built in conjunction with Al J. Schneider, was the first of the new bank buildings to add rental space to the downtown inventory, although it had been preceded in 1965 by the Portland Federal Savings & Loan Association's structure at Second and Broadway.

The tempo increased at the end of the decade when Citizens Fidelity Bank and Trust Company announced its thirty-story tower at Fifth and Jefferson, First National Bank of Louisville a forty-story high-rise (the city's tallest), and Louisville Trust Company (merged later with Liberty National Bank) a twenty-four story structure at Fourth and Main as part of the Riverfront Project. The latter building replaced the Columbia Building, the 1891 ten-story pioneer skyscraper. These new buildings not only significantly altered the downtown skyline, but also helped stem the outflow to suburban office structures by providing hundreds of thousands of square feet of prime office space downtown. All were completed in 1971.

While these building projects and other massive amounts of new construction throughout the central core changed the old familiar face of the city's heart, the hoped-for turnaround in the decline of retail shopping did not follow. Vacant storefronts testified to the attractions of the myriad of suburban shopping centers that had taken on new sophistication with the 1963 opening of The Mall at the Shelbyville Road/Watterson Expressway interchange. That same interchange was chosen for Oxmoor Center, opened in 1971 on part of the historic Oxmoor estate, the last intact local survival of the early slave plantations.

In the search for solutions to downtown's retail decline, Louisville Central Area's 1962 planning document, *Design for Downtown*, had recommended turning three blocks of Fourth Street between Broadway and Liberty into a pedestrian mall with a vehicular lane for buses, taxis, and emergency vehicles. By then such malls had been tried in other cities facing the same problems and early results were encouraging. The retail situation continued to worsen, so that by the latter 1960s merchants and building owners were receptive to the pedestrian mall proposal.

Although funding was an issue, a solution developed by the city and business interests was approved by the 1970 state legislature. It called for the city to issue $1.5 million in twenty-year bonds to be retired by assessments of land along the mall, a financing arrangement that, along with the Riverfront Project, marked the emergence of the public/private partnership in

Above: Guests at the Hyatt Regency Louisville have a breathtaking view from the top of the atrium in the eighteen-story hotel. Opened in 1978, the hostelry was financed by a combination of private and state funding. It is connected to both the Commonwealth Convention Center and the Galleria by skywalks.
Louisville Chamber of Commerce

Right and below: The Galleria, opened in September 1982, was the first successful effort to stem the long-term decline of retail shopping downtown. The glass atrium, spanning the Fourth Avenue Mall, is surrounded by shops, stores, and restaurants on several levels. The exterior view looks south from Liberty Street.
Quadrant/Ted Wathen

Right: The Seelbach Hotel, Louisville's finest when it opened in 1905, fell on hard times and closed in 1975, a victim of the shift to automobile travel and the auto-oriented motel. Its reopening in 1982, with an adjacent city-built parking garage, was directly related to construction of the neighboring Galleria. The $24-million renovation of the hotel restored its original Beaux-Arts elegance.
Quadrant/Ted Wathen

redevelopment. The opening of the pedestrian way with its plantings, fountains, and benches in August 1973 (shortly after completion of the Riverfront Project) boosted hopes that the city's retail heart would regain much of its former vigor. The mall was extended two blocks north to Market Street with the opening of the Commonwealth Convention Center (1977) and the Hyatt Regency Louisville hotel (1978).

The mall, however, did not fulfill the hopes riding on its landscaped length. Stores at cross-street intersections benefitted most, some even reporting increased sales. But those in mid-block did not fare so well. Stores and cinemas continued to close. The Brown Hotel went out of business in 1971, not long after the death of owner/operator James Graham Brown, followed by the Seelbach in 1975. The Brown became administrative headquarters of the Louisville public schools, but the Seelbach stood like a stately ghost at an important intersection. The management of one store that closed was blunt about its decision: The mall "was no help and may have hurt." Part of the problem was undoubtedly the lack of readily accessible parking and of public transportation. Planners felt that the sixty-foot width of the thoroughfare would not permit both vehicular and pedestrian traffic.

But there were positive aspects that outweighed the negative in the long run. The mall, which demonstrated a local commitment to keep the central business district viable, was a factor in gaining state financial support for the Commonwealth Convention Center and the Hyatt Regency Louisville, which then made possible the Galleria, downtown's first successful retail revitalization project. The Galleria, in turn, led to the reopening of the Seelbach Hotel, and stimulated both the development of Theater Square on the south end of the mall as part of the Broadway Renaissance and the reopening of the Brown Hotel. Along the one-mile stretch of Fourth Avenue from the waterfront to Broadway, 59 percent of the buildings existing at the time the mall was opened in 1973 had been replaced by new structures by 1985, and many others had been totally renovated.

The lack of public transit on the mall was remedied in 1987 as a direct outgrowth of the Broadway Renaissance, the revitalization of the Fourth and Broadway area. To connect this project with the developments around the Riverfront Plaza/Belvedere, a frequent bus service has been instituted, using vehicles that resemble old trolley cars. The service, named Toonerville II, recalls the former Brook Street trolley line that was one inspiration for Louisvillian Fontaine Fox, Jr.'s nationally syndicated comic strip, "The Toonerville Trolley."

The Galleria, a $143.5-million development of shops, restaurants, and two high-rise office towers in the heart of downtown, has played a principal role in halting the long-term decline of retail shopping in center city. It has transformed the Fourth Avenue block between Liberty Street and Muhammad Ali Boulevard into a centerpiece of downtown revitalization. It also illustrates how the private sector can act as the coordinating factor in public/private development. The project had its origin in 1975 when, at the suggestion of Mayor Harvey I. Sloane, an informal working group headed by Maurice D. S. Johnson, retired board chairman of Citizens Fidelity Bank, developed a plan for a mixed-use project with emphasis on retailing. The working group, comprised of private-sector senior executives, maintained a close liaison with city and state governments in formulating the plan and choosing a developer. That developer, selected in early 1977, was Oxford Properties, Inc., the United States subsidiary of Oxford Development Group of Canada.

The conversion of Fourth Avenue to a pedestrian mall had created the opportunity to use the thoroughfare as the principal element around which new construction was grouped, and to enclose a portion of the mall

Below: Recalling Louisville's electric streetcar era, the Toonerville II 'trolleys' ply the rebuilt Fourth Avenue Mall between Broadway and the Riverfront. The original Toonerville Trolley nationally syndicated cartoon strip, popular during the 1920s and 1930s, was created by Louisville native Fontaine Fox, Jr. He based it partly on the city's Brook Street trolley line. The new Toonervilles are actually buses modeled on early electric streetcars, which ran on tracks. This one departs Theater Square, near Broadway, for the Riverfront and the two Galt House hotels.
Quadrant/Ted Wathen

in an all-glass, climate-controlled atrium soaring to a maximum height of 110 feet. The Galleria was financed by a combination of private, city, state, and federal funding, with the private sector contributing the largest share — $121 million. Studies by Louisville Central Area before and after opening of the Galleria in 1982 indicated a welcome rise in the number of downtown shoppers between 1981 and 1985.

An immediate by-product of the Galleria was the renovation and reopening of the Seelbach Hotel, Louisville's finest when it opened in 1905. It was agreed that this vacant, ten-story hotel would not be an attractive neighbor to the Galleria. Two Louisville developers were approached by the city's key banks and asked to take on the task of reopening the stately, 350-room edifice. Construction loans were promised, plus assistance in finding long-term financing. The hotel, reopened in April 1982, some six months before the Galleria was completed, restored some of downtown's older elegance.

With the Galleria, the renewal of the central business district took on a new dimension. What had started out at the end of the 1950s as essentially slum clearance on either side of downtown had progressed to the rebuilding and renovation of the core itself. During this time a public/private partnership was being forged that reached maturity with the Galleria — then took a further step with the Broadway Renaissance, a major project initiated by the private sector.

When the Fourth and Broadway area at the south end of downtown was developing rapidly in the 1920s, one Louisville newspaper called it "the magic corner." There was little of that magic left in the 1970s. The once-prestigious Brown Hotel lost even its function as administrative headquarters of the Louisville public schools when city and county schools were merged. Then, when the state agreed in 1977 to provide funding for the proposed Kentucky Center for the Arts in the Riverfront area, the future of the area seemed gloomier than ever. No longer would the Macauley Theatre, neighbor to the Brown Hotel, be the centerpiece for the performing arts.

However, Capital Holding Corporation, a major nationwide insurance-holding company, was also located at Fourth and Broadway in its own twenty-three story corporate headquarters, and was unhappy with the

Above: Recalling the days when "Lit up like Levy's" was a commonplace Louisville expression, the 1893 Levy Building at Third and Market streets has been rejuvenated by developer Frank Metts with apartments on the upper floors and commercial space on the lower.
Quadrant/John Beckman

Above, right: Phoenix Place, a mix of new and renovated older housing east of the central business district, demonstrated that there is a demand for market-rate residential facilities in and near downtown.
Quadrant/Carl Maupin

Below: As Main Street changes character, some of its Victorian commercial structures are being recycled into apartments. One is the Harbison, west of Seventh Street, providing unobstructed river views from its rear windows.
Quadrant/Ted Wathen

decline of its business neighborhood. The corporation, under the direction of its board chairman, Thomas Simon, teamed up with Louisville Central Area in 1978 to form the Broadway Group. This broadly based task force of downtown business leaders looked for ways to infuse new life into the area. The results were announced at the end of 1979 — a plan that called for reopening the Brown Hotel, plus a mix of new low-rise retail and office buildings and adaptive reuse of many older structures. With plans in hand, a package of private and public funding was assembled, and the first phase of what was called the Broadway Renaissance became reality in early 1985.

Reopening the hotel was a bold stroke, but the boldest proposal of all called for construction of 550 market-rate apartments and condominiums to be erected in phases. This was to provide the missing element in downtown renewal: the kind of housing that would counter the appeal of the suburbs. It had been early recognized that an essential ingredient in restoring vitality to the core area was a permanent population of higher income residents. It had been one of Louisville Central Area's first priorities, and The 800 Apartments was the result of that thrust. But when that high-rise structure opened in 1963, downtown was in a state of decline and offered few inducements as a residential area. In the quarter-century following, however, the situation changed greatly, thanks to the dedicated dollar involvement of the private sector. As the cultural and arts center of the region, along with vastly improved shopping, restaurants, transportation, and other amenities, the central core is an attractive living place for many, especially those who work there, a number that is increasing. Between 1968 and 1985, center city employment expanded from 45,000 to more than 60,000, reflecting both the retention of jobs in the area made possible by additional office space, and the shift of the basic Louisville economy from blue- to white-collar employment.

Downtown housing was not entirely neglected before the Broadway Renaissance. The seventeen-story Trinity Towers was completed at Third and Guthrie in late 1962, but was primarily for the retired and elderly. The eighteen-story Kentucky Hotel, converted to apartments and renamed the Kentucky Towers in 1972, found ready rental but offered only smaller units. Not until the early 1980s, when core-area redevelopment was well under way, did the provision of downtown living space take on important dimen-

Top: Belgravia Court in Old Louisville exemplifies the elegance that Victorian planners were capable of producing. Laid out about 1892 as the first of the city's pedestrian-only courts, it was the prototype of many others with differing architectural styles. Some were laid out as late as the 1920s. The pedestrian-only court is found in few other cities than Louisville.
Quadrant/John Beckman

Bottom: The most impressive mansion in Old Louisville, the 1904 Ferguson mansion at 1310 South Third Street, became the headquarters of The Filson Club in 1986. The club, founded in 1884, houses an impressive library and is a center of research on Louisville and Kentucky history and genealogy. Edwin Hite Ferguson, who built the mansion, amassed a fortune in refining cotton-seed oil, but in 1907 was ousted from the Kentucky Refining Company, which he founded. He died in 1924 in reduced circumstances.
The Filson Club

sions — often in the private recycling of older commercial structures into apartments. Examples are The Harbison at Seventh and Main, Billy Goat Strut (named for the alley at the rear) at Main and Clay, and the next-door Abell Apartments.

A more ambitious project was Phoenix Place, a mix of new construction and rehabilitation of older homes in a deteriorating area east of the central business district and near the Medical Center. Initiated in 1976 by a number of business firms in the area who took their case to City Hall, the project was financed by a mix of private, city, and federal funding. The initial phase of 140 garden apartments and townhouses (114 new and 26 in renovated housing) aimed at middle-income tenants was completed in 1984. It was so successful that the developers added another 140 units, completed in 1986.

The new housing in the Broadway Renaissance area, however, is of an entirely different order and designed for higher-income residents. The Crescent Centre takes its name from the two semi-circular, three-story apartment rows facing each other across Third Street and built atop a 346-car ground-level garage. A series of condominiums lines a courtyard modeled after Belgravia Court in Old Louisville. An eleven-story apartment tower completes the 231-unit development, linked directly to Theater Square, north of the Brown Hotel, by ramps and steps. As usual, it was financed by an intricate combination of public and private funding, and the city itself is a limited partner, the first time it has been involved in such a joint venture in redevelopment.

The long-term redevelopment of the central business district meant that old landmarks fell in wholesale lots during the 1960s and the early 1970s, a process accelerated by the demand for automobile parking space. Not surprisingly, this drastic alteration of the familiar cityscape helped crystallize a growing interest in historic preservation. Many Louisvillians had felt dismay as they watched some of the best of the older city give way to what they considered lesser uses, especially parking lots. At the same time, the concern about the future health of downtown kindled a parallel interest in older residential areas that had suffered neglect and changing uses.

The two interests — the better architecture of the past and the desire to halt the creeping decay in some older neighborhoods — were natural allies, and first came together in 1961 with the formation of a group to stir interest in the residential neighborhood immediately south of downtown.

Above: The early development of the
Highlands overlapped the latter years
of Old Louisville's as the architecture
along Cherokee Road demonstrates.
'Gentrification,' the term coined to
describe the move of young professionals
into older neighborhoods with well-built
housing, is especially evident in the
Highlands, Old Louisville, and Crescent
Hill.
Quadrant/John Beckman

Below: Familiar landmark in the
Cherokee Triangle area of the Highlands
is the statue, erected in 1913, of John
B. Castleman on his horse Carolina.
Castleman's former country retreat is
now the nearby Castlewood enclave and
his former stable at Baxter Avenue and
Eastern Parkway has been converted
to a private home. He was for years
president or a member of the Board of
Park Commissioners. Fittingly, his
bronze image looks toward Cherokee Park.
Quadrant/John Beckman

Launched by area churches, once the most prestigious in the city but now
losing membership to the suburbs, the group created the name Old Louisville to describe this neighborhood, that in its earliest years had been
simply the Southern Extension.

The promotional activities of this group, calling itself the Old Louisville Association, struck a responsive chord in a city now old enough to
have a rich community memory and to have developed some interest in
preserving important artifacts of its past. The beginnings of a move back to
Old Louisville by young professionals was a sign that the popular suburban
lifestyles did not appeal to all. Soon the phenomenon of a small, but noticeable, countermove from suburbs to city spread to other older neighborhoods, particularly the Highlands, the Cherokee Triangle, and Crescent
Hill. Accompanying this was a rise in neighborhood consciousness. Associations of residents promoting the improvement of their areas became
common — a kind of city counterpart to the rise of numerous incorporated
municipalities beyond the Louisville boundaries.

This movement was given official recognition in 1973 by the creation
of the city's Historic Landmarks & Preservation Districts Commission to
institute safeguards against indiscriminate destruction and alteration of
structures within designated districts. By the mid-1980s the commission had
created five such districts. Four of these, plus seventeen others, are also on
the National Register of Historic Places, an unusually large number for a
city of Louisville's size. Aiding greatly in the rehabilitation process was the
federal investment tax credit, beginning in 1982, which provided an attractive tax incentive for the renovation of older property. This tax credit, used
in eleven older Louisville neighborhoods, resulted in private investment of
nearly $25 million in housing rehabilitation from January 1982 to mid-1985
— mostly in Old Louisville, the Highlands/Cherokee Triangle, and Crescent Hill, in that order.

The investment tax credit was also applicable to older commercial
property and was a major factor in adaptive reuse of numerous historic
buildings in the central business district, especially in the three-and-one-
half-block West Main Street Historic Preservation District, where the stock
of Victorian commercial structures was virtually intact. Ironically, the
resurgence of this former commercial heart of the city was triggered in large
part by the urban-renewal demolition for the Riverfront Project and the new
developments surrounding it. This new activity center turned attention to
the nearby blocks of West Main Street. The tide turned here in 1974, when

Right: Youngsters at the entry of the Museum of History & Science ponder the giant solar mirror that was part of the Australian exhibit at the World's Fair in Knoxville, Tennessee, in 1982. The mirror can concentrate sufficient solar energy to produce steam to operate a small electric generator. It was a gift of the Australian government to the museum, which opened in 1977 at 727 West Main Street in the former headquarters of wholesaler Carter Dry Goods Company. The museum's location gave a boost to the recycling of commercial structures along Main Street.
Quadrant/Robert K. Hower

the Junior League of Louisville purchased the recently burned-out shell of a building for its headquarters, named Stairways. In 1975 the city chose to locate the new Museum of History & Science in a large building vacated by the Carter Dry Goods Company when it moved to a suburban location. The opening of the museum in 1977 was a giant leap forward in West Main Street's renaissance.

The clear signal that private investors were moving into Main Street property came in 1979 with completion of the first private renovation: the pair of 1855 buildings on the southwest corner of Sixth and Main, which once housed the original Seelbach Hotel. The major breakthrough came in 1980, however, when Kentucky statutes were liberalized to permit use of industrial-revenue bonds, issued by local governments, to be used not only for industrial development but also for a wide range of commercial construc-

tion, including renovation. (Such bonds are not an obligation of government, but of the developer, who gains the advantage of the low interest rates of tax-free bonds.) From 1980 through 1985 a total of $37.1 million in such bonds was issued by Louisville and Jefferson County for purchase and rehabilitation of buildings for office space on West Main Street. These bonds have also been used for the same purpose throughout the central business district. This investment totaled $58.3 million from 1980 through 1985, in addition to the investment on West Main.

The result of the massive public and private investments — over $1 billion in the central business district between 1968 and 1986 — was to increase office-space square footage from less than 4 million to nearly 7 million, most of it new or renovated. Hotel/motel rooms multiplied from 2,291 to 3,625, all new or renovated; the property-tax base rose from $176.6 million to $610 million; and the city's share of property-tax revenue went from $1 million annually to $3.4 million. During the same period, investment in neighborhood housing rehabilitation was about $35 million — $10 million of that total before 1980 without tax incentives or industrial revenue bonds.

While these changes were taking place in the city, the suburban areas outside the Louisville boundaries continued their rapid growth. In 1972 the county population outside the city exceeded Louisville's population for the first time since the early days of settlement. That estimated difference of 3,400 grew to 88,000 by 1980, when the city total stood at 298,450, a decline of some 100,000 over a twenty-year period. As the subdivisions spread to — and beyond — the Jefferson County line, suburbia reveals itself as the latest ring of urban growth around the original heartwood, a place where once-pastoral country lanes are rapidly transformed into busy four-

lane roads. No longer a retreat separate from the city, it is now a diverse mix of single-family dwellings, apartment buildings, office parks, industrial complexes, shopping centers, motels/hotels, even hospitals. Linking it all together and permitting it to function is the expressway system, where road interchanges become the nerve centers of this new form of the urban scene.

As early as 1966 the first concept of a hospital beyond the city limits was initiated by the Hospital Commission of Kentucky Baptists, which purchased fifty-two acres of the J. Graham Brown farm near St. Matthews at the Breckinridge Lane/Interstate 64 interchange. The new 352-bed Baptist Hospital East, opened in 1975, was preceded, however, by the nearby Humana Hospital-Suburban in 1972. This 380-bed facility, the Louisville area's largest at the time, was also the community's first for-profit hospital — a project of Humana, Inc., then still known as Extendicare.

It was significant that this Louisville-based company, which began by operating nursing homes, then switched operation by purchasing existing hospitals across the nation, chose a suburban site for the first new hospital it erected. That both these medical facilities were built in eastern Jefferson County reflected the fact that this area was not only the scene of the most intense development, but also of highest average incomes. (In 1987, in a sign of continuing suburbanization, the long-established Baptist Hospital Highlands on Barret Avenue announced that it would transfer all operations to Baptist East by 1994.)

Southwest Jefferson County, where more modest lower-middle-income subdivisions had proliferated along the Dixie Highway corridor since the 1950s, also clamored for better medical facilities. As development spread south toward Fort Knox and the Hardin County line, residents found themselves farther and farther away from medical facilities, even Sts. Mary & Elizabeth Hospital in Louisville's far South End. The gap was filled by another for-profit hospital operator, American Medicorp, Inc., which

Right: The shopping center with acres of parking space outside is the retail response to the automobile and suburban sprawl. Over one-hundred shopping centers, many small, dot Louisville and Jefferson County. However, suburbia is home to the enclosed or so called 'mall' types, exemplified by Oxmoor (top) in the east and Jefferson Mall (bottom) in the south.
Quadrant/Robert K. Hower, *and*
Carl Maupin

Below: The expressway system in Jefferson County, first envisioned by the Louisville Area Development Association (LADA) in the late 1940s, had developed forty years later into a network far outstripping LADA's more modest proposal. Linking once-isolated areas, the expressways are a major factor in the spread of subdivisions to the Jefferson County border and beyond.
Map by Images

Bottom: The subdivisions continue their outward march as farmland is converted to housing tracts. Typical is Lake Forest along the Shelbyville Road corridor, where concentrated development approaches the Shelby County line. By the mid-1970s, the population of Jefferson County outside Louisville exceeded that within the city. By the mid-1980s surrounding counties were noticeably affected by the outward spread.
Quadrant/Robert K. Hower

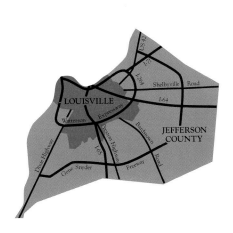

opened the 150-bed Southwest Jefferson Community Hospital in 1977 as the Louisville area's third suburban hospital. The institution faltered financially, however, and was taken over by Humana a year later, becoming Humana Hospital-Southwest.

But it was the eastern area of the county that most attracted developers. Typical of the changes that were to transform the largely rural countryside along Shelbyville Road east of St. Matthews was the Hurstbourne subdivision that had its beginnings in 1965 — and became an incorporated city in 1982. It encompassed in its 1,000 acres the tract that had been pioneer Soldier's Retreat, the home and plantation of Virginian Richard Clough Anderson, Sr. In 1949 the property passed into the hands of Leroy Highbaugh, Sr., and his son, who began developing Hurstbourne in 1965, shortly after the completion of Interstate 64 into downtown Louisville provided easy access via the Hurstbourne Lane interchange. The plan included not only large-sized lots plus shopping facilities, but also the Hurstbourne Country Club and its golf course.

Part of the acreage was utilized as Hurstbourne Park, an office-building development, where the first eight-story structure was completed in 1972. While Hurstbourne was taking shape, the Highbaughs were developing the nearby Bluegrass Research & Industrial Park, also served by the Interstate 64/Hurstbourne Lane interchange. Designed for light industry, warehousing, and the like, it was the Louisville area's first large-scale industrial park, luring not only some new names from out of town, but also established operations from throughout the area, including the city.

Other developers, seeing the potential, also began moving into the area. In the 1970s the Plainview Dairy Farm, immediately east of Hurstbourne Lane, lost its rural aspect as it was transformed into Plainview, a planned community of single-family homes, garden apartments, shopping facilities, and office buildings. The transformation of the Shelbyville Road corridor continues at the end of the 1980s, as new subdivisions stretch eastward toward the Shelby County line. The area around Shelbyville Road and Hurstbourne Lane has become practically a 'city' in its own right, an almost self-contained area of shopping centers, restaurants, housing, and recreation. Similar development, but on a smaller scale, marks Brownsboro Road stretching east to Oldham County. Urbanization, in fact, marks almost all areas of Jefferson County, with the outward thrust along such corridors as Bardstown Road, Newburg Road, Preston Highway, Third Street Road, and others accelerated by the Gene Snyder Freeway (formerly the Jefferson Freeway), the limited-access highway circling the metro area near the Jefferson County limits.

But as it assumes the new form of the city, suburbia develops its own urban problems (including mounting traffic volumes that require constant road widening), and inherits some of the old city's problems. When the financially crippled Louisville public school system was forced to dissolve, the responsibility for continued operation fell upon the county school system. The racial imbalance of the resulting single system led to federally mandated school busing in the fall of 1975. Unfortunately, the experience of 1956 was not repeated. The violent resistance in the southern and southwestern parts of the county was a vivid reminder not only of surviving racial tensions (many of the residents of those areas had been part of the earlier 'white flight' from the city), but that the sense of mutual dependence that marked pioneer Louisville and the outlying stations had eroded over two centuries.

A year earlier, the joint city-county vote on the issue of a public subsidy for mass transit demonstrated differing attitudes. When the privately owned Louisville Transit Company, beset by falling patronage (12 million passengers annually in 1973 vs. 125 million in 1945), announced that it was going out of business in the fall of 1974, it was obvious that public operation was the only way to keep the buses running. A proposed increase in city and county occupational license taxes to subsidize continued operation rolled up a large majority in the city, but failed to carry the automobile-oriented suburbs. The city margin in the November 1974 vote was so large, however, that the measure passed. Ironically, the Transit Authority of River City (TARC) now operates more routes beyond the city boundaries than the former operator did, and has extended service to Oldham and Bullitt counties, and across the Ohio River to southern Indiana.

The change in Jefferson County's demographics (and of other Kentucky urban counties) prompted a move for more home-rule in the 1970s. Counties were not permitted by the state Constitution to exercise the kind of authority granted to cities, even the smallest. The framers of the 1891

Below: The burst of violence that marked the southern and southwestern parts of the county when court-ordered school busing began in September 1975 overshadowed the lack of problems at most schools. The protestors, directing their ire wrongly at local government, were unable to translate their bitter opposition into significant victories at the polls.
Courier-Journal *and* Times

Above: Tornadoes occasionally strike the
Louisville area, usually causing only minor
damage. There are exceptions however, as
1890 demonstrated. On the afternoon of
April 3, 1974, another whirling black
funnel cloud struck the city, cutting a
swath of destruction eastward from
Standiford Field through the Highlands,
Cherokee Park, Crescent Hill, and the
suburbs beyond. This home was in
Northfield.
Courier-Journal and Times

The tornado's sound and fury
*"The tornado hit Northfield yesterday
between 4:30 and 4:45 p.m. Some say it
was over in a matter of seconds; others
said it seemed to last forever. Some of the
residents saw the large black funnel
cloud, with the shingles and boards
swirling around in the top of it. Everyone
remembered the noise, the incredible,
terrifying noise.*

*" 'God, the sound. I'll never forget the
sound,' said Mrs. Bill Sexton, 6601 Roads
Court. 'I don't ever want to hear it again.
It was like a jet plane screaming through
your home.'*

*"The subdivision was leveled.
Everywhere you looked, on Stannye
and Keewood and all the other streets,
there were piles of rubble where homes
used to be."*
The Courier-Journal, April 4, 1974

document could not visualize urbanization outside a municipality. For
years, Jefferson County government was concerned only with such chores
as seeing that the main roads, at least, were kept in some reasonable repair,
that the few schools needed were provided, that the indigent did not starve,
and that taxes were collected. The sheriff and a few deputies handled what
law enforcement was required when state laws were broken. Counties had
no authority to make local law. Finally in 1978, well into the age of urbanization for Jefferson County, the state legislature granted counties the right to
enact ordinances and issue regulations to deal with increasing complexity.

Meanwhile, the awkward situation of a single geographic and economic entity, separated politically into city and county, disturbed many
civic and business leaders. There was no unified approach in economic
development, for instance; rather, city and county competed to attract
new businesses and the tax base they generate. The suburbs had resound-
ingly defeated the Mallon Plan of 1956 to merge Louisville and the heavily
developed fringe around the city boundaries. A second attempt, the
Morton-Wyatt plan of 1970, also failed. This approach, spearheaded by
the Louisville Chamber of Commerce, was developed by former Senator
Thruston B. Morton and former Lieutenant Governor Wilson W. Wyatt.
The plan called for state legislation permitting merger of Louisville and
the unincorporated areas of the county. No popular vote was ever taken,
however, since the bill was killed in the legislature by the opposition of
the county administration.

With the memory of these defeats in mind, a different tack was taken
in 1982. This called for the dissolution of the city of Louisville as an incorporated entity and the formation of a new governmental structure for the
entire geographic area of the county. (A shadow county government would
have remained, since constitutionally a county cannot be dissolved.) The
new government would have been somewhat similar to those adopted by
such neighboring metropolitan areas as Lexington, Indianapolis, and
Nashville. The proposal would have left the nearly one-hundred smaller
incorporated cities intact. In the November 1982 balloting this proposal,
backed by both Mayor Harvey I. Sloane and County Judge/Executive
Mitch McConnell, came closest of any to acceptance. Defeated by only
1,450 votes out of a total of more than 180,000, the plan received approval
by 59 percent of city voters and 43 percent of those in the county.

Oddly, the eastern areas of the county, earlier a stronghold of opposition to merger plans, approved the proposal. Defeat came from an unlikely
combination of black voters in the city's West End and white voters in the
southern and southwestern sections of the county, where resistance to
school busing had turned violent. West End opposition stemmed largely
from the fact that blacks, making steady progress in city politics, feared that
dissolving the city would dilute their influence. Opposition in the largely
blue-collar south/southwestern sections of the county reflected the feeling
there that those areas had been slighted in government services and public
improvements, and that a new government dominated by the "East End" (of
both city and county) would continue to ignore needs there. The plan was
also seen as merely another name for annexation by Louisville. A second
attempt at passage in 1983 was defeated — by 5,600 votes.

The problem of divided governmental authority and its drawbacks
remained, however, and a different approach was initiated by newly elected
Mayor Jerry Abramson and Harvey I. Sloane, now county judge/executive.
This was the city/county 'compact,' approved by the state legislature in 1986
and effective January 1, 1987, freezing Louisville boundaries for twelve years
and alleviating suburban fears of annexation. The two governments also
share occupational tax revenues under a complex formula, as a step to
ending competition for new jobs. A single economic development office has
replaced the two former competing offices, and the county has increased its

share of funding to joint city/county agencies such as health, parks, and planning and zoning.

Meanwhile, suburbia continues its expansive ways, especially commercially. Office buildings are rising at a more rapid rate beyond the Louisville boundaries than in the central business district. From 1971 through 1985, when downtown office space grew at a respectable 57 percent, suburban office space registered a 74 percent gain. Downtown still held the edge in total square footage, however, with 6.9 million square feet in 1985 (excluding buildings totally occupied by their owners), compared to 4.5 million square feet in the suburbs. Vacancy rates have been consistently lower downtown even though average rents are higher. Although center city will never again be the dominant retail shopping area that it was before the automobile age, it continues as the financial, legal, governmental, and cultural heart of a region extending far beyond Jefferson County. As quality housing is brought to market, it is also becoming a residential neighborhood, although one that shares little in common with suburbia's green lawns.

W hile the demographics of city and county were undergoing a radical reversal, another change — even more profound — was under way. The decline of manufacturing as the single most important underpinning of the local economy affected both city and county equally. Manufacturing's 42 percent share of 1963 employment slipped to 26.5 percent in 1982. Yet total employment throughout the city and county increased from 200,000 in 1960 to more than 283,000 in 1984, even while manufacturing was decreasing from its high of 107,000 in 1974 to 75,000 in 1984. The new jobs were primarily in the services category, a broad grouping that includes such diverse fields as advertising and public relations, performing arts, computer services, education, engineering, and health services, among others, as well as such occupations as waiting on tables. This category accounted for 26.3 percent of 1984 employment. When the related finance, insurance, and real-estate category is added, the total climbs to nearly 40 percent of local employment, occupying the niche held by manufacturing in the 1960s. The burgeoning supply of office space is one visible indicator of the trend.

As an industrial center, Louisville had become essentially midwestern in temper and pace, although it once assiduously cultivated a southern image as a sales tool in southern markets. Its decline in smokestack industries matched that of the Midwest, with manufacturing losing market share to foreign imports or moving to lower wage, open-shop states to the south. With automation and robotization (as at General Electric's Appliance Park and at Ford Motor's two truck-assembly plants), factory employment will probably continue to shrink slowly, even with production increases. The Louisville area's diversification in manufacturing, however, provides some cushion against the shocks felt by those metropolitan areas depending largely on one industry.

Manufacturing, although no longer the dominant activity, remains an important factor in the local economy. New industrial jobs are created annually, slowing — but so far not reversing — the general downward trend. The Jefferson RiverPark and its associated Riverport in southwestern Jefferson County provide room for manufacturing growth and a road/rail/river transfer of cargo, as does the Clark Maritime Centre in Indiana near Jeffersonville. The Louisville Enterprise Zone, created in 1983 as the first in Kentucky and among the first in the nation, provides tax incentives for new enterprises and eases zoning restrictions. The 6.7 square-mile area extends along the railroad corridor from the Ohio River south to Standiford Field. Another approach, initiated in 1987 under provisions of a 1986 state law, is tax-increment financing districts that permit 80 percent of occupational license taxes from new jobs in each district to be plowed back into improvements such as roads, sewers, and drainage.

Above: The Louisville City Hall (in background) and the Jefferson County Court House are neighbors at Sixth and Jefferson streets in downtown Louisville, belying the tensions that sometimes develop between them. The city-county 'compact,' effective January 1, 1987, and continuing for twelve years, relieves the most pressing points of contention and perhaps paves the way for a more lasting solution.
Quadrant/John Beckman

Right, top: The landside terminal at Standiford Field, opened June 30, 1985, provides separate levels for arriving and departing passengers to ease traffic flow. Travelers, including more from abroad as overseas capital is invested in Kentucky, are greeted by Kentucky themes in the decorative motifs. The new facility replaced the original Lee Terminal of 1950.
Quadrant/John Beckman

Right, center: United Parcel Service picked Standiford Field as its principal distribution hub because of Louisville's central location and the fact that Standiford is seldom closed by bad weather. The nightly fleet of arriving and departing planes keeps the runways busy.
Quadrant/John Beckman

Right, bottom: Robotization and automation are transforming Louisville's large manufacturing plants, such as General Electric and Ford Motor, as they move to trim production costs to meet foreign competition. This robot device at General Electric's Appliance Park performs routine assembly tasks tirelessly and accurately.
General Electric Company

The major thrust, however, is toward developing a white-collar base built on the information/knowledge/service sector. Representative of the new economic activity are such corporate names as Humana; Capital Holding, one of the nation's largest insurance-holding companies; BATUS, the holding company for Marshall Field, Saks Fifth Avenue, and other properties of the British-American Tobacco Company; Mercer-Meidinger-Hansen, a nationwide employee-benefits consulting firm; Kentucky Fried Chicken; and Chi-Chi's, the Mexican restaurant chain.

Highlighting the new development drive is the successful 1987 effort to bring the national headquarters of the Presbyterian Church (U.S.A.) to Louisville. Although the church's site-selection committee had recommended Kansas City as the headquarters for the merged north and south branches of Presbyterianism, and despite the fact that Louisville's bid had been rejected a year earlier, the city scored a come-from-behind victory. It was a stunning demonstration of public/private cooperation used for the first time for the recruitment of new jobs — nearly 1,000.

Centerpiece of the package that was assembled was the offer of a gift of headquarters space by David Jones, chief executive officer and chairman of Humana. He offered part of the complex of the former wholesale hardware firm of Belknap, Inc., which he had purchased in an unsuccessful effort to keep it operating. Private funding totaling $6.2 million was pledged to convert the two former warehouses into offices. In addition, Mayor Jerry Abramson pledged $1.4 million in public funds for street improvements, including street lighting and landscaping. The Parking Authority of River City agreed to construct a parking garage nearby for more than 1,000 cars. This package, plus intense lobbying at the Presbyterian General Assembly in Biloxi, Mississippi, and a videotape of a downtown rally by more than 5,000 Louisvillians showing the Presbyterians how welcome they would be, turned the tide. On June 16, 1987, the church delegates voted 332 to 309 to choose Louisville. The decision enhances Louisville's opportunities to become the headquarters city for other national organizations.

The medical aspect of the changing economy became national news in 1984 when the world's second artificial-heart implant was performed at Humana Hospital-Audubon. The events that led to that memorable day in November began in the late 1970s when fast-growing Humana purchased the non-profit St. Joseph's Infirmary on Eastern Parkway from the Sisters of Charity of Nazareth. Soon the 1926 hospital was replaced by Louisville's largest, Humana Hospital-Audubon, on Poplar Level Road. Opened in 1980, the 484-bed hospital also became home to the Humana Heart Institute International, founded in 1984.

Meanwhile, in Salt Lake City, Dr. William C. DeVries had implanted the first artificial heart in a human, using the Jarvik-7 device tested previously only in animals. Dr. Allan M. Lansing, head of the Humana Heart Institute, took note of this and soon recruited Dr. DeVries (the only surgeon permitted by the federal Food and Drug Administration to implant the experimental device as a permanent heart replacement) to move the program to Louisville under the Heart Institute. The first candidate was 52-year-old Bill Schroeder of Jasper, Indiana, a diabetic with a fast-failing heart. By the time the implant was made, two-hundred-and-fifty reporters had gathered in Louisville for the event. Schroeder lived a record twenty months with the implant. Two later implant patients succumbed before Schroeder, and in the late 1980s the Jarvik-7 remains an experimental device as modifications continue. But as a result of the Louisville work, it is now frequently used as a temporary expedient for near-death patients awaiting a human heart transplant.

The artificial-heart program received so much attention that it tended to overshadow the expanding scope of the area's medical services:

Below: Louisville is home to two theological seminaries. The chapel at the Presbyterian institution (top) is representative of the contemporary architectural treatment of other buildings on its campus on Alta Vista Road in the city's East End. The Southern Baptist Seminary (bottom), one of the world's largest in enrollment, uses traditional Georgian design on its Lexington Road campus.
Quadrant/Ted Wathen

Above: The Presbyterian Church (U.S.A.) was persuaded to move its national headquarters to Louisville rather than Kansas City largely as a result of the gift of these two buildings at Second and Washington streets near the river. A total of $6.2 million in private funding was raised to convert the former Belknap, Inc. warehouses to modern office space.
Humana, Inc.

Right, top: The Humana Building at Fifth and Main, seen here from the Riverfront Plaza/Belvedere, is both an announcement of the hospital-operating company's success and confirmation of the resurgence of Main Street as a prestige business address. The First National Tower (at left in photo) was completed in 1971 and the Humana Building in 1985.
John Nation

Right, bottom: Humana Hospital-University, part of the expanding Medical Center east of the central business district, replaced aging Louisville General Hospital in 1983. It was planned and constructed by the University of Louisville, but turned over to Humana management even before it was opened. It is one of the nation's few teaching hospitals operated by a for-profit corporation.
Louisville Chamber of Commerce

Top: The Kentucky Center for the Arts, built with a combination of public and private funding, is the focal point of the performing arts in the Louisville area. Opened in November 1983, the $33.75-million center houses two main performance halls and a small one for experimental productions. The center is located at Fifth and Main streets adjacent to the Riverfront Plaza/Belvedere. Quadrant/Ted Wathen

Bottom: The Robert K. Whitney Hall, seating 2,400, is the largest of the performance halls. It is named for the first conductor of the Louisville Orchestra, which is shown on stage. Louisville Chamber of Commerce

human-heart transplants, liver and lung transplants, kidney transplants, reattachment of severed limbs, correction of spinal problems, microsurgery, physical rehabilitation of the severely injured, and other advanced techniques. The University of Louisville School of Medicine, where recently endowed chairs permit expanding the faculty with some of the leading names in both clinical practice and research, is a keystone in the expanding role of medicine locally.

Another important force is Humana, sometimes to the dismay of the non-profit hospitals and many physicians in private practice affiliated with those institutions. With four hospitals in the Louisville area, Humana is a commanding presence. One of those hospitals is 404-bed Humana Hospital-University in the downtown Medical Center, the teaching hospital of the School of Medicine, and one of the few teaching hospitals managed by a for-profit corporation. This development had its origin in 1978 when the university took over operation of the-then teaching hospital, Louisville General, from the Louisville & Jefferson County Board of Health, in anticipation of the new University Hospital that would replace antiquated Louisville General. The new hospital, with its superior facilities, was designed to attract paying patients as well as the charity cases handled by old Louisville General. However, even before the new hospital was completed, the university found that the economic drain of the primarily charity hospital was more than its budget could handle. As early as 1981 it was seeking an outside operator, and in January 1983, several months before the new hospital was opened, agreement was reached with Humana. Under new management, the deficit operation became a profitable one.

Humana's boldest statement of its presence, however, is the twenty-six-story corporate headquarters it erected at Fifth and Main. Completed in the spring of 1985, the Humana Building's post-modern design by architect Michael Graves caused the first public debate about a Louisville building's design in decades. Unlike the glass-and-steel boxlike towers of the modernist school, the Humana Building uses bold colors, sculptural effects, and images of the past to create a monumental effect. It immediately became a Louisville landmark. Architectural critics, while expressing some reservations, have, nonetheless, praised it. *The New York Times* called it "the only downtown building whose design is devoted to knitting this town back together," a reference to the way it makes a visual transition between the low-rise Victorian buildings on its west side and the forty-story First

National Tower on the east.

Significantly, the Humana Building — which its architect approached as a work of art — faces the Kentucky Center for the Arts on the north side of Main Street. Completed in 1983, the $33.5 million home of the performing arts is visible testimony to the growing base of support for the arts in Louisville since 1960. It is also an example of the private sector committing significant amounts of corporate cash to a public project that had financial problems. With its two performance halls — one of 2,400 seats, the other of 625 seats — the Kentucky Center is home to most of the city's performing arts groups: the Louisville Orchestra; the Kentucky Opera; the Louisville Ballet; and Stage One: The Louisville Children's Theatre; as well as the Louisville Theatrical Association, which brings touring Broadway shows to the city. The only major organization which does not present performances at the Kentucky Center is the internationally prominent Actors Theatre of Louisville, housed nearby on Main Street in its own recycled Victorian commercial building with the 1837 Bank of Louisville as its lobby entrance.

The city's arts renaissance, which began in the 1950s, created a need for a better performance center than the boxy Memorial Auditorium. This need was first filled in 1962 when the Brown Theatre on Broadway was refurbished — and in 1972 renamed the Macauley, to recall the city's earlier, much-loved theatre of that name. Though elegant, the Brown/Macauley seated only 1,435 patrons, necessitating multiple performances, with higher expenses, to accommodate all who wished to attend. By the end of the 1960s the need for a larger center was evident, but lack of funding stymied efforts to build a new facility.

In 1974 the Center City Commission, a public/private group, unveiled plans for a 2,400-seat hall and proposed that public funds (most to come from the state) be used to construct it. Governor Julian Carroll agreed to state participation, but wanted commitments for participation from the city and county. Because of personality conflicts between City Hall and Court House, it was not until 1977 that a task force of local arts and business representatives developed a financial proposal that both the mayor and county judge/executive endorsed. With architectural plans in hand, a groundbreaking was held in November 1979, shortly before Carroll was succeeded in office by John Y. Brown, Jr., the man who had made Kentucky

Right, top: The 1914 Belle of Louisville, *owned jointly by the city and county, has brought a touch of the Ohio River's old romance to the downtown wharf since 1962. A genuine steamboat with a genuine steam calliope, the* Belle *is a token of the community's continuing affection for the river. She runs daily excursions to Six Mile Island every summer and annually pits her stamina against the bigger* Delta Queen *in the Great Steamboat Race, an event of the Kentucky Derby Festival.*
Quadrant/Robert K. Hower

Right, center: The Louisville Redbirds brought professional baseball back to Louisville in 1982. A farm club of the St. Louis Cardinals, the Redbirds set a minor-league attendance record in 1983 with over 1 million fans attending home games at the Kentucky Fair & Exposition Center.
Quadrant/John Beckman

Right, bottom: The Louisville Zoological Garden, opened in 1968, follows modern practice by providing as natural a setting as possible for its animal inhabitants. The zoo, on a ninety-eight acre tract on Trevilian Way between Newburg and Poplar Level roads, was made possible by a $1.5-million gift from James Graham Brown.
Quadrant/Ted Wathen

Above: The first-ever turf track at Churchill Downs, inaugurated in April 1987 with the Early Times Turf Classic, was added because racing on the grass is becoming more popular and because it permits the Louisville track to host from time to time the prestigious Breeders' Cup Series of seven races, including turf events. The Breeders' Cup has purses totaling $10 million, with the premier race paying $5 million, the highest ever in racing. The turf track is inside the traditional dirt track.
Quadrant/Carl Maupin

Below: The colorful balloon race is one of the many events of the week-long Kentucky Derby Festival that precedes the annual running of the Derby on the first Saturday in May. The Kentucky Fair & Exposition Center is the usual launching site of the balloons, seen here from above.
John Nation

Fried Chicken a household word throughout much of the world.

The new governor, unhappy with the financial commitments made by his predecessor, moved quickly to change the rules of the game. The state's commitment was limited to $22.4 million and Brown challenged the business community to raise $10 million as an endowment, with the income used to cover shortfalls in operating income. The drive eventually raised some $14 million, part of which had to be used to aid in construction costs. Brown also shepherded an increase in the Jefferson County hotel/motel room tax through the 1980 state legislature, the additional funds generated to go to operation of the Kentucky Center. With its combination of state, local, and private funding, the Kentucky Center for the Arts was opened with gala festivities on November 19, 1983 — not only a home for cultural events, but also an economic development tool.

It has become apparent that as part of the development of a new economic direction, Louisville and Jefferson County must offer a diverse complement of amenities attractive to middle- and upper-income groups, and the arts are an important part of this mix. When Governor Brown was considering the future of the Kentucky Center in 1980, he consulted former business partner Wendell Cherry, chief operating officer of Humana. The principal argument used by Cherry, and David Jones, Humana's chief executive officer, was that the center was related to economic development by helping to create an attractive environment for Louisville and Kentucky. Brown was not only convinced — he persuaded Cherry to take over management of the project.

Sports, too, figure in the mix, with the return of professional baseball in 1982. Although the University of Louisville basketball Cardinals, winners in 1980 and 1984 of the coveted National Collegiate Athletic Association championship, provide exciting sports action during the winter, Louisville sorely missed its summer baseball that ended after the 1972 season. The Louisville Colonels of the International League departed when the stadium at the Kentucky Fair & Exposition Center was rebuilt for University of Louisville football. Determined to remedy the loss, a committee of business executives, spearheaded by Dan Ulmer, president of Citizens Fidelity Bank and Trust Company, began searching in 1981 for a team to bring to Louisville. The committee found what it was looking for in Springfield, Illinois — an AAA team and farm club for the St. Louis Cardinals that was looking for a new home.

Above: An extensive building program in the 1980s, funded by local corporations and individuals, marked Bellarmine College's campus (bottom of photo) between Newburg Road and Norris Place. Quadrant/John Beckman

Below: A massive building program also transformed the University of Louisville's expanded Belknap Campus beginning in the late 1960s. Enrollment at U of L increased sharply after the former municipal institution became a state university in 1970 with lower tuition. Quadrant/Carl Maupin

Finding the team was one thing; bringing it to Louisville was another. It meant finding the money to rebuild Cardinal Stadium again so that it would be suitable for both baseball and football. Again the business community came to the fore, raising $4.1 million for the task. In 1982 the new Louisville Redbirds took to the field, and its sponsors knew that they had hit a responsive chord when more than 19,000 spectators turned out for the first home game. The Redbirds set a new minor-league attendance record in 1983 with over 1 million enthusiastic fans, and won the league championship in 1984 and 1985.

Improving the educational system at all levels has also been a community priority, with the greatest physical evidences of change at the University of Louisville's Belknap Campus and at Bellarmine College. Building construction programs have transformed both campuses almost beyond recognition since the 1960s, and both have been aided by sizeable corporate gifts. Significantly, given the shift toward a white-collar economy, both have erected new buildings to house their schools of business.

Change is endemic in the life of any community; new institutions are continuously created, and old familiar ones that once loomed large, fade away. Two household names that vanished from the local scene in the 1980s were the Louisville & Nashville Railroad (L&N) and *The Louisville Times*; the railroad by merger, the newspaper by ceasing publication. The L&N disappeared into the giant CSX Transportation Corporation (rail, river, and pipelines) on January 1, 1983. That was the end point of a process that began in 1972 when the Seaboard Coast Line, which owned the majority of L&N stock, purchased all remaining shares.

In 1980 the Seaboard and Chessie systems were merged as CSX, leaving the L&N a corporation in name only, which after two years was

Right: The rail system that Louisville developed during the nineteenth century, often with the city's financial aid, remains a vital part of the community's transportation network despite newer competing technologies. CSX Transportation's Osborn Yard, in southern Jefferson County, is a beehive of activity around the clock as freight cars are sorted and assembled into trains for varied destinations.
Louisville Chamber of Commerce

Bottom: Although the Louisville & Nashville Railroad, that once billed itself as 'The Louisville Line,' is now part of CSX Transportation, its neon herald atop the former corporate headquarters at Ninth and Broadway still lights the night sky.
Quadrant/John Beckman

simply retired. The L&N's former corporate headquarters at Ninth and Broadway was sold to the state of Kentucky as an office building. But a city that likes to remember its past by reviving such names as the Galt House and Macauley Theatre was not willing to let the once-potent name 'L&N' vanish completely. The state agreed to repair and maintain the huge neon version of the railroad's herald atop the office building. Now each night it flashes a remembrance of the line that one historian called "Louisville's imperial weapon" in the city's nineteenth-century battle to dominate southern markets.

There is nothing left of the *Times* except the memory and old files of the newspaper that published its final edition on February 14, 1987, only a few weeks short of its 103rd birthday. With the demise of the *Times*, leaving only *The Courier-Journal*, Louisville joined the majority of American cities as a one-newspaper town. Even more significantly for the community, that one newspaper was no longer locally owned, nor were any of the other communications enterprises of the Bingham family that had played a dominant role in that field locally since 1918. Oddly, just as a family quarrel had put the two newspapers on the market in that year, leading to the purchase by Robert Worth Bingham, a family quarrel among third-generation Binghams put the whole communications empire on the block in early 1986 — newspapers, radio and television stations, and other subsidiary enterprises.

The quarrel initially involved Sallie Bingham and her brother, Barry Bingham, Jr., the newspapers' publisher, over management policies. Soon other family members were reluctantly drawn in. Sallie turned down the family's offer of $26.3 million for her stock; she wanted $32 million. Finally, to break the impasse, board chairman Barry Bingham, Sr., announced in January 1986 that all the Bingham properties were for sale. The newspapers

were the first to go, purchased by the expanding Gannett Company chain, with the change in ownership effective July 14, 1986. In short order, WHAS-TV, WHAS-AM, and WAMZ-FM found willing buyers. Seven months to the day after the Gannett purchase, the long-struggling afternoon *Times*, once the financial star of the Bingham properties, ceased publication, a victim of television news that has practically eliminated afternoon newspapers across the nation.

A bronze George Rogers Clark, standing on Louisville's Riverfront Plaza/Belvedere, looks today across an Ohio River that Clark in the flesh would not recognize. The Falls has vanished, tamed behind a wall of concrete. Corn Island has vanished, literally quarried away to pave early Louisville streets and later to make cement. The Indians have vanished. The river, channeled by locks, dams, and floodwalls, is broader and deeper than the one he knew, with no low-water seasons interrupting navigation. Clark looks across the water to the former 'Indian side' and toward the Illinois country, where his brief, brilliant military campaign won him a permanent place in the nation's Revolutionary history.

Behind his bronze image rise the gleaming towers of a Louisville he would not understand — the fortieth largest metropolitan area in a nation that now stretches to the Pacific shore and beyond to Hawaii. The wilderness he knew has given way before the hand of man and man's technology. The elevated Riverside Expressway, blotting out the site of the once-clamorous wharf, sweeps past the sites of Fort Nelson and the first rude fort on shore, carrying a continuous stream of motor vehicles. The roar of the internal-combustion engine and fast-moving traffic, characteristic sounds of the twentieth century, fills the air where eighteenth-century Louisvillians struggled with the problems of sheer survival.

Above: The Louisville skyline seen from the Indiana shore has changed dramatically since 1970 when it still matched a 1937 description of the riverfront as "an old red-brick jumble." The positive change in the area of the city's beginnings dates from the Riverfront Project, completed in 1973, and has been continuous ever since.
Quadrant/John Beckman

Now Louisville is well into its third century, rebuilding itself as it has many times in the past, and will again in the future; building a new economic base as it has in the past, and undoubtedly will again in the future. The one-time western river outpost has been dealing with change since the first axe stroke rang out on Corn Island in 1778. There is continuity, too, that threads through the change. One is geography; whatever else may have changed, the Ohio still flows to the sea. Another is the border position that from the beginning attracted a diverse population, and eventually forged a climate that welcomes the talented, including newcomers, to positions of leadership. It is this openness that Louisville should prize and nourish. That is its greatest strength as it looks to the twenty-first century.

Index

Errata

Page 15, line 16: Read *near* Hurst-bourne, not *at*.
Page 33, line 14: The Catholic church was on *Tenth*, not *Eleventh* street.
Page 38, line 10: Read *1804*, not *1805*.
Page 38, line 35: Portland was laid out in 1811, the first sale of lots was in 1814, and a town charter was secured in 1834.
Page 51, line 13: Read *1818*, not *1811*.
Page 65, line 38: *Samuel* Casseday should be *Benjamin* Casseday.
Page 138, line 4: Read *January 1, 1891*, not *January 1, 1890*.